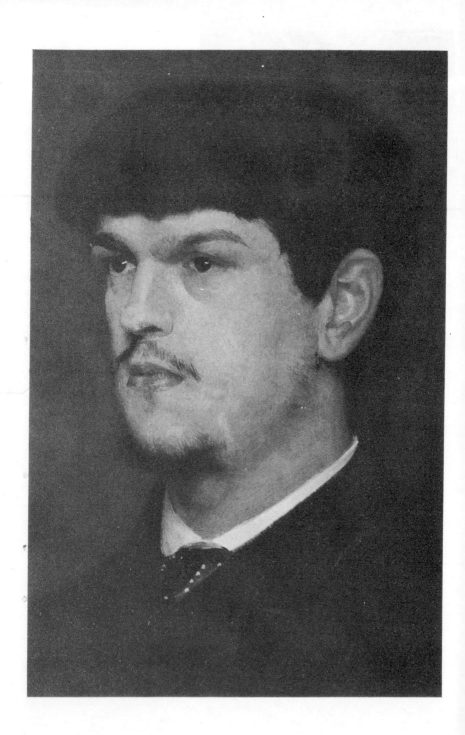

LÉON VALLAS

CLAUDE
DEBUSSY

HIS LIFE AND WORKS

Translated
from the French by
MAIRE and GRACE O'BRIEN

DOVER PUBLICATIONS, INC.
NEW YORK

Published in Canada by General Publishing Com-
pany, Ltd., 30 Lesmill Road, Don Mills, Toronto,
Ontario.
   Published in the United Kingdom by Constable
and Company, Ltd., 10 Orange Street, London WC 2.

   This Dover edition, first published in 1973, is an
unabridged republication of the work originally
published by Oxford University Press in 1933. It is
reprinted by special arrangement with the previous
publisher at 200 Madison Ave., New York 10016.

International Standard Book Number: 0-486-22916-5
Library of Congress Catalog Card Number: 72-93606

Manufactured in the United States of America
Dover Publications, Inc.
180 Varick Street
New York, N. Y. 10014

PREFACE

IN this book on Claude Debussy I have avoided all biographical details the publication of which might be deemed premature and indiscreet. The secrets of his private life belong to those who shared it and who bear his name.

For the purposes of this book I have made use only of such documents as were originally intended for publication or which have by chance become public property. To my mind, the really interesting points in the life of a musician are his works, his activities, and his influence on his contemporaries.

The book which I published in 1928 under the title of *The Theories of Claude Debussy, musicien français*, supplements the present work, revealing as it does the composer's ideas on music given to the public between the years 1901 and 1916.

I have made frequent use of Debussy's published correspondence: his letters to Vasnier and Ernest Chausson (*Revue Musicale*, December 1925 and May 1926) and to the publisher, Durand (Paris, Durand, 1927). I have also drawn on the reminiscences published by the *Revue Musicale*, in May 1926 (articles by: Raymond Bonheur, Paul Dukas, Robert Godet, André Messager, Gabriel Pierné, Henri de Régnier, Marguerite Vasnier, Paul Vidal). I have likewise utilized the recollections to which Maurice Emmanuel refers in his study on 'Pelléas et Mélisande' (Paris, Mellotte, 1926).

DEBUSSY, *by* JACQUES-ÉMILE BLANCHE
(1903)

CONTENTS

LIST OF ILLUSTRATIONS

CHAPTER I

CHILDHOOD. THE CONSERVATOIRE (1862–83)

IN the heart of the Île-de-France, at Saint-Germain-en-Laye, the birthplace of Louis XIV, was born on the 22nd of August 1862 the artist who fifty years later proudly assumed the name 'musicien français' and bore it as though it were a title of nobility. This was the only title to which he could lay claim; though his father used sometimes to boast that he belonged to a noble family because some of his forebears had written their name in two separate words, as *de Bussy*. But this was merely a fancy spelling commonly used in former times. On tracing back the Debussy genealogy in the public records we find that they were humble folk of purely French stock: artisans, workmen, or small farmers.[1]

This royal borough of Seine-et-Oise was Achille-Claude Debussy's cradle, but nearly the whole of his life was spent in Paris. No. 38 rue au Pain, Saint-Germain, the simple, modest little house where he was born, is still to be seen. On the ground floor, Manuel-Achille Debussy and Victorine Manoury, the parents of the future artist, kept a china shop during the years 1862–4. They had settled there immediately after their marriage which took place on the 30th of November 1861, at 'the village of Levallois', a Paris suburb which is now included in Clichy. Of their five children, only the first two were born at Saint-Germain-en-Laye. The eldest was Achille-Claude. He was baptized at the church of Saint-Germain on the 31st of July 1864. Soon after the christening the Debussy family, whose business had evidently not flourished, gave up their little shop to their predecessor and left Saint-Germain. They settled first at Clichy, then in Paris, where the father, after some vicissitudes, obtained a modest post in the

[1] The composer's father, Manuel-Achille Debussy, was born at Montrouge (Seine) on the 10th of May 1836. He was the son of Claude Debussy, carpenter, born in Paris on the 16th of June 1812, and of Marianne-Françoise Blondeau, born at Chelles (Seine-et-Marne) who was a fringe-maker at the time of her marriage at Montrouge, on the 26th of June 1834. Whilst looking up the origins of the Debussy family in the registers, the author found that the composer's great-grandfather was Pierre Debussy, farmer, living at Semur, who left the Côte-d'Or and established himself at Montrouge (1768–1829). His great-great-grandfather was Pierre de Bussy, farrier, living at Semur, and born at Benoisy (Côte-d'Or) on the 2nd of February 1727, his father being Valentin de Bussy, farm labourer at Benoisy, a native of Corcelles-sous-Grignon, who was married at Seigny, on the 31st of January 1724.

Achille-Claude Debussy's mother was Victorine-Joséphine-Sophie Manoury, born in Paris (1st arrondissement) on the 28th of October 1836; daughter of Louis-Amable Manoury and Eulalie-Sophie Delinotte.

employment of the Compagnie Fives-Lille which he held from 1873 to 1906.

Debussy never spoke of his childhood, except for occasional allusions to his sojourns on the Côte d'Azur. The secrecy he maintained on this subject was deliberate. It is not for us to elucidate the mystery. Future historians may attribute it to the fact that the remembrance of the china shop where he was born was not a source of vanity to him; but those who wish to ascertain the real reason for Debussy's silence regarding his childhood at Saint-Germain and Paris must base their investigations on a public document. His baptismal certificate bears two names which he declared later were unknown to him: those of his godfather, Achille-Antoine Arosa, and his godmother, Octavie de la Ferronnière. The identity of the financier, Arosa, will be disclosed some day, and Octavie de la Ferronnière will be despoiled of the high-sounding name she assumed; we shall ascertain what relationships, legal or otherwise, united the two people who held Achille-Claude at the baptismal font: then only shall we know the exact circumstances of his childhood. We do not propose to reveal here any further particulars on the subject.

Although these humble shopkeepers were not altogether lacking in intellectual and artistic interests, they were not in a position to give their children a very high-class education or careful training. Young Debussy was at first called Achille, and for many years he was known by that name. He received a very elementary and incomplete education, which was interrupted at an early age by his entering the Conservatoire. This early neglect was to prove a handicap to him all his life long. The letters which he wrote in his twentieth year have been preserved and published with some corrections. In style and spelling they betray his lack of general education. This is also evident from the fantastic handwriting in which the poems adorning his earliest scores are written. It was only when he reached the age of manhood that he completed his education by reading and by associating with literary friends. His mental development owed much to the companionship and the almost unconscious intellectual influence of the writer Pierre Louÿs.

Like all French children, he must have been lulled to sleep to the sound of the popular melodies; and later, no doubt, he joined in the 'rondes' which the children sing at play. He never lost his love for these simple tunes, and he recalled some of them in his compositions. But his early childhood passed without his hearing any art music but that of the military and other bands to whose open-air concerts he used to listen in the Paris squares and public gardens. When he was older, his father, who was fond of music and one of whose brothers is said to have been a conductor in the provinces, took him to the theatre occasionally. There he heard such operas as Verdi's 'Il Trovatore' which made a great impression on him. Apart from music, he showed his artistic tastes at an early age in various ways, as his companions have recorded. He took a great delight in the brilliant colouring of the butterflies he collected, and loved to decorate his room with charming little ornaments and pictures. We are told that he wanted to become a painter. No doubt this abortive vocation was in some measure due to the influence of his godfather Arosa, who collected the works of modern painters.

From his sixth year, he used to stay occasionally at Cannes. He never spoke much about these visits. But they left his mind stored with enchanting memories: a landscape with the sea, which he had always loved, as an ever-changing background; the road to Antibes all aglow with roses; and in this radiant setting—as he still recalled it in 1908—'a Norwegian carpenter sang from morning till night— perhaps the songs were Grieg's.' It was there, at the age of nine, that he received his first piano lessons. They were probably paid for by his godfather and his godmother (who was also his aunt). As he told his friend, Louis Laloy, his teacher was an old Italian, named Cerutti, who does not seem to have noticed any particular talent in the child. But at any rate, Achille began to play. It used to amuse him to pick out chords on the worn-out instrument to which he had access and to attempt to reproduce any music he happened to hear.

One day he attracted the attention of a pianist who had been a pupil of Chopin, Mme Mauté de Fleurville. This lady was the mother of Charles de Sivry, the operette composer and conductor, who was connected with the *Chat Noir*. By her second marriage with Mauté, she had a daughter called by the 'Carlovingian name' of Mathilde, who was the heroine of Verlaine's 'Bonne Chanson', and who was for some months the wife of that Bohemian poet.[1] Just when the brief married life of her daughter and Paul Verlaine was drawing to a close, Mme Mauté made the acquaintance of little Achille and discovered that he had genuine talent. She taught him gratuitously. She was an excellent teacher, capable of

[1] In his *Confessions*, Verlaine inserted a little poem dedicated 'To Madame Marie M. . . .', i.e. to his mother-in-law, Mme Mauté de Fleurville, in which he sings her praise. Later on, he writes: 'She was a charming soul, an instinctive and talented artist, an excellent musician of exquisite taste, intelligent, and devoted to those she loved.'

transmitting faithfully what she had learned from Chopin, whose ideals, thus assimilated, her young pupil never forgot. Indeed, so excellent was her teaching and so apt the pupil, that after a few months' study Mme Mauté was able to present Achille for the entrance examination to the Conservatoire, which he passed successfully. The child's path was now definitely directed towards music, and he gave up all idea of becoming a painter, especially as his godfather, who had just got married, ceased to have any further connexion with the Debussy family. His parents, who had intended him to be a sailor, now had dreams of his becoming a great pianist. His father accordingly was very strict with him and made him work six or eight hours a day under threat of punishment.

In October 1873, when he was eleven years old, Achille entered the Conservatoire, where he joined a *solfège* class and one of the two advanced piano classes. His companions still remember him as a short, thick set boy, timid and awkward in manner, who was dressed like a child of the working-classes and looked a real little Bohemian. He had a very long head and a low, prominent forehead—his 'double forehead' had caused much surprise in the family at the time of his birth. His headgear consisted of a red-tasselled sailor's cap, a relic of his visits to Cannes and of an earlier vocation, a headgear to which the music student long remained faithful.

Albert Lavignac, the young professor of *solfège*, was agreeably surprised to discover in Achille Debussy a remarkable degree of musical sensibility, a taste for unusual chords, complex rhythms, and unexpected progressions of subtle harmonies. According to Maurice Emmanuel, Lavignac became greatly attached to the boy during the three years he was his pupil. Sometimes he would keep him after the class was over to teach him to know and appreciate good music; and he often lost all count of time in reading over and over with Achille some comparatively new work, such as the Overture to 'Tannhäuser', an opera whose first performance at Paris some twelve years previously had caused quite an uproar in artistic, social, and even political circles. As happens more frequently than people realize, the young professor derived considerable benefit from his intercourse with the boy. He learnt a great deal himself from the indiscreet questions of his inquisitive pupil. For without being aware of it, Achille was practising the maieutic method by suggesting delicate problems whose solution tended to shake the foundations of traditional teaching and the time-honoured routine of the Conservatoire. Thanks to the patience and kindness of this very sympathetic master, Achille Debussy managed to overcome his hatred of theory and all its absurd rules. Indeed, he became such a good scholar that he obtained in succession all the available distinctions, being awarded the third medal for *solfège* at his first examination, in the summer of 1874; the second medal, in 1875; and the first, in 1876. We may take it for granted that, like all really musical pupils, he obtained higher marks for musical dictation and reading than for theory.

But the atmosphere was not so harmonious in the advanced-piano class to which he was admitted in the autumn of 1873; he did not get on very well with his professor. Marmontel was no longer young. Born in 1816, he had won the first prize for piano in 1832, and had been teaching at the Conservatoire for thirty years. Like most able and experienced teachers, he was inclined to be dogmatic, and would not tolerate in any pupil young Debussy's love of argument. This gave rise to numerous conflicts. Besides, Achille was too gifted to be particularly industrious, and he submitted only very unwillingly to the tiresome technical exercises that are so indispensable to the virtuoso. He preferred to devote his study-time to reading the great works of the classical and romantic masters. His favourites were: Bach, for whom he retained a lifelong admiration, though he considered him rather long-winded; Mozart, whose quartets he used to arrange for the piano; Chopin, with whose style Mme Mauté had made him familiar; Haydn, Schumann, Stephen Heller, and Alkan. It would seem that his master was often irritated, but sometimes amused, by the weird little preludes he used to improvise before beginning a piece, as was the custom at that time, and by the uncanny character of the more involved and complex interludes by which he brought the distant tonalities of two consecutive pieces into gear. Speaking one day of his strange pupil, Marmontel is said to have remarked: 'He is not fond of the piano but he is very fond of music.' The first statement was utterly false, for Achille really loved the instrument which he learned to treat with such magic skill and which he always utilized when composing his scores. But the daring manner in which he exploited the resources of the piano was bound to shock the old professor, whose age had strengthened the conservatism of his instincts and training.

In spite of this, Marmontel realized the originality and the exceptional talents of his pupil. With Ambroise Thomas, the director of the school, Achille found even less favour. The composer of 'Mignon' was then an old man; he belonged to another epoch. The boy's whole personality was calculated to irritate him. This was particularly evident on examination days, when he would refuse to sanction or even to tolerate the subtle shades of expression in which the young piano pupil indulged in his renderings of Bach's Preludes and Fugues; for the intolerant director, like many musicians of his day, regarded the 'Well-Tempered Clavichord' as a collection of dry exercises in polyphony. Nor did his fellow students realize that this shy, brusque, elusive boy was a genius. One of them, his senior by four years, a man whose polished culture enabled him to become early in his career the musical critic of the *Revue des Deux Mondes*, has left the following portrait of Debussy as he appeared to him about 1875–6:

'Amongst the rank and file of Marmontel's class, there was one pupil concerning whom his comrades had few illusions. Or rather, they had many, all of them unflattering. Time was to undeceive them markedly to his advantage—to his glory, indeed, and their discomfiture. "Here you are at last, my boy," Marmontel would say, as a small, sickly-looking lad came in, generally late. He wore a belted tunic and carried in his hand a kind of a cap, edged with braid, with a red tassel in the centre like a sailor's cap. Nothing about him suggested the artist, present or future; neither his face, nor his speech, nor his playing. His only remarkable feature was his forehead. He was one of the youngest of the pianists, but by no means one of the best. I remember, in particular, the nervous habit he had of emphasizing the strong beats by a kind of panting or raucous breathing. This exaggerated marking of the rhythm was certainly the very last thing of which he could have been accused later on, as a composer, even if it applied to him as a pianist. You will agree with me when you hear his name. He was Claude Debussy. A very reserved, rather sullen boy. He was not popular with his fellow students.'[1]

Two other companions of his have alluded to his unfriendly manner and to the originality of his playing.

'At Marmontel's Piano class', Pierné writes, 'he used to astonish us with his weird playing. I do not know whether it was due to native awkwardness or to timidity, but he used literally to throw himself on the keyboard and exaggerate every effect. He seemed to be in a violent rage with the instrument—to ill-treat it with his impulsive gestures— breathing noisily as he performed difficult passages. These faults became gradually less noticeable, and at times he produced marvellously soft and delicate effects. These qualities, good and bad, gave his playing a very individual character. '

Paul Vidal knew Achille in 1878, at a time when the latter had won the second prize and was working for the first, an ambition which he did not realize. Vidal remembers him with curly black hair falling over his forehead, glowing eyes, a concentrated, surly,

---

[1] Camille Bellaigue, *Souvenir de musique et de musiciens*, Paris, 1921 (p. 35).

'almost wild' expression. Speaking of him as a pianist, Vidal says: 'His playing, although very interesting, was not technically perfect. He played trills with difficulty, but his left hand was wonderfully agile and had an extraordinary stretch. His talents as a pianist became evident during the following years in Bazille's accompaniment class, where he distinguished himself signally.'

In July 1874 Achille Debussy made his first appearance on the platform of the old hall of the Conservatoire, when he took part in the advanced piano competition. He was then barely twelve years old and had been only eight months at the Conservatoire. The piece set was Chopin's second Concerto in F minor. Achille stood the test very creditably—a severe one for a boy who had not yet completed his twelfth year. He received the second honourable mention. In some of the newspapers and reviews there were sympathetic references to this 'child of twelve' or this 'little boy of eleven, who exhibited a degree of confidence and vigour that were quite remarkable in a child of his age'. But his very obvious defects called forth the following severe criticism from the *Temps*: 'The youngest pupil is not yet twelve years old; he obtained the second honourable mention because to youth much must be forgiven.'

The following year the piece chosen for the competition was Chopin's second Ballade. Achille received the first honourable mention. That year, he impressed the critics greatly, and he is referred to in various papers as: 'a little prodigy of twelve', 'a child who promises to become a remarkable pianist', 'a boy of twelve destined to become a first class virtuoso'. These prophecies were not fulfilled in 1876, when the piece to be interpreted was the first movement of Opus 111. Beethoven's great sonata suited neither his talents nor his taste. He received no prize, nor had he the honour of being mentioned in the papers. Indeed, he probably deserved to share in the harsh criticism which the *Revue et Gazette Musicale* meted out to the class to which he belonged. They were accused of mannerisms, affectation, and showing off—faults with which Marmontel's pupils were often charged.

In 1877 the first movement of Schumann's Sonata in G minor enabled Debussy to take his place once more amongst the prize-winners of the Conservatoire. He shared the second prize with Camille Bellaigue. The editor of the *Journal de Musique* mentions in his notes: 'M. de Bussy, for whom, last year, we predicted a brilliant future and who is fulfilling the promise of his previous performances. He is only fourteen years of age. In his fifteenth year, M. Marmontel's young pupil will surely carry off the first prize.'

Events did not justify this flattering prophecy. In 1878 the test piece was the *Allegro* from Weber's 'Sonata in A flat'. The first prize was awarded to Camille Bellaigue who, a few years later, was appointed musical critic of the *Revue des Deux Mondes*, and who became the merciless censor of musicians of genius such as Richard Wagner and Claude Debussy. Prizes were also given to Camille Chevillard and Gabriel Pierné, both of whom were later on to become conductors, and the interpreters of their less fortunate comrade, Achille, who failed to secure the first prize. One newspaper insisted that the adjudicators had not been fair. Another admitted that the competitor whose name was omitted on the prize list was one of the best in the sight-reading test—a page by Théodore Dubois. A third remarked that although 'M. Debussy, the former winner of the second prize, did not play sufficiently well to be awarded the first prize', there was no need to despair, for 'he has plenty of time to improve his style and his technique, since he has not yet attained his sixteenth year'. But the defeat of 1878 was not to be wiped out.

During the holidays Achille had an opportunity of spending a few days in London, in the month of August. He accompanied some friends of his family, and while he was there he saw a performance of Sullivan's 'H.M.S. Pinafore'. After the holidays he went back to Marmontel's class. But whether he did much work is doubtful. He competed again in 1879, when he played Chopin's 'Allegro de Concert'. Gabriel Pierné took one of the first prizes, Camille Chevillard received none, nor was Achille's name included on the list of prizewinners. According to *La Revue et Gazette Musicale*, Debussy 'seemed to be progressing backwards'. Obviously, in the execution of most pieces, he was handicapped by the serious shortcomings to which his comrades and rivals have referred and which he had not the necessary perseverance to overcome. Possibly too, even at the school competitions, he may have indulged in the exquisite effects of tone-colouring that called forth so much admiration later on, but which were not likely to appeal to his conservative-minded examiners. The set-back of 1879 put an end to his parents' hopes that he would become a great pianist.

In the little world of the Conservatoire, a competitor who has won the second prize in his special subject loses caste if for two years in succession he fails to obtain the first prize. The entire educational system is founded on public competition, other forms of examination being regarded as practically worthless. It is likely enough that young Achille may have become a careless pupil in his sixteenth or seventeenth year, for, like many talented boys, he was not fond of hard work. Certainly, most of the other piano students must have got this impression. It was likewise borne out by the verdict passed on him by the master of the harmony class which he had joined three years previously and which he attended very much against his will. Émile Durand was one of those mediocre, colourless musicians who, merely because they are inoffensive, easily obtain positions which are withheld as long as possible from artists of talent and character. Having won the second Prix de Rome in 1853, he had, in his twentieth year, been put in charge of one of the solfège classes, and had been appointed professor of harmony in 1871. He composed some songs and two minor operas, which were given at some of the smaller theatres in 1868 and 1869. According to Maurice Emmanuel, he was a mere hack, who had not the least interest in music, or in his profession, or his pupils. A slave to routine, he naturally imposed on his class the rigid rules and mechanical exercises which are insisted upon even to-day. At first, there was a weekly conflict between the original pupil and the autocratic master, one inevitable cause of disagreement being the cadence on the chord of the fourth and sixth, which the master regarded as essential, the pupil as negligible. Their mutual irritation was increased by the master's horror of the whims his pupil sometimes indulged in. Not content with disfiguring his exercises with consecutive fifths and octaves, Debussy took delight in seating himself at the piano when the class was over and producing monstrous successions of weird, barbarous chords—that is to say, chords that were not classified in the official treatises of the Conservatoire. Émile Durand was at first driven distracted by Achille's pranks, but, according to Antoine Banès, another pupil of Durand at that time (whose reminiscences on this subject appeared in the Figaro of the 19th of April 1920) the master was gradually tamed by his pupil.

'At the end of the lesson,' writes Banès, ' when he had examined all our exercises with scrupulous care, he would linger over the correction of young Claude's work with almost epicurean enjoyment. Severe criticisms and angry pencil marks rained upon the pupil's head and music paper. However, as soon as the teacher's natural prejudice was overcome, he would reread in silent concentration the pages he had so cruelly mutilated, murmuring with an enigmatic smile: "Of course, it is all utterly unorthodox, but still, it is very ingenious! " '

A token of this tardy sympathy between them is to be found in the dedication of a sonata for three instruments, completely unknown up to the present, which is included in the Legouix collection. It is entitled: 'First Trio, in G, for Piano, Violin, and 'Cello,' and consists of three parts: *Andantino con moto allegro—Intermezzo*, and *Finale appassionata*. It bears the following inscription: 'An offering of many notes and much friendship from the composer to his professor, Monsieur Émile Durand. Ach. Debussy.' However, whether his harmony master was friendly or not, Achille stood not the least chance of winning a prize or even the smallest distinction in this subject either at the tests in accompaniment and practical harmony in 1878, or at the ordinary harmony examinations, in 1879 and 1880. Yet he did not lose interest in this austere science, though he despised its canons. When class was over, he would often improvise, very freely and fantastically, on the exercises that had been set for his young comrades, harmonizing the given basses and melodies, without much attention to rules and with very little respect for the academic style.

In November 1927 the present writer searched the hitherto unexplored sections of the Conservatoire library for the exercises written by the competitors in the harmony examinations of 1878, 1879, and 1880. Under the blank covers of those outwardly anonymous papers the various tests in the harmonization of basses and melodies were found. The unruly pupil had conferred a title of nobility on himself, by signing: *Ach. de Bussy*. Two characteristics are noticeable in the young student's work: a delightful musical quality, that must surely have charmed the examiners; and an abundance of mistakes in musical syntax, which prevented them from placing him amongst the prizewinners. Debussy's harmony exercises of 1878, 1879, and 1880 are now included in the collection of his manuscripts in the Conservatoire library, as well as the Fugue he wrote for the competition of 1881, and for which he received honourable mention.

A quarter of a century later, Durand's former pupil, who had become in turn a celebrated composer, a musical critic, and a member of the Council of the Conservatoire, condemned in the strongest terms this method of teaching, which he considered most injurious. He admitted, without any false pride that never, either in his student days or afterwards, had he been able to discover in the school exercises any key to those conventional, automatic formulas that constitute the composer's 'stock-in-trade'. 'I humbly acknowledge that I was never able to discover *l'harmonie de l'auteur*; but, indeed, that did not worry me very much.' About the same time, he inveighed against the 'useless and even harmful' competition system. Speaking to the editor of the *Figaro* (14th February 1909) he said: 'Take the case of a really good student who is working hard. He may be in bad form on the day of the competition, and so he fails. I know of nothing more absurd than competitions. Many students who never got a single prize or even an honourable mention at the Conservatoire, have become excellent musicians.' This statement is one of the many criticisms which he passed on the school and which will be found in the writer's book, *The Theories of Claude Debussy* (Chapter III).

In spite of the technical imperfections which handicapped him in the competitions, Achille Debussy had become a brilliant pianist. He wished to devote some time also to the study of the organ. César Franck taught organ-playing and improvisation at the Conservatoire, devoting his attention particularly to the latter. The young pianist joined the old professor's class. He liked and admired him. Later on it was said that Debussy had studied composition as well as improvisation with him. Perhaps he did study more seriously with Franck than he was willing to admit. Franck's influence can certainly be traced, as we shall see later. But he soon gave up the contemplated study. According to some reports, the reason was the professor's harmonic vagueness due to his mania for modulating. Later on, indeed, Debussy went so far as to call his former master 'a modulating machine'.

Achille Debussy had already begun to compose in his Conservatoire days. As we have seen, there is still in existence the manuscript of a 'Trio in G', a very immature composition. His fellow students, Paul Vidal and Raymond Bonheur, remember also a 'Rhapsodie' in the Liszt manner; a song, 'Madrid, Princesse des Espagnes'; a 'Ballade à la Lune', to the poem by Alfred de Musset. The latter is in 6/8 time, in the key of G, and similar in style to Gounod's 'Venise.' These early efforts of a youth lacking literary and musical culture were of little value, as may be judged from the three songs dated approximately 1876 and 1878, and only published in 1882 and 1891. They are entitled 'Nuit d'étoiles', 'Beau soir', 'Fleur des blés', and are mere drawing-room music. Their broad curves and the symmetry of their structure give no hint of the future personality of their composer. It is true that in the beginning of the first song (written when the young musician was scarcely fourteen) some ingenious people have, by dint of violent efforts, managed to trace the melodic contour of the far-distant Mélisande. This they discover in five notes which occur quite casually and without rhythmic accent at the top of the commonplace arpeggios which form the accompaniment.

After this series of disappointments, culminating in his double failure at the piano and the harmony competitions both in 1878 and 1879, Achille Debussy found consolation in a remarkable journey which brought him fruitful musical revelations of the highest interest.

He had the good fortune to be recommended by his master, Marmontel, as pianist to a very artistic society lady. Up to the present, no writer has identified this lady, and Debussy's biographers have given her name as Meich or Metch. She was, as a matter of fact, very well known in musical circles as the friend and patron of a celebrated composer, and her name was Madame Nadedja Filaretovna de Meck. The wife of a Russian engineer, she had been left a widow at an early age, and her large fortune enabled her to bestow a pension for a number of years on the artist, Peter-Ilich Tchaikovsky, whom she greatly admired but never met. At the castle of Chenonceau where she often resided, she kept a trio of young musicians—a pianist, a violinist, and a 'cellist. In 1879 Achille Debussy replaced his comrade, Jimenez, in this little group. Whilst at Chenonceau he was required to play classical music, and no doubt, all Tchaikovsky's chamber music; and he improvised at the piano in accordance with the tastes of his hostess. During the summer Mme de Meck went to Florence, Venice, Vienna, and then to Moscow. She took her pianist with her.

Very little is known about Achille's brief tour. At Vienna, he attended a performance of 'Tristan and Isolde' conducted by Hans Richter. This opera, which had then been played in Germany for some fifteen years, always remained a great favourite with Debussy. Such music must surely have been a revelation to him, and must have produced a very deep and lasting impression on his sensitive mind. Its chromaticism cannot have offended a young artist who had been brought up in the love of Chopin. May we not say, indeed, that all modern harmony, and Debussy's in particular, is founded on that of 'Tristan and Isolde'—or rather, is derived directly from that opera?

He did not, as one might have expected, bring back from Moscow any intimate acquaintance with the works of the new Russian composers, the *Five*, then completely unknown in France. Yet, in the spring of 1880, their names and the titles of some of their works, such as 'The Maid of Pskof' and even 'Boris Godunof,' had been mentioned by Bourgault-Ducoudray in his lectures on the history of music at the Conservatoire. Debussy may have attended those gatherings, where the professor was never tired of expatiating on the beauties of the ancient modes, and where he had popular songs from the Balakiref collection performed by Russian artists. But the *Five* were still neglected by their compatriots. They preferred Tchaikovsky, and at the moment it was his art that aroused the young Frenchman's enthusiasm. Mussorgsky was within two years of his death. Yet even in his own country, he had not begun to attain that great celebrity which was soon to be his throughout the whole musical world. The entire musical harvest of the young traveller's Russian trip seems to have consisted of an old opera of Rimsky-Korsakof, and a few songs of Borodin which some of the Russian critics then considered cacophonous. These were not negligible items. Rimsky's orchestration, derived from that of Berlioz, probably attracted his attention to an orchestral colouring more limpid and fluid than that of Wagner, which had been adopted by most musicians of that day. Some songs of Borodin, like the 'Queen of the Sea' or the 'Sleeping Princess', may have led him towards those experiments in harmony in which he soon became so deeply interested. Certainly, the persistant dissonances of the seconds in the last-mentioned song still haunted him ten years later, when, in March 1889, he wrote the accompaniment to Baudelaire's 'Jet d'eau'.

His friends have testified to the homage he paid even then to Borodin's art. A few years later, he gave several of this composer's songs to his friend, Paul Poujaud, who carefully preserved them. Under the Russian text, Debussy had written a French translation. If further proof of his admiration for Borodin were needed, it is to be found in the songs he wrote soon after his return to Paris. As they are much more skilfully written than his other works of that period, it is probable that he touched them up twelve years later, before giving them to a publisher. These songs are: 'Paysage sentimental', 'Voici que le Printemps' ('Romance'), which bear the date 1880, and 'La Belle au Bois dormant', which, like the two former, was sold in 1893, and published only in 1903. With regard to 'Paysage sentimental', the incorrect musical accent on the first syllable in the first three verses would suffice to determine its early date. The refrain reminds one of a theme by Borodin. It also vaguely suggests a melody which occurs in the cantata Debussy wrote later for the Prix de Rome: the 'Air de Lia' in 'L'Enfant Prodigue'. In the first bars of the vocal score two common chords (on C, and D flat) occur in immediate succession, and other equally daring touches are to be found amongst the free and charming harmonies. 'La Belle au Bois dormant' is very characteristic. The name of the poet, Vincent Hyspa, and the use of the ballad form, suggest the Chat Noir—that famous cabaret which Debussy frequented; though, according to his own denial in Comoedia, 19th of February 1908, he did not collaborate there with Paul Delmet, even anonymously. As a matter of fact, in 'La Belle au Bois dormant' Debussy is evidently haunted by a definite memory of Borodin's 'Sleeping Princess', of which he seems to have attempted to make a replica. Yet he utilizes a popular French *ronde*, 'Nous n'irons plus au bois', which he utilizes again later in 'Jardins sous la pluie'. But here he does not limit himself to a passing or fragmentary allusion; the *ronde* serves as a base to the whole ballad, stands out repeatedly in bold relief, and forms a luminous ending. Of equal historical interest is 'Voici que le Printemps', which, like 'Paysage sentimental', is written to verses by Paul Bourget. One notices a series of those common chords linked together in arpeggios, such as later on characterize the 'Chevaux de Bois', as well as festoons of major thirds in the Borodin manner, and successions of ninths. We have also the old E mode, known as the Dorian, serving as the scale on which he constructs the principal theme. In inspiration, this theme is probably Russian, for it is very similar to a song by Borodin entitled 'Prelude'. These songs and the lively 'Mandoline' of the same period, which shows a characteristic sense of humour and a promising skill in modal treatment, are a great advance on the few commonplace songs composed between 1876 and 1878.[1]

Even if we had no other proofs than these to show that the seventeen-year-old composer came under a definite Slav influence in 1879, this Russian trip would still seem to hold considerable significance for the historian. But we find another reminiscence of Rimsky-Korsakof in the 'Divertissement' from the 'Triomphe de Bacchus', written in his student days, when he was in training for the Prix de Rome, a part of which was published recently with a superadded orchestration. Although some of his friends deny it, Achille Debussy seems to have made another musical discovery at this time which, even if it was outside the domain of Russian art, was none the less noteworthy. This was the spontaneous, extempore music of the gipsies, which he heard in the Moscow cabarets and was to hear again ten years later at the Paris exhibition. This languorous dance music, with its supple melodies and fluid rhythms, is rendered melodiously on the violin; whilst other bowed instruments and the tympanum, in strongly contrasting tone-colouring, supply an accompaniment of free harmonies and unrestricted

[1] Debussy sold the three songs, 'La Belle au Bois dormant', 'Voici que le Printemps', 'Paysage sentimental', to the publisher, Paul Dupont, on the 21st of September 1893. He also made over his rights in the three poems which he had only acquired from Paul Bourget on the 29th of October 1892, and from Vincent Hyspa on the 19th of December of the same year. Bourget sold his copyright for fifty francs. Hyspa gave his gratuitously. These songs were only published after 'Pelléas', in December, 1902.

counterpoint based on strange modes. The unruly pupil, chafing
under the too-rigorous discipline of the Conservatoire, was quick
to profit by a lesson in freedom, as precious as it was paradoxical—
a lesson which was to be of inestimable value to him.

On his return from Moscow, Achille Debussy again attended
Durand's harmony classes at the Conservatoire, but he benefited
little by them. He also joined the new piano accompaniment
class which took the place of the practical harmony and accompaniment course. The professorship of this reorganized subject had
been given to a new-comer, Auguste Bazille, an unknown, but
able musician, who had obtained the second Prix de Rome in 1848.
He had previously been accompanist at the Opéra-Comique,
where he still held the post of director of singing. He had specialized in arranging orchestral scores for the piano. His classes,
which Debussy attended for a year, have been highly praised by
Maurice Emmanuel, who enumerates the difficult tasks that were
imposed on the pupils in this important subject: the extempore
harmonization of a figured bass, the improvisation of an accompaniment to a melody, various transpositions at sight, the arrangement of orchestral scores at the piano. He says:

'Debussy, who felt at his ease with the conscientious and broad-minded
Bazille, soon reached the stage when he could extemporize at the piano
harmonic exercises that were well-balanced and finished in style. He
was fond of adding interesting passing notes to his basses; he endeavoured
to break the monotony of harmonic sequences, whose recurrence was
inevitable, by varying the melodic contour of the upper parts—a proceeding which at first scandalized Bazille, who however soon gave way.
. . . Above all, he excelled in solving the musical enigma of the given
melody. Bazille did not always approve of the underlying modulations
in which his pupil indulged. But, just as Marmontel had realized the
spontaneity of Debussy's talent in spite of his carelessness and eccentricity, so Bazille, also, listened, growled, stormed, but ultimately gave
in—*encaissait*, to quote the expression Debussy himself used when
describing his exploits at the accompaniment class.'

This class, where he became familiar with practical, unwritten
harmony, was of the greatest value to Debussy, whereas the
theoretical harmony class had always appeared to him senseless
and irritating.

Bazille, a highly trained specialist, held that it was only at the
piano—where harmonies were easily found—that one could compose well. Debussy, whose introduction to music had been effected
by means of that instrument, was quite ready to accept his master's
point of view, but he very soon found out how dangerous and

exaggerated this theory was. This fact will be apparent to any one who looks through Debussy's early orchestral scores, which we shall examine later on. The unsuccessful candidate of 1878 and 1879 was compensated in 1880 for his repeated disappointments. Three male candidates entered for the accompaniment competition that year. Achille and his fellow student, Kaiser, took the first prize. But that year again, he failed to pass in harmony. This is accounted for by the fact that in his accompaniment of the twenty-seven bars of the given bass, there are at least half a dozen consecutive fifths and octaves.

In spite of his harmonic shortcomings, he was now ready to take up the study of composition. He joined one of the special classes. Not Massenet's as one might have expected from the melodic colouring of his first works—though this versatile artist would have thoroughly understood his youthful genius. He joined the class of Ernest Guiraud, who had been newly appointed to the Conservatoire. This sensitive and intelligent musician became a real comrade and friend to him. They had many interests in common—aesthetic conversations, painting, harmonic combinations, noctambulism, billiards, cigarettes. The master saw that it would be a mistake to subject such a pupil to a strict observance of the traditional school routine, and he realized that such marvellous gifts should be allowed to develop without too much restraint.

Whilst he was pursuing his studies at the Conservatoire, Debussy was obliged to earn a modest income, sadly inadequate for one of his lordly tastes. He was accompanist to a singing-class held by Madame Moreau-Sainti, an artist to whom he dedicated in 1882 his first song, 'Nuit d'étoiles'. There he developed a taste for choral combinations for female voices. Later, he became accompanist to the Concordia Choral Society, under the directorship of Charles Gounod. This composer, then at the height of his glory, openly proclaimed his young colleague a genius, and used all his influence in his favour during the deliberations in connexion with the competition for the Prix de Rome. Debussy's christian name was usually given as Achille at this time, and his surname was still often written in the titled form—Achille de Bussy. In this form we find it on some programmes, reports of Conservatoire competitions, and on the harmony exercises above mentioned. At the Moreau-Sainti classes he made the acquaintance of Mme Vasnier, a society lady, who for some time to come exercised a considerable influence on him. She was the young and very beautiful wife of an old Parisian architect. She had a light, and evidently very high, voice, to judge by several songs written for her by her admirer, to whom she seems to have been a devoted Egeria. Debussy left his parents' roof and became the constant guest of the Vasniers from 1880 to 1884, both in Paris and at their country house at Ville-d'Avray. In the home of these intelligent and generous friends he was surrounded by all the intellectual and material resources which he lacked elsewhere even in his own home. Fully conscious of his ignorance, he tried to educate himself by reading books of every description, including the encyclopedia. The artistic culture of his host and the talent and charm of his hostess had their inevitable effect. He gave music lessons to the daughter of the house and became greatly attached to his adopted family. In fact, later on, he even contemplated renouncing the Prix de Rome with all its advantages rather than leave these friends. His correspondence of 1885–6 shows clearly how hard he found the separation.

Mme Vasnier's daughter has traced the portrait of Debussy as he was at the age of eighteen.

'He was a big, beardless boy, with strongly marked features and thick, black, curly hair, which he wore flat on his forehead. But in the evening, when his hair had become untidy—which suited him much better—my parents used to say that he looked like some medieval Florentine type. . . . I can still see him in the little drawing-room on the fifth floor, in the rue de Constantinople, where for five years he wrote most of his compositions. He used to come there nearly every evening, often too in the afternoons, leaving behind him the unfinished pages which were placed on a certain little table as soon as he arrived. He used to compose at the piano . . . or at times walking about the room. He would improvise for a long time, then walk up and down humming, with the everlasting cigarette in his mouth, or else rolling tobacco and paper in his fingers. When he had found what he wanted, he began to write. He made few corrections, but he spent a long time working things out in his head and at the piano before he wrote. He was rarely satisfied with his work. . . .'

Apart from these recently published particulars about the Vasnier family, little is known of Debussy's life during his preparation for the Prix de Rome. One public incident might have been expected to draw attention to the young artist. On the 6th of March 1882 the first performance of 'Namouna' was given at the Opera. The leader of the ballet, Sangalli, was hostile to Édouard Lalo's music and, for political reasons, the audience shared her feelings of animosity and deliberately moved about and talked during the symphonic interludes. Debussy, who was full of enthusiasm for the music, became exasperated by this stupid behaviour. Seated in the box usually reserved for the Conservatoire pupils, the young composer gave vent to such noisy protests that he was turned out. In later years, he still had a vivid recollection of that scene, which he described in one of his articles in *Gil Blas* (19th January 1903).

'The mention of "Namouna" reminds me that when I was very young, I attended a performance of that ballet, which was given only too rarely. I indulged in noisy but excusable enthusiasm. M. Vaucorbeil, a very gentle man who was then director of the Opera, had me summarily ejected. I bear him no grudge for that, but I recall this episode with feelings of deep emotion; and nothing has lessened the joyous and affectionate enthusiasm with which I still greet the name of Lalo.'

Meanwhile, at the Conservatoire, Achille Debussy was rapidly earning a reputation for eccentricity; indeed, many looked upon him as a dangerous revolutionary. His independent attitude towards traditional teaching marked him out as a troublesome character, as did also, to an even greater degree, the fantastic pranks he indulged in in his improvisations, and which his fellow student, Maurice Emmanuel, has placed on record. One winter's day in 1883, when Professor Guiraud was late as usual, Debussy seated himself at the piano and, in a series of noisy chromatic passages, gave an imitation of the buses rumbling down the faubourg Poissonnière. He hurled taunts at his fellow pupils, who were dumbfounded at these weird strains. 'What are you so shocked about? Can't you listen to chords without wanting to know their status and their destination? Where do they come from? Whither are they going? What does it matter? Listen; that's enough. If you can't make head or tail of it, go and tell M. le Directeur that I am ruining your ears.' M. le Directeur—then Ambroise Thomas —was probably not informed of these outrages, but they often came to the ears of the Secretary of the Conservatoire, Emile Réty. It surprised this official that a musician like Guiraud could have a favourable opinion of so dangerous a pupil, one who held that in appraising music the only essential condition was that it should please the ear.

During the year 1883-4 Debussy often created disturbances not only in Guiraud's class, but also in Delibes's. Here too, the undisciplined pupil introduced his daring and subversive ideas, using them as the basis of theories that were then inadmissable. He used to preach revolt against traditional harmony to his fellow students. 'Dissonant chords', he would say, 'must be resolved. What's that you say? Consecutive fifths and octaves are forbidden. Why? Parallel movement is condemned, and the sacrosanct contrary movement is beatified. By what right, pray?' Maurice Emmanuel often witnessed with keen interest Debussy's attempts to bewilder

NEW YEAR'S GREETINGS TO MADAME VASNIER
(on the music of *Mandoline*)

ACHILLE-CLAUDE DEBUSSY
(in 1867)

VILLA MEDICI (1885)

Centre, leaning against column, ANDRÉ MARTY : *seated on step, in white coat,* DEBUSSY : *seated on right,* THE DIRECTOR, CABAT : *standing up,* PAUL VIDAL *and* MARCEL BASQUET (*in white*)

the pupils of the orthodox Delibes. He thought it worth while to note down in his exercise books the unheard-of progressions of chords which this apostle of revolt used to produce. He thus preserved shorthand notes of his most striking innovations: strings of fifths and octaves in parallel series, sevenths, resolved by ascending or not resolved at all, false relations, chords of the ninth built up on all the degrees of the scale, chords of the eleventh and the thirteenth, and even aggregations of all the notes of the diatonic scale.

One day, in the spring of 1884, when Léo Delibes was absent, Debussy had the audacity to take the master's place in order, as he put it, to feed the little orphaned birds. That day, there was a regular debauch of chords, 'a stream of outlandish arpeggios, a gurgling of triple trills in both hands simultaneously, continuous successions of indescribable harmonies'. The seance lasted more than an hour. It was brought to an abrupt conclusion by the unexpected arrival of a superintendent, who summarily ejected the impossible 'fanatic'.

Previous to this, Maurice Emmanuel had had an opportunity of enjoying an imitation of Achille-Claude Debussy's sacrilegious tricks. Guiraud, the professor of composition, Ernest Reyer, the composer of 'Sigurd' and 'Salammbô', Réty, the Secretary of the Conservatoire, and other artists were in the habit of meeting occasionally in Marmontel's salon in the rue Blanche, Paris. The host, in an ironical mood, was fond of inflicting 'novel harmonies' on his guests. He would play long series of chords chock full of augmented intervals, successions of chords of the ninth, the eleventh, and the thirteenth, which amused Guiraud, horrified Réty, and exasperated Reyer. Thereupon, Marmontel would hastily disclaim all responsibility and explain that the author of these novelties was young Achille Debussy, whom he liked to call 'mon second prix de 1877'.

These daring innovations, which were at first regarded as mere folly, had aroused the curiosity, though not the sympathy, of Théodore Dubois. This future director of the Conservatoire was then professor of harmony there and organist at the church of the Madeleine. He wagered that he could improvise on his organ, with one finger, an accompaniment to a verse of the Magnificat, 'in the Debussy manner', and he carried out his strange bet. One day, in his improvisation during Vespers, he used only the mutation stops—whereby each note was accompanied by its upper harmonics—and the chords thus formed, when played in strict succession, did indeed produce young Achille's favourite device. Thus, in 1883, in sheer mockery, we find Théodore Dubois mimicking the eccentricities of a young pupil from the solemn heights of his organ gallery, at the risk of shocking the congregation! In indulging in the ironical experiment, this grave pedagogue, a strict upholder of traditional harmony, unintentionally provided an *organic* justification for the daring innovations his academic prejudice explicitly condemned.

Thus the young rebel acquired a precocious reputation in the little world of the Conservatoire. Having drawn up the plan of his intended revolution, he now began to make what we may call laboratory experiments, in order to train himself in the practice of his new principles, as well as to irritate and scandalize the intolerant pedants of the school. In his more serious compositions he only dared to give a discreet hint or a passing suggestion of this new style, which was still vague and incoherent. We have met with some such touches in his songs of 1880. Others may be found in songs of the same date which remained unpublished until 1926, and should have been left so. One wonders whether similar traces exist in his unpublished, and entirely unknown works, such as: 'Les Roses', for voice and piano, or the 'Nocturne' and the 'Scherzo' for violin, in the performance of which he took part with Mme Vasnier and the violinist, Thieberg, at Paris, on the 12th of May 1882. Debussy took good care not to show this new tendency too clearly in the compositions he wrote for the Conservatoire. The fact is that at the national Conservatoire of Paris—where the training was indeed excellent—many of the masters made a point of ignoring and even condemning all innovations. More than one music student was forced to leave the State Academy simply because, in the presence of a reactionary pedagogue, he had proclaimed his admiration of new works then considered revolutionary, or professed his faith in new theories, even though these were merely a revival of Greek art. Such was, in fact, the fate of Maurice Emmanuel and of Émile Vuillermoz. In 1886 the former was expelled from the school, where to-day he lectures on the history of music, because he believed in the eternal adaptability of the manifold modes of antiquity—a flagrant heresy in the eyes of his master, Léo Delibes. Émile Vuillermoz was sent away, in 1902, for having disobeyed his harmony professor, Taudou, who had absolutely forbidden him to go and hear a dangerous work that was being performed at the Opéra-Comique—none other than 'Pelléas et Mélisande!'

The broad-minded Ernest Guiraud, who had the courage to introduce unusual successions of chords into his own scores, took the greatest interest in the experiments of his independent-minded pupil. But he was experienced enough to realize that it was unwise for a candidate who aimed at academic distinctions to indulge in unusual idioms. One day, as Louis Laloy relates, Debussy showed his composition master a score he had written to Théodore de Banville's 'Diane au Bois.' Guiraud read it through carefully twice, and admired its many good points. But he gave his opinion quite frankly to the audacious young author: 'It is all very interesting. But you must keep that sort of thing for later on, or else you will never get the Prix de Rome.' So, to all appearances, Debussy renounced his own harmonic instincts and adopted the utilitarian principles of his master and patron.

ACHILLE-CLAUDE DEBUSSY, WHILE AT THE
CONSERVATOIRE
(about 1874)

CHAPTER II

THE PRIX DE ROME (1883–84)

IN 1882 Achille Debussy again took part in the Conservatoire competitions in counterpoint and fugue and was awarded a second honourable mention. The manuscript of his fugue is preserved in the Conservatoire library. Some time previously, about the middle of May, he had gone in for the preliminary examination for the Prix de Rome competition but had not passed. The two tasks set for this preliminary test, a fugue and a chorus with orchestral accompaniment, have been found in the archives and have recently been placed with his other manuscripts. The fugue is written on a theme supplied by Gounod. The chorus—for female voices and orchestra —bears the title 'Printemps'. On the occasion of its ill-timed publication, in May 1928, in order to distinguish it from other works of that name, the title was altered to 'Salut, Printemps', these being the two first words of the poem, by Comte de Ségur: 'Salut, printemps, jeune saison! . . .' This immature work shows no signs of the candidate's originality. The only thing that attracts attention is his fondness for the harp. What this little manuscript does betray is his lack of elementary education: for, in copying out the text of the poem, he made numerous spelling mistakes. We find the following phrase repeated three times with this spelling: 'Dieu rend *au plaine* leur *courronne.*' [1]

Whilst those of his fellow students who had entered for the Prix de Rome were presenting their cantatas to the Institut and the public, Debussy was training himself for the following year's competition by composing a work whose existence has remained unknown up to the present. The manuscripts, both of the orchestral score and of an arrangement for piano duet, are included in the Legouix collection. The composition—an 'Intermezzo', signed 'Ach. Debussy', and dated 21st June 1882—is an interpretation of the following passage from Heinrich Heine's 'Intermezzo', which the musician did not succeed in copying out without spelling mistakes: 'The mysterious isle of the spirits showed faintly in the moonlight; exquisite sounds reached the ear and dancing shapes floated mistily. The music grew ever sweeter, the whirling dance more alluring. . . .' If this subject was Achille's own choice, and not set by the Conservatoire, we may look upon it as a sign of his future impressionistic tendencies.

[1] Should, of course, read: '*Dieu rend aux plaines leur couronne.*'

By the following year, 1883, he was ready for the final competition for the Prix de Rome. In the preliminary examination he took fourth place, coming after Paul Vidal, Charles René, and Xavier Leroux, and before Edmond Missa. As in the previous year, he had to write the customary fugue and chorus. The latter composition, for male voices and orchestra, was written to a poem of Lamartine's entitled 'Invocation'. The fugue is not to be found in the archives of the Conservatoire library. The original score of the chorus was recently bound together with the cantata which he wrote for the competition. This chorus is nothing more than a correct exercise, giving no hint of future characteristics. The composer confessed to his comrades that he lacked the religious feeling requisite for the type of text which had been set for the examination.

The poem chosen for the final competition of 1883 was 'Le Gladiateur', by Émile Moreau. It was considered an excellent choice. Some even thought, as a newspaper remarked, that it had only one fault: 'that of being so harmonious as to make the addition of music almost unnecessary'. The cantatas were performed on the 22nd of June for the musical section of the Institut; and on the following day, they were given again in the presence of the entire Académie des Beaux-Arts. The performances, at which Gounod presided, were considered very brilliant both as regard the standard of the compositions and the manner of interpretation. Paul Vidal's score gave Ernest Van Dyck, an unknown young Belgian singer, the opportunity of making an extempore début in Paris. Achille also availed himself of the assistance of the celebrated Gabrielle Krauss, Taskin, and a Conservatoire pupil, named Muratet.

The struggle lay between Vidal, Debussy, and René, all three of whom were pianists, former pupils of Marmontel, and laureates of his class. When it came to the vote, Paul Vidal headed the list. There was a close contest for the 'premier second grand prix'. At the third ballot, Debussy had sixteen votes, and René the same number. When the fourth ballot was taken, Debussy got four additional votes, and so won the second prize, the third being awarded to his rival.

The musical critics were very sympathetic towards the 'premier second grand prix'. Stoullig considered that he had undoubtedly 'less knowledge, but more personality then M. Vidal'. Gaston Serpette acclaimed his 'remarkable qualities. The final trio, in particular, is so excellent that it looked for a moment as if M. Vidal must lose the first prize. It is true that M. Debussy was fortunate in his interpreters: M. Taskin, M. Muratet, a young tenor of the greatest promise, and above all, the marvellous Gabrielle Krauss, who made the music vibrate with her deep, tragic emotion'. *L'Art musical* registered an equally favourable impression. The editor declared that although Debussy was less expert in the technique of his art, he was more original than Vidal. He regretted that the Institut could not award two first prizes. He considered Debussy in every respect worthy of the highest award and described his success as highly significant, especially in the opinion of musicians.

Charles Darcours, of the *Figaro*, recognized in Debussy 'an exceptionally musical nature, but a rather exaggerated craving for originality'. This critic, whose real name was Charles Réty, was a brother of the Secretary of the Conservatoire. He was a former laureate in *solfège*, had been director of the Théatre Lyrique from 1850 to 1862, and was the author of the poem set for the Prix de Rome competition in 1880. In his reports of these examinations, his remarks probably reflected the opinions of some member of the jury, possibly those of his brother, who had been a student in the harmony and accompaniment class, or of some other well-informed musician. This would account for the accuracy and the musical knowledge shown in his criticisms. He examined the score in detail:

'M. Debussy has written a good instrumental introduction; his processional march is correct in colour; his invocation to Baal is more remarkable for its weirdness than for the correctness of the declamation. The beginning of the duet is exquisite; Fulvia's phrase lacks simplicity, but it ends in a deeply poetical strain which was marvellously rendered by Mme Krauss. The trio is well constructed, but there is too much vocal unison, a device which is not in accordance with the best French traditions. The death scene is remarkable for its solemn, poetical atmosphere.'

Ernest Reyer, Berlioz's successor in the *Journal des Débats*, devoted an important article to the Prix de Rome competition, on the 28th of October 1883. He admitted that Paul Vidal's two rivals had 'run him close. . . . M. Debussy has the temperament of a real musician, but his talents lack balance, and he is far from possessing the deep knowledge of his craft which young Vidal has already acquired'.

The critics were quite right when they pointed out Debussy's technical deficiencies. They are very evident to any one who looks through the score of 'Le Gladiateur', which it is to be found in the library of the Paris Conservatoire where it had been completely forgotten. This composition by an inexperienced pupil is highly

MUSIC FACSIMILE (FROM *LE GLADIATEUR*)

MUSIC FACSIMILE (FROM *LE GLADIATEUR*)

interesting historically. It is scored for full orchestra (two flutes and a piccolo, two oboes, two B flat clarinets, two bassoons, two valve horns in F, two horns in D, two cornets in B flat, two valve trumpets in F, three trombones, one tuba, kettle-drums, and the usual strings). The structure is exceedingly weak, the instrumentation shows great inexperience, and the prosodic treatment is clumsy and incorrect, as was indeed the rule in most of the operas of that day. The whole thing suggests an attempt on the part of a gifted pianist to transport his facile improvisations into the domain of the orchestra without the necessary adjustment.

In the very first pages the awkward writing for the strings betrays Debussy's ignorance of the classic style. We find chromatic passages used as padding, just as they would be dashed off by the fingers of a pianist; parts doubled in the wood-winds, and an overloading of secondary subjects, which cannot possibly produce the required sonority. The literary ideas in the poem are interpreted by light, transient touches; the descriptive effects are cursory, and are not subsequently utilized. The trio, which was so much appreciated at the time, consists of the merest harmonic patchwork; it contains only a few bars in the traditional contrapuntal style. The melodic feeling is on the whole elegant but commonplace.

One naturally hopes to find some hint of his later characteristics in this first orchestral score of the future *Maître*, who was then not quite twenty-one years old. There are perhaps two or three very vague signs. For instance, in the 'Invocation' (page 26), after the first five bars, we have series of simultaneous descending chromatic passages for the wind instruments which, in conjunction with the tremolo of the strings, produce so-called dissonant chords, of rather novel colouring. One notices also a tendency to subdivide the instruments. Again, on page 102, there are a few bars which give a general impression of freedom of line and movement and aim at creating a sonorous atmosphere. Particularly in the scene where Fulvie sings '*Sous ton ciel brûlant au pays des palmes*', the treatment of the flutes, clarinets, horn, and harp is noteworthy, and also the entry of the strings with pedal notes in the extreme parts. That is perhaps the best passage. It is worth reproducing as an example.

There is a wide gulf between this clumsily written score 'Le Gladiateur' and the one Debussy was to write the following year for the Prix de Rome competition. It seems incredible that only twelve months elapsed between the composition of the cantatas of 1883 and 1884. The young musician must have worked hard during that interval. He also came under various influences that were favourable to his development. Chief amongst these were: his professor, Ernest Guiraud, an experienced master and an expert in instrumentation; Gounod, whom he saw every week at the meetings of the Concordia Society, and with whom he had long talks afterwards; Édouard Lalo, whose music he always admired intensely; the works of the classical and romantic authors which he had been advised to study; and above all the instrumentation of Weber's masterpieces. Then came the revelation of two of Massenet's works, which were produced at the Opéra-Comique and the Théâtre des Italiens, in January and February 1884. Whilst listening to 'Manon' and 'Hérodiade', a student in composition might learn many profitable lessons under the pleasantest conditions.

At the preliminary examination for the Prix de Rome competition in 1884 he took fourth place. Before him came Xavier Leroux, Charles René, and a new comer, Kaiser. As had happened the previous year, Edmond Missa was the only candidate who did not take precedence of him on the preliminary list. Achille Debussy's fugue, adorned with the composer's fantastic signature, and the choral test—which, as in 1882, was entitled 'Le Printemps', but the text of which was by Jules Barbier—are preserved in the Conservatoire library and are bound in the same volume as the final cantata. The 'Printemps' of 1884 is the work of a painstaking pupil who had grown considerably in wisdom since the preceding year. The fugue, written on a subject chosen by Massenet, contains some audacious touches which the professors must have regarded as errors, especially his contempt for structural balance which is noticeable in the *stretto*. According to the regulations, the candidate had noted on his manuscript in red ink, the mechanical academic processes: *exposition, subject, answer, counter-subject, subject in the relative key,* &c.[1]

The poem chosen for the final competition for the Prix de Rome was 'L'Enfant Prodigue', by Édouard Guinand. The public performance took place on the 27th of June. Debussy's interpreters were Rose Caron, Van Dyck, and Taskin; he himself and his friend René Chansarel performed the orchestral part at the piano. He had a remarkable success. Out of twenty-eight academicians twenty-two voted for him. Thus, before he had completed his twenty-second year, Achille Debussy won the first 'Grand Prix

---

[1] At one of the meetings of La Musique Vivante (Paris, 25th and 26th of November 1927) the author produced as an interesting historical curiosity this fugue, written for the preliminary competition, whose existence was unknown.

de Rome'. His comrades, René and Leroux, were awarded the first and second 'Second Grand Prix'. This verdict was justified by the fine melodic and dramatic qualities of Debussy's cantata. During the deliberations his cause was strongly supported by his friend Gounod—an influential member of the Academy—and by Guiraud, who acted as a supplementary adjudicator. But the verdict did not satisfy every one. Arthur Pougin, a critic who hated all innovations, wrote a report of the competition for two reviews. His article in the *Ménestrel* was partly devoted to the praise of Charles René's cantata, which he described as: 'charming, elegant, and exceptionally original', and superior, in his opinion, to that of 'M. de Bussy'. He also praised Kaiser's work, which had been awarded no distinction by the Institut, but he did not write a single word about the prize-winning composition. Again, in his notes in the Belgian review, the *Guide musical*, he complained that the prize had been given to a candidate whom he considered inferior to Charles René, and added: 'This is also the opinion of a member of the Academy who is well known in Brussels.' This academician was evidently Ernest Reyer, who was very partial to Charles René, and who gave no report of the competition in his feuilleton in the *Journal des Débats*.

Another critic, Charles Darcours—the complex source of whose sound opinions the author has previously conjectured—discussed the work of the various candidates in an important article in the *Figaro* of the 1st of July. The criticism is judicious and, to some extent, prophetic. It is a sort of differential diagnosis accompanied, in the case of the prize-winner, by a forecast which strikes us as quite remarkable to-day. He describes René's cantata as sound, well-balanced, correct, and impersonal; Missa's, with its old-fashioned Italian formulas, he considers already out of date; Kaiser's is good, but too restrained. But, for Debussy and his score, he has high praise and wise criticism:

'This year's competition has brought to light a young musician of talent, a student who does not, perhaps, surpass his colleagues in actual attainments, but who proves in the very first bars of his composition that he is not one of the common herd. This is worth something in an age when everyone has talent and no one individuality. . . . M. Debussy, the hero of the competition, is a musician who is destined to meet with a great deal of praise . . . and plenty of abuse! At any rate, he is the most *alive* of the candidates this year and for many years past. The very first bars of his score reveal a courageous nature and an outstanding personality.'

The critic of the *Figaro* goes on to praise the short, striking instrumental introduction and the beginning of Azaël's aria, with its delightfully poetical atmosphere. But he does not consider the composition faultless.

'We find nearly all the faults that characterize the work of the musical dreamer. The tonality is often indefinite, the vocal parts are written without much attention to compass or timbre, there are frequent and unaccountable outbursts of violence, and confusion would seem to be a guiding principle. Yet, in spite of all, M. Debussy's cantata is an exceedingly interesting work, by reason of its colouring, the expressive quality of the occasionally over-emphasized declamation—and above all, the exuberant individuality it reveals.... It is up to the young musician now to find his own path, amidst the enthusiasms and the antagonisms he is certain to arouse.'

These good and bad qualities which the critic pointed out in 1884 are much less evident forty or fifty years later. What chiefly strikes one to-day, on reading or listening to this old composition (written in twenty-five days by a young man of twenty-one and a half years), is the Massenet-like character of the melody, then the fashion amongst the pupils of all the composition classes at the Conservatoire. Debussy himself acknowledged that he had deliberately imitated the charming style of the composer of 'Manon' in order to win the favour of the adjudicators, the majority of whom were not musicians. The prize-winner's companions had anticipated that the harmonic tricks he usually indulged in would horrify the Institut. But, in this work, there are practically no traces of his insolent innovations. Achille had behaved with remarkable docility in accordance with the advice of his master, Guiraud. The attention which his work attracted was due chiefly to its rather effeminate grace, its commonplace charm, its orchestral colouring, which imitated that of Lalo and Guiraud, and the slightly oriental character of the dances, probably a reminiscence of Léo Delibes's 'Lakmé', which had been performed in the spring of 1883.

A glance through the complete original score, which is kept in the Conservatoire library, enables us to estimate relatively the standard of the laureate of 1884, and the importance of his discoveries. The first bars, for example, contain an intimation of a tendency that was to characterize some of his later music: an attempt at those colourless chords he achieved in such perfection in 'Le Martyre de saint Sébastien'. The style is no longer awkward as it was in 1883. The orchestral colouring is very different. The frequent division of the strings, and certain light, detached touches, give the composition something of that undecided, vague, hazy atmosphere that was to distinguish his future works and stamp them with a personal charm. Here and there, we have effects of fourths and fifths attenuated by sixths, free successions of sevenths, a transient use of the whole tone scale. . . . In these details, but most of all in its atmosphere, the work shows a subtle but obvious pre-Debussyism. If we but glance through the prelude, and notice the instrumentation woven of harps, of high-pitched, muted violins, and of wood-winds tracing ever-changing patterns, we realize how far we are from 'Le Gladiateur' of 1883, and how very near his future masterpieces.

Debussy cannot have attached much importance to this facile composition of his student days, the seeming orthodoxy of which was evidently due to the fact that it was not advisable to shock his academic judges. He dedicated this cantata to his master, Ernest Guiraud. Debussy did not foresee that, thirty years later the editor, Durand, who had already published the competition score in 1884, would attempt, for very legitimate commercial reasons, to produce this student's work at the theatre, under the new title of 'lyrical drama in one act'. It was given at the Théatre Lyrique de Vaudeville on the 10th of December 1919. In 1907-8 Debussy was obliged to revise the instrumentation of the 'Enfant Prodigue' for concert performances. He himself described it as theatrical, amateurish, and boring. He was surprised and delighted to find thirds and fifths in the part—for the cor anglais! 'It is a great pity,' he wrote, 'that this instrument has not yet been invented!' In his manuscript one can see the old text in black ink and the corrections in red. Thus, we are able to compare two versions of the 'Cortège' and of the 'Airs de danse', as well as of the 'Récit' and 'Air d'Azaël', completely rewritten, after a lapse of twenty-five years, by Debussy's own hand. After 1902, when 'L'Enfant Prodigue' became a drawing-room favourite, the composer was often annoyed by the fashionable success accorded to one page of his cantata, 'L'Air de Lia', whose Massenetism is so obvious, whilst its Debussyism is limited to some equivocal tonalities and a few furtive harmonic successions.

The competition for the Prix de Rome seems to have left a very unpleasant impression on Debussy. Many years later he was still full of rancour when he spoke of it or mentioned it in his articles. He ridiculed the conditions under which the cantata had to be written. 'They expect you to be full of ideas and inspiration at a given time of the year. If you are not in form that particular month, so much the worse for you. It is a purely arbitrary affair, without any significance as regards the future.' He criticized the cantata itself as 'a hybrid form, that partakes clumsily of all that is commonplace in the opera or in the choral symphony. It is, indeed, an invention of the Institut—one of whose authorship no one need boast'. He also censured the preparatory training for the manufacture of the cantata, 'by which the candidates are trained like a horse for the Grand Prix'. He protested against the composition of the adjudicating committee: 'The umpires are the members of the Institut. A curious consequence of this fact is, that Messrs. Bourguereau and Massenet adjudicate the various matches indiscriminately, whether the games are played in music, painting, sculpture, architecture, or engraving. It has not yet occurred to any one to include a dancer on the committee, though this would be logical, for Terpsichore was not the least amongst the nine Muses.' Other criticisms of this nature are quoted in the author's book, *The Theories of Claude Debussy.*

Debussy cannot have been entirely indifferent to his success and 'this little taste of glory'. He admitted that when he arrived at the Villa Medici in 1885 he was almost inclined to think himself 'the darling of the gods of whom the ancient legends speak'. But, although he realized the advantages of his position, he soon saw its drawbacks. Twenty years later, on the 6th of April 1903, he related in *Gil Blas* his 'happiest impression of the Prix de Rome', which he experienced, he said, on the Pont des Arts, the bridge leading to the Institut, when the competition was over and he stood watching the movements of the steamers on the Seine as he waited to hear the results.

'I was not excited', he wrote, 'and I had lost any particularly Roman emotions, so fascinated was I by the exquisite play of the sunlight on the rippling waters—a sight which those picturesque loiterers whom the rest of Europe envies us, watch spellbound for hours from our bridges. Suddenly, some one tapped me on the shoulder and said breathlessly: "You've won the prize!" . . . People may not believe me, but, nevertheless, it is a fact that all my joy was over. I saw clearly the worries and annoyances that the smallest official position brings in its train. Besides, I felt that I was no longer free. . . .'

According to recently published documents, it would seem that the worries and annoyances were chiefly connected with his separation from the Vasnier family, which his departure for Rome necessitated. He was often tempted to renounce his sojourn in Italy in order to remain with his friends, especially his interpreter, the 'melodious fay' to whom he had dedicated, as a mark of eternal gratitude, the series of songs he had written for her during the preceding years.

The manuscript book containing these songs has been preserved, and now forms part of a private collection. It includes five pieces from Verlaine's 'Fêtes galantes' ('Pantomime', 'En sourdine', 'Mandoline', 'Clair de Lune', and 'Fantoches') of which he wrote the first version in 1882 and 1883. To these, he added a 'Chanson espagnole' for two similar voices, a 'Rondel Chinois', and several little songs written between September 1883 and the spring of 1884 to poems by Paul Bourget. The most noteworthy is a 'Romance' ('Silence ineffable'), which should not be confounded with the 'Romance' published in 1881, nor with another, published later on, under the title 'Voici que le printemps'. A careful review of these youthful works, by Charles Koechlin, appeared in the *Revue musicale* of May 1926. Four of the songs were published in the same issue of this review, namely: 'Pantomime', 'Clair de lune' (which, except for the text, has nothing in common with the version which Debussy gave to the publisher, Hartmann, for the first collection of 'Fêtes galantes'), 'Pierrot, and 'Apparition'. Historical curiosity, as futile as it is indiscreet, explains, although it does not justify, the posthumous publication of these songs. The composer himself would have opposed it, as also the publication of other works which have appeared recently or are about to be printed.[1]

[1] Mr. Richard Aldrich of New York is the owner of a manuscript signed A. Debussy, in which, under the general title of 'Poèmes de Paul Verlaine', we find the following sub-titles: *Fêtes galantes*: 1. 'Mandoline', 2. 'En sourdine', 3. 'Pantomime', 4. 'Paysage sentimental'. *Romances sans paroles*: 1. 'Paysage', 2. 'Chevaux de bois'. Then follows the complete musical text of 'Mandoline' (four pages); the first page of 'En sourdine' (without the words); and one other page containing the poetical text alone of: 'Mandoline', 'Pantomime' (i.e. the *Fantoches*: 'Scaramouche et Pulcinella . . .'), and 'Pierrot'.

CHAPTER III

THE VILLA MEDICI (1885-7)
THE 'ENVOIS DE ROME' (1885-90)

ACHILLE DEBUSSY set out for Rome on the 27th of January 1885—seven months, to the day, after his success at the Institut de France. A three-years' sojourn at the Villa Medici was one of the conditions attached to the scholarship he had won so triumphantly in 1884. In the Roman Campagna he was to meet again the laureates of his own year and those of the preceding years engaged in the study of the various arts: painting, sculpture, architecture, engraving, music. The youthful representatives of the last-mentioned subject were Georges Marty and Gabriel Pierné, the winners of the Prix de Rome in 1882, and Paul Vidal, with whom Debussy had competed in 1883.

The pleasant life led by the artists at the Villa Medici does not seem to have suited Debussy as well as might have been expected. Achille, nicknamed 'the Prince of Darkness', was of a very independent character, and resented the slightest restriction of his liberty. He felt the restraint so keenly, and it made so deep an impression on him, that, even twenty years later, he felt an irresistible desire to make a public statement on the subject. He voiced his retrospective complaints in 1903 in two articles which were published in *Gil Blas* on the 6th of April and the 10th of June. The Villa Medici was under the directorship of Louis-Nicolas Cabat, whom Debussy describes as 'an excellent landscape painter and a very distinguished man of the world', who 'never took the least interest in the students, except as regards administrative matters.' He describes the life of the Prix de Rome laureates as a combination of the existence at 'a cosmopolitan hotel, a private college, and a compulsory civilian barracks'. There was no intercourse with Roman society which was 'very aloof, and inhospitable towards the young students whose typically French independence of character did not harmonize with the cold formality of the Romans'. He speaks of aimless journeys throughout Italy visiting towns 'through which we passed as utter strangers'; the conversation of the young artists which consisted entirely of table-talk; deficiencies in the housing arrangements; mediocre artistic standards; a school of *arrivisme*. Even when the centenary of the Académie de France in Rome was celebrated in 1903, the rancour of the former laureate was not dispelled by the festive atmosphere. Debussy's report of the proceedings was confined to some twenty savage lines, ending as follows: 'One could have wished that in honour of the occasion, some improvements had been made in the meals supplied to the Prix de Rome students . . . of the present day. We narrowly escaped poisoning, and dyspepsia is not a necessary addition to the aesthetic equipment of an artist.'

His letters to his friends, the Vasniers, bear out the fact that he felt a real, though not continuous, distaste for the life in Rome. He tells of 'the indescribable discomfort of feeling out of his proper atmosphere'; his antipathy towards his companions, of which many of them were more or less definitely aware; his loathing for the life in common, and of the material conditions at the 'abominable villa'; the sufferings he endured as a result of the heat, and the fevers which often prostrated him; all the unpleasant details connected with the 'life of a non-commissioned officer on full pay'. And yet his sojourn in Rome brought him warm friendships, great advantages, and genuine pleasures which, for obscure sentimental reasons, he concealed from his former hosts in Paris, his 'second family' to whom he wrote such affectionate, tender, almost filial letters. This correspondence, although it has only been partially published, is extremely interesting. It enables us, in some measure, to follow Debussy's career in Rome, the development of his aesthetic ideas, and the progress of his compositions. His deliberately gloomy colouring may, however, be somewhat brightened.

He expressed his disappointment on the very day he arrived at the Villa Medici. With friendly intent, his former companions had come to meet him at Monte-Rotondo. He thought them changed. 'There is none of the warm friendship of the Paris days. They are stiff, and seem to be full of their own importance—there is too much Prix de Rome about these people!' He played his cantata. It was a great success. But as at the Institut the year before, he had the impression that it was not appreciated by the musicians. Yet, these very musicians, his good friends, Marty, Pierné, and Vidal, had already played and sung the new-comer's prize-work amongst themselves. So, from the very start, a feeling of hostility existed—if we can believe Debussy's reports, which were intended to arouse the sympathy of Mme Vasnier. He says: 'The artistic environment and the good comradeship that the older men talk about, are greatly exaggerated.' He tried to work, but found it impossible, both at the official residence, where he was irritated by the general promiscuity, and at the villa of his friend Count Joseph Primoli, at Fiumiselino, by the sea, where he spent

some weeks alone in order to satisfy his love of solitude. He began
'Zuleïma,' to a libretto by Georges Boyer, adapted from Heine's
'Almanzor.' But he soon realized that it was too old-fashioned
and fusty. 'Those great, stupid verses are great only in their length.
They oppress me and my music would surely sink beneath their
weight.' At times, he gave up all idea of writing even the first
of the three parts which the work comprised, though eventually
it became his first *envoi de Rome*. He considered the third part
unsuitable and 'too stupid', and the second not much better.

At the beginning of June 1885 he admitted that he would not
be able 'to imprison his music in any very definite mould'. He
thought he would do better with 'a subject in which the action
was more or less sacrificed to a prolonged description of the
feelings of the soul. I think that in such a work, the music might
become more human, more real; and one could deepen and refine
the means of expression'.

He decided to take up once more Théodore de Banville's 'Diane
au Bois', a composition at which he had already worked at the Conservatoire; the score whose ultra-modern tendencies had aroused the
anxiety of his master, Ernest Guiraud. He intended to make this
work his first *envoi*. He decided to get the poet's permission,
through his godson, Rochegrosse, and to ask him to add some
choruses to complete the libretto. The work appealed to him, 'for
it is not in the least like the poems usually chosen for the *envois*
which are really nothing more than glorified cantatas'. One
cantata was enough for him. He wanted to 'produce something
original and—not always follow the same paths'. Already fore-
seeing an event that was imminent, and wishing to proclaim the
aristocratic ideal to which he always adhered, of writing exclusively
for an élite, he added: 'I am sure the Institut will not approve, for,
naturally, it considers that the path it prescribes is the only right one.
But, it can't be helped! I am too fond of my freedom, and of my
own ideas. This is the only kind of music I can write. The
question is, whether I shall be capable of doing it. I can't say.
At any rate, I shall do my best to satisfy a few people, I don't care
what the rest think.'

This fine declaration of independence was written on the 4th of
June 1885. After a few weeks at Count Primoli's villa, which he
spent in working or in wandering about the beautiful countryside,
he found himself once more a prey to artistic uncertainty. He confessed his difficulties in a letter dated the 24th of November.

'I am working hard. I feel that I must make sure of quantity, since I
cannot count on the quality of my work. "Diana" is giving me a lot of

trouble. I cannot find a phrase that will express her personality as I should wish. Indeed, it is no easy matter, for the phrase I need must have a cold beauty, that suggests no idea of passion. Love does not come to Diana till much later, and is, in reality, only an accident. It should be possible to produce good effects by transforming the phrase whilst keeping its contours, as Diana gradually loses her power in the struggle against love.'

On the 29th of January, he writes:

'the *envoi* keeps me busy and preoccupied. One day, I think I have found what I want, the next day I fear I have been mistaken. No composition has ever given me such anxiety. Besides, you can't imagine how difficult it is to render the thousand and one sensations of a character, whilst keeping the form as clear as possible. And, as the scenes in "Diana" were not planned from the point of view of music, there is a danger that they may seem too long. It is the very mischief to keep up the interest, so that the public may not be bored to tears.'

Nine months went by, and his work had not progressed. He had made a rough plan for 'Salammbô,' but he put aside the few notes he had made with the idea of developing them later in Paris. He did some sketches of songs to poems by Paul Bourget, but he only wrote one new one. 'The rest', he wrote, 'are like the song about Marlborough'. 'Zuleïma' was dead; he would not hear of it; that kind of music did not suit him. He wished to find a type 'supple and mobile enough to adjust itself to the lyrical emotions of the soul, and the whims of dreams'. The wish was not easy to realize. As for 'Diane au Bois', only one scene was finished and he was none too well pleased with it. Later on, his friend Paul Vidal recognized some of its picturesque impressionist touches in the 'Prélude à l'Après-midi d'un Faune.'

'I have, perhaps, undertaken a work beyond my capacity,' wrote Debussy. 'As no precedent exists, I find that I am obliged to invent new forms. I might seek help from Wagner, but I need not tell you how ridiculous it would be for me even to attempt such a thing. I should be merely adopting his manner of linking up the scenes, whereas, my aim is to try and maintain the lyrical atmosphere and not to allow the orchestra to predominate.'

This anxiety about his music, this impression that he was making no artistic progress, often tormented him during the course of his life. It greatly increased the feeling of enervation he experienced in Rome. He used to spend long hours dreaming as he looked out over the town from the windows of his room. He first occupied one that was known as 'the Etruscan tomb'. 'Its walls were painted green, and seemed to recede as one walked towards them.' Later on he had a room that was decorated with frescoes painted by Besnard. The Villa Medici, the beautiful 'maison de France', was a prison to him, and the director—Ernest Hébert, a painter, who had succeeded Cabat—he looked upon as a jailor. But he was a good-natured jailor, surely, for he did not refuse Debussy permission to go to Paris; and at his house, where some Parisian friends used to come on visits, the exile found relaxations that must have proved a powerful antidote to his sentimental sorrows. He constantly entertained the idea of resigning in order to be able to return to Paris. In September 1885 he expected to leave at the end of his first year, which he looked upon as completely wasted. Towards the end of the winter of 1885–6 he planned an escape in a romantic setting, the success of which was facilitated by his talent for acting. He came back a few weeks later, but could not bring himself to complete the regulation period. His longing to leave the Villa became so strong that he returned to Paris in 1887, having spent a little over two years in Rome in his official capacity.

His sentimental troubles were natural enough. His musical worries are easily explained. He was, by nature and instinct, a musician of marked originality with the most individual ideas on art, far in advance of those about him. He had invented a new idiom, the component elements of which he had already collected in his Conservatoire days, yet he did not dare to exploit its treasures; and in addition he was surrounded by influences that were hostile to his natural tendencies. In the company of some of his fellow students, he indulged in music of the most varied types, both classical and modern. Paul Vidal and he used to read through scores of every description with studious and loving care. They played in duet form the organ works of Bach; they performed at two pianos Beethoven's Ninth Symphony, whose praises Debussy was to sing later on in such fitting terms;[1] or again, Emmanuel Chabrier's 'Valses Romantiques', whose harmonic and rhythmic originality must have pleased and interested him. He also devoted time to other arts besides music and visited the museums and galleries. Some of the masterpieces of painting produced a very deep impression on him. Like his Prix de Rome comrades in the other arts, he was attracted by the new style of the pre-Raphaelites. Fascinated, for a time, by this ephemeral aesthetic tendency, he became an enthusiastic admirer of original painters like Whistler, whose *Nocturnes* delighted him, and he devoted himself passionately to questions that were outside the ordinary domain of music. Amongst the

---

[1] See the opinions on Bach and Beethoven quoted in the author's book, *The Theories of Claude Debussy, Musicien français*.

laureates from the École des Beaux-Arts who used to enjoy
listening to his music in the evenings, were his seniors, the architect, Gaston Redon—a flute-player and a good musician—and the
sculptor, Lombard, a friend of Ernest Chausson. Achille and they
managed to bridge over the gulf between arts that are often hostile,
and both men played a considerable part in the artistic and literary
development of the musician. Another companion of his was the
painter, Marcel Baschet, one of the youngest of the laureates. It
was he who painted the fine portrait reproduced in this volume,
thereby rendering an anticipatory homage to a comrade whose
genius he had recognized. Ancient and modern literature also
interested this ignorant, but highly sensitive, *elementary* scholar—
this son of a petty tradesman of Saint-Germain-en-Laye. In the
company of Lombard, Redon, and Baschet, he read Baudelaire,
Verlaine, and even Spinoza. Xavier Leroux and Paul Vidal introduced him to Shakespeare, some of whose tragedies and comedies
they read aloud together. The poems of Rossetti were also
revealed to him—so utterly different from those of Paul Bourget
which he still greatly admired. He discovered a type of old music
which had been unknown to him. For in the simple, severe setting
of the church of S. Maria dell'Anima, he had an opportunity of
listening to the masses of Palestrina and Orlando di Lasso. This
was the only religious music he approved of, and in a letter to
Vasnier he declared that, in comparison with it, 'that of Gounod
and Co. seems the product of hysterical mysticism, and sounds
like a sinister farce'.

He wrote in terms of passionate enthusiasm to his friend,
Vasnier, on the subject of the sacred music of the sixteenth century. In a letter of the 24th of November 1885 he drew a comparison between the masses of Palestrina and those of Orlando di
Lasso. Without being aware of it, he wrote on that occasion a
piece of valuable musicography. He considered Orlando more
decorative, and more human than the great Italian master.

'I think it is a marvellous feat,' he writes, 'to produce such effects
as they did, entirely by means of their vast knowledge of counterpoint.
You probably do not realize that counterpoint is the grimmest thing
there is in music. Yet, in their hands, it becomes exquisite; it brings out
the meaning of the words in the most marvellous manner; and now and
then, there are scroll-like melodic outlines that remind you of ancient
missals. Those were the only occasions when my musical feelings were
at all awakened.'

He always retained his love of counterpoint, although it was
opposed to his own tendencies as a harmonist. Later, in Paris, he

became a fervent admirer of the Chanteurs de Saint-Gervais. On the occasion of the Palestrina centenary, Julien Tiersot related in the *Rivista musicale italiana* of 1925 a reminiscence which testifies to Debussy's enthusiasm for this form of art. He tells that one day his colleague came out of the church of Saint-Gervais 'with a light in his eyes such as I had never seen before, and coming over to me, he expressed his intense emotion in these simple words: '*Voilà la musique!*'

While frequenting the Roman churches his ear probably became attuned to the ancient art of Gregorian chant, with which he would have been more familiar if he had attended César Franck's class at the Conservatoire more regularly a few years previously. He must have noticed the freedom of its rhythm, unhampered by alternating strong and weak accents, and observed its oratorical emphasis. He no doubt appreciated the variety of the ecclesiastical modes, which some Russian melodies had already revealed to him; although their infinite diversity had never been pointed out to him by his professor of harmony. All these points must have impressed this independent young man who instinctively rebelled against all restrictions, whether modal, rhythmic, or harmonic, and who was later to hearken with such passionate interest to similar strange traits in exotic art.

He devoted hours of his day and night to a passionate study of the score of 'Tristan und Isolde' at the piano. His Wagnerism was of the most intense and violent description. Indeed, all the younger musicians were under the spell of Bayreuth. The painter, Hébert, who was director of the Villa Medici, was also an amateur violinist, and Debussy used to play the Mozart sonatas with him. He was surprised to find that this artist, who was passionately fond of music, detested Wagner. Later on, recalling the days of his youthful enthusiasms, he stated in one of his articles on music: 'At that time, I was a Wagnerian to the point of forgetting the most elementary principles of politeness. I little dreamt that I should come to hold much the same opinions as that passionate old man whose clairvoyance has plumbed the depths of all the emotions, whilst we still hardly know what they contain or how we should make use of them.'

As we shall see, some pages of his compositions of 1884–6 are Wagnerian in colour—the wonder is that they are not entirely impregnated with the spirit of Wagner. But in the German master's operas it was the music alone that thrilled him; by a strange contradiction, his natural sensitiveness rebelled against the grandiloquence of these inordinately massive and long-winded works. His friend, Xavier Leroux, the Prix de Rome scholar of 1885, writing in the *Revue des Arts Français*, in 1918, mentions Debussy's horror of over-emphasis. Leroux's brief reminiscences give us the following detailed and flattering portrait of Achille:

'Those who only knew him superficially might have thought him a fantastic, whimsical creature. But on the contrary, he was very strong-willed, and he knew his own mind. He was capable of the most faithful and devoted friendships, was very sensitive and emotional, gay and full of verve. He was quite incapable of dissimulation; his face reflected all his feelings—his joys and his slightest sorrows. Nor could he keep his troubles to himself. It was absolutely necessary for him to have a friend to confide in. He was very extravagant, and could rarely resist any desire or temptation. His moods were very changeable. He had all the caressing ways of the felines and, like them, was given to sudden outbursts of temper. He delighted in all that was refined, delicate, complicated and strange—and that in every domain. This refinement was evident in his dress, in the ornaments with which he surrounded himself, the perfumes he affected, and the bindings of his favourite books. The latter, like his favourite musical compositions, were works that appealed particularly to his love of the exquisite and the complex. In the matter of food there was no happy medium. He either lived on fried eggs and tea (his favourite beverage, which he was an adept at making), or else he indulged in highly *recherché* dishes and famous vintages. He detested pomposity in any of the arts. What appealed to him most of all was the expression of intimate feelings. Human productions that were planned on a grand scale astonished him, without arousing either his admiration or his enthusiasm. . . .'

All his fellow students at the Villa Medici remember his love of Japanese *objets d'art*. He had such a passion for them that he could not refrain from buying a great many more than his very modest resources permitted. In some of his later compositions we find that he has, as it were, transposed into music the impressions produced on him by some Japanese works to which he was particularly devoted. One of his piano compositions, 'Poissons d'or', written in 1907, was inspired by the contemplation of a piece of lacquer he possessed. And on the cover of his symphonic sketches entitled 'La Mer,' he insisted on reproducing a wave, from a print by Hokusai, the sight of which always delighted him.

During his sojourn at the Villa he went out very little. The theatre did not attract him, for the repertoire consisted mainly of such Italian operas, as Donizetti's 'La Favorita,' and the early works of Verdi and his lesser colleagues. But he used to attend the performances of the Neapolitan Polichinelle, a kind of masked Pierrot, with his friend Augustin Savard, a Prix de Rome scholar of 1886, whom he knew for a short time at the Villa Medici, and whose reserved character appealed to him more than the ultra-artistic behaviour of some of the other students. He took the greatest delight in the performance itself and in the resigned attitude of the old double-bass player whose instrument formed the basis of the lamentable little orchestra of this popular theatre. The keen sense of humour which Debussy so often manifested in his later works also found expression in the imitations, parodies, and amusing improvisations to which he sometimes treated his colleagues.

We do not know for certain whether he made any journeys during the intervals of his residence at the Villa Medici. According to the information collected by André de Ternant, the English journalist and musical critic,[1] Debussy whilst he was in Italy met Leoncavallo, then chiefly known as a journalist; he went to Milan to see Boïto, who procured an interview for him with Verdi at Sant'Agata; and he also frequented the house of the pianist-composer, Sgambati, where he met Liszt, who had called there with his friend, Cardinal Hohenlohe. We are told that on that occasion, at the prelate's request, Liszt and Sgambati played at two pianos Saint-Saëns' Variations on a theme of Beethoven, in honour of the young Prix de Rome and as a homage to French art. At any rate, Debussy did hear Liszt in Rome. In a letter, written thirty years later, he recalled with admiration the skill with which the great pianist 'seemed to make the pedal breathe.'

In 1886, practically within the prescribed time, Debussy sent in to the Académie des Beaux-Arts the first of the series of compositions which the Institut requires from the students at the Villa Medici during their three years' sojourn in Italy. After many hesitations which we find recorded in his letters to Vasnier, Debussy had given up 'Diane au Bois' and finished the first part of 'Zuleïma', an adaptation of 'Almanzor', which he described as a 'symphonic ode'.

It would have been surprising if the Academicians of the various sections had expressed themselves as satisfied with this work, which the composer himself destroyed later. The young musician's tendencies were too modern. He insolently advertised the fact that, once a laureate, his first care had been to forget everything he had been taught at the Conservatoire. Massenet used to say: 'Debussy is an enigma.' The academic censure, couched in the strongest terms, smote him ruthlessly. As was customary, it was published in the *Journal officiel* on the 31st of December 1886. The same document contained high praise of the works sent in by Paul Vidal and Gabriel Pierné, and a criticism of those of Georges Marty.

'The work which earned for M. Debussy the first prize in musical composition in 1884', says the *Officiel*, 'gave the Academy reason to expect that this remarkably talented young artist would give further evidence of the melodic and dramatic qualities which he exhibited in the competition piece. The Academy must regretfully record the exact contrary. At present, M. Debussy seems to be afflicted with a desire to write music that is bizarre, incomprehensible, and impossible to execute. With the exception of a few passages that show individuality, the vocal part of his work is uninteresting, both as regards the melody and the declamation. The Academy hopes that time and experience will bring salutary modifications to M. Debussy's ideas and compositions.'

This very narrow-minded judgement is based solely on the melodic and dramatic qualities of the composition. But its rhythm, harmony, and structure surely contained some good points worth mentioning.

Camille Saint-Saëns must have had a hand in this official report. He should have remembered—and recalled to the minds of his colleagues—some of the advanced theories which he himself had submitted to them two years previously. On the 25th of October 1884, at the annual public meeting of the five Academies, he had read a paper on the past, present, and future of music. In this paper he had foretold that owing to its constant state of evolution, musical idiom must inevitably become transformed. He had foreseen an epoch when commas, or ninths of a tone, would be used. He had visualized a new art, beside which that of the nineteenth century would be as a dead language; a form of art that would be incomprehensible if it were to be prematurely revealed. But the *Maître* only regarded it as a creation of the distant future. Meanwhile he and his colleagues rejected what they no doubt considered as mere eccentricity on the part of a young man who was anxious to break away from scholastic discipline.

At the end of 1887, the Académie was more lenient towards the second *envoi*, 'Printemps'. This composition was inspired by Botticelli's 'Primavera', and, apart from the title, has nothing in common with the two choruses written for the Prix de Rome preparatory tests of 1882 and 1884. This symphonic suite in two parts, for orchestra and chorus, bears the date February 1887. It was the last really Roman work, and Debussy played it as a piano duet with his friend, Savard, at one of the receptions given by the

director, Hébert. The Institut did not grant the work its un-
qualified approval. Some of the 'Immortals' were shocked by it.
Probably what upset them most of all was the instrumental treatment of the humming voices, and the use of a key—that of F sharp
major—which was not considered suitable for orchestra. The use
of this key which, in the eighteenth century, was considered likely
'to inspire fear', had caused a passage in César Franck's 'Rédemption' to be condemned in 1873. Possibly the adjudicators were
somewhat indulgent this time because of an accident—genuine or
imaginary—which prevented them from forming an exact opinion
on the instrumentation. The official report of the permanent
secretary of the Académie des Beaux-Arts was as follows:

'M. Debussy has sent in, as his second year's work, a symphonic piece
in two parts, entitled: "Printemps". As the orchestral score of this work
was burnt at the bookbinder's to whom the composer had sent his manuscript, it was only possible to judge of the young student's work from the
point of view of general musical tendencies, and the intrinsic value of his
ideas—except in the case of some portions which he had hastily re-
scored. Certainly, M. Debussy does not transgress through dullness or
triteness. On the contrary, he shows a rather over-pronounced taste for
the unusual. His feeling for musical colour is so strong that he is apt to
forget the importance of accuracy of line and form. He should beware of
this vague impressionism which is one of the most dangerous enemies
of artistic truth. The first movement of M. Debussy's symphonic work
is a kind of prelude—an *adagio*. Its dreamy atmosphere and its studied
effects result in confusion. The second movement is a bizarre, incoherent transformation of the first, but the rhythmical combinations
make it somewhat clearer and more comprehensible. The Academy
awaits and expects something better from such a gifted musician as
M. Debussy.'

Were the Academicians getting accustomed to the peculiar
style of the young deserter from the Roman villa? Their verdict
on the third year's composition, which appeared in the *Officiel* of
the 29th of January 1889, shows a certain degree of qualified appreciation; it even contains some gratifying words of praise for which,
in all probability, the painters rather than the musicians of the
Institut were responsible. Debussy had sent in 'La Damoiselle
Élue'. This lyrical poem, with soli and choruses, which he had
written entirely since his return to Paris, was inspired by Rossetti's
'Blessed Damozel'. Debussy had read this poem in Rome. It
was already forty years old, but Sarrazin's French translation had
recently appeared. The academic report was as follows:

'"La Damoiselle Élue", a lyrical poem, for solo voices and chorus.
The text chosen by M. Debussy is in prose, and rather obscure; but the

music which he has adapted to it is not deficient either in poetry or charm, although it still bears the marks of that systematic tendency towards vagueness of expression and form of which the Academy has already complained. In the present instance, however, these propensities and processes are much less noticeable and seem to some extent justified by the very nature of the subject and its indefinite character.'

By his choice of this libretto, Debussy may possibly have aroused the friendly interest of some of the academicians who were not musicians. He may also have benefited by a comparison with one of his fellow-students, Augustin Savard. This laureate, who was an ardent Wagnerian, had sent in a fragment of a lyrical drama, entitled 'Maldeck,' which had made a most distressing impression on the conservative members of the Institut, and had been ruthlessly censured. We read in the same report of the 29th of January 1889:

'M. Savard has entered upon a path where the Academy cannot follow him, and where it strongly disapproves of his having ventured. Our ears, as well as our feelings and taste, are revolted by the outrageous modulations which this student affects, and by the dissonant chords which follow one another mercilessly and result in an almost incessant racket.'

'La Damoiselle Élue' should have been performed soon after Debussy's return from Rome at the concert which, according to academic tradition, was devoted each year to the compositions sent in by the laureate who had just completed his term of residence at the Villa Medici. According to the established procedure, the Academy concert of December 1889 had been reserved for the *envois* of his predecessor, Paul Vidal. But, in 1890, an incident occurred which put an end to 'the Debussy Festival', as the hero of the prescribed seance ironically called it. He had expected that his 'Printemps' would be performed with his other works. But the Academy forbade the performance of a work which it had condemned three years previously. Debussy stubbornly refused to agree to the exclusion of his score. He perferred to forgo the honour and the advantages resulting from his concert. Such, at least, is the legend which has been officially authorized up to the present. The real history of the incident was possibly somewhat different. The former Prix de Rome broke with his Academic patrons by refusing to provide for a prize-distribution the overture which according to tradition it was his duty to compose. Whatever the reason was, 'La Damoiselle Élue,'—which was published in 1893 in a limited edition of a hundred and sixty copies, with a cover designed by Maurice Denis—had to wait till that year for its first public performance, which was given under the auspices of the Société Nationale. It was not accepted by the Société des Concerts du Conservatoire until the 3rd of April 1909. As for 'Printemps', it met with an even harsher fate. It was only printed in 1904, in the form of a piano duet arrangement, as a supplement to a musical review; and it was not performed until 1913, and then in a new, and purely orchestral version of the original score, arranged by Henri Büsser, according to Debussy's instructions.

A 'Fantaisie' for piano and orchestra, written in 1889–90, and dedicated to the pianist, René Chansarel, who was to have been the first to perform it, is also included in the *envois de Rome* series, although it was composed in Paris and was never sent in to the Institut de France. This composition remained unknown for an even longer period. It had been engraved as early as 1890 by the publisher, Choudens, for his colleague, Hartmann. The proofs, printed on beautiful paper, were the admiration of the composer, who always liked to see his works well turned out. It was not published till 1920, and was not made known to the musical public till December 1919, twenty months after the composer's death and contrary to his wishes. This long delay of thirty years was due to Debussy's own decision. The history of the affair has remained rather vague up to this; the facts are as follows:

In the composition of this work, Debussy seems to have been influenced to some extent by Vincent d'Indy's 'Symphonie Cévenole'. The 'Fantaisie' is a fine composition, remarkable for its clever instrumentation, the elegance of the piano part, and the youthful ardour that animates it. Although written in 1890, it foreshadows the style and many of the details that characterize his later works. This very well-ordered 'Fantaisie' was to have been played at one of the orchestral concerts of the Société Nationale, on the 21st of April 1890, two days after the first performance of César Franck's Quartet by the same Society. Vincent d'Indy conducted the rehearsals of the long programme which, besides the 'Fantaisie', included: Camille Benoît's 'Noces Corinthiennes' (which was omitted at the last moment); the prologues of Léon Husson's 'Azaël,' and of Gabriel Fauré's 'Passion'; an 'Overture' by Lucien Lambert; 'Dansons la Gigue', a song with orchestral accompaniment by Charles Bordes; other songs by Georges Hué and Mme de Grandval; and a 'Prélude' by Jacques Durand. It had been hard work to get up so many items, but Vincent d'Indy, who was to conduct the concert, expected that all would be well. At the end of the last rehearsal but one, Debussy, without saying a word to any one, removed the orchestral parts of his work from the desks and took them away. On leaving the Salle Érard, where the concert was to take place, he wrote a letter to Vincent d'Indy, notifying him that he was withdrawing his score. This withdrawal had, necessarily, to be accepted, although it was very unpleasant for the organizers of the concert, besides being contrary to the statutes of the Société Nationale. From that day the composer would never allow his 'Fantaisie' to be performed. He adhered strictly to this decision as long as he lived, that is, for more than twenty-five years.

There has been much discussion as to the reason for this stubborn refusal. Robert Godet attributes the setting aside of this composition to some complex feelings regarding Catulle Mendès, the author of the libretto, 'Chimène,' which Debussy was about to attempt in vain to set to music. According to Robert Godet, Debussy considered the orchestration of the 'Fantaisie' too heavy, although he always retained a liking for many of its characteristics, especially for the rhythm. Maurice Emmanuel, on the other hand, states that the reason for its withdrawal was the composer's recognition of the fact that his 'Fantaisie' contradicted his own theories regarding the use of the classical forms proper to the sonata; for he always deplored the stereotyped imitation of these forms by modern musicians. This composition is, in fact, a real concerto or orchestral sonata with piano solo, consisting partly of variations, written in a definitely 'cyclical' style. In other words, it is a 'heavy structure', with a very visible framework. Debussy hated variations. This is evident from his critiques of Witowski's First Symphony, Dukas's Variations for the piano, and those of Rhené-Baton for the orchestra. One day, he expressed the following very decided opinion to Robert Godet: 'It is an easy means of getting a great deal out of very little; sometimes, it is a form of vengeance; occasionally, the poor theme gets angry and seems to reject, in disgust, the disguises which the ingenious composer persists in thrusting upon it.' Any one who examined this music would be inclined to accept Maurice Emmanuel's explanation, were it not for the fact that the Quartet of 1893 offers a contrary example. For, in spite of its very marked and obvious classical tendencies, in the manner of Beethoven and Franck, the author did not dream of disowning it, although he soon lost all liking for it. The real reason why Debussy withdrew this work was that he considered the Finale a failure. It was not until some years later that he took a dislike to this composition, probably because it then seemed very immature to such an ultra-modern musician as he had become.

Of the *envois de Rome*, only the unknown 'Zuleïma' and 'Printemps' deserve this title; for 'La Damoiselle Élue' and the

'Fantaisie' were written in Paris. They are all highly interesting
and attractive. They show the development of Debussy's style, his
determination to get out of the ruts, his desire to discover a new
type of beauty—to find a means of expressing his artistic impressions adequately and exquisitely, and his efforts to perfect his
individual style. They also show us that he hesitated between two
different paths. With the exception of the 'Fantaisie' the influence
of Wagner predominates in these works; or rather Debussy unconsciously reflects the colouring of the most brilliant lyrical scenes
in 'Tristan', 'Parsifal', the 'Ring', and especially 'Götterdämmerung'. One feels that he is steeped in the mobile harmonies
of this latter score, where the chords of the ninth abound; he even
seems to be impregnated with the pianistic formulas peculiar to the
current arrangements which he played incessantly. He is evidently
conscious of this deep-seated Wagnerian influence; he tries to
avoid thematic processes, to escape from the very German melodic
line, from tonal definiteness, and a paradoxical fidelity to classical
rules. There is a perceptible suggestion of Massenet in the curve
of many of the melodies, in their rather effeminate grace, in their
suavity—a trait which characterized all Debussy's compositions at
that time.

Both in 'Printemps' and in the 'Fantaisie' the initial melody
escapes from the usual limits and slips into the A mode, transposed
or otherwise, and into an incomplete scale of four or five notes. In
'Printemps' the melody immediately reveals its tonal ambiguity;
in the 'Fantaisie' it at first wavers doubtfully between the ordinary
major and minor. In both compositions the tonality is extremely
mobile, and in the opening bars, whole-tone scales make their
appearance. Some melodic characteristics of 'L'Enfant Prodigue'
are to be found in 'Printemps', and also some of the typical
harmonies of the 'Air de Lia': common chords and chords of the
seventh interlaced; swaying festoons of parallel ninths. There are
continual experiments in novel rhythms, especially in the parts for
female voices; for example, we find two or three groups in opposition to one another, a device that occurs more than twenty years
later in the final chorus of 'Saint Sébastien'. The writing of the
choral parts contains continuous vocalizations—perhaps indirectly
derived from the song of the Rhine Maidens in 'Götterdämmerung'; the daring intervals and the wide distribution of the
parts strike an original note.

'La Damoiselle Élue' is very similar in style. But, in spite of its
very languishing melodies, and all the finery in the fashion of 1887
with which it is bedecked, this work shows still more clearly the

precursory signs of what was later on to be called 'Debussyism'. It exhales a curious, delightfully fragrant perfume, which harmonizes subtly with Dante Gabriel Rossetti's exquisite, but rather effeminate text. The succession of fifths in the very first bars proclaims the young composer's audacious personality. Its mysticism seems to prepare the way for 'Le Martyre de Saint Sébastien'. The spirit of Wagner—the Wagner of 'Parsifal'—hovers over the entire work; there is a faint suggestion of César Franck's 'Rébecca', and Massenet's caressing charm greets one at many a turn. Three themes are exposed in the prelude and are developed, chiefly harmonically, in the course of the composition. The first appears without introduction—its interest lies in its vertical style—the second is sung by the strings, the last, recited by the flute. One notices Debussy's constant care to subordinate the symphony to the poem, to interpret the latter in a flowing style closely resembling the words and, by means of syllabic diction and a choral treatment free from contrapuntal interlacing, to bring out all the words clearly, even those that occur in the united choral parts. There are some attractive and novel effects in the treatment of the female voices, and the instrumentation is light and delicate, though varied throughout. There is a certain amount of padding which betrays the haste with which the composition was written. The score is well known, and all musicians are familiar with it. It is often performed at concerts. In 1919 an attempt was made to have it produced at a theatre, but without success.

Although Debussy remained faithful to some scholastic mannerisms, he began, in these three scores, to elaborate his musical vocabulary and definitely to determine his individual style. He attempted to apply, in an artistic manner, the revolutionary principles he had proclaimed in 1887 in his remarkable conversations with his former master, Ernest Guiraud, which Maurice Emmanuel noted down from day to day. (They took place at the little restaurant to which Ernest Guiraud used to bring his two disciples to lunch. Maurice Emmanuel used to jot down in a little note-book the remarks exchanged by the master and his former pupil, the exceptional interest of which he realized.) During these talks Debussy developed, matured, or improvised a theoretical basis for the experiments in sonority in which he used already to indulge at the Conservatoire before his Prix de Rome days, to the bewilderment of his companions, and the horror of his masters. The principal points discussed were: the necessity of utilizing scales of all kinds, constructed in every possible way; a liberal use of the enharmonic; the production of constant modal ambiguity by

allowing the key to sway between the major and minor; the creation of equivocal tonality by the construction of ambiguous chords;
the advisability of blending the tonalities, which are usually too
definite and crude, so as to be able to enter or leave a key at will;
and the equally urgent need of varying, not only melody and
harmony, but also the rhythmic formulas, with whose uniform
regularity and symmetry people had become so smugly satisfied.

To-day, when we read through these so-called *envois de Rome*,
and take into account the fact that forty years have elapsed since
they were written, we can well understand the uneasiness of the
members of the Académie des Beaux-Arts and the motives which
prompted their harsh verdict. The older composers of the
Institut had been brought up, and had lived all their lives, in an
attitude of absolute, religious respect towards certain harmonic
laws which were then looked upon as unassailable dogmas.
Naturally, they were aghast when they were asked to read or listen
to combinations of chords that were not resolved according to
their rules, and which eluded all scholastic classification. For,
whether the laureate carries out his developments in the classical or
the Wagnerian manner, as in 'Printemps' or 'La Damoiselle Élue;'
or whether, as in the 'Fantaisie', he has recourse to such scholastic
devices as the double theme of the sonata, the cyclical derivation
of motifs, and their superimposition, ordinary variations, the
commonplace expedients of augmentation and diminution, more
or less disguised rosaliae, and persistently monotonous basses—
it is all one. Under the old, worn-out trappings, his individuality stands revealed. And even though some pages are written in
a contrapuntal style that brings him into line with his friends
Ernest Chausson and Vincent d'Indy and their master, César
Franck, the atmosphere of his music is utterly different—full
of charm and individuality. In nearly every page of his scores
his sensibility finds novel means of expression: strange melodies;
delightfully vague harmonies; interwoven chords, in which each
voice faithfully follows the same curve; curiously punctuated
rhythmical gestures—everywhere his genius gushes forth. That
genius of his was soon to cast the world of music into confusion,
by overthrowing those age-old traditions whose chief virtue was
their antiquity.

CHAPTER IV

RETURN TO PARIS (1887). INFLUENCES

THE Prix de Rome laureate of 1884 refused to complete the regulation sojourn in Italy and fled from the Villa Medici. He did not return there until February 1914, and then as a tourist. The joy of his departure was not untinged with regret and emotion. As was customary, he drove to the station in the carriage of the director, Hébert. During that drive, and in the sleeping-car which, in spite of his slender resources, he considered indispensable to his comfort, Debussy must have reflected on the freedom from material cares which he had enjoyed in Italy and the uncertainty of the future that awaited him in France. He was definitely settled in Paris by the beginning of 1887, but much of his life at that period is still veiled in obscurity. It was in Paris that he composed his last *envois de Rome*: 'La Damoiselle Élue'—which, like the 'Printemps', is not mentioned in the published portion of his Roman correspondence—and the 'Fantaisie' for piano and orchestra, the solo part of which was destined for his friend, Chansarel. He was still a dependent of the Académie des Beaux-Arts, but he severed his connexion with the Institut in 1890, by his refusal to provide the traditional overture for the prize-distribution ceremony of 1889. Thus, for the sake of a whim, he deprived himself of his 'Debussy Festival' and of the moral advantages resulting from a public performance of his *envois* in the old hall of the Conservatoire—one of the privileges attaching to the Prix de Rome.

During the year 1887 he made two journeys—one to London, the other to Vienna—of which nothing was known until recently, and then from the sole testimony of André de Ternant,[1] the English writer.

[1] André de Ternant, journalist and musical critic, was born in London of French parents. When Debussy went to London in 1887 Ternant had just published in the *Musical World*—a review published by Franz Hueffer which is no longer in existence—a series of articles on Berlioz's 'Les Troyens', the first study on that subject in the English language. Ternant was assistant to Franz Hueffer on *The Times*.
André de Ternant saw Debussy for the first time in 1887, at the offices of the *Musical World*. He met him again in London on the occasion of the musician's next visit in 1895, and later in Paris. Very friendly relations were established between the two young men. The fact that Ternant was French by birth helped to increase their intimacy in a foreign country. Debussy, indulging in confidences, decribed his travels in Italy which we have already mentioned, and his short visit to Vienna in 1887. Possibly he romanced a little. The confidant was pledged to keep these particulars secret till after Debussy's

He had gone to Vienna with a view to meeting Brahms, a difficult undertaking because of the Austrian master's unsociableness. After several fruitless attempts, he managed to meet him and even to have lunch with him at the house of a lady who was a friend of both artists. The conversation was highly interesting. Brahms declared that a musician should remain faithful to the artistic traditions of his country. He was overjoyed that the French should consider him the most German of all composers, and expressed his unreserved admiration for 'Carmen', that typically French work, which he said he had heard twenty times. He spoke with horror of the people who imitated and copied him unscrupulously, and of the indiscreet flattery and servility he had to endure. The day after this memorable lunch Brahms invited Debussy to dine with him and go on to a performance of 'Carmen' afterwards. A few days later Brahms devoted a whole day to showing his young confrere everything of musical interest in Vienna. The two composers parted as friends. The incident is interesting. But Debussy does not seem to have mentioned it to his other friends, not even when later, in his capacity as critic, he had occasion to pass judgement on Brahms—and that in the most severe and brutal manner.

His visit to London in the autumn lasted a week and had a practical end in view. Debussy was then writing 'La Damoiselle Élue'. We do not know whether his object was to obtain the authorization of Rossetti's heirs, or whether it was merely to find an English publisher for an *envoi de Rome* written to a poem of English origin. At all events, he set out for London with a letter of introduction to the critic, Franz Hueffer, who was a friend of the family of his librettist, the pre-Raphaelite poet-painter. Hueffer, an English writer of German origin, was musical critic to *The Times*, director of the *Musical World*, and a correspondent of the French review, the *Ménestrel*, to which he regularly sent important articles from England until his death on the 19th of January 1889. He was married to a daughter of the painter, Ford Madox Brown, who had been a close friend of Dante Gabriel Rossetti. Hueffer tried to help Debussy to find a publisher for the manuscripts he had brought with him from France. He showed them to Berthold Tours, a Dutch musician who had become a naturalized English-

death, and he did not divulge them until 1924. He then published his reminiscences in the *Musical Times*, in the form of three articles: 'Debussy and Brahms' (July), 'Debussy and some Italian musicians' (September), 'Debussy and others on Sullivan' (December). In addition, in the course of a private correspondence, he has kindly given the present writer some further particulars and supplied him with exact references.

man, and who had a great reputation as adviser to a London publisher. Tours thought the compositions remarkable, but said that no English firm would agree to publish them at its own risk, as the music of a young Prix de Rome was of no commercial value in England. Perhaps we can discover traces of Hueffer's disappointment in the article he published in the *Ménestrel* of the 30th of October 1887. In this article he deplores the fact that French music was unknown in England, excepting the music of Berlioz, of Gounod, whose 'Rédemption' was often given, and of Saint-Saëns, 'who in any case, shows a good deal of affinity with the German genius.' After a week's visit, Debussy returned to Paris.

At first, Debussy resumed his regular intercourse with the Vasnier family; but it soon became intermittent, and eventually ceased. Probably, his independent nature could no longer submit to the intellectual and sentimental bondage which he had so long and so lovingly endured. Life was leading him elsewhere. His youthful love of freedom was less in harmony with the conservative ideas of his old friends than with those of the advanced literary and artistic circles. His choice of 'La Damoiselle Élue' as the subject for his last *envoi de Rome* was in itself a proof that his tastes linked him to these circles. His evolution was in process of completion, and he was endeavouring, not without some effort, to free his personality from previous influences.

His transient Wagerism—a deep and genuine influence, as Debussy himself angrily acknowledged in his violent musical articles[1]—was not yet shared by the general public. It was rife only in those limited circles into which he happened to be drawn on his return to Paris. The composer came into contact with the artists and poets who were attracted to the impressionist and symbolist movements, at Stéphane Mallarmé's, in the back room of the Librairie de l'Art Indépendant; and the publisher, Edmond Bailly—himself an amateur composer—rendered Debussy great service by publishing his first important works. He also frequented other similar groups that met together occasionally in *brasseries*.[2]

The aim of all these young men was to express in their works a free conception of life; they did not wish to represent objects, but rather their reflections—the impression they produced on the

[1] See *The Theories of Claude Debussy, Musicien français*, Chapter VIII.

[2] Debussy's impressionism has been much discussed, and we have not yet heard the end of it. Some of his admirers deny its existence. It is a mere quibble about words. In a musical article in *La Victoire* (4th of May 1926) Paul Landormy has put the gist of the matter in a few lines, and shown that we can call Debussy an impressionist without denying the subjective and emotional character of his art. He developed the same subject in the *Ménestrel* of the 28th of January 1927.

artist. Their dream was to achieve a fusion of all the arts that would
bring out the mysterious connexions between them, and break
down, or render permeable, the watertight partitions that usually
divide them. The conservatives regarded them with the same disapproval and contempt which they meted out to the advanced
musicians who had recently become partisans of Wagner—thereby
uniting them to this latter group. The consequence was that they
became Wagnerians without realizing that Wagnerism and the
neo-classicism of the Franckists, which was indirectly or collater-
ally related to it, did not at all correspond to the literary or plastic
art of their dreams. Of all his contemporaries, Debussy alone (who
had wished to become a painter and who was to try his hand at
poetry later) manifested an artistic sensibility which harmonized
perfectly with that of the impressionists and symbolists. Like them
he aimed at avoiding regular lines and symmetrical rhythms. He
lived in an intimate unity of thought with both these groups, and
often chose his literary collaborators from amongst them. Sometimes he sought inspiration in the aesthetic ideals of certain indivi-
duals, by imitating their poetic style, as in the case of the 'Proses
Lyriques,' the curious poem which was written by himself. It
is strongly reminiscent of various writers, especially of the fantastic
Jules Laforgue, for whom he always entertained a sympathetic
admiration, although he did not know him personally.

Debussy's friend, Paul Dukas, has given us a picture of that
period, which coincided with the days of his own youth. They met
in the autumn of 1885, when Dukas joined Ernest Guiraud's composition class which Debussy had left the year before. Dukas
writes:

'Verlaine, Mallarmé, and Laforgue used to provide us with new sounds
and sonorities. They cast a light on words such as had never been seen
before; they used methods that were unknown to the poets that had
preceded them; they made their verbal material yield subtle and powerful effects hitherto undreamt of. Above all, they conceived their poetry
or prose like musicians, they tended it with the care of musicians and,
like musicians, too, they sought to express their ideas in corresponding
sound values. It was the writers, not the musicians, who exercised the
strongest influence on Debussy.'

Paul Dukas then goes on to speak of the 'Prose pour des Esseintes,'
which appeared in the *Revue Indépendante;* and he mentions the
Revue Wagnérienne, which, in January 1886, suddenly launched out
into symbolism by publishing Mallarmé's and Verlaine's sonnets
to Richard Wagner. He alludes to the paintings of Degas and
Berthe Morizot, the experiments of Renoir and Claude Monet, the

friendship between Ernest Chabrier and Cézanne and Manet, the pre-Raphaelite movement—which was almost as widespread in young France as it was in England; and mentions Gabriel Sarrazin's French translation of *Les Poètes Modernes de l'Angleterre*, which included Dante Gabriel Rossetti's 'Blessed Damozel'. He says: 'Impressionism, symbolism, and poetic realism, were united in one great contest of enthusiasm, curiosity, and intellectual emotion. All these painters, poets, and sculptors, were engaged in analysing matter. They bent over it, scrutinizing it, altering it, and remaking it to suit their fancy; their one endeavour being to make words, sounds, colours, and lines express new shades of feelings.' Smarting under the attacks of unintelligent critics who condemned them all equally, these poets, painters, and musicians became reconciled with one another, like brothers who had quarrelled. The poets and painters took to attending concerts, the musicians endeavoured to understand the new experiments in poetry and the plastic arts.

Claude Debussy kept aloof from his musical colleagues, the most gifted of whom were then devoting themselves to elaborate symphonic works after the manner of Beethoven and Wagner, and adhering faithfully to the mathematical rules of composition. Debussy preferred to mix with those writers and artists whose tendencies were similar to his own. This intercourse, which was more restricted than people realized, enabled him to acquire a degree of culture—not in the least classical, but highly modern—for which his early schooling had in no wise prepared him. How deep and how subtle it was may be gauged from his articles in various papers from 1901. He came to realize the kinship of all the arts, literary, plastic, and sonorous—'perfumes, colours, and sounds correspond to one another.' He foresaw that a fusion of these various modes of expression might give fruitful results. His mental horizon expanded, whilst most of his comrades cramped their art by confining themselves within the limits of the little world of music.

One of his friends, Pierre Louÿs, became in a sense, the director of his literary conscience. He was particularly well fitted for this difficult role, for he was highly sensitive to music, and in his youth he had contemplated devoting himself to composition as well as to literature. These two friends, united by their common love of literature and music, used sometimes to visit the picture-galleries together. A mutual friend of theirs relates how one day, in the *grande galerie* of the Louvre, they all three stopped in front of Titian's 'Jupiter and Antiope'. He noticed Debussy's look of passionate concentration, and describes him as he stood there 'with bared head and tense gaze, bending his great bulging forehead over the water and the grass of that divine landscape, as if he hoped to catch the supreme cadences of the blue mountain on the horizon, the sounds and echoes of the hunter's horn.'[1] Later on, Debussy paid a grateful homage to his initiator, by illustrating three of the 'Chansons de Bilitis' with the most subtle and luminous music. To this writer, who was also an amateur photographer, we owe the fine portrait, taken by flashlight, which is reproduced on another page. Louÿs's friends were all familiar with this picture; Debussy had a copy of it, but he tore it up one day, when he was in a bad humour. The photogravure published here was reproduced from that very copy which was put together again.

Debussy numbered amongst his friends Henri de Régnier, Maurice Vaucaire, Jean de Tinan, Gaston Redon, André Gide, Maurice Denis, Whistler, Viélé-Griffin, and Jacques-Émile Blanche. The last named, when writing an account of Pierre Louÿs's young days, just after that author's death, traced the following unflattering literary silhouette of Debussy, whose pictorial portrait he was to paint formally in 1903:

'That very material-minded fellow, always so taciturn unless he wanted to get good addresses for procuring caviare, of which he was inordinately fond; that sleepy, heavy creature, always on the look out for music publishers, whom Louÿs was constantly extricating from his straitened circumstances; that Prix de Rome who suggested an old-fashioned model for an historical painting. . . .'[2]

The truth is that Debussy, like many artists, had little strength of character, and always remained in some respects a child. He never grew up and was easily led and swayed.

Henri de Régnier, whom Debussy consulted one day on the subject of the poetical text of the 'Proses Lyriques', retained a more favourable impression of his former comrade. He well remembered what he was like when he used to meet him at the Librairie de l'Art Indépendant.

'. . . He used to walk in with a heavy, muffled tread.· I can still see that flabby, indolent figure, the dull pallor of his face, the keen, black, heavy-lidded eyes, the huge forehead with its curious bumps, over which he wore a long wisp of fuzzy hair; there was something feline and at the same time gipsy-like about him, something passionate, yet self-centred. Whilst we talked, Debussy would listen, turning over the leaves of a book

    [1] Ugo Ojetti, 'Souvenirs sur Pierre Louÿs', published in the *Nouvelles Littéraires*, 27th of January 1928.
    [2] Jacques-Émile Blanche, 'La Jeunesse de Pierre Louÿs', in the *Nouvelles Littéraires*, 13th of June 1925.

or examining an engraving. He was fond of books and bibelots, but he always got back to the subject of music. He spoke very little about himself, but criticized his confreres severely. He spared hardly any one but Vincent d'Indy and Ernest Chausson. I do not remember anything in particular about those conversations; any remarks he made were intelligent. He was interesting, though always rather reticent and elusive. . . . It was at Pierre Louÿs's that I came into closer contact with Debussy. . . . I often saw him at the piano. I heard him play his Baudelaire songs, extracts from "Tristan", and most of "Pelléas", while it was in process of composition. . . .'

Pierre Louys's piano was often replaced by an harmonium, a famous instrument, which all his friends well remember. For want of anything better, Debussy often made use of it to introduce his new works, which he used to sing in a very individual manner.

Another of his friends, Raymond Bonheur, a fellow student of his at the Conservatoire, has given his impressions of Debussy in the days before he won the Prix de Rome. He describes him as 'reserved, rather distant, exceedingly fond of rare and precious objects, and very attractive, in spite of a certain brusqueness when one met him first.' He used to see him at the Brasserie Pousset:

'his powerful, faun-like forehead, with its curious profile, projecting like the prow of a ship; his dark eyes, overshadowed by the frowning eyebrows, gazing fixedly, straight before him, at some far-distant, imaginary point; whilst his forefinger, with a characteristic gesture, flicked the ash off his cigarette. As often happens with people who are not content with commonplace remarks, and who think for themselves, his speech was hesitating, and he usually spoke with a slight lisp, in short, detached, unfinished phrases, or in monosyllables, searching impatiently until he found the right word to express the exact shade of an impression or point of view. With his dark hair, his sensual nose, and his pale face framed by a slight beard, Debussy in those days reminded one of the portraits of noblemen that Titian painted, and it was easy to picture him in the sumptuous setting of some Venetian palace. . . .'

Raymond Bonheur completed his physical portrait of Debussy by a sketch of his moral traits which is accurate, in spite of its obviously laudatory intentions.

'Although Debussy was born poor, he began life with the tastes, the needs, and the recklessness of a great nobleman. Nothing gave him greater offence than to be taken for a professional musician—the word filled him with secret horror. Given his remarkable facility and the rare quality of his talents, he could have become a popular composer at an age when few could have resisted the temptation. But his ambition soared higher, and he would more readily have agreed to make counterfeit money than to write three bars of music without feeling an irresistible craving to do so. There was no trace in him of that rather gross self-conceit which is so common in artists, nor of that jolly good-fellowship which so often conceals questionable motives. He was extremely sensitive to the opinion of a few and capable of a high degree of enthusiasm for any new work that interested him; but he was supremely indifferent to the favour of the crowd, and his chief trait was an admirable pride which sprang from a consciousness of the fact that he lived, so to speak, on a higher plane. He was, besides, so free from all spirit of intrigue and what is known as *arrivisme*, that one wonders what would have been the fate of "Pelléas" if he had not been fortunate enough to come across the publisher, G. Hartmann.'

On rare occasions he frequented the famous literary salon of Stéphane Mallarmé, the mysterious poet, for whose 'Après-midi d'un Faune' he was to write such a marvellous preface. It was there that he met Paul Verlaine, whose mother-in-law, Mme Mauté de Fleurville, had been his piano teacher before he went to the Conservatoire. He can hardly have been attracted by poor Verlaine's dissolute bohemianism, but he deeply appreciated his poems, which he, as well as Gabriel Fauré, illustrated in the most subtle and beautiful manner. In his Conservatoire days he had already collaborated with the author of the 'Bonne Chanson,' and also with Mallarmé; and three out of the four songs dedicated to Mme Vasnier, which were so unnecessarily published in 1926, are written to texts by these two authors.

This literary and artistic intercourse, not so much an intercourse with men as with their works—reacted powerfully on the young musician's highly impressionable personality, and the importance of this influence is easily seen even in the composition of 'La Damoiselle Élue' and the 'Fantaisie'. Neither of these scores can be called Roman, except for the sake of expediency; both of them, and especially 'La Damoiselle', are early fruits, forced to maturity in the *serres chaudes* of Parisian symbolist and impressionist circles. As was stated in the official report quoted before, the Académie des Beaux-Arts had already discovered in 'Printemps' alarming traces of 'that vague impressionism which is one of the most dangerous enemies of artistic truth'. Rossetti is not the only painter whose influence was visible in these experiments which were still hampered by other memories both old and recent. One influence—quite as strong and more lasting, was that of Whistler, who often borrowed words from the musical vocabulary for the titles of his pictures, just as Debussy was to choose terms used by painters for the titles of his symphonies. The still-uncertain tendencies of this music were obviously inspired by the aesthetic ideals of the pioneers of 1885–90. In his next compositions Debussy was to prove the soundness of his artistic creed, the perfect agreement between his thought and his executional processes, and his complete mastery of this new musical art—which coincided with the symbolism of the literary group and the impressionism of the painters. These qualities were still more clearly seen when, not without violent effort, he succeeded in freeing himself from the oppressive yoke of Richard Wagner.

Achille Debussy (he still bore the name which was soon to appear ridiculous to him) attended the Wagner performances at Bayreuth for two years in succession—in 1888 and 1889, not, as has always been stated, in 1889 and 1890. He accomplished these two journeys in very different frames of mind. In 1888, a passionate devotion drew him thither; it was a genuine pious pilgrimage, enthusiastically performed by one who was, so to speak, in the state of grace. He was deeply sensitive to the religious atmosphere of the model theatre and, during the long intervals between the acts of 'Parsifal', he was annoyed by the frivolousness of his companions, who spent the time flirting with the waitresses. Their coarse gallantry shocked him; such behaviour seemed like sacrilegious impropriety in the vicinity of a temple. He also heard the 'Meistersinger' on that occasion. In 1889 he heard the same operas, and also 'Tristan und Isolde'. He was deeply moved on hearing this work which he so fervently admired, and yet he was disillusioned by the complicated aestheticism and the oppressive dramatic effects indulged in by the German master. On his return, when discussing the subject with his former master, Ernest Guiraud, he found that he was now capable of pronouncing very personal and severe criticisms on the *Tondichter* he had so passionately admired.[1] His persistent and violent denunciation of Wagner was especially directed against the dramatist or the musician regarded from the point of view of the theatre; but not against the musician as such, for he still admired him and was too deeply impregnated by his influence to indulge in a sweeping censure. As a matter of fact, the harmony of Debussy, the anti-Wagnerian, bears a definite resemblance to that of Wagner—if it is not derived from it. Ernst Kurth, a Swiss musicographer, has recently attempted to trace this relationship in his important German work (*Romantische Harmonik*), published in 1920, which treats of 'Romantic harmony and its crisis in Wagner's "Tristan"'. A French writer, Julien Tiersot, in his book, *Un Demi-siècle de Musique Française entre les Deux Guerres (1870–1917)*, and in an

[1] See Maurice Emmanuel, *Étude sur Pelléas*, pp. 31–6.

article in the *Ménestrel* of the 31st of December 1920, had previously admitted that Debussy's harmony had drawn the best part
of its substance from the super-augmented chords in the prelude to
'Tristan', the transient harmonies in the 'Parsifal' chorus: 'Durch
Mittleid wissend', and the mysterious sonorities of the 'Wald-
weben'. Thus, in accordance with the inexorable logic of history,
Debussy's art—at least in the domain of harmony—could not be
said to represent a reaction against Wagnerian influence, but rather,
the ultimate stage of that influence.

About the date of that second journey to Bavaria—his last pilgrimage to the temple of the god Wagner—certain musical incidents
occurred which were to prove of the highest importance in
Debussy's life. The so-called revolutionary spirit which animated
his discussions on art found favourable soil for its development.
For, whilst he continued to frequent that very limited group of
'advanced' artists and writers whose society he had cultivated since
his return from Rome, he was also given an opportunity of exploring some foreign folk-music, and in addition he discovered some
original scores by various composers, the most noteworthy being
the work of a creative artist who was entirely unknown in France.

In 1889 he was able to make a sort of artistic voyage of discovery through the various countries of the world in the easiest and
most economical conditions, without even having to leave Paris.
This opportunity occurred at the Exposition Universelle, where, in
various corners, groups of popular musicians were gathered
together, representing many different nations. In the company of
his friends, Paul Dukas and Robert Godet, he often went to the
exhibition as a musical explorer. He would listen with the closest
attention to the improvisations of popular musicians, whose talent
had not been fettered or stifled by strict scholastic rules, and who
knew no principle but that of absolute liberty. On the Champ
de Mars and on the Esplanade des Invalides, either in the open
air, or in the shelter of the little booths, Debussy listened to the
tiny Spanish, Chinese, Javanese, or Annamite orchestras, and
learnt from the music of these very different races the useful lesson
of independence which, we are told, he had already acquired from
the gipsies in Moscow ten years before. Here he found a supple
diversity of forms, rhythms, chords, and scales, in marked contrast
to the stereotyped forms and harmonies, the stiff, symmetrical
rhythms, and the modal restrictions which he had been taught in
vain at the Conservatoire. Twenty-four years later, in one of his
last articles, he was to praise the originality and the expressiveness
of some of the Javanese and Annamite music; and he contrasted

the grandiloquent art of Bayreuth with the more direct expressive action of the Oriental theatre which he had frequented at the exhibition.[1]

The principal attraction for Debussy in this exotic art was the *Gamelang*, that weird orchestra which was to be heard in the Javanese village on the Esplanade des Invalides, and which accompanied those lithe and stately dancers, the Bedayas, now swaying to their voluptuous undulations, now emphasizing their stiff, hieratical gestures. This group of instrumentalists, which was calculated to excite the laughter of the ignorant, aroused the curiosity and the interest of musicians. Except for a kind of two-stringed viola, it consisted entirely of percussion instruments: clappers, gongs, and tuned drums or kettle-drums, which produced not noises, but musical sounds, full of rich rhythms and subtle harmonies. The Oriental pentatonic scale was the basis of the musical *divertissement*, during which the percussion instruments occasionally produced long tremolos in ninths. It is extraordinary music, and deserves careful and sympathetic study on the part of composers and writers on music. During the summer of 1887, Julien Tiersot devoted important articles to it in the *Ménestrel*. Undoubtedly the *Gamelang* helped to open up new musical paths for Debussy in the domain of melody, rhythm, and harmony; this soon became evident.

During the period of the great international exhibition, Debussy also availed himself of an opportunity to increase his scientific knowledge. On the 22nd and the 29th of June 1889 he attended the two concerts of Russian music which had been organized by the publisher, Belaïef, under the direction of Rimsky-Korsakof. At a time when the Russians were almost unknown with the exception of Rubinstein and Tchaikovsky, these two programmes provided a bountiful harvest. They included: works by Glinka and Dargomijsky; César Cui's 'Marche Solennelle'; Balakiref's 'Overture on Russian Themes'; Borodin's 'Polovtsian Dances' from 'Prince Igor', and his symphonic sketch 'In the Steppes of Central Asia', which had already been heard at the Concerts Lamoureux; Rimsky-Korsakof's 'Antar' and 'Caprice Espagnol'; Mussorgsky's 'Night on the Bare Mountain'; and Glazounof's 'Stenka Razin'. This three hours' performance at the Trocadéro was nothing less than the revelation of the *Five*; the discovery (or, in the case of one

[1] See *The Theories of Claude Debussy*. It is curious to note that Rimsky-Korsakof, who visited the exhibition, was also interested in the popular orchestras, especially the Hungarian and Algerian ones. He declared that those were the only definite musical impressions which he received in Paris. (Rimsky-Korsakof, *Memoirs*, English edition, p. 4).

or two of these composers, the reminder) of their Oriental sump-
tuousness, and their vivid orchestral colouring; of the untold
riches—almost unknown to modern art—which result from the use
of strange scales taken from folk-music. These were royal treasures,
indeed, and they were further augmented by the concert of choral
music, both popular and religious, which was given at the exhibition, during the same period, by Slaviansky d'Agreneff's National
Slavo-Russian Choir. Furthermore, about this time, Achille had
an opportunity—of which he availed himself little if at all—of
becoming acquainted with the masterpiece of the most original
and powerful of these new composers, whose very name was still
unknown in France; namely, Mussorgsky's 'Boris Godunof'.

In 1874 Camille Saint-Saëns had brought back from Moscow
a copy of the original edition of 'Boris'. The composer of 'Samson
et Dalila', who was too conservative to appreciate such a very
daring work, had given this copy—then unique in France—to
Jules de Brayer, an organist and professor of music, who was
manager of the Concerts Lamoureux, and a contributor to the
Revue Wagnérienne. De Brayer was enthusiastic about the work,
and endeavoured to make his friends share his lively admiration for
Mussorgsky. But his attempts at proselytism were unsuccessful.
Even Debussy, who about the year 1890 had the copy of 'Boris'
in his possession for some time, does not seem to have taken
much interest in this opera; possibly because he did not understand the subject, as the text was in Russian. He looked through
the work, but does not seem to have fully realized its extreme
originality. It was not till a few years later, in 1893, that he read it
through completely at Ernest Chausson's house at Lusancy. In
February 1896 he came into closer touch with the genius of this
composer, during the lecture-concerts which Pierre d'Alheim
organized in Paris, at which the interpreters were the singer
Marie Olénine, and the pianist Foerster. The songs entitled 'Sunless' were for Debussy a further revelation of Mussorgsky's art.
In 1901, on the 30th of March at the Société Nationale, he again
heard Marie Olénine sing the 'Chambre d'Enfants', and he warmly
praised its picturesque beauty in his second musical article in the
Revue Blanche.[1]

This chronology of the connexion between Mussorgsky and
Debussy is in accordance with the detailed evidence recorded by
the Swiss author, Robert Godet, in the second volume of his work,
En Marge de 'Boris Godounow'. Robert Godet, who was an
intimate friend of Debussy, had himself given the composer the

---

[1] See The Theories of Claude Debussy, Chapter VII.

score of 'Boris'. The few who had seen it then, Saint-Saëns in particular, had criticized its clumsy, eccentric originality. Yet it is hard to believe that Debussy experienced no fellow-feeling for Mussorgsky. He must have realized even vaguely that here was a musician who spoke an untrammelled language; whose eloquence was simple and direct; who avoided all Wagnerian pomposity and intricacy; and who had produced in his own manner an original and spontaneous work of art, the equivalent of which the young Frenchman had, for years past, been trying to create, in his utterly different and much more subtle style. One is very much tempted to accept the opinion that was generally held before the publication of Robert Godet's statements, reliable though they be, and to believe that Mussorgsky did, in some small measure, help to wean Debussy from his devotion to Richard Wagner. Probably this aesthetic problem will never be definitely solved. But a hitherto unknown work by Debussy, 'Rodrigue et Chimène', which the writer saw recently, seems to prove beyond doubt that he was familiar with Mussorgsky's works in the spring of 1890.

In any case, the influence which is usually ascribed to Mussorgsky is not the one he actually exercised. Superficial observers are apt to lay stress on certain themes or details of instrumental treatment which Debussy unconsciously borrowed from the Russian composer. These are unimportant and negligible coincidences. Mussorgsky's real, deep, and beneficial influence was one of *de-Wagnerization*. In spite of this influence, however, Debussy's works show no trace of the realistic style adopted by his senior. His art is made up of fine shading, discreet allusions, vague evocations, subtle impressions, faint outlines and touches. In Mussorgsky, there is no delicate shading; the line is hard and sharp, the colouring brilliant or violent; the contrasts are definite, the musical gesture clear cut. One composer lives in a continual dream; the other in the midst of realities. The music of the former insinuates itself delightfully into the souls of the hearers; it satisfies them, unless it absolutely fails to awaken any tender echoes in their hearts. The music of the latter produces a direct impression, dominant and irresistible, from which there is no escape.

Mussorgsky certainly influenced Debussy's harmony too, inasmuch as he encouraged him to disregard scholastic rules. Mussorgsky's use of the modes adopted from the orthodox religious music, and his freedom, which was partly due to his instinctive and deliberate neglect of traditional laws, might be regarded as a retrospective justification of young Debussy's daring. Nor was

Mussorgsky the only non-professional musician whose contempt for so-called essential rubrics encouraged an original genius to choose a path of his own. Emmanuel Chabrier had exercised a similar influence a little earlier.

Chabrier's principal works were published and performed about the time Debussy finished his studies at the Conservatoire and won the Prix de Rome. The 'Dix Pièces' for piano appeared in 1881, and the 'Valses Romantiques' in 1883; as we have seen, the laureate used to play them at the Villa Medici. In December of the same year, the Concerts Lamoureux produced 'España,' and during the two following years, excerpts from 'Gwendoline' and 'La Sulamite'; and later 'L'Ode à la Musique' and 'Le Roi Malgré Lui'. Some of Chabrier's methods, which were then considered crazy (whole tone-scales, series of sevenths and ninths), and his harmonic independence, natural in an undisciplined amateur—were probably regarded by Debussy as a practical ratification of his own attempts, and as sanctioning the musical vocabulary which he was attempting to compile.

It has been alleged with an insistence that is little short of ridiculous that Erik Satie exercised a similar influence. The present writer has persistently denied this. What indications are there that this influence ever existed? In order to prove it, a great deal has been made of some harmonic successions in the 'Sarabandes' composed in 1887 by that poor humorist whom some people attempted to raise to the dignity of a *maître* and leader of thought, immediately after the war of 1914–18. Maurice Emmanuel's recent disclosures with regard to Debussy's revolutionary escapades at the Conservatoire in 1883 confirm the writer's opinion. Emmanuel's statements justify the surmise that, in his first sketches, Satie merely utilized—and that very clumsily—the experiments and discoveries the secret of which had been revealed to him by his generous friend. He merely gathered up the crumbs that fell from a bounteous table. The sham title of 'precursor' was the subsequent invention of a certain group, the intention being to irritate Debussy, although the latter had behaved with great generosity to poor Satie.

Debussy's instinctive love of harmonic freedom had made him appreciate Chopin from his earliest years. Long before the Russians, and perhaps in an equal measure, the Polish master played an important part in revealing to him the rich possibilities of the Oriental scales, and the melodic and harmonic variety they afforded. The same qualities attracted him to Grieg, for this charming Scandinavian *petit maître* was wont to blend, or to

alternate, the major and minor modes in the accompaniments of
songs in the popular style. With the most elegant ease, he, too, had
written forbidden successions of chords, and left sevenths and
ninths unresolved. For the same reason, the young French composer could not but admire the modal flexibility and the subtle
ambiguity of Gabriel Fauré who, harmonically speaking, had
stolen a march on all his contemporaries, but so discreetly that the
fact had passed unnoticed. On one occasion, at least, Debussy paid
formal, though involuntary homage to this composer in the form
of a 'Nocturne' for piano, which he sold to a publisher in 1891, and
in which the theme, movement, and modulations were obviously
inspired by Fauré.

Debussy must also have been interested in the works of Alfred
Bruneau. The harmonic innovations of this former fellow student
of his shocked many music-lovers. But others revelled in them
when, in 1891, the Opéra-Comique produced 'Le Rêve', an
'advanced' work, in which one can even trace signs of the future
polytonality of the twentieth century. About this time, or perhaps
a few years earlier, Ernest Chausson also appeared in the guise
of a precursor. His harmonic tendencies and those of Debussy
were closely related, although the tastes and training of the two
men were so divergent, and they certainly reacted on one another.
A comparison of the works written by the two friends about
1884 reveals traces of their reciprocal influence, though they
are difficult to determine definitely. It was apparently not until
his return to Paris that Debussy became familiar with the works
of his compatriots—with the exception of Lalo, whose 'Namouna'
he appreciated, as we saw, even in 1883, and the memory of which
possibly haunted him still in 1892, when he composed his 'Fêtes
Nocturnes'.

Some traces of César Franck's influence are to be met with
in Debussy's works, especially in the String Quartet of 1893. In
spite of his antipathy for the exaggerated use of modulation in
which his former professor of improvisation indulged, the young
musician had not been able to resist the charm of some harmonic
effects and daring sequences which adorn the scores of Franck.
Besides, there is reason to suspect that he was Franck's pupil in
a more direct and permanent sense than he admitted later. In the
Belgian papers of 1894, which reported Debussy's first concert
at Brussels, we find statements of this kind: 'M. Debussy belongs
to the Franck school, but his relationship with the master is a
degree more distant than that of MM. Vincent d'Indy, Ernest
Chausson, Gabriel Fauré, and Pierre de Bréville. In fact, it was

only for six months that he was a disciple of the composer of the "Béatitudes"' (*Art moderne*, 4th of March 1894). 'A. de Bussy . . . a pupil of Guiraud and of César Franck, has given himself up to his own experiments since the death of the *Maître* . . .' (*Le Patriote*, 5th of March 1894). It is possible that Debussy, who had gone to Brussels to take part in the concert, may have supplied the newspapers with information other than that which he gave his friend and biographer, Louis Laloy, in 1909. It is also possible, and more likely, that the newspaper reports were inspired by Vincent d'Indy, who was desirous of linking up a young composer whom he admired with the school of his own master, César Franck.

Gounod too, whose artistic influence was very marked and wide-spread, may be regarded as having reacted, at least in an indirect manner, on Debussy. For one thing, he gave him advice in the course of their frequent conversations; and again, he showed him the example of a limpid instrumentation and, what was still more important, accurate declamation.

The creator of 'Faust' had a keen sense of the musical possibilities of the French language. His young colleague and friend may have sometimes recalled a certain passage from the famous opera where Marguerite declaims 'Je voudrais bien savoir . . .' on one immutable note sustained by mobile harmonies. Besides, in spite of the statements Gounod made at the Académie des Beaux-Arts in condemnation of modern art, he must surely have realized that some of the daring touches by which Debussy proclaimed his harmonic freedom were quite legitimate. Did not Gounod himself write a defence of Rossini, in order to justify a passage in 'William Tell' where 'the night falls' in a series of four common chords of different tonalities?

These then were the French and the foreign composers from whom Debussy received a more or less definite impetus. In addition to those already mentioned, we must not forget Wagner, whose influence we have already noted; nor Borodin, whose art left on him, even as early as 1879, the very visible marks we have already described, and which are also to be traced in the string Quartet of 1893. To these names must be added those of the other Russians he heard in 1889, especially Balakiref. The appeal of the latter composer resided chiefly in the pianistic processes of 'Islamey', and in the colouring of his symphonic poem, 'Thamar'— a highly original composition which, according to 'L'Ouvreuse', made Debussy turn 'pale with emotion', when he heard it again at the Concerts Lamoureux, in November 1895. So keenly sensitive was the young Frenchman, that he was affected by music of the most varied types and countries. And although it is true that here and there, by dint of more or less close analysis, we can discover, in compositions that hail from diverse countries, some elements of the musical tongue he was destined to speak, we are nevertheless forced to acknowledge the originality of the peculiar syntax and individual style he was able to create for himself. Nor does the discovery of these complex influences diminish the greatness of his genius.

CLAUDE DEBUSSY
(about 1895)

CHAPTER V

THE FIRST COMPOSITIONS (1888–93)

IN 1888 Girod published for Achille Debussy a set of 'Ariettes' for voice and piano, two of which were sung by the tenor, Bagès, at the Société Nationale on the 2nd of February 1889. In an article in the *Ménestrel*, Julien Tiersot praised the 'very delicate and refined artistic feeling' of these two songs, whose titles were not given on the programme. They attracted the attention of musicians, who from that time forward were on the look-out for young Achille Debussy's compositions; they were not, however, noticed by the general public. The songs changed publishers, passing from Girod to Fromont; and fifteen years after their first appearance, immediately after the production of 'Pelléas', they reappeared under a new title which betrays ironical disappointment. Henceforward, they were known as the 'Ariettes Oubliées' ('The Forgotten Ariettes'), by Claude, no longer Achille, Debussy. This new edition was dedicated 'to Miss Mary Garden, the unforgettable Mélisande'. The 'Chevaux de Bois', as well as 'Mandoline' and 'Fantoches', had already been favourites of the Prix de Rome students at the Villa Medici in 1885; indeed, none of these six songs, not even the earliest, was unworthy of the artist who was to become so famous on the appearance of 'Pelléas'.

The 'Ariettes Oubliées' include three 'Ariettes' properly so-called, a 'Paysage Belge', and two 'Aquarelles'. Although their melodic curves may occasionally evoke the shade of Massenet—who at that time strongly influenced all the Conservatoire pupils, old and new—still, as regards their colouring, feeling, and harmonic style, some of the 'Ariettes' are genuine Debussy. 'Green', for instance—so delightfully expansive and so subtle in style; and 'C'est l'Extase'—a broad and truly ecstatic melody, completely enveloped in ninths and series of common chords; its continuous modulations which steep the hearer in everchanging tonalities seem to suggest 'the embrace of the breezes' and the 'chorus of small voices'. 'Spleen' is equally characteristic, although its essential melodic and rhythmic elements are definitely reminiscent of Chabrier's 'Bénissez-nous, mon père, avec vos bras tremblants', from the 'Épithalame' in 'Gwendoline'. 'L'Ombre des Arbres' modulates with a daring which must have seemed alarming, if not insane, in 1888. In the 'Chevaux de Bois'—written about 1885, when the young composer was twenty-three or twenty-four

years old—the gallop sets in motion series of parallel common
chords; and the melody—unconsciously borrowed from the
'Parsifal' bells, though the whirling rhythm completely alters it—
undergoes a startling harmonic transformation, an effect which
used to delight Debussy's fellow students in Rome—possibly the
former pupils of the Conservatoire were disconcerted, but not so
those of the École des Beaux-Arts.

Another composition of that period is the 'Petite Suite', which
until now has been dated 1894. It was published by Durand in
February 1889, and a few weeks later was played in a musical
salon by the composer and his fellow student, Jacques Durand,
a son of the publisher. It seems incredible that it did not immediately attract the attention and approval of the public. It is very
popular to-day both in its original form as a piano duet, and in
its various transcriptions for full and small orchestra. No music-
lover could resist the charm of the syncopated 'Barcarolle', or fail
to admire the animation of the brilliant 'Cortège', with its conflicting, but balanced rhythms. There is nothing revolutionary
here, but we notice some daring touches in the harmonies and
accents, a facile flow of charming melodies, and a remarkable
spontaneity—a felicitous quality which is not to be found in
another important work of the same period, the 'Cinq Poèmes
de Baudelaire', for voice with piano accompaniment.

Debussy's biographers have always assigned to this composition the date 1890, that of its first publication. The composer
himself, who had left some of his manuscripts at the publisher's
and presented others to friends such as Paul Poujaud, did not
remember that they supplied proof that the songs had been composed between 1887 and 1889. 'La Mort des Amants' is the earliest.
It was written in December 1887. 'Le Balcon' was completed in
January 1888, its initial *motif* being taken from the contemporary
score, 'La Damoiselle Élue'. 'Harmonie du Soir' belongs to
January 1889, and the 'Jet d'Eau' to March of the same year.
'Recueillement' alone is not dated, or rather, the page bearing
the date has disappeared. This new chronology explains the complex, elaborate character of these Baudelairian compositions—for
1888–9 was the period of the Bayreuth pilgrimages; from the first
of which he returned full of enthusiasm, from the second, entirely
disillusioned. Debussy had reached the crisis of his transformation at the time he wrote these songs; consequently, the 'Cinq
Poèmes' may be regarded in a sense as laboratory experiments of
a complicated chemical nature.

Achille Debussy (who now begins to prefer his other Christian name, Claude) is haunted by Wagner's elaborate art and sumptuous orchestration as he weaves and intertwines his melodic garlands; they are often artificial—he is trying to escape from Massenet! He is full of memories of Bayreuth. We can trace them both in his style and in his developments. Sometimes, the reminiscence is definite, as in the beginning of 'Recueillement', where we hear the horn *motifs* from 'Tristan und Isolde'. They seemed to haunt him, for we find them again in a later work. Nevertheless, the effort to free himself from the dominion of German art is apparent, especially in his transcription of French diction which, though not yet smooth, is broadly melodic, in contrast to the rough, bouncing declamation imitative of German diction, to be found in so many contemporary works. The Debussyism of the future manifests itself in another manner, and that chiefly harmonical. Sometimes it can be traced very clearly, as in certain irregular arpeggios which are possibly atonal; in the harsh modulations of 'Le Balcon'; in the common chords which occur in 'Recueillement' and which produce at the words 'Et comme un long linceul . . .' a tonal and modal vagueness that is curiously arresting. That same work shows another instance of his talent for creating an atmosphere, for in it he achieves a most effective rendering of 'the obscure atmosphere' that 'envelops the town'—an evocation of that nocturnal Paris, so dear to the young artist, the sounds of which were to be transcribed in a similar manner, some twelve years later, in Gustave Charpentier's 'Louise'. Debussy's struggle to liberate his personality seems most successful in 'Le Jet d'Eau', the earliest and the most finished of the 'Cinq Poèmes'. The persistent double pedal-note in seconds, in the opening bars, is reminiscent of Borodin. The composer himself seems to have demonstrated his own belief in the superiority of this piece, when he scored the piano part for full orchestra twenty years later. In spite of their extreme delicacy and fluidity, these pages are full of melodic interest.

There was no likelihood of the 'Poèmes' being accepted by any publisher, although a second series had already been projected and announced. The words were of a nature to alarm the timorous, the music was calculated to frighten the average amateur, and the writing of the vocal part to dismay the singers. No one would undertake to publish or perform them. The composer had to content himself with ordering a *de luxe* edition for a few subscribers. It was limited to a hundred and fifty copies, one-third of which were printed on hand-made paper. The subscriptions were collected by Gaston Choisnel, a former pupil and laureate of the Conservatoire, who had become one of the principal employees of the publisher Durand. The ordinary copies of this edition were sold at twelve francs, a very high price at that time, when the piano score of an opera, which was fifteen or twenty times as voluminous, cost twenty francs. The edition was on sale without the publisher's name at the Librairie de l'Art Indépendant. It was dedicated to Étienne Dupin, a rich young amateur and a great friend of Debussy's, who probably helped to finance the publication. The composer was well aware that, owing to the aristocratic nature of his work in general, he could not hope for widespread popularity. In fact, as we shall see later, when planning the production of his future opera, 'Pelléas', he did not anticipate anything more than a few special performances at a private theatre. Consequently he put aside the plates of the 'Cinq Poèmes' and of 'La Damoiselle Élue' after the first edition had been published. But, acting on the advice of Gabriel Fauré—who proclaimed the 'Poèmes' to be a work of genius—the publisher, Hamelle, entered into negotiations with Debussy with a view to purchasing these songs, as well as the *envoi de Rome*. The matter dragged on until the production of 'Pelléas'; in 1902, it was taken up again, and eventually concluded by the firm of Durand.

Soon after the publication of the 'Cinq Poèmes', Debussy had the good fortune to meet with an exceptionally intelligent publisher who was to be of invaluable service to him in the future. This was Hartmann. He was of foreign origin, but a naturalized Frenchman. In 1873 Hartmann had founded the Concerts de l'Odéon, which next became the Association artistique, and then the Concerts Colonne. It was he who had discovered or adopted Bizet, Franck, Lalo, Castillon, Reyer, Saint-Saëns, Massenet, Bruneau, Charpentier, and Vidal. Debussy was to be one of his last discoveries. He was an active and daring publisher, and had done some unobtrusive literary work, having for instance collaborated in the libretto of 'Marie-Madeleine', and in the translation of the 'Ring' edited by Alfred Ernst. He had been obliged to sell his publishing business, but it was only the outward show of his profession that he gave up. He became the representative of the Wagner family in France, and of the Mayence firm of Schott, and he remained a publisher, to all intents and purposes, though he had the name of his colleague, Fromont, printed on the works he published. Consequently, all those compositions of Debussy which bear Fromont's name really belonged in the first instance to Hartmann, who proved himself a faithful and devoted friend and became, in a sense, the banker of the capricious young composer.

In 1890, 1891, and 1892 Debussy sold a considerable number of small pieces, most of which did not appear until some ten or fifteen years later. The purchasers were Hartmann, and several other publishers, such as: Durand, Hamelle, Dupont, Girod (whose business was bought up by Fromont), Choudens (who engraved the 'Fantaisie' for piano and orchestra in 1890, though he did not publish it). In 1890 Debussy sold five piano pieces of more or less recent date, some of which had no doubt been composed a good deal earlier. These were: 'Rêverie', 'Ballade Slave', 'Tarentelle Styrienne', 'Valse Romantique', and 'Nocturne'.

The 'Rêverie', with its orthodox counterpoint, is written in a pleasant style. It contains some unusual harmonies and a certain amount of pianistic padding, and reveals the composer's taste for recurring designs. It was sold to the publisher Choudens on the 4th of March 1891, and bought from him by Hartmann. Its publication, which occurred after a delay of fifteen years, was deplored by Debussy. On the 21st of April 1905 he wrote as follows to the publisher Fromont: 'It was a mistake to bring out the "Rêverie". It is an unimportant work which was written in a great hurry to oblige Hartmann; in other words, *It is bad.*' The 'Ballade Slave', which was republished later under the simple title of 'Ballade', suggests a study. There are endless repetitions and sequences, amongst which we find some harmonies of a new type, and certain *arpeggio* figures that we meet with again in the 'Toccata' from 'Pour le Piano'. Its principal interest lies in one characteristic melody and in the ending, both of which justify the epithet *Slav*. The typically slavonic theme is written in the A mode, on a gapped scale, and the ending reminds one of Borodine and Balakiref. The 'Tarentelle Styrienne', which reappeared later under the title of 'Danse', is similar in style to the 'Fantaisie' for piano and orchestra. It modulates with daring ease, contains free interlacings of chords of the seventh and ninth, and is full of new rhythms. It does not seem to have attracted attention on the occasion of its performance at the Société Nationale on the 10th of March 1900. But, thirty-five years after its composition, Maurice Ravel thought it sufficiently original to be worth orchestrating. Nothing about the 'Valse Romantique', except its title, is reminiscent of Emmanuel Chabrier's celebrated pieces for two pianos; it would be very commonplace, were it not for the abruptness of its modulations. Debussy had probably given the title of 'Interlude' to the 'Nocturne', for this name occurs in parenthesis, as a sub-title, on the sale contract which was concluded on the 27th of July 1892, for the sum of one hundred francs. Its few pages are written in a composite style and show fugitive characteristic touches. Some lines foretell the future String Quartet, or remind us of the Cantata of 1884. Others suggest Franck or Borodin. But, alone amongst all Debussy's compositions, the general aspect of this 'Nocturne', both as regards its principal theme and its modulations, is reminiscent of Fauré, as we have already observed. Indeed, all these early piano pieces bear the marks of the period to which they belong; and many a passage might be attributed to Saint-Saëns, or Massenet, or even Benjamin Godard. It seems probable that Debussy had composed, or at least sketched them at the Conservatoire, and that he revised and finished them in days of financial stress. In any case, we cannot entirely trust the accuracy of the dates which Debussy indicated, quite approximately, to the critic, Jean Aubry, when the latter was drawing up the first catalogue of his works. The composer had no love for musicography, and he did not think that any one could attach much importance to determining the exact year in which he had written his compositions. The date of the 'Cinq Poèmes' has already been rectified. Other chronological corrections[1] will be made in the course of the present work.

Two other piano pieces are ascribed to the year 1891: a 'Mazurka, and a 'Marche Écossaise'. The 'Mazurka' is certainly much older than is officially stated. It probably dates from the Conservatoire days and the journey to Russia, that is to say, from about 1880. It has no particular individuality except its modal uncertainty. The influence of Chopin is very clear, and that of Borodin more definite still (the 'Intermezzo' from the 'Petite Suite'). The history of its publication is difficult to trace. The composer had absent-mindedly sold it to two different publishers: to Hamelle, who printed it; and to Choudens, who bought it on the 14th of March 1891, with the 'Rêverie'. Hartmann bought it back, and in 1902 it came into Fromont's hands. In spite of the composer's disapproval, the latter published it in 1905.

The 'Marche Écossaise sur un Thème Populaire' is written in the form of a piano duet. Its first title was the very high-sounding one of 'Marche des Anciens Comtes de Ross, dédiée à leur Descendant, le Général Meredith Read, Grand-Croix de l'Ordre Royal du Rédempteur'. The following historical note was added: 'The origin of the Earls of Ross, Chieftains of Clan Ross of Rosshire, Scotland, dates back to the remotest times. The Chief-

[1] See the author's article in the review *Musique* (Paris), 15th of November 1927.

tain's band of Pipers used to play this March for their Laird before and during battle, as well as on festival days. The primitive March tune forms the refrain of the composition.' This note reveals the fact that the composition was written to order, the air having been supplied by the afore-mentioned personage, a Scottish officer, who was a descendant of the noble Earls, and who wished to have the air arranged. The 'Marche' is a very brilliant piece, which is correctly worked out according to scholastic formulas, and even contains a canon. Debussy arranged it for orchestra about 1908, and developed the Finale. The piano version now available is an arrangement by Gustave Samazeuilh which corresponds to the orchestral score. The author himself did not hear the piece in its orchestral form until 1913, during a rehearsal of the Nouveaux Concerts, at the Théâtre des Champs-Élysées, under the conductorship of D. E. Ingelbrecht. This conductor performed the 'Marche Écossaise' on two occasions at least: on the 19th of April and on the 22nd of October 1913. As he listened, Debussy could not help saying: '*Mais c'est joli.*'

Two songs for voice and piano, 'Romance' and 'Cloches' appeared in 1891, at the same time as the 'Marche' and the 'Mazurka'. Several others were to have been published about that time, such as: 'Les Angélus', 'Dans le Jardin', 'La Mer est plus Belle', 'Le Son du Cor s'afflige', and 'L'Échelonnement des Haies'. The two first-named songs, 'Romance' and 'Cloches', are pleasant but mediocre, with their persistent themes, and their rather Massenet-like style. The date of their composition has always been given as 1880, and that of their publication as 1887. But, as a matter of fact, the manuscript is dated June 1891, and they were published the following December. Debussy had given them to the publisher without separate titles, calling them 'Deux Romances, Poésies de Paul Bourget'. Judging by their melodic curve and the style of the writing, both of them are probably somewhat older than is stated. That year the same firm published the two pleasant 'Arabesques' for piano, which up to the present have been ascribed to the year 1888. *Arabesque* is a word to which Debussy was later on to assign a more definite meaning in connexion with the works of Bach, whose 'adorable arabesques' delighted him.[1]

The chief charm of 'Les Angélus' consists in a delicate notation of the harmonics of bells, which already creates what was to be known later on as 'a Debussy atmosphere'. 'Dans le Jardin' has a graceful subtlety, and one notices certain touches that are to be

[1] See *The Theories of Claude Debussy*, Chapter VIII. (O.U.P.)

met with again in 'Pelléas'. Thus, around the words 'les yeux
bleus ombrés' he has woven the same *atmosphere*—once more the
word is necessary—that envelops Mélisande as she passes along
the terrace, in the third scene of the dramatic work. In 'La
Mer est plus Belle' we notice common chords in changing
tonalities, and it concludes audaciously on a chord of the dominant seventh. 'Le Son du Cor s'afflige' is like a new version of
the 'Ariettes'. At the point where 'la neige tombe a longs traits
de charpie', we hear the very Debussyist effect of six descending
common chords. 'L'Échelonnement des Haies' is full of life.
Charles Bordes also produced this effect of luminous brilliance and
pulsating rhythm when he in his turn set the same poem to music.

At that time Debussy had lost his taste for Paul Bourget's
poetry, and was entirely taken up with the art of Paul Verlaine.
'*Je n'aime plus que ça*', he said one day to the publisher, Hamelle,
as he handed him over the manuscripts of some songs and a volume
of Verlaine's poems, asking him to pick out what he wished him
to set to music. Wherever the fault lay, the volume remained at
the publisher's. He did not make the proposed choice, and only
decided rather tardily, in 1901, to publish the works he had bought
so long before. In 1893 Debussy, who was always short of money,
made at Hamelle's request a piano solo arrangement of Raff's
'Humoresque en Forme de Valse', which was engraved and brought
out. He also offered to write a set of Verlaine songs, easy pieces
for children, and even a Piano Method. But none of these schemes
materialized.

The three songs which eventually formed the first volume of
the 'Fêtes Galantes' were also left lying for a long time at the
publishers'—first at Hartmann's and then at Fromont's. Although
the *Courrier Musical* announced in May 1903 that they were 'about
to appear', they did not see the light of day until the following
year. But they were written in 1892. In fact, as we have seen,
the first version was written some ten years earlier. The three
songs are entitled: 'En Sourdine', 'Fantoches', and 'Clair de Lune'.
The versions of 1892 are a great improvement on the earlier ones.
'Fantoches', however, was but little altered. Its sprightly humour
and its delightful spontaneity seem to have gushed forth in a single
stream. It bears all the characteristic marks of the type of art that
was to be known as Debussyism. The first song, 'En Sourdine',
is written in the orthodox *Lied* form. The song of the nightingale,
which is evoked at the end of the poem, opens and closes the little
score; and the melodic inspiration of this theme—both as regards
its rhythmical outline and its colouring—is very similar to that

of the String Quartet (the opening phrase) and the 'Prélude à l'Après-midi d'un Faune'. The declamation adapts itself to the poetical text, but is occasionally carried away by the music, and imitates its syncopations even when the resulting effect is absurd—as in the passage 'de ce silence . . . fondons nos âmes'. In 'Clair de Lune' we find the entire Debussy of the future. The serene melancholy of a very sustained melody is enveloped in the genuine moonlight atmosphere of the accompaniment achieved by means of persistent patterns, a certain modal colouring, unexpected successions of accumulated intervals, and the daring manner in which he blends and links the mobile harmonies which succeed one another with absolute freedom.

An important piano work, the 'Suite Bergamasque', is connected with the same period. This set of pieces, the title of which is evidently reminiscent of Verlaine, was originally to have consisted of a 'Prélude', a 'Menuet', a 'Promenade Sentimentale', and a 'Pavane'. It formed part of the manuscripts which were sold to Fromont in 1902, by Hartmann's heirs. It was then announced that the series was to include 'Masques', 'L'Isle Joyeuse'—which was published separately in 1904—and a 'Deuxième Sarabande', which was probably transformed into 'Hommage à Rameau' in 1905. In 1904 an advertisement of Fromont's in the musical papers announced that it was 'in the press', and was to retain its original form. It eventually appeared at the end of June 1905, and consisted of four pieces: 'Prélude', 'Menuet', 'Clair de Lune'—which may possibly be the piece originally entitled 'Promenade Sentimentale'—and 'Passepied' which, in spite of its title which suggests a brisk tempo, is probably very similar to the original 'Pavane', if not identical with it. In the course of fifteen years the 'Suite Bergamasque' obviously underwent many alterations. When selling it to Fromont, on the 21st of April 1905, the composer wrote these significant words: 'It would be both absurd and futile to give it to you in its present form.' A minute examination of its pages enables the musical expert to distinguish the material that was added, at fairly distant intervals, although the essentials date from about 1890. In this elegant and fascinating composition we find the most varied elements: charming trivialities in the Godard style, fugitive allusions, reminiscent of such composers as Grieg, Massenet, and Saint-Saëns, as well as some very original touches. The 'Menuet' and the 'Passepied' are very individual in colouring in spite of the intentional 'pastiche', and the 'Clair de Lune' floods the third piece with an exquisite atmosphere, unmistakably

Debussyist in character. All these pieces belong to a period of transition, and show evidence of his familiarity with the works of many of the older masters, such as Schumann, and more particularly Chopin. Outside the little group of writers and painters who believed in his talents, Debussy still remained unknown. One realizes how far he was from being a celebrity, when one glances through the 'Lettres de l'Ouvreuse' written, from 1890 on, by Willy, with the collaboration of Alfred Ernst and a number of musicians. These humorous chronicles, in which the musical life of Paris was whimsically depicted week by week, rarely allude to the young composer. On the 9th of March 1890 he is mentioned for the first time, in the following equivocal terms: '. . . Debussy, who fertilizes Baudelaire's "Flowers" with his music.'

On the 1st of November 1891, after a performance of Liszt's 'Valse de Mephisto' at the Concerts Lamoureux, the chronicler unkindly remarks: 'The vertiginous Debussy, who is more Fleur-du-mal than ever, listened with disdainful pity. But, by Jove, Monseigneur, there is something in that music after all. Ask Saint-Saëns or, better still, consult his "Danse Macabre".' We find a little more sympathy, and even a note of ironical admiration, in 1893, when the Société Nationale produced the 'Damoiselle Élue', which is described as 'a symphonic stained-glass window by Fra Angelico Debussy (somewhat perverse however)'. Two weeks later, he is alluded to as the 'damoiseau élu'. It was not until the end of that year, when his String Quartet was performed, that he succeeded in attracting the serious attention of the little musical world of Paris.

He should have won the admiration of music-lovers and the esteem of professional musicians long before this. His early works deserved recognition, both those that were written for piano solo and those that embellished the verses of various poets. As we have pointed out, these little pieces, which the publishers refused and the public disregarded, often contain more than a promise. We find in them, in fact, the germ of nearly all those characteristics that give his great scores their value. Like the Roman compositions, they display the first-fruits of the Debussyism of the future. But the limited public that creates reputations in Paris was still being carried along on the flood of a romanticism that had gone out of fashion elsewhere. The select shrines were still consecrated to the cult of a fierce, grandiloquent, philosophical art: Beethoven's last quartets, the new works of César Franck—discovered very late in the day—and Richard Wagner's great operas. . . . These complex, ambitious works, so full of noble beauty, were alone capable of arousing an enthusiasm that bordered on delirium. Delirium—the word actually occurs in an article by Paul Landormy published not long since, in the Paris journal, *La Victoire*. In the course of his article, this critic, who has followed the evolution of music during the last forty years with a close and intense interest, makes a reference to the 'nineties, the days of his own youth.

'The taste in those days', he says, 'was all for Beethoven's last Quartets, Wagner's operas, and Franck's Quintet and Quartet, which were accorded an excessive admiration, romantic in its violence. When Lekeu attended the Bayreuth performances, he fainted from emotion at the end of the Prelude to "Tristan", and had to be carried out of the theatre. That was the sort of enthusiasm people indulged in then. They listened to music in a state of delirium. We are very far from that sort of thing nowadays. Debussy and Fauré have taught us a different manner of feeling, one that is much more concentrated and reserved. Sobriety and restraint are the fashion now.'

In spite of his Wagnerism, now on the wane, Debussy had already begun to react against the universal craze for passion, and to avoid the romantic excesses of his contemporaries. He had some difficulty in resisting this tendency, especially as even the intellectuals, who were alive to the dangers of the German influence, could not conceive of any other form of dramatic aesthetics but that of the god of Bayreuth. A very significant article appeared in the *Revue Wagnérienne* on the 8th of June 1885, which was reproduced later by its author, Catulle Mendès, as an epilogue to his book on Richard Wagner. One is inclined to think it refers to Claude Debussy, especially when one considers the date of the article, its title ('Le Jeune Prix de Rome et le vieux Wagnériste'), and when one remembers the cordial relations that existed between the composer (a Prix de Rome of the previous year), and Mendès, who depicted himself under the aspect of the old Wagnerian. This verbose document, which proclaims the need for a national reaction—but within Wagnerian limits—would, therefore, seem to deserve our serious consideration.

The old Wagnerian—forgetting his Jewish origin, and remembering only his acquired nationality—manifests a fervent French nationalism. He warns the Prix de Rome student against the imitation of Wagner, and points out that, in their instrumental works, composers are already giving evidence of 'the increasingly penetrating influence of Germanic inspiration'. He calls on composers to listen to folk-songs and 'seek in them the characteristics of *our own* music and thus achieve—by the aid of inspiration and individual labour—a perfect artistic expression of the unconscious musical soul of our country'. He advises composers to imitate Wagner the aesthetic dramatist, rather than Wagner the poet-musician. Thus, 'musical drama in France would be the product of intensely French inspiration developed according to laws adopted from the Wagnerian system'.

Mendès waxed enthusiastic over this international compromise, for he saw in it the realization of his artistic ideals regarding music and the drama.

'This signal and novel glory', he wrote, 'is in store for the first musician of genius in France who will steep himself in the musical and poetical atmosphere that fills our legends and songs, whilst adopting all the Wagnerian theories that are compatible with the spirit of our race. Such a man will succeed—either alone or with the aid of some poet—in freeing our opera from the ridiculous, old-fashioned conventions that fetter it. Let him bring poetry and music into intimate union, not with the object of making the one heighten the effect of the other—but for the sake of the drama alone. Let the poet in him sternly repress all literary embellishments, and let the musician in him reject all such vocal and orchestral affects as would interrupt the dramatic emotion. Let him forgo all recitatives, arias, *strettos*, and even ensembles, unless the dramatic action—to which everything must be sacrificed—requires the union of several voices. Let him break the framework of the old symmetrical melody. Without Germanizing his melody, let him prolong it indefinitely to suit the rhythm of the poetry. In a word, let his music become speech, but a speech that is all music. In particular, let the orchestra use all the resources of science and inspiration, so as to blend and develop the themes which represent the various emotions and personages, until it becomes like a great vat, in which all the molten elements of the drama may be heard seething together. Meanwhile, enveloped in the emanating atmosphere of tragedy, the lofty heroic action—which, in spite of its complexity, is the logical outcome of one single idea—will hasten onwards, amidst violent passions and unexpected incidents, amidst smiles and tears, towards some great final emotion. Whoever creates such a work will be a great man and he will earn our love. For, even though he borrow his forms from Germany, he will modify them and, in his inspiration, he will remain a Frenchman. Then when the Germans extol the great name of Richard Wagner, we shall proudly acclaim this name—as yet, unknown—but which we shall soon hear greeted with cries of applause and welcome.'

Inspired by this dim, but splendid hope, 'the old Wagnerian' thought it well to provide librettos for various composers. For the 'young Prix de Rome' of 1884 he prepared a drama or tragedy entitled 'Chimène et Rodrigue'. This heroic subject was utterly

unsuited to the advanced young artist, who was an avowed enemy
of romanticism, and an apostle of pre-Raphaelitism, symbolism
and impressionism. Debussy accepted it, however, possibly because
Catulle Mendès promised to facilitate the publication of his other
works. During the year 1891 he worked at the uncongenial task
of putting this new 'Cid' to music. He laboured hard, struggling
against his own artistic feelings which could not rally loyally to
the support of his dramatist's grandiloquence. In January 1892
he wrote to his friend Robert Godet: 'I am kept in a state of
feverish anxiety by this opera in which everything is against me.
I should like you to hear the two acts I have finished, for I am
very much afraid that I have been victorious over myself.' He also
acknowledged to his friends that he felt a real repulsion for the task
he had undertaken. 'It is the exact opposite of everything I should
like to express', he confided to his friend, Gustave Charpentier.
'The traditional nature of the subject demands a type of music
that I can no longer write.'

Three scenes of this work were written, or at least, according
to his usual custom, Debussy made a rough draft on three or four
lines and added notes regarding the instrumentation. This un-
natural collaboration soon came to an end. Contrary to what has
been stated, Debussy did not destroy the hundred pages or so he
had written. But he kept them concealed. The only existing copy
has been intentionally withdrawn. It is no longer to be found
amongst the mass of papers which the musician kept until his
death, the most important of which are scattered throughout the
world to-day, many being in America. 'Rodrigue et Chimène'
now belongs to a celebrated French pianist and remains hidden
in his private collection. In this instance, the intention of Debussy's
heirs coincides with the wishes of the musician. In spite of its
historical interest, they will not allow this valuable document to
be made public. If it should one day be placed in the library
of the Paris Conservatoire, writers on music will be able to
indulge their very legitimate curiosity. They will then be free
to study this remarkable manuscript composed by a musician not
yet thirty years old, during an unsettled period of artistic transition.

In the dedication, dated April 1890, they will find the real
Christian name and the surname of a certain green-eyed lady
who was for some years the composer's devoted companion.
This name is not the one by which she was known to her intimates,
neither is it her *nom de guerre*. In the score itself, they will find
many admirable pages which bear the stamp of such fascinating
originality that, in spite of everything, it will be impossible to

resist the temptation to publish the work one day. The experts will discover here, as in all the works Debussy wrote about that time, rather obvious reminiscences of the Russian *Five*, particularly of Mussorgsky whose influence was evident even in 1890, as we mentioned on page 60. They will not fail to notice a *motif* from Chabrier—a heroic theme, sounded on Rodrigue's horn, which is developed at length as a guiding theme; it is the same seven-note melody which, as we saw, Debussy had already borrowed from 'Gwendoline' when he composed 'Spleen' ('Ariettes Oubliées'). The musicographers may also find curves suggestive of Massenet. But above all, they will see to what an extent the young French master was still under the dominion of Wagner, in spite of his genius and his deliberate anti-Wagnerian tendency. Thus, we are reminded of 'Tristan' when he wished to render pensive sadness or to write a love duet (syncopations in the accompaniment, intervals of the ninth in the vocal parts); his expression of heroic sentiment suggests 'Götterdämmerung'; and the sparkling song of the Flower Maidens in 'Parsifal' obsessed him whenever his librettist—who was equally impregnated with Wagnerism—provided him with the intermingled stanzas of the Filles de Bivar.

But all this was of little account. Claude Debussy was about to discover the very different art of Maurice Maeterlinck. All his energies were now to be devoted to the slow and successful musical development of a masterpiece that harmonized with his sensibility, namely, 'Pelléas et Mélisande'.

CHAPTER VI

BEFORE 'PELLÉAS': THE 'QUARTET' AND THE 'PROSES LYRIQUES' (1892–9)

THE first important event which attracted the attention of the musical public to the young composer occurred when he was just thirty-one years old. This was the performance of 'La Damoiselle Élue' by the Société Nationale, on Saturday, the 8th of April 1893, at an important orchestral and choral concert, held in the Salle Érard, under the conductorship of Gabriel Marie. Some purely symphonic works by young composers of the day were also given, such as: Paul Dukas's Overture to 'Polyeucte', another Overture by Raymond Bonheur, a symphonic tale, entitled 'Iris', by Paul Fournier; several vocal works, such as: Ernest Chausson's 'Poème de l'Amour et de la Mer', Pierre de Bréville's 'Medeia', Henri Duparc's 'Phidylé'—a song that was already known, but which was then given for the first time with orchestral accompaniment—and lastly, 'La Damoiselle Élue', in which the solo parts were taken by Julia Robert and Thérèse Roger.

The *envoi de Rome*, now heard at last, was also to be seen in print, for it was published at the same time by Bailly, at the Librairie de l'Art Indépendant. A coloured cover by Maurice Denis adorned the volume, 'in a rare and exquisite manner' to quote Debussy's words in a dedication to the painter. Only a hundred and sixty copies were printed. The fact that the edition was so strictly limited shows how little hope Debussy had that his works would be widely circulated.[1] There were few critiques in the papers. Two of them, those by Julien Tiersot and Charles Darcours, are worth mentioning.

' ... I do not know', Tiersot wrote in the *Ménestrel*, 'whether it was his masters who taught him the principles of which he has shown us the practical application. I do not think so, although his work gives evidence of a skill which is the result of deep and serious study. As regards

---

[1] In April 1895 the catalogue of the Librairie de l'Art Indépendant contained the following note: 'This edition, which is limited to a hundred and sixty copies, including those printed on special paper, will not be reprinted. At the present moment it is nearly exhausted.' The original MS. contains a number of minor corrections which were probably made in 1902, with a view to a second edition. This MS. is to be found in the Paris Conservatoire library, together with a rough copy which drifted there in some mysterious way. A comparison of these two documents, which are both from Debussy's hand, enable us to note some interesting points which we shall record later on.

the general feeling, it is essentially original and highly modern. The music is artistically wrought, in concise and delicate forms, with a rare and subtle skill. The whole of the first part is exquisite, with its alternating verses of dialogue between the female chorus and the solo recitative. And although, towards the end, the length of the solo part rather damped the ardour of the general public, the work was nevertheless received with rapturous applause by the more enthusiastic portion of the audience.'

The originality of 'La Damoiselle Élue' so impressed Charles Darcours—or rather, his anonymous prompters—that this critic, in an article in the *Figaro*, contrasted it in vehement terms with the old-fashioned works that had been performed on the same day. He mercilessly censured the compositions of Raymond Bonheur, Pierre de Bréville, and Ernest Chausson, and ruthlessly condemned the Société Nationale, which he stigmatized as dead and alive: 'a school of belated mutual admiration which, if it possessed any influence, would lead French music into a blind alley where no one would follow it—the public, least of all'. Then followed praise of Debussy whom, as we have seen, Charles Darcours had already championed in 1883 and 1884, on the occasion of the Prix de Rome competitions in which the composer had taken part. He considered that 'La Damoiselle Élue' constituted a 'remarkable antithesis to the fuliginous productions of the forefathers of the Cénacle' (who, as a matter of fact, were of the same age as Debussy). Debussy's score, he went on to say,

'is not a masterpiece, but there is more life in it than in the whole series of compositions that preceded it on the programme. "La Damoiselle Élue" is at any rate an original work. It is very insinuating and extremely modern. After listening only a few days ago, with such heartfelt admiration to the lofty beauty of Palestrina's music, we experienced an almost guilty delight on hearing this composition. For it is very sensual and decadent, rather corrupt in fact, but it has pages of exquisite, sparkling beauty. How refreshing is a touch of youth! We are told it was quite by accident that M. Debussy was admitted to the Société Nationale. And yet, new blood such as his is just what that venerable institution needs. This sub-cutaneous injection may possibly produce dangerous eruptions in the young musicians of the near future. But, after all, for the Société Nationale such an incident would be less serious than death.'

In this article the critic of the *Figaro* showed an insight and a sound prophetic sense of which he had already given proof in his report on the 'Enfant Prodigue'. As we saw before, the cantata for the Prix de Rome competition had enabled him to foretell, as early as 1884, that young Achille was a musician who was 'destined to meet with a great deal of praise . . . and plenty of abuse', and that a laureate, who had made such a remarkable début, only needed 'to find his own path amidst the enthusiasms and the antagonisms he is certain to arouse'. We find this admirable forecast repeated in the critique of 1893. The rich blood which Debussy transfused into the worn-out organism of the antiquated Society did, in fact, very soon rejuvenate that valetudinarian body; but in the process it provoked some cases of toxic-poisoning amongst those who imitated him too closely.

This enthusiasm for the new-comer's art was not universal. Many conservative musicians were shocked by the tendency that Charles Darcours himself designated as 'rather corrupt'. One of the strongest partisans of 'La Damoiselle Élue' was Vincent d'Indy. He praised the composition in the highest terms and did everything in his power to procure further performances, especially in Brussels.

A few days after his triumph, Debussy took part in an important public function. The atmosphere of mystery that still surrounded him was soon to be dispelled. In preparation for the first performance of the 'Walküre', a special 'avant-première' had been organized at the Opéra, for the 6th of May 1893. It took the form of a lecture on 'Rheingold' by Catulle Mendès. Musical examples were given to illustrate the remarks of this poet and critic, who was one of the best-known representatives of Wagnerism in France, if not the most highly qualified. Two artists played extracts from the first part of the 'Ring', arranged for two pianos. These were Raoul Pugno, who as virtuoso was very soon to take a conspicuous place in the musical world, and Claude Debussy, who was that day quite as much admired as his partner for his pianistic interpretation of Wagner's orchestration. Yet, at that very time, the drama was being chosen which Debussy—animated by an anti-Wagnerian spirit— was gradually to transform into a masterpiece of operatic art.

During the summer of 1892 Claude Debussy had bought in Paris a book by Maurice Maeterlinck, which had been published in Brussels on the 4th of May, namely, 'Pelléas et Mélisande'. He read it immediately with enthusiasm. The thought of setting this mysterious tragedy to music occurred to him. He then and there wrote down some of his musical impressions, and the first of these ideas, which he communicated to his friend, Godet, were utilized in the final version. They include: Golaud's rhythm, the five-note arabesque which describes Mélisande, and a sketch of the theme in 6/4 time which accompanies these words sung by Pelléas: 'On dirait que ta voix a passé sur la mer au printemps.' It was not until the following year that he made up his mind to write the score of this drama, probably after he had seen the work performed at the Théatre des Bouffes-Parisiens, on the 17th of May 1893.

On the occasion of the first production of Maeterlinck's drama in France, the song in the third act had been put to music by Gabriel Fabre, a young amateur, very much in vogue in literary circles at that time. This drama, with its unusual form and its vague philosophy, had not been very favourably received by the critics. In fact, the majority had not understood it at all. Francisque Sarcey had cut it to pieces in his feuilleton in the *Temps*. He had even gone so far as to conclude his review with lines which show a mediocrity of thought and feeling that is only equalled by his style: 'You emerge from that gloom utterly stupefied, as if you had a leaden weight on your head. Oh, what a voluptuous joy it was to get out into the fresh air. You don't catch me listening to Maeterlinck again.' Even Pierre Louÿs, Debussy's confidant and literary adviser, did not approve of the project of his friend and disciple. However, the musician induced Louÿs to accompany him when he went to ask Maeterlinck for the authorization he so ardently desired.

On his way to Ghent, where his future collaborator resided, Debussy stopped at Brussels. There he visited the violinist, Eugène Ysaÿe, and, to the great joy of the virtuoso, showed him the 'Cinq Poèmes', 'La Damoiselle Élue', and the notes that he had made for 'Pelléas et Mélisande'. As for the interview, during which he asked the Belgian dramatist's permission to transform 'Pelléas' into a lyrical work, Debussy has described the scene in a letter to Ernest Chausson.

'I saw Maeterlinck and spent a day with him in Ghent. At first he behaved like a girl meeting an eligible young man. Afterwards, he thawed and became charming. He talked about the theatre as only a very remarkable man could. As regards "Pelléas", he has given me full authorization to make any cuts I wish, and has even pointed out some very important and very advisable ones. As far as music is concerned he says he does not know a thing about it, and when he goes to hear a Beethoven symphony, he is like a blind man in a museum. But he is really very nice, and talks with a delightful simplicity of the wonderful things he discovers. When I was thanking him for entrusting "Pelléas" to me, he did his utmost to prove that it was he who was indebted to me for so kindly writing music to it! As my opinion is the exact opposite, I had to use what little diplomacy nature has endowed me with. . . .'

In spite of the discretion with which Debussy used the author's permission to revise the drama and make the necessary cuts—in a word, to adapt it for the purposes of the musical version—Maeterlinck had nevertheless occasion later on to regret this authorization keenly, for purely personal reasons that had nothing to do with art.

Debussy was overjoyed to be able to set 'Pelléas et Mélisande' to music. It had been a most distressing labour to write those two acts to Catulle Mendès's libretto, 'Chimène et Rodrigue'. And although we see from a letter which he wrote during the summer of 1893, to his friend, Ernest Chausson, that even at the age of thirty-one he was not quite sure of his aesthetic ideals, still the play 'Pelléas', and Maeterlinck's dramatic style in general, were in harmony with his feelings and in complete agreement with his hopes and aspirations.

It almost looks, indeed, as if Claude Debussy had foreseen the artistic tendencies of his future collaborator several years before he came to know his works. There is something strangely prophetic in one of those remarkable talks he had after his return from Rome with his former professor, Ernest Guiraud, which Maurice Emmanuel quotes in his book on 'Pelléas'. The theories are so appropriate that one would be inclined to suspect they had been fabricated after the event, were it not for the fact that the historian is absolutely trustworthy and took notes of his comrade's words, almost in the form of a dictation. In October 1889, when the last pilgrimage to Bayreuth had destroyed his faith in Wagner, Debussy made the following statement: 'I do not feel tempted to imitate what I admire in Wagner. My conception of dramatic art is different. According to mine, music begins where speech fails. Music is intended to convey the inexpressible. I should like her to appear as if emerging from the shadowy regions to which she would from time to time retire. I would have her always discreet.' When he was asked what poet would provide him with a suitable libretto, he answered:

'One who will only hint at things, and will thus enable me to graft my thought on his; one who will create characters whose history and abode belong to no particular time or place; one who will not despotically impose set scenes upon me, but will allow me, now and then, to outdo him in artistry and to perfect his work. And he need have no fear! I shall not follow the usual plan of the lyrical drama, in which the music predominates insolently, whilst the poetry is relegated to the background and smothered by elaborate musical trappings. There is too much singing in musical dramas. The characters should sing only when it is worth while, and the pathetic note should be held in reserve. The intensity of the expression should vary in degree. At times, it is neces-

A FEW PAGES FROM THE NOTE-BOOK OF
MAURICE EMMANUEL

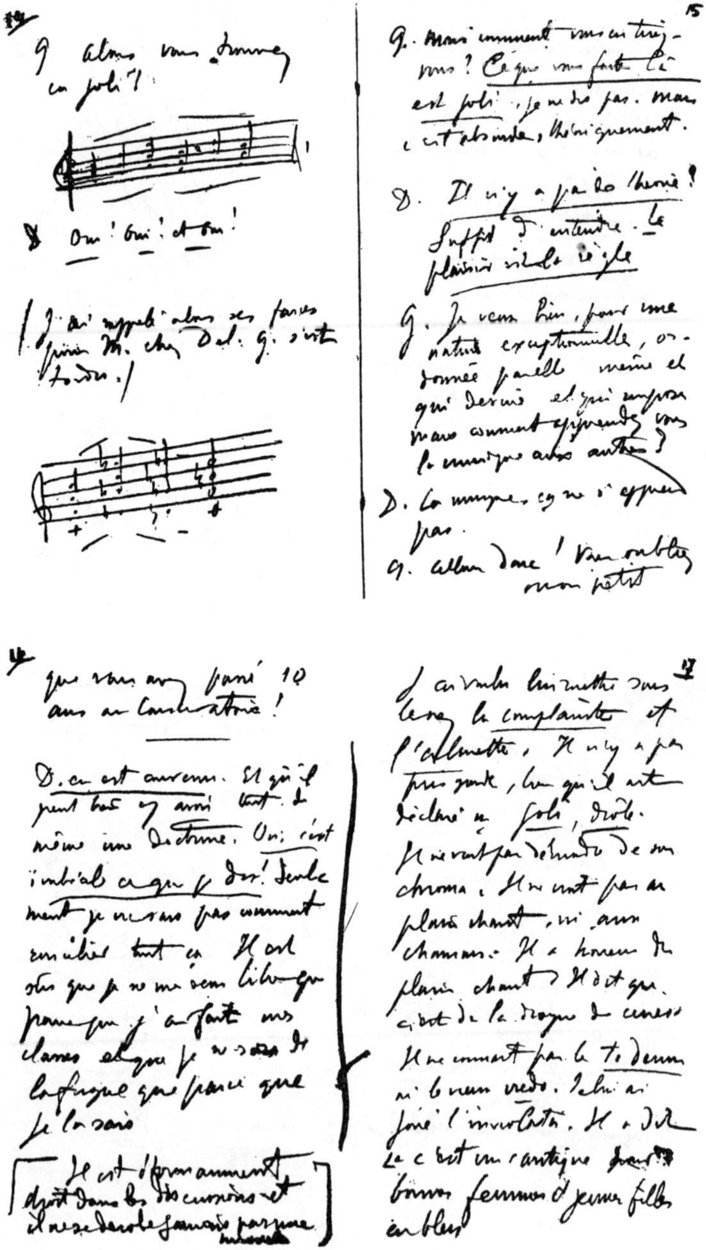

A FEW PAGES FROM THE NOTE-BOOK OF
MAURICE EMMANUEL

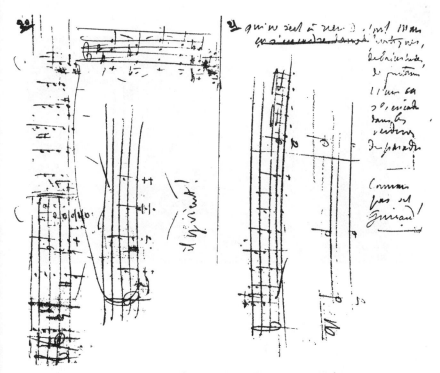

A PAGE FROM THE NOTE-BOOK OF
MAURICE EMMANUEL

DEBUSSY AT THE HOUSE OF ERNEST CHAUSSON, 1893
Leaning against mantelpiece, RAYMOND BONHEUR: *standing up,*
against piano, ERNEST CHAUSSON: *at the piano*, DEBUSSY

DEBUSSY AT THE PIANO
(about 1898)

CLAUDE DEBUSSY
(about 1895)

sary to paint in monochrome and limit oneself to grey tones. . . . Nothing should retard the progress of the dramatic action: all musical development that is not essential to the text is incorrect. Apart from the fact that any musical development which is at all protracted cannot possibly correspond to the mobile words. . . .'

In the course of the same conversation he once more specified his ideal, thereby expressing his distaste for Wagner or rather for the dramatic system of Bayreuth. '. . . My dream is to find poems that will not condemn me to perpetrate long, ponderous acts; poems that will provide me with changing scenes, varied as regards place and atmosphere, in which the characters will not argue, but live their lives and work out their destinies.'

Debussy must have forgotten this casual conversation, and he had no idea that a résumé of it had been carefully written down by one of his comrades. Yet fifteen years later he elaborated these valuable ideas in a statement which he handed over for publication to the General Secretary of the Opéra-Comique. He mentioned the reasons for his collaboration with Maeterlinck in 1893:

'For a long time, I sought to compose music for the theatre. But the form I wished to employ was so unusual, that after various efforts I had almost abandoned the idea. Previous research in pure music had led me to hate classical development, whose beauty is merely technical and of interest only to the highbrows of our class. I desired for music that freedom of which she is capable perhaps to a greater degree than any other art, as she is not confined to an exact reproduction of nature, but only to the mysterious affinity between Nature and the Imagination.

'After several years of passionate pilgrimage to Bayreuth, I began to entertain doubts as to the Wagnerian formula; or rather, it seemed to me that it could serve only the particular case of Wagner's genius. He was a great collector of formulas. He assembled them all into one which appears individual to those who are ill acquainted with music. And without denying his genius, one may say that he placed a period to the music of his time in much the same way as Victor Hugo did for poetry. The thing, then, was to find what came *after Wagner's time* but not *after Wagner's manner.*

'The drama of "Pelléas", which, in spite of its fantastic atmosphere, contains much more humanity than the so-called *documents on life*, appeared to me to be admirably suited to my purpose. The sensitiveness of the suggestive language could be carried into the music and orchestral setting. I have tried to obey a law of beauty which appears to be singularly ignored in dealing with dramatic music. The characters of this drama endeavour to sing like real persons, and not in an arbitrary language built on antiquated traditions.'

The composition of 'Pelléas' was not scamped. On the contrary it was very slowly evolved. Debussy's correspondence with Ernest

Chausson reveals the composer's long deliberations and constant hesitations. One day, probably at the beginning of 1894, he apologizes for having left his friend so long without news:

'The fault is Mélisande's, but please forgive us both. I have spent days in the pursuit of those airy trifles of which she (Mélisande) is made, and I sometimes lacked the courage to tell you about it all. In any case, you know what those struggles are like. But I don't know whether, like me, you have ever gone to bed with a vague desire to weep, feeling as if you had not been able to see some beloved friend during the day. Now it is Arkel who is tormenting me. He belongs to the world beyond the grave, and he is full of the disinterested and far-seeing affection of those who are about to pass away. And one has to express all that with do, ré, mi, fa, sol, la, si, do. What a life!'

On the 6th of September 1893, he was able to announce triumphantly that he was finishing the fourth scene of the fourth act, 'Une Fontaine dans le Parc'. But he realized almost immediately that he had boasted too soon. He exercised his keen critical sense upon himself, and was obliged to acknowledge, in a letter dated the 2nd of October, that 'it isn't at all right. It is like a duet by Mr. So and So, or any one at all. And worst of all, the ghost of old Klingsor, alias R. Wagner, appeared at a turning in one of the bars. So, I tore up the whole thing, and set off in search of some more characteristic compound of phrases, and I tried to be as Pelléas as Mélisande. I went in search of music behind all the veils in which she hides herself even from her most ardent devotees....' Debussy then tells of the result of his quest. 'I have quite spontaneously utilized a medium which seems a rather unusual means of expression, namely, silence (don't laugh). I think it is sometimes the only way to emphasize the emotion of a phrase. For though Wagner employed it, I think he did so only for purely dramatic purposes....'

By astonishing good luck, we have recently come to know what were the fruits of this new effort to free himself from Wagnerian domination and to discover an individual means of expression. The first version of an important scene from the future opera, 'Pelléas et Mélisande', has been partly preserved in the form of a rough copy containing rather more than half of this attempt of 1893. The document is authentic, being entirely from the young composer's own hand. One hopes that this unique manuscript will soon be published with a short notice explaining its aesthetic and historical importance. It consists of twelve sheets. According to Debussy's invariable habit, the accompaniment is written on three staves with notes in green pencil which indicate the instrumentation. These pages correspond to pages 208–15, and 230–42 of the vocal score. At the end of the scene, we find Debussy's serpentine monogram forming his initials, C.A.D., and the date, *Sept.-Oct.* 93, which corresponds exactly to the dates of his above-mentioned letters to Chausson. Very little of the original sketch was transmitted intact to the final version. Here and there, of course, they have some points in common, though these have been more or less modified. Many elements are entirely different. Portions of Maeterlinck's libretto which were originally utilized were eventually abandoned by the composer. There is no connexion between the suggested instrumentation in the first project and the subsequent orchestration. Even the vocal declamation is almost entirely different. In the 1893 version it is more commonplace, less accurate and exact as regards accentuation and rhythm. The role of Pelléas is written in a higher *tessitura*. A minute comparison of the two musical texts reveals points of considerable interest to which we can only allude here.

Debussy is obsessed by a desire to dispel the memory of Wagner and to avoid imitating him. He tries to persuade his composer friends to join him in withdrawing deliberately beyond the reach of this oppressive Wagnerian influence. He begs Chausson to give up troubling about the framework. He considers that 'we have been taken in' by the great German; 'we too often decide upon the frame before we have acquired the picture, and sometimes the richness of the former causes us to overlook poverty of ideas; not to mention cases where magnificent trappings are used to decorate ideas that are not worth a sixpenny doll'. He wishes to proceed in the contrary manner: 'To discover the perfect design for an idea, and to add only what is absolutely necessary in the way of ornament; for, indeed, some composers are like those priests who clothe wooden idols with peerless gems.'

However, in the spring of 1895, Debussy was able to give Robert Godet the joyful news that 'Pelléas et Mélisande' was completed, in its first form—only to be begun again immediately. Two years later, the new version was finished and offered to the Opéra-Comique, where it was accepted in principle. But the work was taken back and altered and remodelled so often, that it was not really finished until 1902, on the eve of its production. During the rehearsals, it had to be revised again and lengthened by the addition of extensive interludes which make it heavy but which allow time for the scenery to be changed. The instrumentation, too, which had only been sketched on a few staves, was written at the eleventh hour, in the space of a month, at the beginning of 1902. Thus, in accordance with the statement of which we have reproduced a facsimile, this masterpiece represents ten, if not twelve, years of the composer's life. The formation of a new operatic style in the middle of the Wagnerian period meant a hard struggle. We find allusions to it in the report of an interview which Robert de Flers had with Debussy in May 1902 and which he published in the *Figaro* of the 16th of May. As we shall see, the composer took the opportunity of replying to the principal criticisms that had been levelled against him and defined the object he had in view in creating this work.

'I wished that the action should never be arrested, that it should be continuous and uninterrupted. I tried to dispense with parasitic musical phrases. When listening to an opera, the spectator usually experiences two distinct kinds of emotion—the emotion of the music, and the emotion of the character; as a rule, he experiences them in succession. I have attempted to blend these two emotions absolutely and to make them simultaneous. Melody is almost anti-lyrical, if I may so express myself. It is incapable of reproducing such mobile elements as life and the soul. It is essentially suited to the song, which confirms a definite sentiment. I have never allowed my music for the sake of technical requirements to hurry or to delay the course of the feelings and passions of my characters. Whenever it becomes advisable to give free course to their gestures, their cries, their joy or their sorrow, my music effaces itself. . . .'

He believed that he had entirely shaken off the haunting obsession of Wagner's elaborate art from which he had striven so diligently to free himself. He further declared to Robert de Flers:

'My process consists chiefly in doing without Wagner, it owes nothing to Wagner. In his operas, every character has, so to speak, his *prospectus*, his photograph, his *leit-motif*, by which he is always preceded. I must confess, I think that a rather crude method. Again it seems to me that the symphonic development which he has introduced into lyrical drama, interferes constantly with the moral conflict in which the characters are engaged, and hampers the emotional expression which alone is of consequence. . . .'

Although Debussy had formally repudiated all symphonic display, and had used the accepted methods with great discretion, he was somewhat deceived when he imagined that he had rid himself completely of the *leit-motif* system. As a matter of fact, his censure of the Wagnerian style was always directed against the over-elaborate thematic and symphonic treatment of the 'Ring', and in particular of 'Götterdämmerung'—a treatment which may be necessary or at least advisable, in the case of the German public which is disinclined to accept anything that has not been demonstrated to it at considerable length. But Debussy still admired 'Tristan und Isolde'. He himself stated in his conversations with Guiraud, as reported by Maurice Emmanuel, that he noticed a constant equilibrium between the musical requirements and the thematic reminiscences; the latter intervened only in order to give the orchestra the appropriate colouring for its decorative functions.[1] In the composition of 'Pelléas', instead of accumulating and interlacing a number of *motifs*, Debussy made use only of some dozen characteristic themes—definite melodies, expressive accents or typical harmonies. And we may say that, generally speaking, he treated them in Wagner's 'Tristan' manner, bending their outlines to suit his fancy and avoiding all academic precision or definite style of writing.

Even Wagner's orchestration seemed unacceptable to Debussy, although this ponderous instrumentation had been adopted by a great many French composers. The German composer himself, realizing that it was too powerful, had attempted to moderate its excessive sonority by the use of the covered orchestra, the famous 'mystical gulf', as it was then called. Debussy's ideal was a discreet, fluid instrumentation that would give the singers a chance of making themselves heard without effort. As he stated in April 1902, in an interview which was reported at the time in the *Revue d'Histoire et de Critique Musicale*, he saw no need for the bass drum or the triangle, although these instruments were usually considered indispensible in expressing emotion: he wished to return to the orchestra of Mozart. In spite of his reputation for artistic intricacy, he made a point of stating, in the course of the same interview, that no musician could be more enamoured of simplicity than he. He added that he did not approve of a sonorous syllable being more stressed in music than it would be in conversation. As regards musical declamation, what he aimed at was a very simple notation of the words in keeping with the smooth fluency of the French language. Even the most Wagnerian among his early works showed signs of a continuous and very successful attempt to strike out in an absolutely contrary direction to that of Wagner, whom too many French composers were unfortunately following blindly—or deafly.

In the course of his long task, Debussy often sang and played some pages from his score for his friends, in particular the duet

---

[1] With reference to Wagner and Debussy, see the author's book, *The Theories of Claude Debussy, Musicien français*, Chapter VII.

in the fourth act which he had written in 1893. In a previously
mentioned article, J.-É. Blanche relates how Debussy used to
accompany himself on Pierre Louÿs's harmonium—a wretched
instrument which the writer kept till his death—and 'murmur, in
his curious, timbreless voice, the freshly written scenes from
"Pelléas".' Then, 'the Sunday-school harmonium was transformed
into a supernatural instrument'. A few painters and poets, and
a very few musicians, were thus vouchsafed a revelation of the
new art for which the general public had to wait ten years. Camille
Mauclair, Henri de Régnier, Robert Godet, René Peter (who had
even registered Mélisande's death-scene on a phonographic record
that is now worn out) and many others, have described their
recollections of these intimate auditions which Debussy gave at
the piano at the houses of various friends. Blanche adds: 'Imagine
what it meant to us then, at the height of the symbolist movement,
to hear this combination of Maeterlinck's stammerings and the
mysterious sonorities with which Claude Debussy sustained
them. . . .'

During those unforgettable auditions, in which fragments of
this very remarkable opera were rendered at the piano or harmonium to an audience of artists and writers with independent
ideas on music, those present probably received a much more
favourable impression of the new art than did the limited audience
of musicians—chiefly of Wagnerian and Franckist tendencies—
who listened to the performance of Debussy's String Quartet by
Ysaÿe, Crickboom, Van Hout, and J. Jacob, on the 29th of
December 1893. This audience, consisting of the musical élite of
Paris, comprised, in the first place, those whom the composer
called 'the Mandarins of our class', that is to say, the specialists
who appreciated above all the technical beauties of classical
development which Debussy—who sought instinctively and
deliberately for the mysterious relationship between nature and
the imagination—had come to hate intensely. In addition to these
artists—who were enlighted, it is true, but only by the blinding
rays of a few stars—the audience of the Société Nationale
included many unprejudiced musicians who kept clear of narrow-
minded categories and shunned the 'petites chapelles'; a few small
groups of snobs, and some amateurs of indefinite tendencies; as
well as a considerable number of 'sound music lovers'—a type
that is fast disappearing in France, and which deserves the attention of the historian.

On fixed days these good people meet together and perform
famous String Quartets for their own satisfaction. By dint of

cultivating solely the gardens of Haydn, Mozart, Beethoven, and their closest and dullest imitators, these excellent musicians end by appreciating no other musical flowers but those they gather themselves or those that habitually bloom between their often skilful fingers. They develop a peculiar state of mind, they become purists, and their sense of hearing acquires certain definite cravings. This special and exclusive training renders them austere, formal, and dogmatic, and limits their sensibility to a domain which is bounded by the landmarks of celebrated names and further restricted by the barricades of high-class conventions. Their cult of Beethoven makes them more Beethovenian than Beethoven. It was they who christened his tenth quartet the 'Harp' Quartet. And there is a subtle hint of reproach in this title, for they are shocked by the charming fancifulness of all the *pizzicati* which pass backwards and forwards between the 'cello, the viola, and the violins. Nor can they fully appreciate the only work which the ultra-classical Saint-Saëns wrote, very tardily, for four strings, because of the abuse of the same *pizzicato* effect. They also profess a certain contempt for Gabrial Fauré because, until the eve of his death, he never consented to deprive his quartets of the help of the piano, an instrument that is accounted impure.

It was inevitable that these pure-minded ones should look upon Debussy's composition as a freakish fancy, quite unsuited to such a high-class form. This time it was not a 'Harp' Quartet they were asked to listen to, but a guitar and mandoline quartet full of persistent *pizzicati*. Indeed, it was nothing less than a miniature orchestra in which the timbres of flute, horn, and trumpet were often heard. And they had to listen to this at one of those Nationale concerts which Chausson himself compared to an examination for a Doctor's Degree. They were utterly disconcerted by the novelty of the details and bewildered by the harmonic daring of this revolutionary style of writing, by all the effects that seemed to them like a fine powdering of sounds. Consequently they could not immediately grasp the paradoxical classicisms that were to be found in the work, especially in its form and structure. The first movement, for instance, has the two themes of the sonata with their exposition, development, and recapitulation; the Scherzo and Andante are both moulded on the *Lied* form, that is to say, they consist mainly of the interplay of two alternating principal subjects. In the Finale, too, we can distinguish characteristics that bear an unexpected likeness to Beethoven and Franck. The beginning reminds one of the last part of Beethoven's Ninth Symphony or of Franck's Quartet, with its repetitions—veiled or obvious—of the rhythms of the first movement, and its reminiscences of the Scherzo. Besides, the whole plan of the work is cyclical; for, thanks to the musicographer's magnifying glass, we can discover the origin of the melodic elements in one insignificant triplet figure of prodigious fecundity.

Those musicians who had specialized too closely, and who had always trained on the same tracks, took particular exception to the extraordinarily brilliant and original manner in which some brief rhythm or scanty theme was embroidered or illuminated with rich and varied details. They were scandalized by the style of this audacious composer who had not thought it expedient to imitate Beethoven's pathetic lamentations, and who had managed to pour new ideas into an old mould though not without distorting it somewhat. Even some of the 'forewarned' members of the audience could not understand, or rather could not follow the unfolding of the more original and lengthy themes, such as that very delicate and insinuating melody at the beginning of the Andante which is given alternately by muted violin and viola. The only thing they noticed was the strange colouring of the very first notes; on hearing the exposition of the 'generating theme' they were disconcerted by its obscure mode—a revival from the Greeks —by its complex rhythms, and its unprecedented harmonies. Even after ten years' training, we find a critic writing in the *Revue Bleue*, on the 26th of April 1902, the following words, which sound very strange to-day: 'It would be difficult to be more vague without being incoherent.'

The ordinary public would have received a very different impression, as was demonstrated later on. The quartet-strummers and a great many habitués of the so-called classical concerts are victims of their musical training and slaves of their unconscious habits. They suffer real tortures if an innovator attempts to unwind the myriad bands in which long habit or honest prejudice has swathed them, whereas the ignorant general public is quite ready to enjoy new pleasures without delay. No exacting habits impede the exercise of its musical sensibility. Its lack. of culture, its very ignorance, is an advantage. It does not need to hear several performances like the 'Mandarins', who are ill prepared because they are too well prepared. Debussy's works immediately cast their spell on the general public which gave itself up without restraint to the charm of his countless impressionistic novelties: delightful harmonic caresses produced by persistent throbbings and unvarying accompaniments; the piquant contrast between certain passages in rough consecutive fifths and others of the most exquisite suavity; the ineffable sweetness and the insinuating rhythmical qualities of the Scherzo—a 'serenade to fair listeners'; the attractive tone-colouring due to novel aggregations or to simple chords whose unusual successions give them a peculiar charm. It is a feast of harmony and a feast of rhythm; a joy of the senses and of the mind to which one must yield in all simplicity, as one enjoys the voluptuous atmosphere of that hour when

> Les sons et les parfums tournent dans l'air du soir.

As the majority of the critics either did not understand the bearing of the new quartet or did not dare to give a definite opinion about it, very few mentioned its first performance. The number of articles that were devoted to it may be counted on one's fingers. J. Guy Ropartz, a young composer of the Franck school whose aesthetic ideals were and always remained the very antithesis of Debussy's, praised his colleague's Quartet briefly but unreservedly, in the *Guide Musical* of the 7th of January 1894: 'A very interesting work in which the influence of young Russia predominates; poetical themes and rare tone-colouring; the two first movements are particularly noteworthy.' 'L'Ouvreuse du Cirque d'Été', the mouthpiece of the 'vanguard' musicians, confessed to having been disconcerted by this quartet which is described as: 'bewildering, full of originality and charm (the Scherzo has delightful *pizzicati*, the Finale is rather abrupt), but it is diabolically difficult, and I must confess I did not greatly relish the middle of the Andante'.

Those among the Nationale audience who had at first objected to this baffling quartet were destined to grow accustomed to it very soon. It was frequently played at the performances of that Society, which is dedicated to *Ars Gallica*. The Quartet made its appearance again on the 20th of April 1895, the 9th of January 1897, and the 8th of January 1898. Thus it soon became in a sense part of the repertoire, more so, indeed, than any other work of the kind. But it did not achieve great success—not to speak of popularity—until after the production of 'Pelléas et Mélisande'. Meanwhile the score, which had appeared in the autumn of 1894, was offered in vain by the publisher Durand to the various Quartet societies: they pronounced it unplayable. The Guarnieri Quartet, however, performed it in Paris that year, and on that occasion Paul Dukas reviewed the work for the *Revue Hebdomadaire* in an important and very judicious article, which must, however, have seemed inspired rather by friendship than by the spirit of criticism.

Paul Dukas, who had been for many years a close friend of

Debussy, hailed his comrade as 'one of the most gifted and
original artists of the young generation of musicians', one of those
composers 'who look upon music as an end rather than as a means,
who regard it not as a lever of expression, but rather as expression
itself'. He proclaimed him to be 'a lyricist in the full sense of
the term'. He declared that in spite of the Conservatoire training
which should have given him an operatic bent, such a musician
was bound to end by writing pure music; he did not belong to
the Beethoven lineage, but to the race of composers who regard
with horror all exaggerated dramatization of music.

Proceeding to a detailed examination of this work which had
startled so many musicians, the professionals in particular, Paul
Dukas wrote:

'M. Debussy's Quartet bears the definite stamp of his manner. Everything is clearly and concisely drawn, although the form is exceedingly
free. The melodic essence of the work is concentrated, but of a rich
flavour. It impregnates the harmonic tissue with a deep, original poetic
quality. The harmony itself, although greatly daring, is never rough or
hard. M. Debussy takes a particular delight in successions of rich
chords that are dissonant without being crude, and more harmonious in
their complexity than any consonances could be; over them, his melody
proceeds as on a sumptuous, skilfully designed carpet of strange colouring that contains no violent or discordant tints. One single theme forms
the basis of all the movements of the work. Some of the transformations
it undergoes have an unexpected charm that is particularly fascinating,
as, for example, the passage that occurs in the middle of the Scherzo.
(This movement is simply an ingenious variation of the theme.) Nothing
could be more charming than the very effective reappearance of the
rhythmical theme to the accompaniment of the delicate quivering
throbbings of the second violin and the viola, and the *pizzicato* of the
'cello. If I were called upon to say which of the four parts I liked best,
I should pick out the first movement and the Andante, which are exquisitely poetical and most delicate in conception.'

Ernest Chausson did not share Paul Dukas's enthusiasm, and
Debussy was grieved by his friend's disapproval. In an undated
letter, written at the end of February 1894, Debussy remarked
that the Quartet seemed to have awakened Chausson's appreciation for certain compositions which he had hoped the new score
would make him forget. 'Well', wrote the composer of the much-
discussed work, 'I shall write another quartet for you, entirely
for you, and I shall try to give dignity to my forms'. It would
seem that Debussy really meant to add a second quartet to his
'Premier Quatuor en sol. Op. 10'—as the title of the original
manuscript reads. In the beginning of March 1894 a Brussels

paper published a note by Octave Maus to the effect that the
third movement of this work was already written, but nothing
more was ever heard of this composition.

Soon after the first performance of his String Quartet, other
new works by Debussy were produced at the Société Nationale:
namely two of his 'Proses lyriques', entitled 'De Fleurs', and 'De
Soir'. He accompanied these songs at the piano on the 17th of
February 1894. (They were sung by Mlle Thérèse Roger, a very
talented young singer, the daughter of a well-known pianist, to
whom he was then engaged. But a few weeks after this concert
the engagement was broken off.) J. Guy Ropartz gave a very
favourable critique of these songs in the *Guide Musical*.

'M. Debussy', he wrote, 'is one of the most promising of the young
composers whom we have reason to hope will add to the glory of the
French school. These two new compositions are quite exquisite. They
have a rare distinction of feeling and are intensely emotional; and the
instrumental tissue which the piano part weaves about the voice is
absolutely individual. M. Debussy played the accompaniments himself
in a manner that could not have been improved upon.'

But the 'Proses Lyriques' did not receive such a warm welcome
from all. To the ordinary amateur, the literary text was quite as
startling as the music, if not more so. Debussy had written these
four poems himself, and it seems that he had also planned to write
five others of the same type and unite them all under the title of
'Nuits Blanches'. These very poetical, but far-fetched 'Proses' were
full of the verbal affectations and studied abstruseness so fashionable in the *cénacles* of that day, and their hermetical character
was too closely reminiscent of Mallarmé's mannerisms and Jules
Laforgue's humour to be congenial to the average amateur. The
music, too, seemed strange in parts even to those who were capable
of appreciating its charm and the really deep and vivid beauty
of some pictures or passages the writing of which was admirable.
In the *Courrier Musical* of the 15th of December 1900 a very clever
critic, disguised under the pseudonym of 'Boîte à Musique'
described with witty candour the mingled feelings of horror and
fascination which the majority of sincere musicians experienced
on reading this score. Further on we shall see what bewilderment
a Belgian critic expressed on hearing the 'Proses Lyriques'.

The amateurs and even the professional musicians were out of
their depth in all these pieces, in spite of the signposts provided
by melodic phrases of definite meaning which acted more or less
as *leit-motifs*. The first of the 'Proses', 'De Rêve', in which
delicate arpeggios produce a real Debussy atmosphere from the

very beginning, contains three such themes which reappear as often as six or seven times in the piano commentary, and which could easily be christened like Wagner's *leit-motifs*. In spite of its 'awe-inspiring' harmonies, it may be assumed that this song is older than the others by reason of its complex and rather incoherent symphonic style. (According to a letter written to Ernest Chausson, the last of the 'Proses', 'De Soir', was finished in August 1893.) The last words of the poem: 'Mon âme, c'est du rêve ancien qui t'étreint', can be applied to the song in a purely musical sense. For, in spite of the novelty of the harmony and the melopoeia, its style remains rightly clasped by old formulas, those of Wagner in particular. One can even hear the echoes of Tristan's horn, as in 'Le Recueillement' of 1888–9. The second 'Prose', 'De Grève', with its mixture of humour and poetic meditation, is one of Debussy's most perfect songs. It is a delightful sea piece, entirely new in colouring. Each of the three verses has a character of its own, although all three are written in the same manner. The accompaniment is a piece of genuine piano music, floating and splashing amidst the nimbly fleeting words, and winding around the long sustained pedal notes of the recitative. The third verse gives a most harmonious and serene rendering of the peaceful impression produced by 'les cloches attardées des flottantes églises'. The effect, which is as simple as it is subtle, results from the slow repetition of one note amid continuously swaying successions of sixths in changing harmonies. The third of the 'Proses lyriques', entitled 'De Fleurs', opens with common chords—each suggestive of a new tonality—which introduce the obscure, chromatic initial melody. The prosodic incoherence of certain passages and their far-fetched alliterations ('les grands iris *violets violèrent* méchamment mes yeux . . .') almost incline one to accept Charles Koechlin's fragile hypothesis that the literary text may have been written 'après et d'après la musique'. As for the last of the four 'Proses', it has a delightfully humorous text, and ranks with the second as the finest of these songs. Its form is novel and exquisitely varied. First, we have a vivid picture of a Parisian Sunday. The principal melodic trait, with its entangled rhythm like that of Couperin's 'Barricades Mystérieuses', is taken from the popular song, 'Tour prend garde', and represents 'les rondes obstinées où les bonnes tours n'en ont plus que pour quelques jours'. Then follows a peaceful nocturne which ends in a contemplative prayer to the Virgin, in tones of 'or sur argent'. The whole of this section is based on a sort of chime whose cadence remains mysteriously suspended.

Soon after their production at the Société Nationale, Debussy's new compositions were given in Brussels. His name had never appeared before on a programme in the Belgian capital. The Libre Esthétique, an advanced artistic society, under the directorship of Octave Maus, had decided to devote the entire matinée performance of the 1st of March 1894 to the French composer. Vincent d'Indy, Maus's intimate friend and musical mentor, strongly urged him to include 'La Damoiselle Élue' in the programme. In one of his letters he wrote: 'It is really delightful. I gave myself the pleasure of re-reading this delicate and exquisite work.' At the beginning of September 1893 he had written to the composer himself in such terms of praise 'as would bring a blush to the lilies that lie asleep between the fingers of the Blessed Damozel'. Debussy had joyfully transmitted this news to Ernest Chausson. An important programme was drawn up, and entrusted to the Ysaÿe Quartet, a symphony orchestra about fifty strong, a choir of thirty female voices, and the Brussels singer, Demest. The programme consisted of the String Quartet, 'La Damoiselle Élue', 'Recueillement', and 'Jet d'Eau', which the composer himself was to accompany. The last item was to be an unknown and unpublished work: 'Prélude, Interlude et Paraphrase Finale pour "L'Après-midi d'un Faune".' It had been announced under this title both in the recent newspaper notices and on the score of 'La Damoiselle Élue' which had been engraved in 1893. This important work, which was soon reduced to the form of a simple 'Prélude', had to be omitted, as Debussy had not finished revising it. An incident occurred at the last moment which occasioned further changes. The two 'Poèmes de Baudelaire' were replaced by two 'Proses Lyriques' the proofs of which Debussy corrected in Brussels during the intervals of the rehearsals of his 'Festival'; and Mlle Thérèse Roger sang instead of Demest.

Eugène Ysaÿe had undertaken the direction of this concert and considered it an event of great importance. He had specially invited the Belgian musician of highest standing, F. A. Gevaert, Director of the Brussels Conservatoire. But when the time came for the concert to begin, this musician had not arrived. Ysaÿe, who was already installed on the platform with the other members of his Quartet, waited a long time for the guest of honour. At last he decided to begin the first movement of the Quartet, and when Gevaert entered the hall, he recommenced it. The rest of the concert went off without a hitch. Much interest was aroused not nly by Debussy's music, but also by his personal appearance, which was bound to impress an audience largely composed of painters and art-lovers.

A few critiques appeared in the Brussels press. Naturally, Octave Maus praised Debussy in his review, *L'Art Moderne*, the organ of La Libre Esthétique, and his words probably expressed the opinions of his friend, Vincent d'Indy, quite as much as his own. Having called attention to the young composer's kinship with Franck, in the words we have already quoted at the end of Chapter IV, he particularly stressed the classical character of the Quartet which 'follows a logical, clearly defined course in spite of the fantastic caperings of the modulations which seem to be enticing it away at a venture. This fact particulary struck the musicians, in the midst of this torrent of youthfulness, harmonic audacity, and unexpected resolutions'. Lucien Solvay, the Brussels correspondent of the Paris *Ménestrel*, was almost as eulogistic. But he considered the 'Proses Lyriques' *unsingable*, and availed himself of the opportunity to make a general statement on the maltreatment of the voice by young composers.

Two dailies, the *Patriote* of the 5th of March and *L'Indépendance Belge*, published critiques on the new composer. The first paper referred only to the Quartet. The writer praised its impressionism, its attractive tone-colouring and the daring originality of its rhythms and harmonies; but he complained of the constant artificiality of the music and its lack of balance. In his opinion, Debussy's personality seemed 'to sway between the influence of Bruneau which was very evident in some harmonic progressions, and that of Borodin, with suggestions of Grieg and reminiscences of Wagner'. The notice which appeared in the other paper was likewise anonymous, but it is easy to determine the author; for this was a short, preliminary version of the important and memorable article which Maurice Kufferath published on the 4th of March in his *Guide Musical*.

This highly intelligent and very cultured writer confessed that he had listened to the new works with feelings of surprise and alarm. There was not one of the compositions but caused him uneasiness. The Quartet struck him as strange and bizarre. Its Oriental quality reminded him of

'the rue du Caire at the Exhibition of 1889. Bounding rhythms, violent harmonic jerks, alternating with languid melodies on the violin, viola, and 'cello, which recall the chromatism of oriental melodies; *pizzicato* effects suggestive of guitars and mandolines; copious floods of rich, sustained harmonies that evoke the memory of the *Gamelang*. The four movements of this Quartet contain a curious collection of tonal effects that are now charming, now irritating. . . . It is neither banal nor commonplace. On the contrary, it is very *distingué*, but one does not know how to take hold of it. It is more like an hallucination than a dream. Is it a work? One hardly knows. Is it music? Perhaps so, in the sense that the canvases of the neo-Japanese of Montmartre and its Belgian suburb may be called paintings.'

Kufferath made a great many reservations with regard to 'La Damoiselle Élue'.

'The orchestration has a singular charm of colouring, but the constant changes of rhythm, the unexpected modulations and the accumulation of superimposed themes, subjects, and patterns, as well as the straining after rare and unforeseen combinations produce, at the first hearing, a vagueness of expression which must surely be the very opposite of what the composer aimed at.'

He censured the 'Proses Lyriques' in particular. Their dissonances suggested to him a far-fetched comparison with an old musical joke.

' Two songs ', he says, ' in which the piano and the voice trace chromatic patterns that are at variance with one another, at such close or such distant intervals that one experiences the painful sensation of a complete absence of tonality. The effect reminds one of the occasion when Rubini and Lablache sang the duet from "I Puritani" at the interval of a second instead of a third. At times, the result is pure cacophony. If this was not done for a wager, one must seriously conclude that it points to a defect of the auditory sense, similar to the defect of sight which is responsible for the distorted vision of certain painters.'

In his general summing-up of the three works he had heard, the Belgian critic paid homage to Debussy's talent. 'Very unusual qualities, wonderful refinement of tone-colouring, great richness in the combinations, here and there a very effective pathetic accent.' But he soon reiterated his predominant impression of bewilderment. 'At first sight, everything is completely submerged in a flood of deliberate eccentricities, and these compositions leave one with a curious impression of discomfort, a strange uneasiness such as one feels on waking after a nightmare.' He considered the music too novel, 'more studied than inspired, more deliberate than deeply felt . . . very tedious, on account of the excessive accumulation of the subtlest artifices of harmony . . . often more literary than really musical, tending entirely, in fact, towards purely external effect, whilst claiming to be intimate and symbolistic'. According to him, Claude Debussy was an adept of 'the new school of musical stippling and universal amorphism'.

This verdict is very valuable, as it plainly shows the state of mind of most musicians when Debussy's music was first revealed to them. But Maurice Kufferath was too intelligent and too well acquainted with history to imagine that his verdict could be final. Although in 1894 he himself did not feel capable of accepting in its entirety the artistic manifestation of this very daring composer, he left it to the future to pronounce a definite judgement. 'Our grand-children will be in a position to judge, and perhaps they will call us old fogies for not understanding Debussy, just as we did in the case of our predecessors because they did not appreciate Wagner.' The critic of the *Guide Musical* had not to wait two generations to see his verdict completely set aside.

CHAPTER VII

'L'APRÈS-MIDI D'UN FAUNE'; THE 'NOCTURNES';
CRITIQUES (1894–1901)

BY the end of the summer of 1894 Claude Debussy had finished a minute revision of his symphony to Mallarmé's 'Après-midi d'un Faune'. He had reduced it to the form of a simple 'Prélude', omitting the 'Interlude' and the 'Paraphrase Finale' originally announced but which had been barely sketched. The manuscript of his orchestral score, which has been preserved by the publisher, Jobert, Fromont's successor, bears two dates. Beside the title we read 1892, and on the last line, 1894. As we saw before, the entire triptych—of which only one panel was destined to remain—had been announced as early as 1893 by the publisher of 'La Damoiselle Élue', and in the spring of 1894 by the organizers of a concert at Brussels.

The Société Nationale produced the 'Prélude' on the 22nd of December 1894, exactly a year after the Quartet. This purely orchestral work had been looked forward to with keen interest. It had been slowly matured and carefully revised, and further corrections were made in details of the instrumentation during the course of the rehearsals. It was the first symphonic work of this kind written by the young composer who still signed himself 'C. A. Debussy'. So far the public had only been able to judge of his orchestral talents from 'La Damoiselle Élue', a work which was at the same time vocal, choral, and instrumental. Curiosity was intensified by the fact that the Société Nationale, setting aside its traditions, opened its doors for the first time to the general public. Two performances of the same programme were given on consecutive days, Saturday, the 22nd and Sunday, the 23rd of December, in the Salle d'Harcourt, 40 rue Rochechouart. Thus, the 'petite chapelle' was transformed into a vast temple of music.

Contrary to the regrettable rule which ordains that original works shall not be understood at their first hearing, this little composition was such a brilliant and immediate success that the conductor, Gustave Doret, had to repeat it. The appreciation with which it was received has endured. The 'Prélude' was again performed at the following day's concert. Soon after, André Messager and Édouard Colonne placed it on the programmes of the Vaudeville and Châtelet concerts, and a few years later this symphonic piece, which was not engraved until the summer of 1895,[1] was included in the repertoires of all orchestral societies. On the 1st of April 1902 it was given for the first time in the United States (Boston Orchestral Club, conducted by Longy). Yet it was not until eleven years later, at the end of December 1913, that it was accorded the honour of being adopted by the Société des Concerts du Conservatoire de Paris. No one had ventured to offer the highly conservative habitués of that old society the delightful commentary in which Debussy contrived to interpret in terms of music the burning sensuality and the intense delight of an utterly pagan demi-god pursuing his not very intellectual pleasures on a sunny day.

When Stéphane Mallarmé heard it for the first time at the piano before the public performance, he confessed that it far exceeded his expectations. According to a letter written by Debussy to Jean Aubry, Mallarmé said to the composer: 'This music prolongs the emotion of my poem and fixes the scene much more vividly than colour could have done.' One must not, however, look for any strict connexion between the music and the poetry. Mallarmé himself acknowledged that he could not discover any, although he was musical and frequented orchestral concerts. He expressed his thanks to his collaborator in the following little verse which he wrote on a copy of his 'Après-midi':

> Sylvain d'haleine première,
> Si ta flûte a réussi,
> Ouïs toute la lumière
> Qu'y soufflera Debussy.

The composer's artistic sensibility had filtered the music that is diffused throughout the poet's words and imagery. The score is as subtle as the poetical text, but it is clearer. It is a kind of free illustration, a commentary; or, to be more exact, as the title itself indicates, it is an introduction, a preparation. According to a note which Debussy probably wrote himself, it evokes 'the successive scenes of the Faun's desires and dreams on that hot afternoon'.[2]

The analysis of the work can be reduced to a few simple lines. There are two essential themes; one is softly uttered by the flute

[1] The library of the Eastman School of Music at Rochester, U.S.A., contains a proof of the orchestral score corrected by Debussy, which is signed by him and dated 3rd of July 1895. The date on which the engraver entered the corrections is given as 26th of July 1895.

[2] In April 1895 the Mercure de France published 'Le Petit Vapereau des Musiciens', consisting of two pages of satirical definitions of contemporary composers. There we read: 'Debussy, (C. A.) Aspires to be Mallarmé's successor.'

at the very beginning, the other boldly chanted by the wood-winds. The former, describing the 'bosquets arrosés d'accords', is of a cloudy colour, uncertain as to mode and undecided in rhythm. The latter is very definite, and its comparatively clear tonality is fixed by the syncopated chords of the quartet. The very free interplay of these two themes constitutes the whole of the prelude as far as the concluding bars. There two stopped horns take up in thirds the pattern of the flute-theme which gradually fades away. Whereupon the harmonies of the harps and the silvery tinkling tones of antique cymbals softly sound the notes of a major chord in conclusion.

The development is something entirely new. It is remarkable for the very fragmentary treatment of the material and for the fact that its movements are controlled by the significance of the music, which itself conforms to the spirit of the poem. There is no trace of the traditional 'official' symmetry that characterizes the well-known symphonies. No sooner are the themes stated than they break up, divide, and contract. The lively fragments spread rapidly throughout the orchestra. They change their rhythm and their nature, they amalgamate in original and unexpected ways. The most varied accents jostle one another, and from their impact new rhythms spring, an independent life is born. The harmony moves with the complete freedom which Debussy always aimed at, and he utilizes it with a facility hitherto unknown. There is continuous modulation throughout the most remote tonalities, which are linked together with perfect ease and delightful spontaneity. The instrumentation, which is for a small symphony orchestra (there are neither trumpets nor trombones), is very individual in character, owing to novel combinations of timbres and the subdivision of the parts, with occasional contrasting effects of massive unison. It is as different as possible from Wagner's heavy scoring and César Franck's organ effects.

This short 'Prélude' remains one of Claude Debussy's most perfect and most typical works. The numerous reviews that appeared later form quite a considerable literature; but the annotators never succeeded in conveying the impression of its exquisite charm. This work shows that the composer has rid himself of his former doubts and attained to perfect mastery. The traces of old influences which were easily discernible in the preceding scores are here so blurred as to be almost undistinguishable. The most definite reminiscence is that of Balakiref's 'Tamara' which occurs in the middle of the composition. (As we mentioned before, this original work affected Debussy deeply when he heard it at the Concerts Lamoureux in November 1895). His new musical language is now completely formed—a language with an utterly novel syntax. Further on, in speaking of the 'Nocturnes', we shall discuss its characteristic elements. A few years later its idioms and its vivid style were somewhat unceremoniously adopted by all musicians. What is particularly noticeable is the perfect artistry with which the new expressive mediums of this eclogue are utilized. To use a phrase which has become stereotyped because of its exactness and truth—they enable Debussy to *create an atmosphere* unprecedented in its fluidity and vibration. This work is undoubtedly a masterpiece of musical impressionism. Many years have gone by since its creation, but time has not lessened its originality nor dimmed its tints and colours.

The musical press indulged in a discreet chorus of praise in which there were a few discordant notes hardly worth recording. We may, however, mention the peculiar criticism of Hugues Imbert, the chief critic of the *Guide Musical*. A work, entitled 'Prière', by Guy Ropartz, having been performed on the same evening as Debussy's 'Prélude', the critic classed the two new works together, in spite of the fact that they belonged to utterly different aesthetic types. With reference to both scores, he made the following extraordinary statement: 'The Wagnerian influence is so preponderating that it deprives the artist of such style as he might have achieved.' Another noteworthy opinion was that expressed by Charles Darcours of the *Figaro*. This journalist was either ill-disposed or ill-advised on the occasion of the concert, and his only comment was to the effect that the young composer seemed to be entirely taken up with experiments in timbre effects. He concluded his very brief critique with the following remark which sounds surprising, and even ridiculous to-day: 'Such pieces are amusing to write but not to listen to.'

One could not expect the audience to be unanimous in its enthusiasm. This feeling was not shared by such people as the author or inspirer of Darcours' article, who are always on the look out for sustained cantabile passages and definitely marked rhythms to which they can beat time by swinging their feet or nodding their heads. There were music-lovers, neither prejudiced nor custom-ridden, who were able to appreciate the charm of this new art, but some even of these wondered anxiously if such music could be approved of, or whether it should not be condemned by respectable people. They solemnly asked themselves if this new art was based on a firm foundation which could be built on without fear; if the artistic conception of this innovator had not made the means an end; and whether it was seemly to give themselves up without remorse to the enjoyment of an art so utterly different from the *soulful music* to which the classics had accustomed them. Such were the anxieties of the people who insist on analysing their pleasures and who like to indulge in subtle aesthetic distinctions. For Debussy's 'Prélude' has not much in common with the sentimental intimacy of a Schumann song, the substantial structure of a Beethoven symphony, or the tender contemplativeness of César Franck. Owing to their long training in the works of Beethoven, Wagner, and Franck, the conservatives in particular were not inclined to recognize as genuine any but the music of yore, or such music of their own day as was unquestionably derived from it. They could not permit an art that was definitely impressionistic and sensual to be classed in the same select category. To people of a certain type of mind, classification, even in the domain of artistic sensibility, is an absolute necessity; and such people naturally took exception to Debussy's aesthetic ideas. The composer had those dogmatic amateurs in mind when, in 1901, he recorded in a newspaper article the following profession of faith which shows that he had no illusions: 'As my music was made with the object of serving that art to the best of my ability, it was only logical that it should run the risk of displeasing those who like only one brand of music and remain faithful to it despite its wrinkles and its paint.'

This natural fidelity to old loves in artistic matters is very legitimate, but it does not last. Little by little, in spite of our instinctive and involuntary opposition, the new forms of art exercise their subtle charm without our realizing it. They tend to create new habits of mind. Soon we begin to make comparisons which are not always entirely favourable to the works whose beauty we formerly proclaimed in so arbitrary a manner. The present weans us from the past. The slow but inexorable evolution proceeds. After a few years, the sincere devotee abandons his former gods, or at least he ceases to worship them. Then one day he is greatly surprised to find himself in an attitude of adoration before idols which, under the influence of his old, ruthless creed, he formerly longed to destroy.

After the appearance of the Quartet and the 'Prélude' to Mallarmé's 'Après-midi d'un Faune', Debussy was greatly looked up to by the advanced musicians. Some of the young composers were already attempting to imitate details of his style and manner. But even the most modern of the critics showed a certain reserve in their appreciation of his somewhat disconcerting art. At this juncture, a study by Georges Servières appeared in the *Guide Musical*, and

Gustave Robert published in the *Revue Illustrée* of the 1st of November 1895 a detailed analysis of the 'Après-midi d'un Faune', which betrayed anxious sympathy. Other critics, not wishing to make a direct attack on the creator of a new type of art, impeached his imitators and copiers. The state of mind of most music lovers can be gauged from certain of the 'Lettres de l'Ouvreuse', published by the *Écho de Paris* in 1895 and 1898, which were written by Willy and several friendly collaborators.

On the 21st of April 1895, the day after a Société Nationale concert at which the Quartet had again been performed, 'L'Ouvreuse' wrote these very significant lines: 'There was prolonged applause after the four picturesque pieces by de Bussy, entitled, "Quartet". They are more interesting than expressive— I adore the "Scherzo".' The following week the same writer expressed his regret that these words should have grieved the young composer—whom he again called de Bussy. He added:

'I regard him as a true-born musician, intuitive, nervous, passionate, never commonplace. It sometimes happens that I do not understand the reason for some of his effects, and then I say so. But I say too that his "Scherzo" contains a most appealing lamentation, oriental in character, G, F sharp, D, F . . . for which I would give all that Loti ever wrote. And I say that the subtle polyrhythmics of the *pizzicati* in 15/8 time, and the gentle, dreamy atmosphere of the "Andantino" in D flat, console me for some rather aggressive sonorities, suggestive of cats on the roof, which make one long for the sound of a common chord. Wagner, who was tonal when he thought fit, speaks somewhere in terms of disgust of unnecessary *orgies of modulation*. . . . But then, I realize that Wagner is rapidly becoming terribly reactionary.'

On the 5th of April and the 24th of October 1898, Willy stated in reference to one of his own friends, Pierre de Bréville, who was one of the principal contributors to his 'Lettres', that it was advisable to leave 'those aggressive rasping noises to the conservatorial foetus which float aimlessly in a jar of Debussy alcohol, swollen with pride in their own unresolved *appoggiaturas*'. Again, he inveighed against 'those nice little young men with long hair and short ideas who pick up the cigarette-stumps of Claude Achille Debussy'. The sentiments of the 'Ouvreuse', that mouthpiece of the neo-classic Franckist school, were not in perfect harmony with those of the enemy of all academic tradition. However, on the 18th of July 1898, there was a friendly allusion to the yet unknown music of 'Pelléas' 'by Claude Debussy, which his intimate friends declare to be exquisite. That does not surprise me, for that slanderer of the "Ouvreuse" is simply rotten with talent.'

Although Debussy was now taking his place in the front rank, his material position was not in keeping with his genius and his newly won fame. He was still poor. Fortunately he was helped by his family and friends. In particular his publisher, Hartmann, and Ernest Chausson proved themselves very devoted friends. He supported himself partly on the slender income which he earned from his profession as composer, teacher, and pianist. On the 19th of October 1899, the day of his marriage to Mlle Rosalie Texier in Paris, he was obliged to give a piano lesson in order to have enough to pay for a modest wedding breakfast for himself and his wife at the Brasserie Pousset. (This authentic anecdote was made public thirty years later in the course of a trial.) His wife, whom the musician and his friends looked upon as the personification of the Mélisande type, proved an affectionate and devoted companion to him. She was able in some measure to guide this great child—for such he always remained—to curb his Bohemian fancies and to regularize his work. He wrote various transcriptions for the publishers Fromont and Durand: duet arrangements of Schumann's 'Am Brunnen', and of several of Saint-Saëns's works, such as the second symphony and the Ballet from 'Étienne Marcel'—a personage whom in his correspondence Debussy jokingly calls an ex-Municipal-Councillor. As we saw, he had offered to set any of Verlaine's poems to music for the publisher Hamelle, or to compose easy pieces or even a Piano Method. Meanwhile, he made a piano solo arrangement of a work which Raff had written for four hands. Like all his comrades, he undertook small musical jobs that were irksome to one of his independent nature. A letter which he wrote to Chausson on the 8th of January 1894 shows that he was looking for a permanent position. The conductor Jehin offered him a post at Royan. Debussy thought he would be able to 'play about with an orchestra'. But it amounted to nothing more than the 'deadly job of accompanist in all its horror' which, in return for a monthly salary of three hundred and fifty francs, would have kept the artist at the piano all day long and all the evening. There was nothing tempting about such a post, although the salary would have provided the young man with a meagre livelihood. Debussy confessed to his correspondent: 'Just now my thoughts are very grey, and melancholy bats fly around the belfry of my dreams. My only hope is in "Pelléas et Mélisande" and heaven alone knows whether that hope too is not a vain one.'

His triumphs, especially the success of the Quartet, had given Debussy the entry into fashionable circles about which he used to joke. 'I hardly know myself,' he wrote to Ernest Chausson in February 1894. 'I am to be seen in drawing-rooms, bowing and smiling, or conducting choruses at Comtesse X's. . . . Yes, sir! and so impressed am I by the beauty of the choir, that I tell myself it is a fitting punishment for such wretched music that it should be murdered by intrepid society ladies. . . .' The cruel irony of fate forced this scorner of Wagner to give fashionable concerts devoted to the works of this composer who appeared to him more than ever a 'very tiresome man'.

Apart from these triumphs, which were limited to a few small circles, the new music remained unknown to the general public. The songs were not sung, nor were the piano pieces played. As we have seen, even the 'Petite Suite' and the 'Arabesques' were not more widely known than the Quartet itself, although these works, which had been published in 1889 and 1891, were decidedly attractive, normal in structure, and easy to perform. If Debussy happened to have one of his smaller works published in a periodical no notice was taken of it. For instance, on the 17th of February 1896, the *Grand Journal du Lundi*, an ephemeral Paris publication, printed his beautiful, characteristic 'Sarabande', which was later to form part of the suite, 'Pour le Piano'; but there was no mention of it. Except for a few drawing-rooms, the Société Nationale remained the only field for Debussy's exploits. But he was *persona grata* there. On the 20th of February 1897 he induced them to perform his orchestral arrangement of the two 'Gymnopédies' by his friend Eric Satie whom the 'Ouvreuse' describes, in one of the 'Lettres' in the *Écho de Paris*, as: 'a Debussy who had spent a while in Charenton' (the French equivalent of Colney Hatch). He sometimes appeared as pianist at the Société Nationale, as for instance on the 1st of February 1896, at the first performance of Lekeu's 'Quatuor Inachevé'. He took part in another performance of the work on the 23rd of January 1897, playing, as he said to Chausson, 'with all my usual contempt for principles'. He was an original virtuoso, remarkable for the delicacy and mellowness of his touch. He made one forget that the piano has hammers—an effect which he used to request his interpreters to aim at—and he achieved particularly characteristic effects of timbre by the combined use of both pedals. The musical critics, being for the most part mere amateurs who were engaged in other less interesting but more remunerative professions and whose principal object was to secure free admission to theatres and concerts, did nothing to make Debussy's name or his works known. Georges Servières was almost the only one who at that early stage paid just homage to Debussy's talents. He devoted an intelligent and sympathetic article to his songs in the *Guide Musical* of the 15th of September 1895.

Debussy made another journey to London early in 1895, possibly in the hope of improving his finances by making his works known abroad. He was away three weeks. We only know of this journey from the testimony of André de Ternant, with whom Debussy exchanged several visits and held long conversations. He stayed at Hampstead with the family of a French professor. During the journey to England, he met his venerable confrère, Camille Saint-Saëns, on the steamer. There was no love lost between the two musicians. Their meeting was, however, friendly. It resulted in Saint-Saëns taking Debussy to the Royal College of Music at South Kensington and introducing him to the director, Sir Hubert Parry. This journey does not seem to have been any more fruitful in practical results than the preceding one.

Debussy, who was always scornful of success, did nothing to push his works. Besides, the interpretative artists, the singers especially, were not inclined to undertake the troublesome task of performing such difficult works which, if they are to be properly rendered, demand a very supple technique, careful study, and a really masterly execution. One realizes this from the fact that the 'Chansons de Bilitis', written to three poems by Pierre Louÿs and published in August 1899, had to wait several months for their first performance. Although Debussy was connected with the Société Nationale in his double role of composer and pianist, no opportunity of hearing these songs occurred until the 17th of March 1900, a week after the first performance of an early work of his, the 'Tarantelle Styrienne'. But in spite of all practical difficulties these songs should have been performed earlier. Neither the interpreter on that occasion, Blanche Marot, an Opéra-Comique artiste, nor the few singers who subsequently performed these songs, succeeded in introducing them beyond a very limited public, although their renderings were often exquisite. They did not achieve success in Paris until nearly ten years later, when Lucienne Bréval, an opera singer and *tragédienne*, sang them on several occasions. On the 26th of December 1909, in the unsuitably vast setting of the Concerts Colonne at the Châtelet, she gave a passionate, romantic, theatrical interpretation which was not perhaps quite in keeping with Debussy's artistic ideals. But renderings of this kind have the best chance of commanding success, especially when sung to the very faithful and delicate orchestral accompaniment recently arranged by Maurice Delage.

The 'Chansons de Bilitis' are amongst the composer's most

110 CLAUDE DEBUSSY: LIFE AND WORKS

significant and perfect works. They are very much akin to 'Pelléas' in the general style of writing, the harmony, the skilful notation of the words—now prosodized, now psalmodized—and also in the subtlety of their atmosphere. The first song, 'La Flûte de Pan', has a charming, naïve simplicity which is in keeping with Louÿs's chaste poem. It is based on a syrinx melody sustained by a mobile accompaniment of alternating common chords. The scene changes with 'the song of the green frogs', which is rendered by *appoggiaturas* in complex rhythms. Then, after a touching half-spoken declamatory passage accompanied by a succession of fifths, the song ends with a repetition of the flute refrain. The second song, 'La Chevelure', which is so often caricatured by over-romantic singers, is utterly different both in emotional character and harmonic treatment; it is agitated and obscure, like the dream of love which constitutes its subject. The musical ending is very simple and remarkably effective: a phrase overflowing with tenderness and voluptuousness, in which the words are treated with absolute fidelity to oratorical rhythm. The final touch is a simple triad, which by reason of its isolation acquires an extraordinary musical value, and its 'resolution' seems to convey the precise emotional significance of a consent or avowal. The 'Tombeau des Naïades' is a magnificent fresco expressed in a few brief pages, by unobtrusive means. Against the background of a continuously moving pattern in semi-quavers which suggests a solemn march, we have festoons of major thirds, fifths, series of sevenths, common chords, clusters of ninths, whole tone-scales, and the rasping dissonances of minor seconds vibrating like cymbals. All this musical magic evokes a dazzling procession of olden days, whilst the voice of Bilitis pours forth a broad, thrilling, irresistible melody. It is a masterpiece of music, of poetry, and one might say, of painting too; in this type of art, neither Debussy nor any other musician has surpassed this supreme standard.

Debussy composed another short piece of incidental music under the same title of 'Chanson de Bilitis'. It was intended as an accompaniment to some poems of Pierre Louÿs which were recited and staged one day at the offices of the *Journal* in Paris. This music, written for two harps and two flutes, consisted of some hundred and fifty hastily written bars divided into a dozen numbers. It was a mere improvization, pleasant and elegant, but of no great importance. Three diminutive notebooks contain the little score of this unknown work, written out by a copyist, but at the last moment the composer himself added the fifteen bars which constitute the last piece but one ('Le Souvenir de Mnasidica'). Fifteen years later,

Debussy arranged and developed the material somewhat, and transformed it into a series of pieces for piano duet under the title of
'Épigraphes Antiques'.

These three songs, as well as the Quartet and 'La Damoiselle
Élue', were successfully performed at the official concerts at the
Universal Exhibition of 1900. The governmental sanction was
further confirmed by a flattering allusion to the compositions in a
report to the Ministre de l'Instruction Publique, which in the name
of the musical section had been entrusted to Alfred Bruneau. This
musician, who was drawn to Debussy both by his own harmonic
audacity and a feeling of personal sympathy, gave him high, though
not unrestricted praise. He hailed 'the very exceptional, the very
peculiar, the very solitary M. Claude Debussy' and gave the following report of 'La Damoiselle Élue':

'I must confess that I had looked forward with the greatest curiosity
to this work of which I had heard much, but which I did not know. It
interested me enormously, but it alarmed and saddened me too. It is an
orchestral and vocal setting of a poem by Dante Gabriel Rossetti,
translated into rather bizarre French by M. Sarrazin. . . . M. Debussy's
talent is beyond all question. "L'Après-midi d'un Faune" is one of the
most exquisite instrumental fantasies which the young French school
has produced. This work too is exquisite, Alas! it is too exquisite. The
harmonic refinements and the perpetual modulations in which the composer delights, dwarf his work and make it flabby and insipid. I have
no objection to an art being rendered intricate by daring and original
innovations, but it must remain virile and human, otherwise it will only
be of passing interest and can leave no lasting emotion. Pre-Raphael-
ism is already going out of fashion and its vogue amongst us was very
short-lived, because it was utterly unsuited to our character and temperament. The lily-bearing ladies soon grew old in this fruitful land of ours.
M. Debussy has written the kind of music that suits the poem. I com-
mend him for it and I consider that it is eminently successful. I wish he
would now write music in keeping with the spirit and the genius of his
race. He would thus emphasize the exceptional originality of which he has
so often given proof, and to which once more, I gladly render homage.'[1]

A symphonic triptych for orchestra and female chorus, entitled
'Nocturnes', definitely established Debussy's reputation. The
first two parts were heard at the Concerts Lamoureux on the 9th of
December 1900. The entire composition was not given until ten
months later, on the 27th of October 1901. On that occasion the
same concert society performed the complete triptych, including

[1] Pp. 241–2 of the 'Rapport sur les Grandes Auditions Musicales de l'Exposition', published in La Musique Française by Alfred Bruneau (Paris, Bibliothèque
Charpentier, 1901).

the third panel, 'Sirènes', which contains a female chorus without words, similar to that in the 'Printemps' of 1887, the intonation of which is difficult.[1] In spite of his declared aversion to explanatory notices which tend to 'destroy the mystery,' the composer published the following lines in order to define the meaning of the title he had chosen and explain his artistic intention.

'The title "Nocturnes" is to be interpreted here in a general and, more particularly, in a decorative sense. Therefore, it is not meant to designate the usual form of the Nocturne, but rather all the various impressions and the special effects of light that the word suggests. "Nuages" renders the immutable aspect of the sky and the slow, solemn motion of the clouds, fading away in grey tones lightly tinged with white. "Fêtes" gives us the vibrating, dancing rhythm of the atmosphere with sudden flashes of light. There is also the episode of the procession (a dazzling fantastic vision) which passes through the festive scene and becomes merged in it. But the background remains persistently the same: the festival with its blending of music and luminous dust participating in the cosmic rhythm. "Sirènes" depicts the sea and its countless rhythms and presently, amongst the waves silvered by the moonlight, is heard the mysterious song of the Sirens as they laugh and pass on.'

These lines remind one of the 'Harmonies in blue and silver' of Whistler's 'Nocturnes'. The painter was a favourite with Debussy, and their art has often been compared. The comparison is a legitimate one, for in the work of both these artists the lines seem to resolve themselves into an atmosphere, luminous or sonorous, coloured or harmonic, that seems more essential to the composition than either the subject or the landscape.[2]

The 'Nocturnes' are dated 1897–9. But, unless Gustave Charpentier showed Debussy the score of 'Louise' before its production at the Opéra-Comique, a remarkable musical coincidence allows us to conjecture that at least one of the 'Nocturnes' was probably written after the 2nd of February 1900, the date of that *première*. The 'Nocturne' in question is the second. The movement of the initial theme, the rhythm and melody of another *motif*, punctuated by bassoons with an accompaniment of horns, in fact the whole atmosphere, is obviously reminiscent of 'Louise'. Again, an unconscious souvenir, very different in origin, is to be found in

---

[1] The choir generally sings this chorus out of tune. To some ears their discords give additional pleasure. In a critique published in *La Revue Musicale*, in November 1901 (p. 44) Louis Laloy wrote the following somewhat ironical account of the 'Sirens'' song on the occasion of the first performance: 'The enchantresses, confused by the chromatic inflections, sing augmented semi-tones and diminished semi-tones that are not unpleasing. I thought of the flat diatonic and the sesquialteral chromatic so dear to the contemporaries of Pericles.'   [2] See App. A, p. 274.

DEBUSSY AT THE HOUSE OF PIERRE LOUŸS
(about 1895)
(*Photograph taken by* LOUŸS)

LETTER TO PIERRE LOUŸS

'Nuages'. At the very beginning, without preamble, a melodic curve in typical intervals is traced by the clarinets, bassoons, and muted strings, every note of which is taken from one of Mussorgsky's songs, 'Sunless'. There the theme (which Stravinsky also used in the prelude of his 'Rossignol') evoked vague memories of a vanished happiness; here it describes the slow, solemn movement of clouds.

It is interesting to note these coincidences and reminiscences —Debussy was always a borrower—but they do not lessen the originality of the symphonic triptych, 'Nocturnes'. Both in feeling and treatment, it is quite individual. The work clearly belongs to the impressionist school. The composer himself seems to suggest this in his preliminary notice. There are no definite descriptions, but rather interpretations; no rough strokes, but finely powdered sonorities shaded into one another by transient harmonies; and a minute, detailed instrumentation which, for all its extreme subdivision, does not mar the unity of the composition. In 1900 an experienced musician might have noticed an exotic touch, as did 'L'Ouvreuse' of the *Écho de Paris*: 'Flutes *à la Russe, pizzicati* from the Far East'. Reminiscences of Slav themes and of the instrumentation of Rimsky and Balakiref were the only influences which could be clearly traced in these pictures. They seemed exotic merely because they were utterly different from the works of other painters in music. One perceived the vibration of the air, the quivering of the atmosphere, that luminous glitter which had never been rendered in such a sustained and effective manner before the appearance of the 'Prélude à l'Après-midi d'un Faune'. In the new score, these effects were achieved by characteristic Debussyist processes, carried out with a very subtle sense of the colouring of each instrument. These processes included the distribution of themes; the portioning-out of the harmonies amongst the various groups of instruments in succession or else, in very much subdivided parts, amongst the violin family muted or otherwise; frequent doubling of solo instruments—for instance, the violin, viola, and 'cello uniting to state a theme that has already been given in unison by the flute and harp; frequent employment of muted brass; constant use of the harps both for special effects and for reinforcing the lower strings. And we find once again the device, already attempted in 'Printemps', of treating the choral part instrumentally in order to blend some unusual vocal sounds into the delicate orchestral texture.

This orchestra, with its clear, light, transparent sonorities, contained no new instruments, no unnecessary overloading. It was a palette on which the colours were blended in such unusual proportions that they seemed entirely novel. It delighted a certain number of music-lovers—the most sensitive but perhaps not the most cultivated, paradoxical as this may seem—but a great many others were disappointed. The professors who respected classical usage and the conservatives who were faithful to traditional habits were once more horrified. They were bewildered by an instrumentation that was so utterly different from the opaque style to which they were accustomed.

The absolute freedom of the harmony caused even more amazement than the other elements of this music. There were so many strange modes, irregular scales, forbidden successions of doubled chords or aggregations strung together in defiance of rules, above all, so many consecutive ninths. This wealth of harmonic invention, which many musicians mistook for incoherence, was carefully studied by a very able critic. In his frequently mentioned articles Jean Marnold demonstrated that this harmony was really orderly, logical, and even historically inevitable. He traced the evolution of the dissonant chord throughout the centuries. He pointed out the gradual increase in the number of chords that were considered consonant, and their eventual acceptance as such, which occurred in the order of the harmonic sounds themselves. According to his theory, the seventh and the ninth should have been accepted, as they actually were, after the fifth and the third, and before the eleventh and the thirteenth. The history of harmony, thus reduced to a progressive piling up of thirds, became an article of faith to musicians. Henceforward Debussy's innovations could be regarded as normal and inevitable. In the land of Rameau, the mathematical ideal is always paramount.

Owing to the success of the 'Nocturnes' even those musical analysts who were most antagonistic to progress found themselves obliged to take the new art into consideration. The composer himself, as he wrote to Pierre Lalo, was only timidly endeavouring 'to rid music of the legacy of clumsy, falsely interpreted traditions, under whose weight the art seemed likely to succumb'. The professors, on the other hand, after minute scrutiny and merciless dissections that greatly exasperated their victim, instinctively sought to bring his art into line with the stereotyped classics with which they were familiar. They emphasized the cyclical character of the composition and discovered, for example, that all the melodic elements in 'Fêtes' were derived from the themes in 'Nuages'. They pointed out that each piece was almost normal in form. Thus, they claimed to discern in 'Fêtes' the general plan of the traditional *Allegro*:

introduction, exposition, and development, with the trio introducing a new idea (the fanfare of muted trumpets) and a coda
in which the themes of the exposition reappeared. They even
forced themselves to admit that the tonality showed signs of careful
and logical treatment, in spite of its apparent uncertainty and
vagueness.

A better understanding of the significance of the new art might
have been arrived at if the experts had noticed that, whilst its essential qualities were the fruit of a very individual artistic sensibility,
the peculiar style of writing had its origin in Debussy's constant,
almost exaggerated determination to react against all the symphonic mannerisms of his day, especially those that were traceable
to Beethoven, Franck, and Wagner. Even such regularly planned
compositions as the 'Nocturnes' and the 'Prélude à l'Après-midi
d'un Faune' show in every line unmistakable evidence of a spirit of
contradiction that is both instinctive and deliberate. Symmetrical
melodies confined within limited modes, straightforward rhythms,
and regular harmonies; all these various elements of the old traditional art are replaced respectively by irregular patterns traced in the
most varied modes, rhythms that conform to no strict measure, and
free progressions of chords. The tonal stability of former days
gives place to the perpetual vagueness of keys that melt into
one another; the inevitable succession of tonalities, ponderously
regulated in cycles of fifths or according to the strict conventions
of relationship or proximity, is replaced by a continual, capricious
modulation treated with a supreme sense of freedom and a disturbing tendency towards the equivocal. Obvious and imposing
architectural structures, built on broad imposing lines, are abandoned in favour of a loose, mobile type of composition whose
plan does not inflict geometrical designs on our attention. Dogmatic statements and definite reminiscences of formal themes are
replaced by discreetly mysterious allusions, romantic bombast by
refined effects and delicate murmurs. The logical processes of classical development and the abuse of the triad are condemned, as well
as all oratorical amplification and grandiloquence; and in their
stead we have a rather lazy tendency to repetition—after the
manner of some of the Russians—a peculiar form of eloquence,
discursive, in fact diffuse, and a fantastic structural plan which
builds up real *divertissements* by utilizing fragments of secondary
importance rather than those elements which might be considered essential. The whole tendency is exactly similar to that
of the symbolistic and decadent writers who, in a reaction against
the stiff forms of the Parnassians, made war on poetical tradition,

violating laws that should have already fallen into disuse, breaking
up the Alexandrine, escaping from its uniform rhythms and strict
stanzas; thus overthrowing the ancient metrical laws and attaining
to free verse.

Owing to their lack of perspective, these numerous articles by
scholars and critics lacked clearness of vision and freedom of
judgement. It was once again a case of not being able to see the
wood for the trees. Nevertheless, the painstaking labour of these
conscientious analysts is the clearest proof that the most cultivated
and enlightened musicians acknowledged the genius of Claude
Debussy, though it was some years before he obtained universal
recognition.[1]

The 'Nocturnes' were received with great applause in the
concert hall and almost unanimous praise in the Press. There were
very favourable critiques in the *Guide Musical* and the *Mercure de
France*; flattering allusions in the *Ménestrel* and the *Monde Artiste*
(which considered 'Fêtes' 'as entertaining as one of Léandre's[2] pictures'); and long eulogistic articles in the *Courrier Musical* and the
Revue Hebdomadaire, to mention only the reviews.

In the *Mercure de France* Pierre de Bréville, a composer of the
Franck school, declared that Debussy's music might be described
as the *despair of the critics*, and that the term 'to defy analysis' and
the epithet 'indefinable' seemed to have been specially invented
for it; for it was '*pure music*, conceived beyond the limits of
reality, in the world of dreams, amidst the ever-moving architecture that God builds with the mists, the marvellous creations of the
impalpable realms'. He described it as translating 'delightfully
superficial, almost phantom-like, impressions. M. Debussy does
not demand of music all that she can give, but rather, that which she
alone is capable of suggesting. He looks upon music as the art of the
inexpressible, whose role begins where inadequate words fail. . . .'

The musical critic of the *Courrier Musical* was Jean d'Udine.
Later on this writer was to make a deliberate attack on Debussy,
a kind of *procès de tendances*, accusing him of writing works that

---

[1] At an early stage, articles in the encyclopaedias included systematic,
academic inventories of Debussy's innovations in harmony: scales, modes,
successions or concatenations of chords. This technical analysis has recently
been very accurately worked out by Maurice Emmanuel in his study on 'Pelléas
et Mélisande' (pp. 97–114, and 216–18). Although confined to this dramatic
work, the analysis can be applied to Debussy's works in general. An English
writer, F. H. Shera, has published a detailed comparative list dealing with
several compositions by Debussy and Ravel (*Debussy and Ravel*, London,
Oxford University Press, 1925).

[2] Léandre (Charles-Lucien), French painter and caricaturist who contributed
to *Le Rire* and the *Figaro*.

were *morally* bad! But the 'Nocturnes' aroused his boundless enthusiasm. 'One cannot imagine', he wrote, 'a more delightful impressionist symphony. It is entirely made up of splashes of sound. It does not trace the sinuous outlines of definite melodic curves, but its treatment of timbres and chords—its harmony, as the painters would say—maintains nevertheless a certain strict homogeneity which replaces the beauty of line by the equally plastic beauty of a sonority skilfully distributed and logically sustained....'

He analyses 'Nuages' by giving a fine literary transcription of the work and adds:

'It is all expressed with an indescribable variety of nuances and the deepest poetic feeling; it is the most finely sifted music imaginable. And yet, I almost think I prefer "Fêtes". Oh, what lively gaiety there is in the atmosphere, what fairy-like effects the light produces as it plays through the furbelows of the cirrus clouds that whirl until they fray. And how subtly naïve it was to render these ethereal frolics in dance rhythms; such an infinite variety of old-world rhythms, with their skilful syncopations, suggesting dainty gavottes and rigaudons, and expressing infectious gaiety, full of peals of laughter and delightful fun, with sudden flourishes of the bassoons or a sparkling harp scale ending in a joyful clash of cymbals. It represents the French taste of a century ago, with all its delicate tenderness, its wit and elegance; the rustling dresses of the "Embarquement pour Cythère" and the charm of the "Nymphe Endormie". It is Verlaine à la Fragonard, and the effect is accentuated when the fantastic vision of a procession in old-world costumes passes through the festive scene, heralded by a discreet and harmonious fanfare on two short trumpets.'

Alfred Bruneau and Paul Dukas took advantage of the occasion to write an appreciation of the personality of their friend and colleague.

'This musician whose works are so rarely performed,' wrote the former, 'is one of the most original and remarkable artistic personalities of the day. He is little known by the crowd, goes nowhere, composes, I fancy, only when he feels inclined, and lives like a recluse, scorning all noisy advertisement. What an admirable and rare example! and what a lot of valuable time some men waste nowadays in preparing their publicity, in writing and distributing notices that proclaim their own glory. Having shut himself up in this haughty seclusion, M. Debussy seems intent on expressing the transient impressions of the dream he is in quest of, rather than the eternal passions of the world which he shuns. There is a certain amount of danger in this tendency for, sooner or later, truth and reality must triumph over illusion, be it ever so seductive. But no matter. It is these very tendencies frankly displayed, which place the author of "La Damoiselle Élue" in a class apart. The two pieces which we have just heard indicate that he continues in the same state of mind. In the first, entitled "Nuages", drifting vapours pass across a mysterious sky and assume the various forms that our imagination suggests. In the second, which is called "Fêtes", the quivering dust atoms dance and scintillate in the atmosphere across which move fantastic beings born of the countless unions of sounds and lights. It has a marvellous and singular charm. Themes there are none in the ordinary sense of the word, but the harmonies and rhythms adequately translate the composer's thoughts and that in the most original and striking manner. A seemingly "padded" orchestra envelops these pictures in music. They recall the strange, delicate, vibrating "Nocturnes" of Whistler, and like the canvases of the great American painter, they are full of a deep and poignant poetry. I do not hesitate to place the man who signed them in the very front rank.'

According to Paul Dukas's article in the *Revue Hebdomadaire*, Debussy occupies henceforward a unique place amongst his contemporaries. It is impossible to classify him in any category, and each new work differs so much from the preceding ones that his most fervent admirers are perplexed. Avoiding any direct translation of feeling, the composer endeavours to reproduce the most remote harmonics suggested by poems or by his own impressions; he thus creates symbols of symbols. For instance, the first of the 'Nocturnes' depicts the clouds 'by means of sumptuous, continuously floating chords whose rising and falling progressions suggest the movements of aerial structures. There is a slight hint of imitation. But the ultimate significance of the piece remains symbolical. . . . This "Nocturne" . . . translates one analogy by another by means of a music in which all the elements—harmony, rhythm, and melody —seem to have been, as it were, volatilized into the very ether of symbolism and reduced to a state of imponderability. We may add that, as is always the case with M. Debussy, the subtlety of this music is justified by its genuinely musical quality.'

Amongst the notices in the daily press Gaston Carraud's article is worthy of mention. This musician, who was a former Prix de Rome (1890), had just taken up musical criticism and made his debut in *La Liberté*. He wrote: 'I shall not attempt to give you any idea of this music. It is both mysterious and definite: It is almost baffling in its refinement and yet leaves an ultimate impression of clarity and simplicity.' Carraud looked upon Debussy as 'one of the most original artists of the day. . . . He is one of those musicians— rare in any epoch—who impress one as being endowed with spontaneous originality, and whom it is difficult to connect with any of his predecessors. . . . Guided by a refined and unerring taste, he knows how to combine harmonies and timbres in ever-changing ratios, as a painter treats the colours of the prism. . . . To-day, he seems to have attained to complete lucidity of thought and accuracy of expression.' The critic deplored the fact that 'Pelléas et Mélisande' was not to be produced at once at the Opéra-Comique, especially as it had been announced two years previously. Meanwhile, a few months after the first performance of the 'Nocturnes', Debussy, then thirty-nine years of age, made an unexpected début in musical criticism after the example of his friend Gaston Carraud. The *Revue Blanche* offered him the post of critic for concerts and operas. During a period of six months, Debussy held forth in this very modern periodical, as from an open tribunal, in terms that were generally considered blasphemous. (This was the opinion of Sâr Peladan, who accused him of 'disrespect to the iconostases'.) His first article, dated the 1st of April 1901, is a profession of faith. He proclaims his fervent love of music, nature, and liberty, his contempt for that type of criticism that indulges in the dissection of compositions, and his hatred of academic prejudices. It was there that he sketched the silhouette of the imaginary 'Monsieur Croche', modelled on Paul Valéry's 'Monsieur Teste'. His ideas were not widely circulated, for the *Revue Blanche* was not read outside advanced literary and artistic circles, but they were—and still appear—highly original, full of delicate sensibility and keen intelligence. Most paradoxically and quite unconsciously he here drew up a complete aesthetic doctrine, both novel and courageous, which we have endeavoured to set forth in a separate book.

In order duly to appreciate these theories, which we cannot analyse here, one must consider the state of mind of the composer in 1901. Debussy, the former pupil of the Conservatoire de Paris, the Prix de Rome, was a favourite with writers, painters, and some few musicians, but he was ignored by the general public and detested by reactionary artists who condemned, anathematized, and excommunicated him. We must also allow for his spirit of contradiction, his love of mockery, his attitude of boyish impertinence towards all established reputations, and all those personal elements which prompted him to exaggerate his opinions. It is also well to remember the prevailing musical conditions in France to which we have already alluded. The majority of musicians were strongly influenced by Wagner and Franck, and thus unintentionally, and even unconsciously, they came under the dominion of German art. Whilst devoting themselves with passionate ardour to the renewal of national art, that *Ars gallica* whose triumphs were celebrated at the Société Nationale, they were actually receiving their strongest impetus, directly or indirectly,

from Germany. These almost unconscious tendencies aroused
in Debussy a lively and aggressive hostility to laboured intricacy
of style, exaggerated sentimentality, and all adherence to false
traditions. He urged the return to a simpler, more discreet type
of art, more in keeping with the character of the French nation
and with its past history. Thus, almost unintentionally, he took
up a nationalist attitude. His articles were an improvised answer
to the challenge Wagner made when he put into the mouth of
Hans Sachs the condemnation of 'foreign insincerity and frivolity'
as the moral of the 'Meistersinger'. Debussy often took but little
interest in these notes which he never wrote except from sheer
necessity, in order to earn a little money. His friends did not think
them so original, or so varied and vivid, as his casual remarks on
art or the impertinent sallies in which he indulged in the *promenoir*
of the Concerts Lamoureux and in the *brasseries* he frequented.
Nevertheless, they deserve to be taken into consideration.

Although they often took the form of humorous chaff Claude
Debussy's harangues were quite seriously meant; they were moreover highly opportune, in spite of his whimsical exaggerations and
the protests they called forth. These theories were a continuation
and development of the propaganda which he had begun in the Conservatoire and which he continued after his return from Rome for
the benefit of a limited circle of composition students consisting of
some of Guiraud's disciples and old school-companions of his own.
This propaganda only lasted till the end of 1901. But two years
later, in 1903, it was continued in the daily paper, *Gil Blas*, after
the production of Debussy's principal work at the Opéra-Comique
had given him almost sovereign authority over the musical opinions
of a great number of his contemporaries.

CLAUDE DEBUSSY
(about 1900)

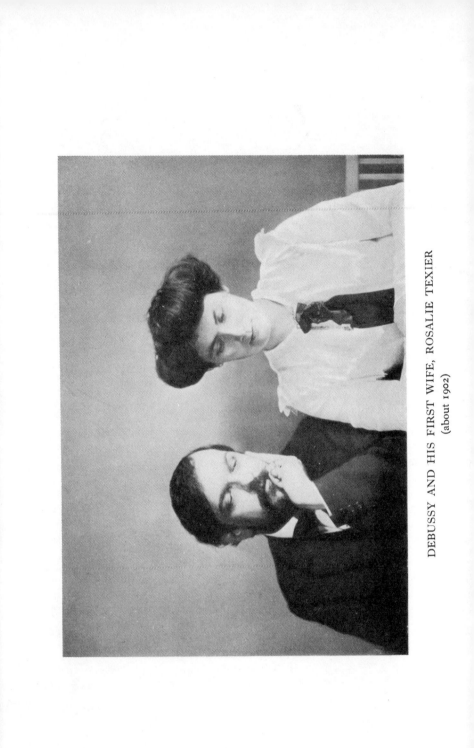

DEBUSSY AND HIS FIRST WIFE, ROSALIE TEXIER

(about 1902)

CHAPTER VIII[1]

'PELLÉAS ET MÉLISANDE' (1892–1902)—DEBUSSYISM

BY 1898, the score of 'Pélleas et Mélisande' was finished and already accepted by the Opéra-Comique, although the date of the first performance had not been fixed. But the work was not definitely completed till three or four years later, for the composer, who was constantly trying to improve it, revised it continually. It was written in the form of a big score for piano and voice with notes on the orchestration, and was not quite finished until the end of 1901 or the beginning of 1902, when it had become absolutely necessary to have the complete score.

The principal conductor and musical director at the Opéra-Comique was André Messager, a highly sensitive and intelligent musician. He was almost the only one of his generation and training who had abstained from the heavy, elaborate style of composition then in vogue, and who had deliberately devoted his talents to a lighter type of music. He had always taken a friendly interest in Debussy's compositions and had been the first to perform 'L'Après-midi d'un Faune' at the Vaudeville concerts immediately after the 'Prélude' was produced by the Société Nationale. Although he had not been shown the various scenes of 'Pélleas' as they were composed, he had seen them at a fairly early stage, and the new opera aroused his enthusiasm. He showed it to Albert Carré, the director of the Opéra-Comique, who at first demurred, but eventually decided, as a matter of principle, to produce this tragedy, the joint work of Maurice Maeterlinck and Claude Debussy.

There was some hesitation as to the manner of the production. While Debussy was slowly developing his musical drama, he had never dreamt that it would be given as one of the regular performances. At first, he had not anticipated more than a couple of performances before a select audience at the house of a rich dilettante, Comte Robert de Montesquiou. Indeed, as his correspondence proves, he always professed the greatest contempt for the crowd. Amongst many characteristic passages, we may quote the following from a letter to Ernest Chausson dated the 26th of August 1893:

'In modern civilizations, the utility of the artist will never be appreciated until after his death and then only for the purposes of idiotic boasting or shameful speculation. It would be better therefore if he had

[1] See also App. B, pp. 274–5.

nothing to do with his contemporaries. Besides, what is the use of arranging performances to enable them to participate in joys that so few are capable of appreciating? It would be better to be *discovered* a long time afterwards, for some of our recent celebrities are assuming a terrible responsibility towards posterity.'

In another letter of the 6th of September 1893 he writes: 'Instead of spreading art amongst the public, I would suggest founding a *Society of Musical Esotericism.*'

The authorities of the Opéra-Comique had contemplated limiting themselves to a few special matinées for the benefit of those who frequented the big symphony concerts. They eventually decided to take the risk of producing the work as one of the regular Opéra-Comique performances. This decision was facilitated by the fact that the creators of the principal roles had become quite enamoured of their parts. Messager has described the circumstances under which the first reading of the opera to the artists took place. It was held at the conductor's own house.

'Debussy played his score at the piano, and sang all the roles in that deep, sepulchral voice of his which often necessitated his transposing the parts an octave lower, but with an expression that grew more and more irresistible. The impression produced by his music that day was, I think, a unique experience. At first, there was an atmosphere of mistrust and antagonism; then gradually the attention of the hearers was caught and held; little by little emotion overcame them; and the last notes of Mélisande's death-scene fell amidst silence and tears. At the end, they were all quite carried away, and eager to set to work as soon as possible.'

It took all the goodwill and enthusiasm of the director, the conductor, and the artists to make the opera a success; so many circumstances seemed to threaten failure. Maeterlinck, who had just married Georgette Leblanc, had expected that his wife would sing the role of Mélisande which she had played in the spoken drama. On hearing that another singer was to create the role of his heroine, he severed his connexion with Debussy and the Opéra-Comique. He protested publicly against the alterations for which he had given a general authorization ten years previously, and called down anathemas on all those who were responsible for the coming performance. In his wrath, he went so far as to wish for the 'immediate and utter failure' of a work which he was no longer willing to recognize as his. Some members of the orchestra were exasperated by the countless mistakes in their instrumental parts—the copying of which Debussy had entrusted to an inexperienced confrère; they were annoyed by the lengthy partial rehearsals and the twenty-one ensemble rehearsals, and they were altogether so bewildered by the unusual style of the music that they declared the score to be unplayable, outrageous, and doomed to failure. This was in accordance with the inevitable tradition which so nearly proved fatal to all innovators from Rameau to Wagner. It is true, however, that some of the instrumentalists displayed the greatest enthusiasm for this new art which was so different from the usual repertoire works. Maeterlinck's libretto came in for a great deal of ridicule on the part of witty members of the theatrical world. They thought it ridiculous. Some unknown persons, either enemies or ignorant fools, drew up a programme entitled the *Select Programme*, that was sold at the doors of the Opéra-Comique, and which parodied the drama in a would-be witty, grotesquely worded, satirical analysis. In spite of rumours to that effect, it is impossible to believe that it was inspired by Maeterlinck himself. With a view to counteracting all these unfavourable impressions a special article was published in the *Journal* of the 27th of April 1902. The writer, Octave Mirbeau, who had been present at one of the last rehearsals, described, in the most appreciative terms, the overwhelming impressions he had experienced.

Claude Debussy, in making his debut, had a formidable role to play. One wonders what his state of mind was during the long weeks of rehearsals which he spent in the company of Albert Carré, André Messager, the scene-painters, Jusseaume and Ronsin, and the interpreters: Miss Mary Garden (Mélisande) and Mademoiselle Gerville-Réache (Geneviève); Jean Périer (Pelléas), Hector Dufranne (Golaud), and Félix Vieuile (Arkel). What were his feelings on the day of the first performance, or rather, the public dress rehearsal? His friends have described his impressions, and they can be clearly read between the lines of an article in praise of his principal interpreter which appeared in *Musica* in January 1908. This acknowledgement of his emotion, attenuated though it was after an interval of six years, deserves to be reproduced in full. Here it is:

'The scenic realization of a work of art, no matter how beautiful, is always contrary to the inner vision which drew it in turns from its alternatives of doubt and enthusiasm. Think of the charming life in which your characters and you yourself dwelt for so long, when it sometimes seemed that they were about to rise, tangible, from the silent pages of the manuscript. Is it any wonder if you are bewildered on seeing them come to life before your eyes through the intervention of such and such an artist? It is almost fear that is experienced; and one hardly dares to speak to them. In truth, they are like phantoms.

'From this moment, nothing remains of the old dream. The mind of another interposes between you and it. The setting materializes under the deft movements of scene-shifters, and the birds of the forest find their nests in the orchestral wood-wind. The lights are turned on. The play of the curtain curtails or prolongs emotion. Applause—aggressive noises resembling the sounds of a distant fête where you are but the parasite of a glory which does not always prove to be what you desired. For to succeed in the theatre most often implies a response to anonymous desires and assimilable emotion. . . .

'In 1902, when the Opéra-Comique staged "Pelléas et Mélisande" I experienced some of these impressions, although the production was carried out with the most scrupulous care. Perhaps my anxiety was futile, but at any rate, it will bear out what I wish to say later. I had always realized that the personality of Mélisande would be difficult to interpret. I had done my best to express in terms of music her fragility and her elusive charm; there was also her attitude to be considered, her long silences, which a single wrong gesture might frustrate or render meaningless. The most difficult point of all was Mélisande's voice which sounded so gentle to my inward ear—for the most beautiful voice in the world may be unconsciously fatal to the individual expression of a given character. It is neither my business nor my intention to describe here the various phases through which one passes during the period of the rehearsals. As a matter of fact, those were the pleasantest hours I spent in the theatre; I saw examples of admirable unselfishness and I came in contact with great artists. Amongst them one lady of very marked individuality stood out. I hardly ever had to make any remark to her; little by little the character of Mélisande took shape in her; and I waited with a strange confidence mingled with curiosity.

'At last we came to the fifth act—the death of Mélisande—and I cannot describe the amazement I experienced. That was, indeed, the gentle voice I had heard in my inmost soul, with its faltering tenderness, the captivating charm which I had hardly dared to hope for, and which has since forced the public to acclaim the name of Miss Mary Garden with ever-increasing fervour.'

The aggressive noises which Debussy mentions in connexion with the dress rehearsal were not mere figments of an artist's imagination, exasperated by untoward circumstances. There were disgraceful scenes both at the matinée rehearsal on the 27th of April 1902 and at the first performance, on the 30th of April. At the dress rehearsal, the first act passed off in comparative calm. During the second scene in Act Two people began to laugh at Mélisande's words: 'Oh! Oh! je ne suis pas heureuse!' which Mary Garden pronounced with an English accent. After that, all unusual phrases excited the hilarity of the spectators and some indulged in jokes and vulgar sarcasms. This very select audience consisted of invited guests and of the people who were entitled to admission—the most unintelligent set in Paris. The majority understood very little about the poem and pratically nothing about the music. They condemned the work both from the dramatic and musical standpoint, simply because the utter novelty of the opera reduced them to such a state of stupefaction that they were incapable of understanding it. According to a gossiping paper, the *Cri de Paris*, there was 'almost a riot' in the *couloirs*. Men of letters like Henri de Régnier, Octave Mirbeau, Pierre Louÿs, Paul Valéry, J. P. Toulet, Curnonsky, some professional musicians, and a few dilettanti, broke lances in favour of Debussy. But, as for the rest of the audience! It would be both cruel and futile to record the anathemas that were hurled against the score that day by certain composers and famous singers. Some were so outraged that a number of cuts had to be made after the dress rehearsal. One was in Yniold's scene with the sheep in the fourth act, another in the scene between Golaud and Yniold at the end of the third act where fifteen bars were omitted in order to suppress the word *bed*, which was vetoed by the majority of the audience, including an official personage, the Under-Secretary of State for Fine Arts. Debussy only permitted this cut as a last resort, in order to save the scene, as the government representative was insisting that it should be entirely suppressed. This ridiculous cut of fifteen bars (pp. 164–5, piano and vocal score, first edition) became permanently accepted, for the passage was omitted in the orchestral score (p. 244). It consisted of this fragment of dialogue between Yniold and his father: 'Non, petit père. — Et le lit? Sont-ils près du lit? — Le lit, petit père? Je ne vois pas le lit. — Plus bas, ils t'entendraient.' [1]

Things were a little calmer at the first performance. Most of the people in the stalls and the dress circle were probably not in the least interested either in the drama of 'Pelléas' or in the music, but enthusiastic applause came from the upper galleries. Some of the young men were beginning to support the new work—an intellectual group consisting of artists, students, Conservatoire pupils, and literary men who gradually succeeded in obtaining recognition for this masterpiece by Maeterlinck and Debussy. At the first performances when Albert Carré, the director of the Opéra-Comique, noticed that the subscribers were leaving the theatre, he filled up the orchestral stalls and balcony with a number of the habitués of the gallery who were delighted to undertake the

[1] 'No, father.—And the bed? Are they near the bed?—The bed, father? I don't see the bed.—Hush, they might hear you.'

duties of *claque* and secure at least a semblance of success for the much-discussed composer. In addition, some favourably-disposed musicians took it upon themselves to defend 'Pelléas', and undertook to convert some of the critics who at the dress rehearsal sided with the unappreciative public. Amongst these courageous supporters of the new art were Paul Dukas and Gustave Doret, both of whom were composers and critics, and Paul Poujaud, an amateur musician of keen sensibility and vast culture whose unobtrusive influence still remains considerable. If the critiques had appeared the day after the dress rehearsal, many of them instead of being favourable would have been absolutely scathing.

'There will be mirth in the halls of the Bibliothèque Nationale, the day our grandchildren, in turning over the dusty newspaper files, come upon the articles which appeared after the first performance of "Pelléas et Mélisande". There will be mirth . . . but also amazement and shame.' This forecast formed the first lines of an article published in May, in the *Revue Dorée*, by a new critic, Émile Vuillermoz, whose enthusiasm for 'Pelléas' had caused him to quarrel with his professor of harmony at the Conservatoire. His statement was justified, for many an article published in the Paris press on the last day of April or the beginning of May was a disgrace to its author.

A few of the principal papers contained the most incredible nonsense. In some cases, those responsible were writers from whom one would have expected more sense. It seems hardly worth while mentioning such absurd remarks as those of the critic to whom this delicate music suggested the 'noise of a squeaking door, of a piece of furniture being moved, or of a child wailing in the distance'. Some other critiques were equally worthless. For instance Louis de Fourcaud, an experienced art critic, professor of aesthetics and history of art at the École Nationale des Beaux-Arts in Paris, ventured to write in the *Gaulois*:

'This score is the outcome of special theories of which I could never, under any circumstances, approve. By dint of indulging in cerebral subtleties and an unwholesome craving for novelty, the composer has attained to a doctrine of complete negation. He renounces melody and its development, he renounces the symphony and its deductive resources. . . . The only really interesting elements in the work are the harmonic combinations. I do not deny that in this respect M. Debussy often achieves rare and even beautiful effects. . . . This nihilistic art, which curtails everything, which throws off the bonds of tonality and liberates itself from rhythm, may distract ears that are *blasé*, but it cannot arouse any deep emotion in our hearts. . . .' His concluding words are note-worthy: 'What we aspire to is a really deep, human art, not continual effects of titillation which are fundamentally morbid. One cannot serve ideals without ideas. One cannot quench the thirst of souls with questionable pharmaceutical beverages.'

In the *Petit Journal*, Léon Kerst proclaimed his utter lack of comprehension:

'All I heard—for even when you don't understand a thing, you can't go to the theatre without hearing something—well, all I heard was a series of harmonized sounds—I don't say harmonious—which succeeded one another uninterruptedly, without a single phrase, a single *motif*, a single accent, a single form, a single outline. And to this accompaniment, unnecessary singers droned out words, nothing but words, a kind of long-drawn-out, monotonous recitative, unbearable, moribund. . . .'

The 'constant nebulosity' of the score gave Eugène d'Harcourt an opportunity of contrasting it with Wagner's 'perfect limpidity' in his article in the *Figaro*:

'M. Debussy's present work is the inevitable outcome of theories which a definite group of musicians have been intent on propagating for some years past. This performance of "Pelléas et Mélisande" proves once more that the world is divided into two camps. On one side we have a group of *arrivistes* whose noisy friends are determined to support them at all costs. On the other side are the fervent disciples of art who look upon music as a holy trinity whose three elements—melody, harmony, and rhythm—are governed by laws which cannot be constantly violated except to the detriment of our reason and our hearing.'

Camille Bellaigue, too, thought the 'Trinity' somewhat dislocated. This writer, who was critic to the *Revue des Deux Mondes*, had been a fellow pupil of Debussy's in Marmontel's class at the Conservatoire. He gave it as his opinion that 'Pelléas et Mélisande' was 'absolutely unbearable during the whole of the first four acts'. In the whole score 'where there is no design', he had only discovered one single sonorous line: the song Mélisande sings while she combs her long hair. He found no melody, no *leit-motifs* (but then, he found no *motifs* at all) and no rhythm. 'The music of "Pelléas et Mélisande" has no more symphonic value than it has melodic or rhythmic qualities to justify its existence; for since symphonic treatment means development, it can only be used where there is something to develop.' Declamation and harmony were the only remaining points: 'As regards the verbal treatment, M. Debussy's work is perhaps not altogether without value.' The harmony, he goes on to say, is treated in a haphazard manner;

the composer seems 'qualified to preside over the decomposition of our art. . . . Everything is wasted and nothing is created in M. Debussy's music. . . . Art of this kind is morbid and pernicious. We are dissolved by this music because it is in itself a form of dissolution. Existing as it does with the minimum of vitality, it tends to impair and destroy our existence. The germs it contains are not those of life and progress, but of decadence and death'.

Arthur Pougin, a former violinist and a fervent reactionary, who instinctively upheld every form of mediocrity, expressed similar opinions in the *Ménestrel*:

'Rhythm, melody, and tonality, are three things which are unknown to M. Debussy, and which he deliberately scorns. His music is vague, irresolute, colourless, and shapeless; it lacks movement and life. . . . There is never any shading, never the slightest contrast of any description. The orchestra itself is always uniform, it has neither energy nor consistency. It is full of sustained sounds and there are continual *tenuti* in the wind instruments: horns, clarinets, and bassoons, during which the brilliant, vibrating, rich tones of the violins are never heard.'

Pougin goes on to criticize the writing, and draws the attention of music-lovers to 'a certain chord of the ninth on page 10 of the score, over which the voice sings the fifth of that ninth, so that only one more note is needed to complete the entire scale on that chord. Queer music, after all'.

Pougin, who was a historian, and Fétis's successor on the supplement to the *Biographie Universelle des Musiciens*, was not particularly well informed on the subject of this 'anarchist of music', to whom the Opéra-Comique audience had listened 'with mournful eyes and bowed heads like the horses of Hippolytus' [1] This is how he speaks of him:

'. . . A composer whose name has not yet reached the general public, but whom some of his confrères seem to regard as a kind of leader of a new school of musical thought. We are all familiar with that sort of school. It aims at overthrowing everything that has existed up to the present and seeks to regenerate art by obscure, symbolic methods. In such matters M. Debussy is a prophet, but a prophet who says very little, one must allow. It may have been the quality of his works that attracted attention to him—though that remains to be seen—but it was certainly not their quantity. . . . His known compositions are few in number. Two lyrical works, "La Damoiselle Élue" and "Chimène"; a "Prélude" to Stéphane Mallarmé's "L'Après-midi d'un Faune", performed at the Concerts Colonne in 1895; a String Quartet which was played at the Société Nationale; a number of songs, some to words

[1] 'L'œil morne maintenant et la tête baissée . . .' (Racine's *Phèdre*).

by Verlaine, others (Proses Lyriques) to poems by Baudelaire (*sic*); and three "Nocturnes", which were sung (*sic*) a few months ago at the Concerts Lamoureux and had a fair success. That is all. . . .'

Two or three articles in the daily press mingled censure with praise. In *L'Éclair*, the composer, Samuel Rousseau, wrote: '. . . There are too many harmonies, unquestionably. But how refined and how novel they are! Whether they are expressive is another matter. . . . They form a harmonious haze which envelops the voices and softens indiscriminately the most varied situations. Idyll and tragedy alike become blurred in a mist in which outlines and colours disappear.' The *Écho de Paris* published an article by 'L'Ouvreuse'. As was customary in the case of critiques of first performances, it was signed with the writer's real name, Henry Gauthier-Villars. This notice was less favourable than might have been expected, and was full of reservations. Willy deplored the harmonic harshness of some rasping dissonances, but realized himself that such a complaint sounded conventional: 'I am wrong. I am behaving like those painters who were so accustomed to the most mournful bituminous colours, that they revolted against the luminosity of the impressionists. Forget what I have said.'

Side by side with these articles full of misunderstanding and censure, there were many others that expressed warm praise and enthusiasm; some of these, however, were not particularly spontaneous or sincere. André Corneau, who had been musical critic to the *Revue Blanche* before Debussy, gave the following report in the *Matin*: '. . . A work of art, original in its impression, and subtle in expression; one is overjoyed to find no imitation of Wagner, Gounod, or Massenet. . . . M. Debussy's very poetical music is unlike anything we have yet heard. . . . One is overcome by the haunting sorcery and the subtle intoxication of this music. . . .' In the *Soleil*, O'Divy praised the admirable manner in which the poem and the music are blended: 'I cannot distinguish between the various elements at all; and no statement could better express the emotion I experienced.' In his feuilleton in the *Journal des Débats*, Adolphe Jullien called Debussy a '*tachiste*, and musical impressionist', and whilst admitting that the composer was 'at present completely under the influence of Mussorgsky', the critic stressed his originality and dramatic vigour, and confessed that he would not have thought it possible that such a musician could have successfully treated such a subject. Catulle Mendès, who was no doubt greatly disappointed, gave a very fanciful report in the *Journal*. He declared that he came away from the performance with two wishes (the first of which is absurd). He longed to hear the score by itself in the concert hall, and the play by itself at the theatre.

Henry Bauer sang the praises of the new opera in the *Figaro* and tried to account for the lack of understanding shown by so many of the audience: 'To-day or to-morrow, Claude Debussy's music will prevail ... this intensely artistic work, so youthful, pure, and tender, in which the subject, inspiration, and expression are so full of originality.' Gustave Bret wrote as follows in the *Presse*:

'This music grows on you. You are impressed by the very force of this art, for which I, personally, have more admiration than comprehension. From beginning to end, there is a very restrained declamation, not one word of which is lost, and a marvellously discreet orchestration, which produces exquisite and unusual sonorities. There is never any violence or display. No means are utilized but such as are absolutely legitimate. This lengthy score flows on to the end without causing a moment's weariness, without ever seeming monotonous, without the inspiration weakening even for an instant. The joy with which it was written illuminates it. . . .'

In a few exceptional cases the critics were particularly alive to the richness and fluidity of the rhythms which, as Camille de Sainte-Croix pointed out in the *Petite République*, 'are renewed for each detail, and follow the melopoeia of the language, syllable by syllable, adapting themselves very subtly to the diversity of the words, by their own continual diversity. . . .' In an important feuilleton article in the *Temps*, Pierre Lalo also remarked on this admirable quality of the new music, amongst many others:

'It has that utter refinement, which betrays no sign of effort, and which seems inborn and instinctive with M. Debussy; so much so, that one fancies he could not write otherwise. . . . A lively, subtle, almost intangible rhythm animates it with an undulating, quivering life. Its brief, delicate, melodic ideas are expressed in the most individual manner, in the most persuasive accents and the most suggestive idiom. Finally, it has the virtue of being always *musical*, a very characteristic and felicitous quality, thanks to which, amongst all the musicians of the day, M. Debussy stands out as a born musician. . . .'

One of the most noteworthy articles was that published in the *Liberté* by Gaston Carraud, and which probably influenced some of the other critics whose reports appeared later. Carraud praised Debussy's absolute originality. The only artistic relationship he could trace was with some Russian composers:

'In his score, everything seems subordinate to the words. Throughout the work, the declamation, which is remarkable for its fluency and ease,

CATALOG OF DOVER BOOKS

SIR HARRY HOTSPUR OF HUMBLETHWAITE, Anthony Trollope. Incisive, unconventional psychological study of a conflict between a wealthy baronet, his idealistic daughter, and their scapegrace cousin. The 1870 novel in its first inexpensive edition in years. 250pp. 5⅜ × 8½. 24953-0 Pa. $5.95

LASERS AND HOLOGRAPHY, Winston E. Kock. Sound introduction to burgeoning field, expanded (1981) for second edition. Wave patterns, coherence, lasers, diffraction, zone plates, properties of holograms, recent advances. 84 illustrations. 160pp. 5⅜ × 8¼. (Except in United Kingdom) 24041-X Pa. $3.50

INTRODUCTION TO ARTIFICIAL INTELLIGENCE: SECOND, EN-LARGED EDITION, Philip C. Jackson, Jr. Comprehensive survey of artificial intelligence—the study of how machines (computers) can be made to act intelligently. Includes introductory and advanced material. Extensive notes updating the main text. 132 black-and-white illustrations. 512pp. 5⅜ × 8½. 24864-X Pa. $8.95

HISTORY OF INDIAN AND INDONESIAN ART, Ananda K. Coomaraswamy. Over 400 illustrations illuminate classic study of Indian art from earliest Harappa finds to early 20th century. Provides philosophical, religious and social insights. 304pp. 6⅜ × 9⅜. 25005-9 Pa. $8.95

THE GOLEM, Gustav Meyrink. Most famous supernatural novel in modern European literature, set in Ghetto of Old Prague around 1890. Compelling story of mystical experiences, strange transformations, profound terror. 13 black-and-white illustrations. 224pp. 5⅜ × 8½. (Available in U.S. only) 25025-3 Pa. $5.95

ARMADALE, Wilkie Collins. Third great mystery novel by the author of *The Woman in White* and *The Moonstone*. Original magazine version with 40 illustrations. 597pp. 5⅜ × 8½. 23429-0 Pa. $9.95

PICTORIAL ENCYCLOPEDIA OF HISTORIC ARCHITECTURAL PLANS, DETAILS AND ELEMENTS: With 1,880 Line Drawings of Arches, Domes, Doorways, Facades, Gables, Windows, etc., John Theodore Haneman. Sourcebook of inspiration for architects, designers, others. Bibliography. Captions. 141pp. 9 × 12. 24605-1 Pa. $6.95

BENCHLEY LOST AND FOUND, Robert Benchley. Finest humor from early 30's, about pet peeves, child psychologists, post office and others. Mostly unavailable elsewhere. 73 illustrations by Peter Arno and others. 183pp. 5⅜ × 8½. 22410-4 Pa. $3.95

ERTÉ GRAPHICS, Erté. Collection of striking color graphics: *Seasons, Alphabet, Numerals, Aces* and *Precious Stones*. 50 plates, including 4 on covers. 48pp. 9⅜ × 12¼. 23580-7 Pa. $6.95

THE JOURNAL OF HENRY D. THOREAU, edited by Bradford Torrey, F. H. Allen. Complete reprinting of 14 volumes, 1837–61, over two million words; the sourcebooks for *Walden*, etc. Definitive. All original sketches, plus 75 photographs. 1,804pp. 8½ × 12¼. 20312-3, 20313-1 Cloth., Two-vol. set $80.00

CASTLES: THEIR CONSTRUCTION AND HISTORY, Sidney Toy. Traces castle development from ancient roots. Nearly 200 photographs and drawings illustrate moats, keeps, baileys, many other features. Caernarvon, Dover Castles, Hadrian's Wall, Tower of London, dozens more. 256pp. 5⅜ × 8¼. 24898-4 Pa. $5.95

THE ART NOUVEAU STYLE BOOK OF ALPHONSE MUCHA: All 72 Plates from "Documents Decoratifs" in Original Color, Alphonse Mucha. Rare copyright-free design portfolio by high priest of Art Nouveau. Jewelry, wallpaper, stained glass, furniture, figure studies, plant and animal motifs, etc. Only complete one-volume edition. 80pp. 9⅜ × 12¼. 24044-4 Pa. $8.95

ANIMALS: 1,419 COPYRIGHT-FREE ILLUSTRATIONS OF MAMMALS, BIRDS, FISH, INSECTS, ETC., edited by Jim Harter. Clear wood engravings present, in extremely lifelike poses, over 1,000 species of animals. One of the most extensive pictorial sourcebooks of its kind. Captions. Index. 284pp. 9 × 12.
23766-4 Pa. $9.95

OBELISTS FLY HIGH, C. Daly King. Masterpiece of American detective fiction, long out of print, involves murder on a 1935 transcontinental flight—"a very thrilling story"—NY Times. Unabridged and unaltered republication of the edition published by William Collins Sons & Co. Ltd., London, 1935. 288pp. 5⅜ × 8½. (Available in U.S. only) 25036-9 Pa. $4.95

VICTORIAN AND EDWARDIAN FASHION: A Photographic Survey, Alison Gernsheim. First fashion history completely illustrated by contemporary photographs. Full text plus 235 photos, 1840–1914, in which many celebrities appear. 240pp. 6½ × 9¼. 24205-6 Pa. $6.00

THE ART OF THE FRENCH ILLUSTRATED BOOK, 1700–1914, Gordon N. Ray. Over 630 superb book illustrations by Fragonard, Delacroix, Daumier, Doré, Grandville, Manet, Mucha, Steinlen, Toulouse-Lautrec and many others. Preface. Introduction. 633 halftones. Indices of artists, authors & titles, binders and provenances. Appendices. Bibliography. 608pp. 8⅜ × 11¼. 25086-5 Pa. $24.95

THE WONDERFUL WIZARD OF OZ, L. Frank Baum. Facsimile in full color of America's finest children's classic. 143 illustrations by W. W. Denslow. 267pp. 5⅜ × 8½. 20691-2 Pa. $5.95

FRONTIERS OF MODERN PHYSICS: New Perspectives on Cosmology, Relativity, Black Holes and Extraterrestrial Intelligence, Tony Rothman, et al. For the intelligent layman. Subjects include: cosmological models of the universe; black holes; the neutrino; the search for extraterrestrial intelligence. Introduction. 46 black-and-white illustrations. 192pp. 5⅜ × 8½. 24587-X Pa. $6.95

THE FRIENDLY STARS, Martha Evans Martin & Donald Howard Menzel. Classic text marshalls the stars together in an engaging, non-technical survey, presenting them as sources of beauty in night sky. 23 illustrations. Foreword. 2 star charts. Index. 147pp. 5⅜ × 8½. 21099-5 Pa. $3.50

FADS AND FALLACIES IN THE NAME OF SCIENCE, Martin Gardner. Fair, witty appraisal of cranks, quacks, and quackeries of science and pseudoscience: hollow earth, Velikovsky, orgone energy, Dianetics, flying saucers, Bridey Murphy, food and medical fads, etc. Revised, expanded In the Name of Science. "A very able and even-tempered presentation."—The New Yorker. 363pp. 5⅜ × 8.
20394-8 Pa. $6.50

ANCIENT EGYPT: ITS CULTURE AND HISTORY, J. E Manchip White. From pre-dynastics through Ptolemies: society, history, political structure, religion, daily life, literature, cultural heritage. 48 plates. 217pp. 5⅜ × 8½. 22548-8 Pa. $4.95

CATALOG OF DOVER BOOKS

CHRISTMAS CUSTOMS AND TRADITIONS, Clement A. Miles. Origin, evolution, significance of religious, secular practices. Caroling, gifts, yule logs, much more. Full, scholarly yet fascinating; non-sectarian. 400pp. 5⅜ × 8½.
23354-5 Pa. $6.50

THE HUMAN FIGURE IN MOTION, Eadweard Muybridge. More than 4,500 stopped-action photos, in action series, showing undraped men, women, children jumping, lying down, throwing, sitting, wrestling, carrying, etc. 390pp. 7⅞ × 10⅝.
20204-6 Cloth. $19.95

THE MAN WHO WAS THURSDAY, Gilbert Keith Chesterton. Witty, fast-paced novel about a club of anarchists in turn-of-the-century London. Brilliant social, religious, philosophical speculations. 128pp. 5⅜ × 8½.
25121-7 Pa. $3.95

A CEZANNE SKETCHBOOK: Figures, Portraits, Landscapes and Still Lifes, Paul Cezanne. Great artist experiments with tonal effects, light, mass, other qualities in over 100 drawings. A revealing view of developing master painter, precursor of Cubism. 102 black-and-white illustrations. 144pp. 8¾ × 6⅝.
24790-2 Pa. $5.95

AN ENCYCLOPEDIA OF BATTLES: Accounts of Over 1,560 Battles from 1479 B.C. to the Present, David Eggenberger. Presents essential details of every major battle in recorded history, from the first battle of Megiddo in 1479 B.C. to Grenada in 1984. List of Battle Maps. New Appendix covering the years 1967–1984. Index. 99 illustrations. 544pp. 6½ × 9¼.
24913-1 Pa. $14.95

AN ETYMOLOGICAL DICTIONARY OF MODERN ENGLISH, Ernest Weekley. Richest, fullest work, by foremost British lexicographer. Detailed word histories. Inexhaustible. Total of 856pp. 6½ × 9¼.
21873-2, 21874-0 Pa., Two-vol. set $17.00

WEBSTER'S AMERICAN MILITARY BIOGRAPHIES, edited by Robert McHenry. Over 1,000 figures who shaped 3 centuries of American military history. Detailed biographies of Nathan Hale, Douglas MacArthur, Mary Hallaren, others. Chronologies of engagements, more. Introduction. Addenda. 1,033 entries in alphabetical order. xi + 548pp. 6½ × 9¼. (Available in U.S. only)
24758-9 Pa. $11.95

LIFE IN ANCIENT EGYPT, Adolf Erman. Detailed older account, with much not in more recent books: domestic life, religion, magic, medicine, commerce, and whatever else needed for complete picture. Many illustrations. 597pp. 5⅜ × 8½.
22632-8 Pa. $8.95

HISTORIC COSTUME IN PICTURES, Braun & Schneider. Over 1,450 costumed figures shown, covering a wide variety of peoples: kings, emperors, nobles, priests, servants, soldiers, scholars, townsfolk, peasants, merchants, courtiers, cavaliers, and more. 256pp. 8⅜ × 11¼.
23150-X Pa. $7.95

THE NOTEBOOKS OF LEONARDO DA VINCI, edited by J. P. Richter. Extracts from manuscripts reveal great genius; on painting, sculpture, anatomy, sciences, geography, etc. Both Italian and English. 186 ms. pages reproduced, plus 500 additional drawings, including studies for *Last Supper*, *Sforza* monument, etc. 860pp. 7⅞ × 10¾. (Available in U.S. only) 22572-0, 22573-9 Pa., Two-vol. set $25.90

CATALOG OF DOVER BOOKS

DEGAS: An Intimate Portrait, Ambroise Vollard. Charming, anecdotal memoir by famous art dealer of one of the greatest 19th-century French painters. 14 black-and-white illustrations. Introduction by Harold L. Van Doren. 96pp. 5⅜ × 8½.
25131-4 Pa. $3.95

PERSONAL NARRATIVE OF A PILGRIMAGE TO ALMANDINAH AND MECCAH, Richard Burton. Great travel classic by remarkably colorful personality. Burton, disguised as a Moroccan, visited sacred shrines of Islam, narrowly escaping death. 47 illustrations. 959pp. 5⅜ × 8½.   21217-3, 21218-1 Pa., Two-vol. set $17.90

PHRASE AND WORD ORIGINS, A. H. Holt. Entertaining, reliable, modern study of more than 1,200 colorful words, phrases, origins and histories. Much unexpected information. 254pp. 5⅜ × 8½.   20758-7 Pa. $5.95

THE RED THUMB MARK, R. Austin Freeman. In this first Dr. Thorndyke case, the great scientific detective draws fascinating conclusions from the nature of a single fingerprint. Exciting story, authentic science. 320pp. 5⅜ × 8½. (Available in U.S. only)   25210-8 Pa. $5.95

AN EGYPTIAN HIEROGLYPHIC DICTIONARY, E. A. Wallis Budge. Monumental work containing about 25,000 words or terms that occur in texts ranging from 3000 B.C. to 600 A.D. Each entry consists of a transliteration of the word, the word in hieroglyphs, and the meaning in English. 1,314pp. 6⅜ × 10.
23615-3, 23616-1 Pa., Two-vol. set $27.90

THE COMPLEAT STRATEGYST: Being a Primer on the Theory of Games of Strategy, J. D. Williams. Highly entertaining classic describes, with many illustrated examples, how to select best strategies in conflict situations. Prefaces. Appendices. xvi + 268pp. 5⅜ × 8½.   25101-2 Pa. $5.95

THE ROAD TO OZ, L. Frank Baum. Dorothy meets the Shaggy Man, little Button-Bright and the Rainbow's beautiful daughter in this delightful trip to the magical Land of Oz. 272pp. 5⅜ × 8.   25208-6 Pa. $4.95

POINT AND LINE TO PLANE, Wassily Kandinsky. Seminal exposition of role of point, line, other elements in non-objective painting. Essential to understanding 20th-century art. 127 illustrations. 192pp. 6½ × 9¼.   23808-3 Pa. $4.50

LADY ANNA, Anthony Trollope. Moving chronicle of Countess Lovel's bitter struggle to win for herself and daughter Anna their rightful rank and fortune—perhaps at cost of sanity itself. 384pp. 5⅜ × 8½.   24669-8 Pa. $6.95

EGYPTIAN MAGIC, E. A. Wallis Budge. Sums up all that is known about magic in Ancient Egypt: the role of magic in controlling the gods, powerful amulets that warded off evil spirits, scarabs of immortality, use of wax images, formulas and spells, the secret name, much more. 253pp. 5⅜ × 8½.   22681-6 Pa. $4.50

THE DANCE OF SIVA, Ananda Coomaraswamy. Preeminent authority unfolds the vast metaphysic of India: the revelation of her art, conception of the universe, social organization, etc. 27 reproductions of art masterpieces. 192pp. 5⅜ × 8½.
24817-8 Pa. $5.95

A CONCISE HISTORY OF PHOTOGRAPHY: Third Revised Edition, Helmut Gernsheim. Best one-volume history—camera obscura, photochemistry, daguerreotypes, evolution of cameras, film, more. Also artistic aspects—landscape, portraits, fine art, etc. 281 black-and-white photographs. 26 in color. 176pp. 8⅜ × 11¼. 25128-4 Pa. $12.95

THE DORÉ BIBLE ILLUSTRATIONS, Gustave Doré. 241 detailed plates from the Bible: the Creation scenes, Adam and Eve, Flood, Babylon, battle sequences, life of Jesus, etc. Each plate is accompanied by the verses from the King James version of the Bible. 241pp. 9 × 12. 23004-X Pa. $8.95

HUGGER-MUGGER IN THE LOUVRE, Elliot Paul. Second Homer Evans mystery-comedy. Theft at the Louvre involves sleuth in hilarious, madcap caper. "A knockout."—Books. 336pp. 5⅜ × 8½. 25185-3 Pa. $5.95

FLATLAND, E. A. Abbott. Intriguing and enormously popular science-fiction classic explores the complexities of trying to survive as a two-dimensional being in a three-dimensional world. Amusingly illustrated by the author. 16 illustrations. 103pp. 5⅜ × 8½. 20001-9 Pa. $2.25

THE HISTORY OF THE LEWIS AND CLARK EXPEDITION, Meriwether Lewis and William Clark, edited by Elliott Coues. Classic edition of Lewis and Clark's day-by-day journals that later became the basis for U.S. claims to Oregon and the West. Accurate and invaluable geographical, botanical, biological, meteorological and anthropological material. Total of 1,508pp. 5⅜ × 8½. 21268-8, 21269-6, 21270-X Pa. Three-vol. set $25.50

LANGUAGE, TRUTH AND LOGIC, Alfred J. Ayer. Famous, clear introduction to Vienna, Cambridge schools of Logical Positivism. Role of philosophy, elimination of metaphysics, nature of analysis, etc. 160pp. 5⅜ × 8½. (Available in U.S. and Canada only) 20010-8 Pa. $2.95

MATHEMATICS FOR THE NONMATHEMATICIAN, Morris Kline. Detailed, college-level treatment of mathematics in cultural and historical context, with numerous exercises. For liberal arts students. Preface. Recommended Reading Lists. Tables. Index. Numerous black-and-white figures. xvi + 641pp. 5⅜ × 8½. 24823-2 Pa. $11.95

28 SCIENCE FICTION STORIES, H. G. Wells. Novels, *Star Begotten* and *Men Like Gods,* plus 26 short stories: "Empire of the Ants," "A Story of the Stone Age," "The Stolen Bacillus," "In the Abyss," etc. 915pp. 5⅜ × 8½. (Available in U.S. only) 20265-8 Cloth. $10.95

HANDBOOK OF PICTORIAL SYMBOLS, Rudolph Modley. 3,250 signs and symbols, many systems in full; official or heavy commercial use. Arranged by subject. Most in Pictorial Archive series. 143pp. 8⅛ × 11. 23357-X Pa. $5.95

INCIDENTS OF TRAVEL IN YUCATAN, John L. Stephens. Classic (1843) exploration of jungles of Yucatan, looking for evidences of Maya civilization. Travel adventures, Mexican and Indian culture, etc. Total of 669pp. 5⅜ × 8½. 20926-1, 20927-X Pa., Two-vol. set $9.90

PLANTS OF THE BIBLE, Harold N. Moldenke and Alma L. Moldenke. Standard reference to all 230 plants mentioned in Scriptures. Latin name, biblical reference, uses, modern identity, much more. Unsurpassed encyclopedic resource for scholars, botanists, nature lovers, students of Bible. Bibliography. Indexes. 123 black-and-white illustrations. 384pp. 6 × 9. 25069-5 Pa. $8.95

FAMOUS AMERICAN WOMEN: A Biographical Dictionary from Colonial Times to the Present, Robert McHenry, ed. From Pocahontas to Rosa Parks, 1,035 distinguished American women documented in separate biographical entries. Accurate, up-to-date data, numerous categories, spans 400 years. Indices. 493pp. 6½ × 9¼. 24523-3 Pa. $9.95

THE FABULOUS INTERIORS OF THE GREAT OCEAN LINERS IN HISTORIC PHOTOGRAPHS, William H. Miller, Jr. Some 200 superb photographs capture exquisite interiors of world's great "floating palaces"—1890's to 1980's: *Titanic, Ile de France, Queen Elizabeth, United States, Europa,* more. Approx. 200 black-and-white photographs. Captions. Text. Introduction. 160pp. 8⅜ × 11¾. 24756-2 Pa. $9.95

THE GREAT LUXURY LINERS, 1927–1954: A Photographic Record, William H. Miller, Jr. Nostalgic tribute to heyday of ocean liners. 186 photos of Ile de France, Normandie, Leviathan, Queen Elizabeth, United States, many others. Interior and exterior views. Introduction. Captions. 160pp. 9 × 12. 24056-8 Pa. $9.95

A NATURAL HISTORY OF THE DUCKS, John Charles Phillips. Great landmark of ornithology offers complete detailed coverage of nearly 200 species and subspecies of ducks: gadwall, sheldrake, merganser, pintail, many more. 74 full-color plates, 102 black-and-white. Bibliography. Total of 1,920pp. 8⅜ × 11¼. 25141-1, 25142-X Cloth. Two-vol. set $100.00

THE SEAWEED HANDBOOK: An Illustrated Guide to Seaweeds from North Carolina to Canada, Thomas F. Lee. Concise reference covers 78 species. Scientific and common names, habitat, distribution, more. Finding keys for easy identification. 224pp. 5⅜ × 8½. 25215-9 Pa. $5.95

THE TEN BOOKS OF ARCHITECTURE: The 1755 Leoni Edition, Leon Battista Alberti. Rare classic helped introduce the glories of ancient architecture to the Renaissance. 68 black-and-white plates. 336pp. 8⅜ × 11¼. 25239-6 Pa. $14.95

MISS MACKENZIE, Anthony Trollope. Minor masterpieces by Victorian master unmasks many truths about life in 19th-century England. First inexpensive edition in years. 392pp. 5⅜ × 8½. 25201-9 Pa. $7.95

THE RIME OF THE ANCIENT MARINER, Gustave Doré, Samuel Taylor Coleridge. Dramatic engravings considered by many to be his greatest work. The terrifying space of the open sea, the storms and whirlpools of an unknown ocean, the ice of Antarctica, more—all rendered in a powerful, chilling manner. Full text. 38 plates. 77pp. 9¼ × 12. 22305-1 Pa. $4.95

THE EXPEDITIONS OF ZEBULON MONTGOMERY PIKE, Zebulon Montgomery Pike. Fascinating first-hand accounts (1805–6) of exploration of Mississippi River, Indian wars, capture by Spanish dragoons, much more. 1,088pp. 5⅜ × 8½. 25254-X, 25255-8 Pa. Two-vol. set $23.90

THE BLUE FAIRY BOOK, Andrew Lang. The first, most famous collection, with many familiar tales: Little Red Riding Hood, Aladdin and the Wonderful Lamp, Puss in Boots, Sleeping Beauty, Hansel and Gretel, Rumpelstiltskin; 37 in all. 138 illustrations. 390pp. 5⅜ × 8½. 21437-0 Pa. $5.95

THE STORY OF THE CHAMPIONS OF THE ROUND TABLE, Howard Pyle. Sir Launcelot, Sir Tristram and Sir Percival in spirited adventures of love and triumph retold in Pyle's inimitable style. 50 drawings, 31 full-page. xviii + 329pp. 6½ × 9¼. 21883-X Pa. $6.95

AUDUBON AND HIS JOURNALS, Maria Audubon. Unmatched two-volume portrait of the great artist, naturalist and author contains his journals, an excellent biography by his granddaughter, expert annotations by the noted ornithologist, Dr. Elliott Coues, and 37 superb illustrations. Total of 1,200pp. 5⅜ × 8.
Vol. I 25143-8 Pa. $8.95
Vol. II 25144-6 Pa. $8.95

GREAT DINOSAUR HUNTERS AND THEIR DISCOVERIES, Edwin H. Colbert. Fascinating, lavishly illustrated chronicle of dinosaur research, 1820's to 1960. Achievements of Cope, Marsh, Brown, Buckland, Mantell, Huxley, many others. 384pp. 5¼ × 8¼. 24701-5 Pa. $6.95

THE TASTEMAKERS, Russell Lynes. Informal, illustrated social history of American taste 1850's–1950's. First popularized categories Highbrow, Lowbrow, Middlebrow. 129 illustrations. New (1979) afterword. 384pp. 6 × 9. 23993-4 Pa. $6.95

DOUBLE CROSS PURPOSES, Ronald A. Knox. A treasure hunt in the Scottish Highlands, an old map, unidentified corpse, surprise discoveries keep reader guessing in this cleverly intricate tale of financial skullduggery. 2 black-and-white maps. 320pp. 5⅜ × 8½. (Available in U.S. only) 25032-6 Pa. $5.95

AUTHENTIC VICTORIAN DECORATION AND ORNAMENTATION IN FULL COLOR: 46 Plates from "Studies in Design," Christopher Dresser. Superb full-color lithographs reproduced from rare original portfolio of a major Victorian designer. 48pp. 9¼ × 12¼. 25083-0 Pa. $7.95

PRIMITIVE ART, Franz Boas. Remains the best text ever prepared on subject, thoroughly discussing Indian, African, Asian, Australian, and, especially, Northern American primitive art. Over 950 illustrations show ceramics, masks, totem poles, weapons, textiles, paintings, much more. 376pp. 5⅜ × 8. 20025-6 Pa. $6.95

SIDELIGHTS ON RELATIVITY, Albert Einstein. Unabridged republication of two lectures delivered by the great physicist in 1920–21. Ether and Relativity and Geometry and Experience. Elegant ideas in non-mathematical form, accessible to intelligent layman. vi + 56pp. 5⅜ × 8½. 24511-X Pa. $2.95

THE WIT AND HUMOR OF OSCAR WILDE, edited by Alvin Redman. More than 1,000 ripostes, paradoxes, wisecracks: Work is the curse of the drinking classes, I can resist everything except temptation, etc. 258pp. 5⅜ × 8½. 20602-5 Pa. $4.50

ADVENTURES WITH A MICROSCOPE, Richard Headstrom. 59 adventures with clothing fibers, protozoa, ferns and lichens, roots and leaves, much more. 142 illustrations. 232pp. 5⅜ × 8½. 23471-1 Pa. $3.95

SUNDIALS, Albert Waugh. Far and away the best, most thorough coverage of ideas, mathematics concerned, types, construction, adjusting anywhere. Over 100 illustrations. 230pp. 5⅜ × 8½. 22947-5 Pa. $4.50

PICTURE HISTORY OF THE NORMANDIE: With 190 Illustrations, Frank O. Braynard. Full story of legendary French ocean liner: Art Deco interiors, design innovations, furnishings, celebrities, maiden voyage, tragic fire, much more. Extensive text. 144pp. 8⅞ × 11¾. 25257-4 Pa. $9.95

THE FIRST AMERICAN COOKBOOK: A Facsimile of "American Cookery," 1796, Amelia Simmons. Facsimile of the first American-written cookbook published in the United States contains authentic recipes for colonial favorites—pumpkin pudding, winter squash pudding, spruce beer, Indian slapjacks, and more. Introductory Essay and Glossary of colonial cooking terms. 80pp. 5⅜ × 8½. 24710-4 Pa. $3.50

101 PUZZLES IN THOUGHT AND LOGIC, C. R. Wylie, Jr. Solve murders and robberies, find out which fishermen are liars, how a blind man could possibly identify a color—purely by your own reasoning! 107pp. 5⅜ × 8½. 20367-0 Pa. $2.50

THE BOOK OF WORLD-FAMOUS MUSIC—CLASSICAL, POPULAR AND FOLK, James J. Fuld. Revised and enlarged republication of landmark work in musico-bibliography. Full information about nearly 1,000 songs and compositions including first lines of music and lyrics. New supplement. Index. 800pp. 5⅜ × 8¼. 24857-7 Pa. $14.95

ANTHROPOLOGY AND MODERN LIFE, Franz Boas. Great anthropologist's classic treatise on race and culture. Introduction by Ruth Bunzel. Only inexpensive paperback edition. 255pp. 5⅜ × 8½. 25245-0 Pa. $5.95

THE TALE OF PETER RABBIT, Beatrix Potter. The inimitable Peter's terrifying adventure in Mr. McGregor's garden, with all 27 wonderful, full-color Potter illustrations. 55pp. 4¼ × 5½. (Available in U.S. only) 22827-4 Pa. $1.75

THREE PROPHETIC SCIENCE FICTION NOVELS, H. G. Wells. *When the Sleeper Wakes, A Story of the Days to Come* and *The Time Machine* (full version). 335pp. 5⅜ × 8½. (Available in U.S. only) 20605-X Pa. $5.95

APICIUS COOKERY AND DINING IN IMPERIAL ROME, edited and translated by Joseph Dommers Vehling. Oldest known cookbook in existence offers readers a clear picture of what foods Romans ate, how they prepared them, etc. 49 illustrations. 301pp. 6⅛ × 9¼. 23563-7 Pa. $6.50

SHAKESPEARE LEXICON AND QUOTATION DICTIONARY, Alexander Schmidt. Full definitions, locations, shades of meaning of every word in plays and poems. More than 50,000 exact quotations. 1,485pp. 6½ × 9¼. 22726-X, 22727-8 Pa., Two-vol. set $27.90

THE WORLD'S GREAT SPEECHES, edited by Lewis Copeland and Lawrence W. Lamm. Vast collection of 278 speeches from Greeks to 1970. Powerful and effective models; unique look at history. 842pp. 5⅜ × 8½. 20468-5 Pa. $11.95

ILLUSTRATED GUIDE TO SHAKER FURNITURE, Robert Meader. All furniture and appurtenances, with much on unknown local styles. 235 photos. 146pp. 9 × 12.   22819-3 Pa. $7.95

WHALE SHIPS AND WHALING: A Pictorial Survey, George Francis Dow. Over 200 vintage engravings, drawings, photographs of barks, brigs, cutters, other vessels. Also harpoons, lances, whaling guns, many other artifacts. Comprehensive text by foremost authority. 207 black-and-white illustrations. 288pp. 6 × 9.
24808-9 Pa. $8.95

THE BERTRAMS, Anthony Trollope. Powerful portrayal of blind self-will and thwarted ambition includes one of Trollope's most heartrending love stories. 497pp. 5⅜ × 8½.   25119-5 Pa. $8.95

ADVENTURES WITH A HAND LENS, Richard Headstrom. Clearly written guide to observing and studying flowers and grasses, fish scales, moth and insect wings, egg cases, buds, feathers, seeds, leaf scars, moss, molds, ferns, common crystals, etc.—all with an ordinary, inexpensive magnifying glass. 209 exact line drawings aid in your discoveries. 220pp. 5⅜ × 8½.   23330-8 Pa. $4.50

RODIN ON ART AND ARTISTS, Auguste Rodin. Great sculptor's candid, wide-ranging comments on meaning of art; great artists; relation of sculpture to poetry, painting, music; philosophy of life, more. 76 superb black-and-white illustrations of Rodin's sculpture, drawings and prints. 119pp. 8⅜ × 11¼.   24487-3 Pa. $6.95

FIFTY CLASSIC FRENCH FILMS, 1912–1982: A Pictorial Record, Anthony Slide. Memorable stills from Grand Illusion, Beauty and the Beast, Hiroshima, Mon Amour, many more. Credits, plot synopses, reviews, etc. 160pp. 8¼ × 11.
25256-6 Pa. $11.95

THE PRINCIPLES OF PSYCHOLOGY, William James. Famous long course complete, unabridged. Stream of thought, time perception, memory, experimental methods; great work decades ahead of its time. 94 figures. 1,391pp. 5⅜ × 8½.
20381-6, 20382-4 Pa., Two-vol. set $19.90

BODIES IN A BOOKSHOP, R. T. Campbell. Challenging mystery of blackmail and murder with ingenious plot and superbly drawn characters. In the best tradition of British suspense fiction. 192pp. 5⅜ × 8½.   24720-1 Pa. $3.95

CALLAS: PORTRAIT OF A PRIMA DONNA, George Jellinek. Renowned commentator on the musical scene chronicles incredible career and life of the most controversial, fascinating, influential operatic personality of our time. 64 black-and-white photographs. 416pp. 5⅜ × 8¼.   25047-4 Pa. $7.95

GEOMETRY, RELATIVITY AND THE FOURTH DIMENSION, Rudolph Rucker. Exposition of fourth dimension, concepts of relativity as Flatland characters continue adventures. Popular, easily followed yet accurate, profound. 141 illustrations. 133pp. 5⅜ × 8½.   23400-2 Pa. $3.50

HOUSEHOLD STORIES BY THE BROTHERS GRIMM, with pictures by Walter Crane. 53 classic stories—Rumpelstiltskin, Rapunzel, Hansel and Gretel, the Fisherman and his Wife, Snow White, Tom Thumb, Sleeping Beauty, Cinderella, and so much more—lavishly illustrated with original 19th century drawings. 114 illustrations. x + 269pp. 5⅜ × 8½.   21080-4 Pa. $4.50

HOW TO WRITE, Gertrude Stein. Gertrude Stein claimed anyone could understand her unconventional writing—here are clues to help. Fascinating improvisations, language experiments, explanations illuminate Stein's craft and the art of writing. Total of 414pp. 4⅝ × 6⅜. 23144-5 Pa. $5.95

ADVENTURES AT SEA IN THE GREAT AGE OF SAIL: Five Firsthand Narratives, edited by Elliot Snow. Rare true accounts of exploration, whaling, shipwreck, fierce natives, trade, shipboard life, more. 33 illustrations. Introduction. 353pp. 5⅜ × 8½. 25177-2 Pa. $7.95

THE HERBAL OR GENERAL HISTORY OF PLANTS, John Gerard. Classic descriptions of about 2,850 plants—with over 2,700 illustrations—includes Latin and English names, physical descriptions, varieties, time and place of growth, more. 2,706 illustrations. xlv + 1,678pp. 8½ × 12¼. 23147-X Cloth. $75.00

DOROTHY AND THE WIZARD IN OZ, L. Frank Baum. Dorothy and the Wizard visit the center of the Earth, where people are vegetables, glass houses grow and Oz characters reappear. Classic sequel to *Wizard of Oz*. 256pp. 5⅜ × 8. 24714-7 Pa. $4.95

SONGS OF EXPERIENCE: Facsimile Reproduction with 26 Plates in Full Color, William Blake. This facsimile of Blake's original "Illuminated Book" reproduces 26 full-color plates from a rare 1826 edition. Includes "The Tyger," "London," "Holy Thursday," and other immortal poems. 26 color plates. Printed text of poems. 48pp. 5¼ × 7. 24636-1 Pa. $3.50

SONGS OF INNOCENCE, William Blake. The first and most popular of Blake's famous "Illuminated Books," in a facsimile edition reproducing all 31 brightly colored plates. Additional printed text of each poem. 64pp. 5¼ × 7. 22764-2 Pa. $3.50

PRECIOUS STONES, Max Bauer. Classic, thorough study of diamonds, rubies, emeralds, garnets, etc.: physical character, occurrence, properties, use, similar topics. 20 plates, 8 in color. 94 figures. 659pp. 6⅛ × 9¼. 21910-0, 21911-9 Pa., Two-vol. set $15.90

ENCYCLOPEDIA OF VICTORIAN NEEDLEWORK, S. F. A. Caulfeild and Blanche Saward. Full, precise descriptions of stitches, techniques for dozens of needlecrafts—most exhaustive reference of its kind. Over 800 figures. Total of 679pp. 8⅛ × 11. Two volumes. Vol. 1 22800-2 Pa. $11.95
Vol. 2 22801-0 Pa. $11.95

THE MARVELOUS LAND OF OZ, L. Frank Baum. Second Oz book, the Scarecrow and Tin Woodman are back with hero named Tip, Oz magic. 136 illustrations. 287pp. 5⅜ × 8½. 20692-0 Pa. $5.95

WILD FOWL DECOYS, Joel Barber. Basic book on the subject, by foremost authority and collector. Reveals history of decoy making and rigging, place in American culture, different kinds of decoys, how to make them, and how to use them. 140 plates. 156pp. 7⅞ × 10¾. 20011-6 Pa. $8.95

HISTORY OF LACE, Mrs. Bury Palliser. Definitive, profusely illustrated chronicle of lace from earliest times to late 19th century. Laces of Italy, Greece, England, France, Belgium, etc. Landmark of needlework scholarship. 266 illustrations. 672pp. 6⅛ × 9¼. 24742-2 Pa. $14.95

ILLUSTRATED DICTIONARY OF HISTORIC ARCHITECTURE, edited by Cyril M. Harris. Extraordinary compendium of clear, concise definitions for over 5,000 important architectural terms complemented by over 2,000 line drawings. Covers full spectrum of architecture from ancient ruins to 20th-century Modernism. Preface. 592pp. 7½ × 9⅜. 24444-X Pa. $14.95

THE NIGHT BEFORE CHRISTMAS, Clement Moore. Full text, and woodcuts from original 1848 book. Also critical, historical material. 19 illustrations. 40pp. 4⅝ × 6. 22797-9 Pa. $2.50

THE LESSON OF JAPANESE ARCHITECTURE: 165 Photographs, Jiro Harada. Memorable gallery of 165 photographs taken in the 1930's of exquisite Japanese homes of the well-to-do and historic buildings. 13 line diagrams. 192pp. 8⅜ × 11¼. 24778-3 Pa. $8.95

THE AUTOBIOGRAPHY OF CHARLES DARWIN AND SELECTED LETTERS, edited by Francis Darwin. The fascinating life of eccentric genius composed of an intimate memoir by Darwin (intended for his children); commentary by his son, Francis; hundreds of fragments from notebooks, journals, papers; and letters to and from Lyell, Hooker, Huxley, Wallace and Henslow. xi + 365pp. 5⅜ × 8. 20479-0 Pa. $5.95

WONDERS OF THE SKY: Observing Rainbows, Comets, Eclipses, the Stars and Other Phenomena, Fred Schaaf. Charming, easy-to-read poetic guide to all manner of celestial events visible to the naked eye. Mock suns, glories, Belt of Venus, more. Illustrated. 299pp. 5¼ × 8¼. 24402-4 Pa. $7.95

BURNHAM'S CELESTIAL HANDBOOK, Robert Burnham, Jr. Thorough guide to the stars beyond our solar system. Exhaustive treatment. Alphabetical by constellation: Andromeda to Cetus in Vol. 1; Chamaeleon to Orion in Vol. 2; and Pavo to Vulpecula in Vol. 3. Hundreds of illustrations. Index in Vol. 3. 2,000pp. 6⅛ × 9¼. 23567-X, 23568-8, 23673-0 Pa., Three-vol. set $37.85

STAR NAMES: Their Lore and Meaning, Richard Hinckley Allen. Fascinating history of names various cultures have given to constellations and literary and folkloristic uses that have been made of stars. Indexes to subjects. Arabic and Greek names. Biblical references. Bibliography. 563pp. 5⅜ × 8½. 21079-0 Pa. $7.95

THIRTY YEARS THAT SHOOK PHYSICS: The Story of Quantum Theory, George Gamow. Lucid, accessible introduction to influential theory of energy and matter. Careful explanations of Dirac's anti-particles, Bohr's model of the atom, much more. 12 plates. Numerous drawings. 240pp. 5⅜ × 8½. 24895-X Pa. $4.95

CHINESE DOMESTIC FURNITURE IN PHOTOGRAPHS AND MEASURED DRAWINGS, Gustav Ecke. A rare volume, now affordably priced for antique collectors, furniture buffs and art historians. Detailed review of styles ranging from early Shang to late Ming. Unabridged republication. 161 black-and-white drawings, photos. Total of 224pp. 8⅜ × 11¼. (Available in U.S. only) 25171-3 Pa. $12.95

VINCENT VAN GOGH: A Biography, Julius Meier-Graefe. Dynamic, penetrating study of artist's life, relationship with brother, Theo, painting techniques, travels, more. Readable, engrossing. 160pp. 5⅜ × 8½. (Available in U.S. only) 25253-1 Pa. $3.95

CATALOG OF DOVER BOOKS

THE BOOK OF BEASTS: Being a Translation from a Latin Bestiary of the Twelfth Century, T. H. White. Wonderful catalog real and fanciful beasts: manticore, griffin, phoenix, amphivius, jaculus, many more. White's witty erudite commentary on scientific, historical aspects. Fascinating glimpse of medieval mind. Illustrated. 296pp. 5⅜ × 8¼. (Available in U.S. only) 24609-4 Pa. $5.95

FRANK LLOYD WRIGHT: ARCHITECTURE AND NATURE With 160 Illustrations, Donald Hoffmann. Profusely illustrated study of influence of nature—especially prairie—on Wright's designs for Fallingwater, Robie House, Guggenheim Museum, other masterpieces. 96pp. 9¼ × 10¾. 25098-9 Pa. $7.95

FRANK LLOYD WRIGHT'S FALLINGWATER, Donald Hoffmann. Wright's famous waterfall house: planning and construction of organic idea. History of site, owners, Wright's personal involvement. Photographs of various stages of building. Preface by Edgar Kaufmann, Jr. 100 illustrations. 112pp. 9¼ × 10. 23671-4 Pa. $7.95

YEARS WITH FRANK LLOYD WRIGHT: Apprentice to Genius, Edgar Tafel. Insightful memoir by a former apprentice presents a revealing portrait of Wright the man, the inspired teacher, the greatest American architect. 372 black-and-white illustrations. Preface. Index. vi + 228pp. 8¼ × 11. 24801-1 Pa. $9.95

THE STORY OF KING ARTHUR AND HIS KNIGHTS, Howard Pyle. Enchanting version of King Arthur fable has delighted generations with imaginative narratives of exciting adventures and unforgettable illustrations by the author. 41 illustrations. xviii + 313pp. 6⅛ × 9¼. 21445-1 Pa. $5.95

THE GODS OF THE EGYPTIANS, E. A. Wallis Budge. Thorough coverage of numerous gods of ancient Egypt by foremost Egyptologist. Information on evolution of cults, rites and gods; the cult of Osiris; the Book of the Dead and its rites; the sacred animals and birds; Heaven and Hell; and more. 956pp. 6⅛ × 9¼. 22055-9, 22056-7 Pa., Two-vol. set $21.90

A THEOLOGICO-POLITICAL TREATISE, Benedict Spinoza. Also contains unfinished *Political Treatise*. Great classic on religious liberty, theory of government on common consent. R. Elwes translation. Total of 421pp. 5⅜ × 8½. 20249-6 Pa. $6.95

INCIDENTS OF TRAVEL IN CENTRAL AMERICA, CHIAPAS, AND YUCATAN, John L. Stephens. Almost single-handed discovery of Maya culture; exploration of ruined cities, monuments, temples; customs of Indians. 115 drawings. 892pp. 5⅜ × 8½. 22404-X, 22405-8 Pa., Two-vol. set $15.90

LOS CAPRICHOS, Francisco Goya. 80 plates of wild, grotesque monsters and caricatures. Prado manuscript included. 183pp. 6⅞ × 9⅜. 22384-1 Pa. $4.95

AUTOBIOGRAPHY: The Story of My Experiments with Truth, Mohandas K. Gandhi. Not hagiography, but Gandhi in his own words. Boyhood, legal studies, purification, the growth of the Satyagraha (nonviolent protest) movement. Critical, inspiring work of the man who freed India. 480pp. 5⅜ × 8½. (Available in U.S. only) 24593-4 Pa. $6.95

A CATALOG OF SELECTED DOVER
BOOKS IN ALL FIELDS OF INTEREST

DRAWINGS OF REMBRANDT, edited by Seymour Slive. Updated Lippmann, Hofstede de Groot edition, with definitive scholarly apparatus. All portraits, biblical sketches, landscapes, nudes. Oriental figures, classical studies, together with selection of work by followers. 550 illustrations. Total of 630pp. 9⅛ × 12¼. 21485-0, 21486-9 Pa., Two-vol. set $25.00

GHOST AND HORROR STORIES OF AMBROSE BIERCE, Ambrose Bierce. 24 tales vividly imagined, strangely prophetic, and decades ahead of their time in technical skill: "The Damned Thing," "An Inhabitant of Carcosa," "The Eyes of the Panther," "Moxon's Master," and 20 more. 199pp. 5⅜ × 8½. 20767-6 Pa. $3.95

ETHICAL WRITINGS OF MAIMONIDES, Maimonides. Most significant ethical works of great medieval sage, newly translated for utmost precision, readability. Laws Concerning Character Traits, Eight Chapters, more. 192pp. 5⅜ × 8½. 24522-5 Pa. $4.50

THE EXPLORATION OF THE COLORADO RIVER AND ITS CANYONS, J. W. Powell. Full text of Powell's 1,000-mile expedition down the fabled Colorado in 1869. Superb account of terrain, geology, vegetation, Indians, famine, mutiny, treacherous rapids, mighty canyons, during exploration of last unknown part of continental U.S. 400pp. 5⅜ × 8½. 20094-9 Pa. $6.95

HISTORY OF PHILOSOPHY, Julián Marías. Clearest one-volume history on the market. Every major philosopher and dozens of others, to Existentialism and later. 505pp. 5⅜ × 8½. 21739-6 Pa. $8.50

ALL ABOUT LIGHTNING, Martin A. Uman. Highly readable non-technical survey of nature and causes of lightning, thunderstorms, ball lightning, St. Elmo's Fire, much more. Illustrated. 192pp. 5⅜ × 8½. 25237-X Pa. $5.95

SAILING ALONE AROUND THE WORLD, Captain Joshua Slocum. First man to sail around the world, alone, in small boat. One of great feats of seamanship told in delightful manner. 67 illustrations. 294pp. 5⅜ × 8½. 20326-3 Pa. $4.95

LETTERS AND NOTES ON THE MANNERS, CUSTOMS AND CONDITIONS OF THE NORTH AMERICAN INDIANS, George Catlin. Classic account of life among Plains Indians: ceremonies, hunt, warfare, etc. 312 plates. 572pp. of text. 6⅛ × 9¼. 22118-0, 22119-9 Pa. Two-vol. set $15.90

ALASKA: The Harriman Expedition, 1899, John Burroughs, John Muir, et al. Informative, engrossing accounts of two-month, 9,000-mile expedition. Native peoples, wildlife, forests, geography, salmon industry, glaciers, more. Profusely illustrated. 240 black-and-white line drawings. 124 black-and-white photographs. 3 maps. Index. 576pp. 5⅜ × 8½. 25109-8 Pa. $11.95

A CATALOG OF SELECTED
DOVER BOOKS
IN ALL FIELDS OF INTEREST

IV ŒUVRES LITTERAIRES

1901-1916 La liste des articles de critique écrits par Debussy est publiée à la fin de notre livre: *LES IDÉES DE CLAUDE DEBUSSY, MUSICIEN-FRANÇAIS.*

1910 *MASQUES ET BERGAMASQUES,* livret (non mis en musique); Durand, 1910.

Paris, Imp. Française
de musique. XXXII

III. ŒUVRES INÉDITES

La Bibliothèque du Conservatoire de Paris possède le manuscrit des devoirs que Debussy fit pour divers concours:

1878	Basse et chant (Concours d'accompagnement).
1879	Basse et chant (Concours d'accompagnement).
1880	Basse et chant (Concours d'harmonie).
1882	Fugue pour le concours d'essai de Rome.
	Chœur du *PRINTEMPS* (publié en 1928), pour le même concours.
»	Fugue pour le concours de contrepoint.
1883	*INVOCATION* (publiée en 1928),pour le concours d'essai de Rome.
»	*LE GLADIATEUR*, cantate pour le concours de Rome.
1884	Fugue pour le concours d'essai de Rome.
»	*PRINTEMPS* (Barbier), chœur pour le même concours *L'ENFANT PRODIGUE*, cantate pour le concours de Rome (publiée en 1884).

1880-1884	Recueil de mélodies, dédiées à Mme Vasnier, dont quatre ont été publiées par la *REVUE MUSICALE* (collection Henri Prunières).
»	Trois mélodies: a) *RONDEL CHINOIS* (vers 1882), b) *PIERROT* (Th.de Banville), c) *APPARITION* (S. Mallarmé), datée de Ville d'Avray, 8.2.84. Library of Congress, Washington.
»	*AIMONS NOUS* (Th.de Banville), pour chant et piano, collection Paul Vidal.
»	*LA FILLE AUX CHEVEUX DE LIN*, pour chant et piano.
»	Diverses mélodies disparues, citées dans notre ouvrage (chapitre Ier)
»	*EGLOGUE*, duo pour soprano et tenor, poésie de Lecomte de Lisle "Chanteurs mélodieux..." partition chant et piano avec quelques indications d'orchestre. Collection de Mme Texier-Debussy.
?	Carnet de croquis musicaux contenant avec diverses notes deux mélodies chant et piano (*L'ARCHET* de Ch.Cros et *FLEUR DES EAUX* de Maurice Bouchor) Coll. de Mme Texier-Debussy.
?	Cahier d'esquisses. Coll.de Mme Debussy.
1891-1892	*RODRIGUE ET CHIMENE*, trois actes, livret de Catulle Mendès; brouillon. Coll. Alfred Cortot.
Novembre 1900	*CHANSONS DE BILITIS*, pour deux flûtes, deux harpes et célesta (musique de scène arrangée en *EPIGRAPHES ANTIQUES*, 1914); Coll. de Mme Texier-Debussy.
1908	Berceuse pour la *TRAGÉDIE DE LA MORT* de René Peter. Collection Réne Peter.

(Cette liste est forcément incomplète: un certain nombre d'inédits se trouvent,inconnus, dans des collections particulières).

1912 *SYRINX*, pour flûte seule· Jobert 1927.

1916-1917 *ODE A LA FRANCE*, (Louis Laloy) pour solo, chœur et orchestre, esquisse arrangée par Marius-François Gaillard ; Choudens, 1928.

Le sommeil de Lear

1904 *LE ROI LEAR,* musique de scène pour orchestre: *FANFARE, SOMMEIL DE LEAR* (Concerts Pasdeloup, 30 octobre 1926); Jobert, 1926. Ms. Coll. Mme Debussy.

Fanfare

Avril 1901 *LINDARAJA*, pour deux pianos a quatre mains; Jobert 1926

1903-1905 *RAPSODIE* pour orchestre avec saxophone en *mi* bémol (Société nationale, 11 mai 1919); Durand, 1919.

Ms. Bibl. Conservatoire Nº 41 (partie de saxophone et de piano et saxophone). Le manuscrit d'orchestre conservé sous le même numéro est de Roger Ducasse. Brouillon d'orchestre inachevé, Coll. Elise Hall.

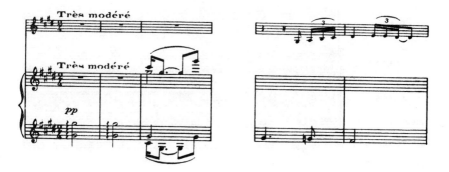

1889 *FANTAISIE* pour piano et orchestre (Royal Philharmonic Society de Londres avec Alfred Cortot, 20 novembre 1919; Concerts Lamoureux avec Marguerite Long et Grands Concerts de Lyon avec Alfred Cortot, 7 décembre 1919);Jobert 1919.

1882(?) *TRIOMPHE DE BACCHUS* divertissement pour orchestre réduction pour piano 2 mains par M. F. Gaillard, Choudens, 1928.

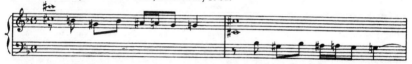

1883 *INVOCATION* (Lamartine), chœur pour le concours d'essai de Rome. Chœur pour voix d'hommes et orchestre. Partition pour piano quatre mains par l'auteur. Choudens 1928.

PIERROT (Th.de Banville)

Le   bon pier _ rot___

APPARITION (S Mallarme)

La lu _ ne s'at _ tris _ tait

1882 *PRINTEMPS:* "Salut,printemps..." (Comte de Segur) chœur pour le concours d'essai de Rome. Réduction pour piano 2 mains et chœur de voix de femmes par
M.F. Gaillard. Choudens 1928.

II. ŒUVRES POSTHUMES

1882-1884 (?) Quatre mélodies pour chant et piano; *REVUE MUSICALE,* mai **1926**
PANTOMINE (Paul Verlaine) *CLAIR DE LUNE* (Paul Verlaine) *PIERROT* (Théodore
de Banville) *APPARITION* (Stéphane Mallarmé).

PANTOMINE (Paul Verlaine).

CLAIR DE LUNE (Paul Verlaine) première version.

1912 *KHAMMA,* légende dansée (Concerts Colonne, 15 novembre 1924);partition piano, Durand 1916. L'orchestration est de Charles Koechlin.

Prélude

Modérément animé
(*comme un lointain tumulte*)

1912 *JEUX,* poème dansé de Nijinsky (Théâtre des Champs-Elysées, 15 mai 1913); Durand 1913.
Ms. Bibl. Conservatoire Nº 82 (partition de piano) et Nº 45 (partition d'orchestre) brouillon orchestre, Coll. Legouix.

1911 *LE MARTYRE DE SAINT SÉBASTIEN,* musique de scène pour le mystère de Gabriele d'Annunzio (Théâtre du Châtelet, mai 1911); Durand, 1911.

Prélude

1909-1911 *PREMIÈRE RAPSODIE,* pour orchestre avec clarinette principale en *si* bémol; Durand 1911.

Ms. Bibl. Conservatoire, N.º 41.

Rondes de printemps

(*) Le Contrebasson est écrit a l'octave réelle

Ibéria

Assez animé (dans un rythme alerte mais précis) (♩=176)

1906-1912 *IMAGES,* pour orchestre: *GIGUES,* 1909-1912 (Concerts Colonne, 26 janvier 1913); Durand, 1913; *IBERIA,* 1906-1908 (Concerts Colonne, 20 février 1910); *RONDES DE PRINTEMPS,* 1906-1909 (Concerts Durand, 2 mars 1910); Durand, 1909. Ms. Bibl. Conservatoire Nᵒˢ 29,30,47. Brouillon d'orchestre de *GIGUES,* Coll. Legouix; brouillon orchestre *IBERIA* Coll. Straram.

Gigues

1904 *DANSES,* pour harpe chromatique et orchestre d'instruments à cordes: *DANSE SACRÉE, DANSE PROFANE* (Concerts Colonne, 6 novembre 1904).
Ms. partition orchestre et réduction piano à quatre mains, Bibl. Conservatoire N°27.

III. Dialogue du vent et de la mer

II. Jeux de vagues

LXIII

1903-1905 *LA MER*, trois esquisses symphoniques: *DE L'AUBE A MIDI SUR LA MER, JEUX DE VAGUES, DIALOGUE DU VENT ET DE LA MER* (Concerts Lamoureux, 15 octobre 1905); Durand, 1905. Ms. piano à quatre mains, Bibl. Conservatoire, N? 34; brouillon d'orchestre Bibl. Eastman School of music de Rochester (U.S.A.)

I. De l'aube à midi sur la mer

Nº III. Sirènes

Nº II. Fêtes

Animé et très rythmé

1897-1899 *NOCTURNES (NUAGES, FÊTES, SIRÈNES)*, pour orchestre(Concert Lamoureux, 9 décembre 1900 et 27 octobre 1901); Fromont (Jobert), 1900. Ms. Coll. Jean Jobert; brouillon orchestre, Library of Congress, Washington.

Nᵒ I. Nuages

1892-1902 *PELLÉAS ET MÉLISANDE,* drame lyrique en cinq actes et douze tableaux, paroles de Maurice Maeterlinck (Opéra-Comique, 30 avril 1902); Fromont (Jobert), 1902; puis, Durand, 1905.
Ms. de la partition d'orchestre, en cinq volumes, Bibl. Conservatoire. Brouillon de la troisième scène de l'acte ÏV (septembre-octobre 1893), Coll. Legouix. Ms. partition piano, Bibl. Conservatoire de Boston.

1892-1894 *PRÉLUDE A L'APRÈS-MIDI D'UN FAUNE*, églogue d'après le poème de Stéphane Mallarmé, pour orchestre (Société nationale, 22 décembre 1894); Fromont (Jobert), 1895.

Ms. Partition d'orchestre et réduction piano à quatre mains, Collection Jean Jobert. Brouillon d'orchestre, Collection Alfred Cortot.

1887-1888 *LA DAMOISELLE ÉLUE*, poème lyrique, voix et orchestre; Librairie de l'Art indépendant, 1893; puis, Durand, 1902. (Société nationale, 8 avril 1893). Mise au théâtre (Théâtre lyrique du Vaudeville, 10 décembre 1919).
Ms. brouillon d'orchestre et grande partition Bibl. Conservatoire, N° 8.

1887 *PRINTEMPS,* voix et orchestre; réduction pour voix et piano à quatre mains, publiée en 1904 dans la *REVUE MUSICALE* (de Combarieu), puis par Durand. Orchestration refaite (suite symphonique, sans voix) par Henri Büsser (Société nationale, 18 avril 1913). Durand 1913.

4. ŒUVRES SYMPHONIQUES

1884 *L'ENFANT PRODIGUE*, cantate pour le concours de Rome; Durand, 1884.
Ms. de *CORTÈGE ET AIRS DE DANSE* et du *RÉCIT D'AZAËL*, Bibl. Conservatoire Nᵒˢ 26 et 28 (version refaite en 1907 1908).

Eté 1915 *SONATE* pour violoncelle et piano; Durand, 1916.
Ms. Bibl. Conservatoire N°.42.

1915 *SONATE* pour flûte, alto et harpe; Durand, 1916.
Ms. Bibl. Conservatoire N°. 43.

Hiver 1916-1917 *SONATE* pour piano et violon; Durand, 1917.
Ms. et épreuve corrigée par Debussy, Bibl. Conservatoire N°.44.

3. MUSIQUE DE CHAMBRE

1893 *QUATUOR A CORDES*; Durand, 1894.
Ms. Bibl. Conservatoire Nº 40.

Animé et très décidé 63 = o

1909-1910 *PREMIÈRE RAPSODIE* pour clarinette et piano; Durand, 1910.
Ms. Bibl. Conservatoire Nº 41.
Orchestrée (voir plus loin: Œuvres symphoniques).

1910 *PETITE PIÈCE* pour clarinette en si bémol et piano ou orchestre; Durand, 1910.
Ms. Bibl. Conservatoire Nº 19 (le titre du manuscrit est *MORCEAU A DÉCHIFFRER POUR LE CONCOURS DE CLARINETTE DE 1910*).

LII

XI. pour les Arpèges composés

dolce e lusigando

XII. pour les accords

Décidé, rythmé, sans lourdeur

1915 *EN BLANC ET NOIR,* trois pièces pour deux pianos à quatre mains; Durand 1915.
Ms. Bibl. Conservatoire N.º 11.

I. Avec emportement (♩. = 66)

VII. pour les degrés chromatiques

Scherzando animato assai

VIII. pour les agréments

Lento, rubato e leggiero

IX. pour les notes répétées

X. pour les sonorités opposées

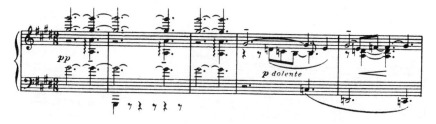

III. pour les Quartes

Andantino con moto

IV. pour les Sixtes

Lento

V. pour les Octaves

Joyeux et emporté, librement rythmé

VI. pour les huit doigts

Vivamente, molto leggiero e legato

Novembre 1914 *BERCEUSE HÉROÏQUE POUR RENDRE HOMMAGE A S.M.ALBERT Ier DE BELGIQUE ET A SES SOLDATS;* Durand, 1915.
Orchestration de Debussy (Concerts Colonne-Lamoureux 26 octobre 1915).
Ms.partition de piano Bibl.Consevatoire N? 3; Ms.partition d'orchestre,Bibl.de l'Opéra

Eté 1915 *DOUZE ÉTUDES;* 1er volume: *POUR LES CINQ DOIGTS, POUR LES TIERCES, POUR LES QUARTES, POUR LES SIXTES, POUR LES OCTAVES, POUR LES HUIT DOIGTS;*
    2me volume: *POUR LES DEGRÉS CHROMATIQUES, POUR LES AGRÉMENTS, POUR LES NOTES RÉPÉTÉES, POUR LES SONORITÉS OPPOSÉES, POUR LES ARPÈGES, POUR LES ACCORDS;* Durand, 1916. Ms. Bibl. Conservatoire N? 12.

I. pour les "cinq doigts" *d'après Monsieur Czerny*

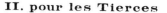

II. pour les Tierces

Pour que la nuit soit propice

Lent et expressif (♩. = 48)

Pour la danseuse aux crotales

Andantino *(souple et sans rigueur)* (♩ = 112)

Pour l'Egyptienne

Très modéré (♩ = 58)

Pour remercier la pluie au matin

Modérément animé (♩ = 60)
sempre leggierissimo

Feux d'Artifice

Modérément animé
léger, égal, et lointain

1913 *LA BOITE A JOUJOUX;* Durand, 1913.
Orchestrée et transformée en ballet sur un livret d'André Hellé (Théâtre lyrique du Vaudeville, 10 décembre 1919.)
Ms. partition de piano et partition d'orchestre, Bibl. Conservatoire, N° 4.

Prélude - le sommeil de la boîte

Très modéré (♩ - 60)

1914 *SIX EPIGRAPHES ANTIQUES,* pour piano à quatre mains (existent aussi à deux mains, transcrites par Debussy): *POUR INVOQUER PAN DIEU DU VENT D'ÉTÉ, POUR UN TOMBEAU SANS NOM, POUR QUE LA NUIT SOIT PROPICE, POUR LA DANSEUSE AUX CROTALES, POUR L'EGYPTIENNE, POUR REMERCIER LA PLUIE AU MATIN,* Durand, 1915.
Ms. des deux versions, Bibl. Conservatoire, N° 9.

Pour invoquer Pan

Modéré dans le style d'une pastorale (♩ = 80)

Pour un tombeau sans nom

Triste et lent (♩ = 60)

Hommage à S. Pickwick Esq. P. P. M. P. C.

Canope

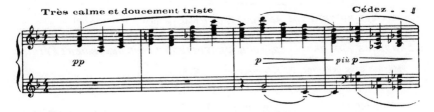

Les tierces alternées

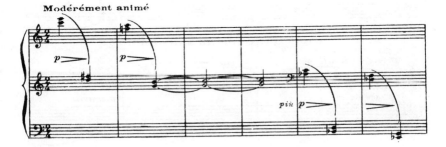

General Lavine - eccentric

Dans le style et le mouvement d'un Cake-Walk

La terrasse des audiences du clair de lune

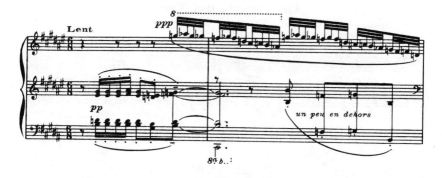

Ondine

Feuilles mortes

Lent et mélancolique

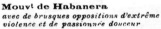

La Puerta del Vino

Les Fées sont d'exquises danseuses

Bruyères

La Cathédrale engloutie

Profondément calme (*Dans une brume doucement sonore*)

La danse de Puck

Capricieux et léger (♩ = 138)

Minstrels

Modéré (*Nerveux et avec humour*)

p les "gruppetti" sur le temps

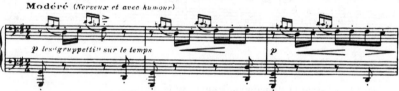

1910-1913 *DOUZE PRÉLUDES,* 2me livre: *BROUILLARDS, FEUILLES MORTES, LA PUERTA DEL VINO, LES FÉES SONT D'EXQUISES DANSEUSES, BRUYÈRES, GÉNÉRAL LAVINE ECCENTRIC, LA TERRASSE DES AUDIENCES AU CLAIR DE LUNE, ONDINE, HOMMAGE A S. PICKWICK ESQ. P. P. M. P. C., CANOPE, LES TIERCES ALTERNÉES, FEUX D'ARTIFICE;* Durand, 1913.
Ms. Bibl. Conservatoire N° 39.

Brouillards

Modéré
extrêmement égal et léger
la m.g. un peu en valeur sur la m.d.

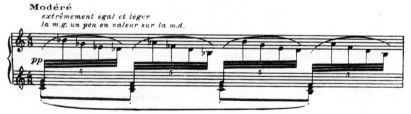

Des pas sur la neige

Ce qu'a vu le vent d'ouest

La fille aux cheveux de lin

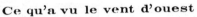

La sérénade interrompue

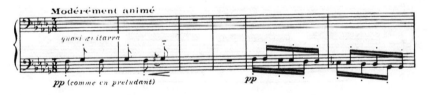
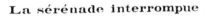

Voiles

Le vent dans la plaine

Les sons et les parfums tournent dans l'air du soir

Les collines d'Anacapri

Golliwog's cake walk

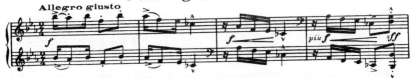

1909 *HOMMAGE A HAYDN; REVUE S. I. M.* janvier 1910; Durand 1911.

1910 *LA PLUS QUE LENTE,* valse; Durand, 1910.
Orchestration de Debussy; Durand, 1912.
Ms. des deux versions Bibl. Conservatoire N° 36.

1910 *DOUZE PRÉLUDES,* 1er livre: *DANSEUSES DE DELPHES, VOILES, LE VENT DANS LA PLAINE, LES SONS ET LES PARFUMS TOURNENT DANS L'AIR DU SOIR, LES COLLINES D'ANACAPRI, DES PAS SUR LA NEIGE, CE QU'A VU LE VENT D'OUEST, LA FILLE AUX CHEVEUX DE LIN. LA SÉRÉNADE INTERROM-PUE, LA CATHÉDRALE ENGLOUTIE, LA DANSE DE PUCK, MINSTRELS;* Durand, 1910
Ms. Coll. Alfred Cortot.
Orchestration de *LA CATHÉDRALE ENGLOUTIE* par Henri Büsser (Concerts Straram, 28 avril 1927).

Danseuses de Delphes

Jimbo's lullaby

Serenade for the doll

Snow is dancing

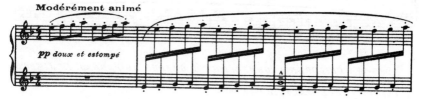

The little shepherd

Et la lune descend...

Poissons d'or

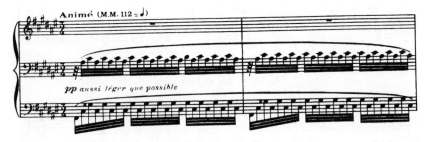

1906-1908 *CHILDREN'S CORNER: DOCTOR GRADUS AD PARNASSUM, JIMBO'S LULLABY, SERENADE FOR THE DOLL, SNOW IS DANCING, THE LITTLE SHEPHERD, GOLLIWOG'S CAKE-WALK;* Durand, 1908.

Orchestration d'André Caplet (Cercle musical, 25 mars 1911).

Ms. Bibl. Conservatoire N° 7.

Gradus ad Parnassum

Hommage à Rameau

Lent et grave
(dans le style d'une sarabande mais sans rigueur)

pp expressif et doucement soutenu

Mouvement

Animé (avec une légèreté fantasque mais précise)

pp

plus pp *la m.d. en valeur sur la m.g.*

1907 *IMAGES*, 2ᵐᵉ série: *CLOCHES A TRAVERS LES FEUILLES, ET LA LUNE DESCEND SUR LE TEMPLE QUI FUT, POISSONS D'OR;* Durand, 1908.

Cloches à travers les feuilles

Lent (M.M. 92 = ♪)

doucement sonore

un peu en dehors

pp

pp

m.g.

1903 *D'UN CAHIER D'ESQUISSES;* publié d'abord sous le titre *ESQUISSE* dans *L'ALBUM DE MUSIQUE*, Librairie Manzy-Joyant, mars 1904; puis par Schott frères (Bruxelles) 1904

Juillet 1904 *MASQUES;* Durand, 1904.
Ms. Bibl. Conservatoire N° 14.

Eté 1904 *L'ISLE JOYEUSE;* Durand, 1904.
Orchestration de Molinari (Concerts Colonne, 11 novembre 1925).
Ms. Bibl. Conservatoire N° 18.

1905 *IMAGES,* 1ʳᵉ série: *REFLETS DANS L'EAU, HOMMAGE A RAMEAU, MOUVEMENT,* Durand, 1905.
Ms. Bibl. Conservatoire N°ˢ 15, 16, 17.

Reflets dans l'eau

XXXIV

Toccata

1903(?) ***ESTAMPES: PAGODES, SOIRÉE DANS GRENADE, JARDINS SOUS LA PLUIE;*** **Durand, 1903.**

Ms. Bibl. Conservatoire, Nº 10.

Pagodes

Soirée dans Grenade

Jardins sous la pluie

1891 *MARCHE DES ANCIENS COMTES DE ROSS*, pour piano à quatre mains; Choudens 1891; publiée ensuite sous le titre de *MARCHE ÉCOSSAISE (SUR UN THÈME POPU-LAIRE)* Fromont (Jobert), 1903.

Orchestration de Debussy.

Ms. partition d'orchestre chez Legouix.

1896-1901(?) *POUR LE PIANO: PRÉLUDE, SARABANDE, TOCCATA;* Fromont (Jobert), 1901. *SARABANDE,* orchestrée par Maurice Ravel (Concerts Lamoureux, 18 mars 1903).

Prélude

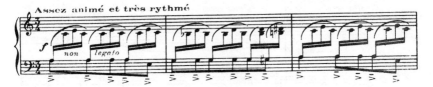

Sarabande

Menuet

Clair de lune

Passepied

1891 *MAZURKA*; Hamelle, 1904; Fromont (Jobert), 1905.

1890(?)*TARENTELLE STYRIENNE*, publiée d'abord sous ce titre chez Choudens 1890, puis sous le titre *DANSE* chez Fromont (Jobert), 1903.
Orchestration (*DANSE*) par Maurice Ravel (Concerts Lamoureux 18 Mars 1923).

1890(?)*VALSE ROMANTIQUE*; Choudens, 1390; puis, Fromont (Jobert), 1903.

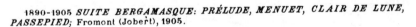

1890(?)*NOCTURNE*; publié dans le *Figaro musical* puis par la Sirene musicale janvier 1903

1890-1905 *SUITE BERGAMASQUE: PRÉLUDE, MENUET, CLAIR DE LUNE, PASSEPIED*; Fromont (Jobert), 1905.

Prélude

Ballet

1890(?)*REVERIE;* Choudens, 1890; puis Fromont (Jobert), 1905.

1890(?)*BALLADE SLAVE,* publiée d'abord sous ce titre chez Choudens 1890, puis sous le titre *BALLADE* chez Fromont (Jobert), 1903.

Cortège

Menuet

2.— ŒUVRES DE PIANO
(sauf indications contraires ces œuvres sont écrites pour piano à deux mains)

1888 *DEUX ARABESQUES;* Durand, 1891.
Ms. Bibl. Conservatoire N? 2.

1ʳᵉ Arabesque

2ᵐᵉ Arabesque

1889 *PETITE SUITE,* pour piano à quatre mains: *EN BATEAU, CORTÈGE, MENUET, BALLET;* Durand, 1889.
Transcription d'orchestre par Henri Büsser.
Ms Bibl. Conservatoire N? 20.

En bateau

Eventail

Décembre 1915 *NOËL LES ENFANTS QUI N'ONT PLUS DE MAISON* (Claude Debussy),
Durand, **1916**. Version chant et piano, version chœur d'enfants à deux voix et piano.
Ms. des deux versions Bibl. Conservatoire, N° 35.

Été 1913 *TROIS POÈMES DE STÉPHANE MALLARMÉ: SOUPIR, PLACET FUTILE, ÉVENTAIL;* Durand, 1913.

Ms. Bibl. Conservatoire N⁰ 37.

Soupir

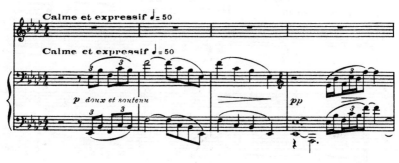

Placet futile

Ballade que feit Villon à la requeste de sa mère...

Da_me du ciel, re_gen_te ter_ri_en_ne,

Ballade des femmes de Paris

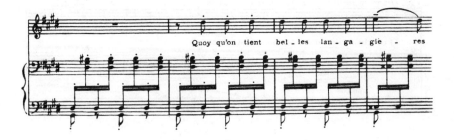

Quoy qu'on tient bel_les lan_ga_gie_res

III.— Yver, vous n'estes qu'un villain

Mai 1910 *TROIS BALLADES DE FRANÇOIS VILLON: BALLADE DE VILLON A S'AMYE, BALLADE QUE FEIT VILLON A LA REQUESTE DE SA MÈRE POUR PRIER NOSTRE DAME, BALLADE DES FEMMES DE PARIS;* Durand 1911.

Orchestration de Debussy, octobre 1910 (Concerts Sechiari, 5 mars 1911).

Ms. des deux versions, Bibl. Conservatoire, N° 1.

Ballade de Villon à s'amye

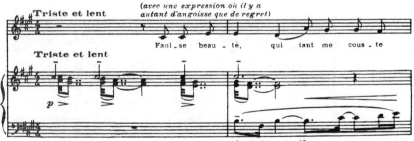

XXIII

1908 *TROIS CHANSONS DE CHARLES D'ORLÉANS*, pour voix mixtes, sans accompagnement : *DIEU, QU'IL LA FAIT BON REGARDER; QUAND J'AI OUY LE TABOURIN; YVER, VOUS N'ESTES QU'UN VILLAIN;* Durand, 1908 (Concerts Colonne, 9 avril 1909). Ms. Bibl. Conservatoire, N° 5.

I.– Dieu! qu'il la fait bon regarder!

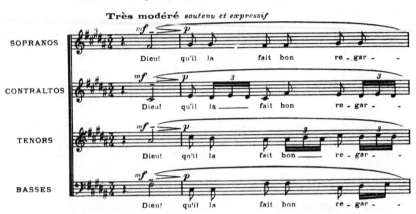

II.– Quand j'ai ouy le tabourin

1904-1910 *LE PROMENOIR DES DEUX AMANTS* (Tristan l'Hermitte): *AUPRÈS DE CETTE GROTTE SOMBRE* (Cette mélodie n'est autre que *LA GROTTE* des *TROIS CHANSONS DE FRANCE*, 1904), *CROIS MON CONSEIL, JE TREMBLE·EN VOYANT TON VISAGE*; Durand, 1910.

Orchestration de Louis Beydts (Concerts Pasdeloup, 15 octobre 1927).

Ms. Bibl. Cons. N° 38.

Crois mon conseil, chère Climène...

Je tremble en voyant ton visage...

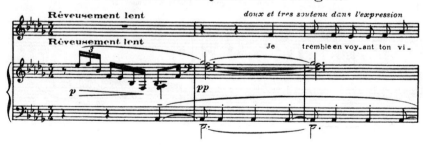

Au - pres de cet-te grot-te som - bre Où l'on res-pire un-

Rondel: *Pour ce que Plaisance est morte...*

Pour ce que Plaisance est mor _ _ te

1904 *TROIS CHANSONS DE FRANCE*: *RONDEL* (Charles d'Orléans), *LA GROTTE*
(Tristan l'Hermitte), *RONDEL* (Charles d'Orléans); Durand, 1904.
Ms. Bibl. Cons. No 6.

Rondel: *Le temps a laissié son manteau...*

Joyeux et animé

Le temps a lais - sié son manteau De vent, de froi-dure_ et de

La grotte

Très lent et très doux

Le Faune

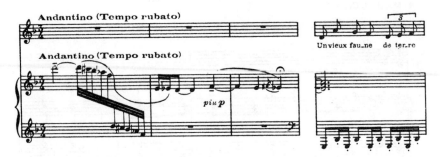

Un vieux fau_ne   de ter_re

Colloque sentimental

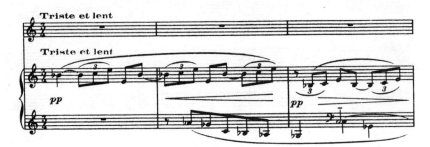

Dans   le_vieux parc so_ li _ taire   et   gla_cé   Deux

La chevelure

Le Tombeau des Naïades

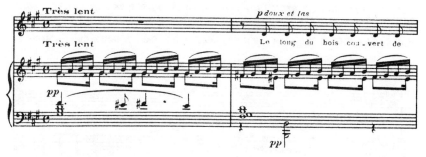

1904 *FÊTES GALANTES* (Paul Verlaine), 2me recueil: *LES INGÉNUS, LE FAUNE,
COLLOQUE SENTIMENTAL*; Durand, 1904. Orchestration du *FAUNE* par Roland Manuel
(Concerts Colonne, 27 janvier 1924); orchestration du *COLLOQUE SENTIMENTAL* par Louis
Beydts (Concerts Lamoureux, 12 janvier 1929).

Ms. Bibl. Cons. N? 13; autre ms. (avec quelques corrections) du *Colloque sentimental* chez
Legouix.

Les Ingénus

De soir

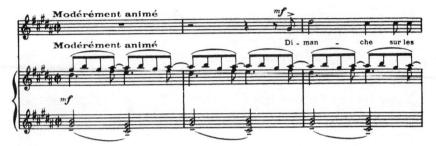

1897 *CHANSONS DE BILITIS* (Pierre Louys): *LA FLÛTE DE PAN, LA CHEVELURE, LE TOMBEAU DES NAÏADES;* Fromont (Jobert), 1899. Orchestration de Maurice Delage (Concerts Colonne, 20 février 1926).
Ms. de *LA FLÛTE DE PAN* et de *LA CHEVELURE* Bibl. Cons. Collection Charles Malherbe.

La flûte de Pan

De fleurs

1892-93 *PROSES LYRIQUES* (Claude Debussy): *DE RÊVE, DE GRÊVE, DE FLEURS, DE SOIR*; Fromont (Jobert), 1895. Debussy aurait écrit pour *DE GRÊVE* et *DE SOIR* une orchestration restée inconnue; les quatre *PROSES* ont été orchestrées par Roger Ducasse (Concerts Colonne, 5 décembre 1926).

De rêve

De grève

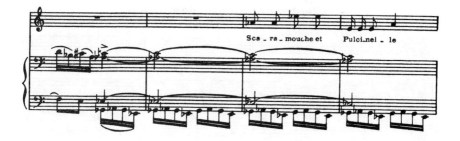

Sca _ ra _ mouche et   Pulci_nel _ le

Clair de lune

Très modéré

pp très doux

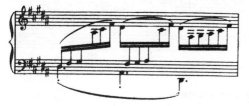

p

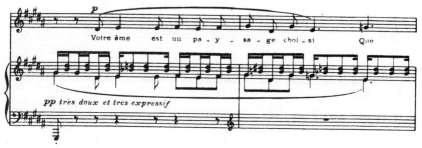

Votre âme   est un pa _ y _ sa _ ge choi _ si   Que

pp très doux et très expressif

L'échelonnement des haies

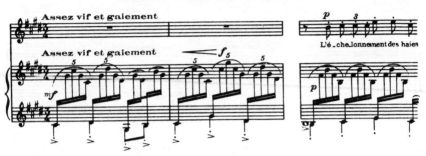

Assez vif et gaiement

L'é_chelonnement des haies

1892 *FÊTES GALANTES* (Paul Verlaine), 1ᵉʳ recueil: *EN SOURDINE, FANTOCHES, CLAIR DE LUNE;* Fromont, 1903 (Jobert).

En sourdine

Rêveusement lent

Cal _ mesdans le

pp doux et expressif

Fantoches

Allegretto scherzando

f > p

Le son du cor s'afflige...

1891 *LES ANGÉLUS* (G. le Roy); Hamelle, 1901.

1891 *DANS LE JARDIN* (Paul Gravolet), du recueil *LES FRISSONS*; Hamelle, 1905.

1891 *TROIS MÉLODIES* (Paul Verlaine) *LA MER EST PLUS BELLE, LE SON DU COR S'AFFLIGE, L'ÉCHELONNEMENT DES HAIES*; Hamelle, 1901. Les deux dernières ont passé en 1907 chez Fromont (Jobert) en échange de *SOIR* et *D'UNE PRISON* de Gabriel Fauré.

La mer est plus belle...

Spleen

1891 *DEUX ROMANCES* (Paul Bourget): *ROMANCE (L'AME ÉVAPORÉE), LES CLOCHES*
Durand, 1891. Ms. Bibl. Cons. N°. 46.

Romance

Les Cloches

L'ombre des arbres...

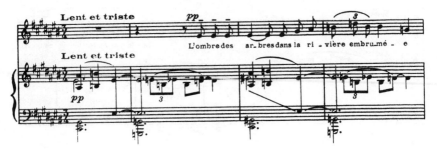

Chevaux de bois

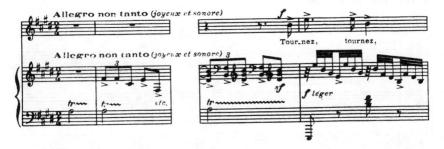

Green

La Mort des Amants

1888 *ARIETTES, PAYSAGES BELGES* et *AQUARELLES* (Paul Verlaine), six mélo-
dies: *C'EST L'EXTASE, IL PLEURE DANS MON CŒUR, L'OMBRE DES ARBRES,
CHEVAUX DE BOIS, GREEN, SPLEEN;* Veuve Girod, 1888; puis sous le titre *ARIETTES
OUBLIÉES,* Fromont, (Jobert) 1903.
Ms. de *C'EST L'EXTASE, CHEVAUX DE BOIS, GREEN, SPLEEN* chez Legouix.

C'est l'extase...

Il pleure dans mon cœur...

Le Jet d'Eau

Recueillement

1887-1889 *CINQ POÈMES* (Charles Baudelaire): *LE BALCON, HARMONIE DU SOIR, LE JET D'EAU, RECUEILLEMENT, LA MORT DES AMANTS;* édition par souscription, sans nom de firme (Librairie de l'Art indépendant), 1890; puis Durand, 1902.

LE JET D'EAU orchestré par Debussy en janvier 1907 (Concerts Colonne, 24 février 1907); partition d'orchestre, Durand, Copyright 1907.

LE BALCON orchestré par Louis Aubert.

Ms. Bibl. Cons. Paris, Nᵒˢ 21 à 25 (chant et piano) et Nᵒ 33 (orchestration du *JET D'EAU*).

Le Balcon

Harmonie du Soir

V

Voici que le printemps

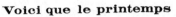

Andantino

p et légèrement

Voi - ci que le prin - temps, ce fils lé - ger d'A - vril

Paysage sentimental

Allegretto ma non troppo

pp legg.

p doux

Le ciel d'hi - ver, si doux, si

pp

IV

1880-1883 *MANDOLINE* (Paul Verlaine); Revue Illustrée, 1ᵉʳ septembre 1890 (avec un dessin de Willette); puis Durand, 1890. Orchestration de Louis Beydts (Concerts Lamoureux, 12 janvier 1929).

1880-1883 Trois mélodies *LA BELLE AU BOIS DORMANT* (Vincent Hyspa); *VOICI QUE LE PRINTEMPS* (Paul Bourget), appelée aussi *ROMANCE ; PAYSAGE SENTIMENTAL* (Paul Bourget); Société nouvelle d'éditions musicales, ancienne maison Paul Dupont, 1902; puis Sirène musicale.

La belle au bois dormant

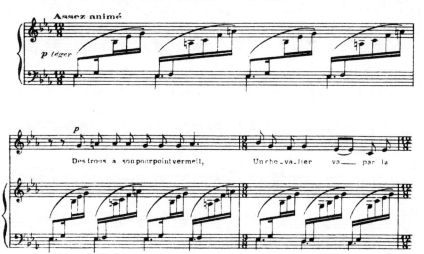

1. ŒUVRES VOCALES

(sauf indication contraire, ces œuvres sont écrites pour chant et piano)

1876(?) *NUIT D'ÉTOILES* (Théodore de Banville); Société artistique d'éditions, d'estampes et de musique (E. Bulla), 1882; puis Coutarel, 1918.

1878(?) *BEAU SOIR* (Paul Bourget); Veuve Girod, 1891; puis Fromont (Jobert).

1878(?) *FLEUR DES BLÉS* (André Girod); Veuve Girod, 1891; puis Leduc, 1919.

AMERICAN CLIPPER SHIPS: 1833–1858, Octavius T. Howe & Frederick C. Matthews. Fully-illustrated, encyclopedic review of 352 clipper ships from the period of America's greatest maritime supremacy. Introduction. 109 halftones. 5 black-and-white line illustrations. Index. Total of 928pp. 5⅜ × 8½.
25115-2, 25116-0 Pa., Two-vol. set $17.90

TOWARDS A NEW ARCHITECTURE, Le Corbusier. Pioneering manifesto by great architect, near legendary founder of "International School." Technical and aesthetic theories, views on industry, economics, relation of form to function, "mass-production spirit," much more. Profusely illustrated. Unabridged translation of 13th French edition. Introduction by Frederick Etchells. 320pp. 6⅛ × 9¼. (Available in U.S. only)
25023-7 Pa. $8.95

THE BOOK OF KELLS, edited by Blanche Cirker. Inexpensive collection of 32 full-color, full-page plates from the greatest illuminated manuscript of the Middle Ages, painstakingly reproduced from rare facsimile edition. Publisher's Note. Captions. 32pp. 9⅜ × 12¼.
24345-1 Pa. $4.95

BEST SCIENCE FICTION STORIES OF H. G. WELLS, H. G. Wells. Full novel *The Invisible Man*, plus 17 short stories: "The Crystal Egg," "Aepyornis Island," "The Strange Orchid," etc. 303pp. 5⅜ × 8½. (Available in U.S. only)
21531-8 Pa. $4.95

AMERICAN SAILING SHIPS: Their Plans and History, Charles G. Davis. Photos, construction details of schooners, frigates, clippers, other sailcraft of 18th to early 20th centuries—plus entertaining discourse on design, rigging, nautical lore, much more. 137 black-and-white illustrations. 240pp. 6⅛ × 9¼.
24658-2 Pa. $5.95

ENTERTAINING MATHEMATICAL PUZZLES, Martin Gardner. Selection of author's favorite conundrums involving arithmetic, money, speed, etc., with lively commentary. Complete solutions. 112pp. 5⅜ × 8½. 25211-6 Pa. $2.95

THE WILL TO BELIEVE, HUMAN IMMORTALITY, William James. Two books bound together. Effect of irrational on logical, and arguments for human immortality. 402pp. 5⅜ × 8½. 20291-7 Pa. $7.50

THE HAUNTED MONASTERY and THE CHINESE MAZE MURDERS, Robert Van Gulik. 2 full novels by Van Gulik continue adventures of Judge Dee and his companions. An evil Taoist monastery, seemingly supernatural events; overgrown topiary maze that hides strange crimes. Set in 7th-century China. 27 illustrations. 328pp. 5⅜ × 8½. 23502-5 Pa. $5.95

CELEBRATED CASES OF JUDGE DEE (DEE GOONG AN), translated by Robert Van Gulik. Authentic 18th-century Chinese detective novel; Dee and associates solve three interlocked cases. Led to Van Gulik's own stories with same characters. Extensive introduction. 9 illustrations. 237pp. 5⅜ × 8½.
23337-5 Pa. $4.95

Prices subject to change without notice.
Available at your book dealer or write for free catalog to Dept. GI, Dover Publications, Inc., 31 East 2nd St., Mineola, N.Y. 11501. Dover publishes more than 175 books each year on science, elementary and advanced mathematics, biology, music, art, literary history, social sciences and other areas.

seems to be entirely concerned with accuracy of expression. It is more rapid and flowing than the Wagnerian declamation, more uniform too, and more intimately connected with the music. It is faithfully modelled upon the simplicity of our gentle tongue. Though closely akin to the spoken word, it is yet tuneful; it merges in the accompanying symphony, tingeing it with the shimmering reflections of its harmonies and sonorities. The symphony itself is marvellously discreet and rich, I hardly know how to describe it. The harmonic concatenations defy analysis, yet they sound natural and clear. The tonality is often impossible to determine, and yet one has the impression of tonality. The short, arresting, suggestive *motifs* are no sooner formulated, than they vanish to make way for others, and then flash back for an instant. The musical subject-matter is subdivided to the utmost degree, yet nothing could be more uniform or consistent. This music makes not the slightest concession to tradition, convention, or custom; it repudiates all that is hackneyed, showy, or commonplace; it seems to roam with the same vagabond freedom as thought itself; and yet it has a proportion, a balance and a progression of its own. It has a form which is subject to the laws of symmetry, as all music should be; but this symmetry remains a secret; one is conscious of it without being able to ascertain its form....'

The following opinion expressed by Carraud must have sounded startling in 1902:

'In order to satisfy the noblest and most courageous of artistic ideals, M. Debussy has created a music of his own. His work overflows with it, everything in it is music. The words form a framework which sustains but never dominates. Significant expression seems to be the sole aim: yet as a matter of fact, it remains a means. The music exists for the sake of its own beauty, its own delight. M. Debussy takes his place, more definitely even than Wagner, amongst the sensualists in music, of whom Mozart was the greatest.'

A few weeks later, in the review *Minerva* of the 15th of July, Gaston Carraud declared that the composer was a classicist, a statement which at that time seemed paradoxical.

'M. Debussy is really a classical composer. I am not speaking paradoxically. After the unbridled romanticism to which music had fallen a prey, he has the lucidity, the tact, the restraint, and the sense of proportion that characterize the classical composers. He has the same controlled emotion as they; he has their charm and dignity of expression, their scorn of emphasis, exaggeration, and mere effect.'

When 'Pelléas' was revived in the beginning of the season of 1902-3, Carraud again extolled Debussy's genius in the *Liberté* of the 1st of November 1902, in the following enthusiastic terms:

'The music of an artist who belongs to the same lineage as the great men of every type; one of those who have been able to discern the

touching charm of suffering humanity rather than its contortions; who
have listened to its songs rather than to its cries; who have expressed
human emotion in the most novel, original, exquisitely beautiful, and
intense manner; one who has also been able to interpret the mystery of
the atmosphere and the horizon, and to express their maternal sympathy with us poor human beings. . . .'

The most varied echoes resounded throughout the musical
reviews. Hugues Imbert, whose god was Brahms, and who was
consequently incapable of appreciating the importance of 'Pelléas
et Mélisande', was careful not to give a definite verdict in the *Guide
Musical*. He confined himself to expressing his uneasiness with
regard to this

'disconcerting work which borders on the morbid. It is thoughtfully
and carefully worked out according to principles which can be dimly
traced, yet its form lacks definite outlines, it is as mysterious as the
poem . . . some musicians declare it to be a work of art, others say that
it is a mistake and that it will bewilder the public. . . . Yet, in spite of
everything, in spite of oneself, one is carried along into the action of
the drama—a work which inevitably raises the question: "Whither are
we tending?" '

Auguste Mangeot published a sympathetic report in his review,
the *Monde Musical*, though his article relegated Debussy's score
to a role of secondary and quite external importance. He gave the
composer high praise for having

'managed to create *invertebrate* music to a structureless drama. Just as
the characters have neither minds, nor energy, nor wills, the music has
neither rhythm, nor time, nor tonality. It is as vague and indefinite and
uncertain as they are. What can one put around a tapestry? Nothing
but a border. M. Debussy's music supplies such a border. He has made
something very discreet and intentionally monotonous, calculated not
to offend the eye—I mean the ear. There are a multitude of charming
little transient details, the colours are uncommon, but harmonious; it
is never showy, and rarely melodious; in a word, it is perfectly suited to
the character of the work. The orchestra is quite right not to worry
about what is happening on the stage, for most of the time nothing
happens. It does not even notice when the curtain falls, but flows on
while the scenery is being changed, without a single jerk or jolt. It is
never hackneyed, but never eccentric; always discreet, restrained, calm,
innocuous, restful, like white clouds. Now and then, a sudden ray of
sunshine brings some outline into relief. That means that something
has happened on the stage. A spark has suddenly flashed forth and is
reflected in the orchestra like the light of a lantern in the water. . . .'

In the *Courrier Musical*, which, in those days, was edited by
sincere, independent-minded artists, two articles appeared, one on

the 15th of May by Victor Debay, the other by Paul Locard on the 1st of June. In the first article Victor Debay described very candidly the state of mind of an unbiased person on hearing the new music drama.

'A really original and individual work, in listening to which one must renounce one's tastes, habits, and theories. I approached it with an open mind, but quite determined not to yield to any influences, not to allow myself to be affected either by the enthusiasm of the audience or by the criticisms in the *couloir*. I confess that at first I was rather disconcerted. Even in the so-called music of the future, we are accustomed to find more definite forms and clearer outlines, well-defined formulas which reappear periodically, at times tyrannically, and impose themselves on our attention, in order to fix the composer's creative projects in our memories. Here, we find ourselves at once in quite a different sonorous world. The very first pages take us by surprise. For, slaves of routine that we are, we seek in vain for the elements that other types of music have always given us; and, so intent are we on this pursuit of things that are not to be found here, that we at first fail to perceive what this music really contains. During the first scenes, I lost my way, like Mélisande and Golaud, in the forest where they met. But gradually the spell began to work, and I was able to understand the perfect relationship, the intimate union, that exists between the work of the poet and that of the composer; I realized that the musician's aim was to evoke rather than describe. To a dream poem, M. Debussy has written dream music, exquisitely melancholy, so subtle that it is sometimes morbid. It produces the exact effect he intended, namely: to help us to escape from all that is commonplace and conventional, from real life; without ever losing sight of his artistic mission to arouse our emotions, which he achieves by novel means entirely his own. . . .'

In an article written after one of the first performances, Paul Locard mentions that on that evening 'the musicians had managed to monopolize the theatre and applauded with an enthusiasm that paralysed all opposition'. In the audience he recognized Alexandre Guilmant and Vincent d'Indy, the founders of the Schola Cantorum, Pierre de Bréville, Charles Koechlin, and Édouard Colonne. He goes on to speak of those musicians

'who are indifferent, if not definitely hostile to M. Debussy's work because of what they call his contempt for form, his vagueness of line, rhythm, and tonality—this last more apparent than real—and his obstinate dissonances; in a word, the mongrel imperfections of an art that has been debased and distorted to suit the requirements of literature. People forget that music does not follow the same rule as philosophy, a science in which every new system destroys the preceding ones. M. Debussy's formula does not claim to be universal, and it leaves ample room beside it for pure musical thought with its spacious, logical

forms. Besides, "Pelléas et Mélisande" does contain themes and rhythms. I may add, that the most distressing dissonances are softened by the ingenious and charming blending of the timbres, and that one could not wish for a more accurate declamation, or a musical idiom that would reflect more faithfully the remote, vague chiaroscuro of the poem. . . .'

Paul Locard concludes his judicious critique with an ironical appeal for peace and prudence:

'Timorous souls need not be uneasy. The composer of "Pelléas et Mélisande" is an excellent musician. He knows what he wants and where he is going. Perhaps for that very reason, there may be danger in imitating him, if one is not very sure of oneself. It will be more prudent to wait.'

There were numerous articles full of intelligent appreciation in the non-musical reviews. In the *Revue de Paris* (June 1902) André Hallays protested against the reproach of lack of melody levelled at Debussy. In the *Mercure de France* Jean Marnold once more emphasized the fact that his harmony, which was considered so revolutionary, was really logical and based on the unrestricted use of natural resonance. He also pointed out that its derivation was normal: 'Without Schubert, Chopin, and perhaps Schumann, without Liszt, Wagner, Franck, Fauré, and Vincent d'Indy, Claude Debussy's harmony would have been not only unrealizable, but unthinkable.' Then, taking advantage of the fact that the production of 'Pelléas' at the Opéra-Comique coincided with the first performance of 'Götterdämmerung' in Paris, he went on to remark that 'the music of the future gradually becomes the music of the past, and the art of sounds proceeds imperturbably on its way. According as it advances, one theory after another collapses; the forgeries of the *epigonoi*, the parodies of the pedagogues and their docile pupils, perish along with the systems. Nothing remains standing but the masterpieces which serve as glorious landmarks and testify to the distance that has been covered'.

Another article in the *Revue de Paris*, from the pen of Fernand Gregh, anticipated the coming of Debussyism, and distinguished between the artist and his imitators. The writer asked himself wherein lay the bewitching charm of 'Pelléas et Mélisande'. He did not attribute it to the innovations or the *tours de force* that shocked the adherents of the old school, and aroused the rather aggressive joy of the advanced musicians. He prophesied an inevitable evolution in this respect:

'The principle of the violation of laws will be codified some day, and will become a law in its turn. The forbidden harmonies with which Claude Debussy has experimented will be accepted in time, and will

eventually be employed to prohibit the Debussys of the future from utilizing other harmonies of which we have no conception. Thus, the most revolutionary innovations will gradually become reactionary *formulas*. "Pelléas" in its turn will grow old, will be imitated and vulgarized. . . . But there is something in "Pelléas" that will not grow old . . . that deep, natural, almost divine element which, because it was alive and young when the composer put it into his music, will always remain so: the soul which we find expressed there, the human feeling that informs the work.'

Two other critiques are particularly noteworthy, both on account of their intrinsic value and the personality of the writers: the article by Paul Dukas in the *Gazette des Arts*, and that by Vincent d'Indy in *L'Occident*.

Paul Dukas regretted that he had to treat as a distinct art music that was so closely incorporated with the action of the drama. In reply to the statements of certain journalists who had not been able to discern any melody, rhythm, harmony, or thematic development in the new score, he declared that Debussy's music was on the contrary very melodic, very rhythmic, and both novel and daring in its harmonic treatment.

'But this melody, this rhythm, and this harmony are not the kind which have become public property owing to the constant imitation of the masters. They are his own, especially the harmony, in respect of which there have been protests against his continual infringement of the rules; whereas, in reality, his harmony is simply a skilful expansion of recognized principles. The same is true of his economical use of thematic development, the plan of which is not merely musical, but profoundly psychological, and entirely novel. The same can be said of his logical orchestral commentary, which maintains an admirable unity. All these elements are his own, entirely his own, and it is amusing that he should be blamed for them, when his confrères have so often been reproached with contrary faults which, in the present case, seem to be regarded as praiseworthy qualities.'

It is possible that Vincent d'Indy may have been somewhat shocked by the first performance, given his whole-hearted admiration for certain types of musical structure and his love of symphonic development. He is said to have betrayed his feelings during one of the intervals by exclaiming: 'It has no form; it cannot live!' The anecdote is not unlikely. But the verdict he expressed in the little review, *L'Occident*, was very different—most enthusiastic in fact. He began by giving a careful definition of this astounding work:

' "Pelléas" is obviously neither an opera, nor a lyrical drama, in the ordinary sense of the term, neither is it a realistic play nor a Wagnerian

drama. It is both less and more than these. It is less, because, most of
the time, the music itself plays a secondary role, the role that illumina-
tion plays in medieval manuscripts, or polychromy in the sculpture of
that period. It is more, because, unlike modern opera, or even the
lyrical drama, the text is here the principal interest. The sonorous
rendering of that text is marvellously adapted to the inflections of the
language; and it is steeped in many coloured waves of music which
enhance its design, reveal its hidden meaning, and intensify its expression, whilst always allowing the words to be visible through the fluid
element that envelops them. . . .'

The symphony composer, who was naturally rather disappointed
that Debussy should have deliberately renounced the symphonic
plan in his operatic music, proceeded to draw a parallel between
Debussy's art and that of Monteverdi. He pointed out that,
although an interval of three centuries separated them, the masterpiece of each of these composers had met with the same measure
of misunderstanding. It was at the beginning of this article that
Vincent d'Indy pronounced his very vigorous censure on musical
critics, the following sentence of which has often been quoted:
'With the exception of bankers and politicians, I do not believe
there is a sorrier or more useless calling in the world than that of
critic. . . .'

One other article is often quoted in connexion with 'Pelléas'—
that of Romain Rolland, which appeared in the Berlin review,
Morgen, on the 29th of November 1907. The original French
version was published in 1908 in the author's book *Musiciens
d'aujourd'hui*. This brief, but very remarkable study indicates the
important place Debussy's opera occupies in the history of music,
and points out the features of the work that are modern and French
as well as its general musical characteristics.

Various writers undertook a criticism of the critics, as did
Debussy himself in the course of an interview he granted to
Robert de Flers, for the *Figaro*, at the beginning of May and which
has already been mentioned in connexion with his theories on
dramatic composition. It shows how clearly the musician realized
the importance of his creation, and how sensitive he was to the
verdict of the leading journalists.

'For the last ten years, monsieur, "Pelléas et Mélisande" has been my
daily companion. I do not complain of this long labour. It has given
me a joy, an intimate satisfaction, which no mere words, no criticism,
can diminish. Besides, some of the critics have understood me perfectly and divined my intentions. I owe my thanks to M. Gaston
Carraud (*La Liberté*), M. Camille de Sainte-Croix (*La Petite République*), M. Gustave Bret (*La Presse*), M. André Corneau (*Le Matin*);

and to M. Henry Bauer for his fine article in the *Figaro*. After an almost embarrassing amount of praise, M. Catulle Mendès states that I have not adequately rendered the "poetic essence of the drama" and that my music is "independent of it". And yet, in all sincerity, I made every effort to identify the two. In particular, I respected the characters and the lives of my personages. I wanted them to express themselves individually, independently of me. I let them sing within me, and I tried to hear them and to interpret them faithfully. That was all. M. Gauthier-Villars finds fault with my score because the melodic pattern is never to be found in the voice, but always in the orchestra. I wished that the action should never be arrested, that it should be continuous and uninterrupted. . . . I know that I have very much alarmed M. d'Harcourt. I greatly regret it. In speaking of me, he mentions "noisy *arrivistes*". He need not be uneasy. He evokes the *Holy Trinity* of music: *melody, harmony*, and *rhythm*, whose laws may not be violated. That is very well put. But is there any law in existence that forbids a musician to blend these three elements? I think not. In any case, although I have read through his critique carefully twice, I have not been able to fathom the meaning of all M. d'Harcourt's remarks. No doubt they are exceedingly profound. This same critic alludes to the "awakening of Mélisande". Perhaps he is confusing it with the awakening of Brunhilde. . . .'

Further criticism both of the critics and of the public is to be found in a statement which Debussy made on the occasion of a revival of 'Pelléas', part of which has already been quoted.

'. . . I have tried to obey a law of beauty which appears to be singularly ignored in dealing with dramatic music. The characters of this drama endeavour to sing like real persons, and not in an arbitrary language built on antiquated traditions. Hence the reproach levelled at my alleged partiality for monotone declamation, in which there is no trace of melody. . . . To begin with, this is untrue. Besides, the feelings of a character cannot be continually expressed in melody. Also, dramatic melody should be totally different from melody in general. . . . The people who go to listen to music at the theatre are, when all is said and done, very like those one sees gathered around a street singer! There, for a penny, one may indulge in melodic emotions. . . . One even notices greater patience than is practised by many subscribers to our state-endowed theatres and even *a wish to understand* which, one might even go so far as to say, is totally lacking in the latter public.

'By a singular irony, this public, which cries out for *something new*, is the very one that shows alarm and scoffs whenever one tries to wean it from old habits and customary humdrum noises. . . . This may seem incomprehensible; but one must not forget that a work of art or an effort to produce beauty are always regarded by some people as a personal affront.

'I do not pretend to have discovered everything in "Pelléas"; but I

have tried to trace a path that others may follow, broadening it with individual discoveries which will, perhaps, free dramatic music from the heavy yoke under which it has existed for so long.'

Those musicians who had followed the development of Debussy's art during the previous ten years in 'La Damoiselle Élue', the 'Prélude à l'Après-midi d'un Faune', the Quartet, the 'Nocturnes', and the various piano pieces and songs, were surprised by his original musical adaptation of Maeterlinck's strange drama, although his previous scores had prepared the way for this new style. But if the astonishment of musicians was great, that of the general run of music-lovers was even greater; and in addition they experienced real grief and disappointment, which few were able to conceal, and the cause of which is easily determined. Like all these manifestations of pained surprise, which we find repeated in every age on the appearance of original works, this disappointment was the inevitable result of the aesthetic habits which fettered amateur musicians. We have already mentioned this point in connexion with Debussy's Quartet. It will bear elaboration with regard to 'Pelléas' which, being an opera, reached a much wider public—an audience comprising not only the little world of musicians, but also the huge clientèle of the opera houses.

The public of twenty-five or thirty years ago was made up of elements very different in their origins. It included the older generations who had been fortunate enough to enjoy the vanished delights of the old repertoire, and who had undergone a gradual and normal evolution; and the later generations whose introduction to the opera had coincided with the invasion and triumph of Bayreuth, and who had arrived on the scene too late to admire the bygone beauties of Meyerbeer's grand opera. These various elements had gradually become merged and united in the universal worship of Richard Wagner. Music-lovers had grown familiar with the gloomy Scandinavian legends, which now held no secrets for them. They had become accustomed to this substantial, luxurious music with its entangled themes, and its bold melodies, which, subject to the sovereign will of the dramatist, sounded now clearly, now dimly, through the sumptuous and magnificent polyphony of the rich, compact orchestra-blending of every conceivable timbre, ringing out powerfully, at full blast, with a noble, solemn, splendid massiveness. After much labour, they had learnt the complex and yet facile art of unravelling the tangled skein of the *leit-motifs* with their definite though variable meanings. Day by day, they had come to take an ever keener pleasure

AT THE TIME OF 'PELLÉAS ET MÉLISANDE'
From the left: PAUL POUGARD, DEBUSSY, PIERRE LALO, MADAME
DEBUSSY-TEXIER, PAUL DUKAS

LETTER TO JACQUES DURAND

(August 1903)

DEBUSSY AND HIS FIRST WIFE, ROSALIE
TEXIER, AT BICHAIN

(about 1902)

in these difficult games and, with increasing ease, they revelled in a succession of more and more complicated works. 'Lohengrin' and 'Tannhäuser' had been followed by the 'Walküre', and the 'Meistersinger', and after 'Tristan' they had finished up with 'Götterdämmerung' and the entire 'Ring'. 'Parsifal', that sublime and touching, though somewhat senile effort, had not yet furnished them with the opportunity of witnessing the decay of this pompous art. The Wagnerian impregnation was complete; the process of poisoning had been accomplished. By indulging in these habits, they had developed definite artistic cravings, and curious musical prejudices; their chief delight was to hear the music of Wagner, and such German or French music as belonged to the same symphonic type. Yet, being persistently 'progressive', they constantly demanded new pleasures of the same order, new joys that could only be achieved by worse complications. . . . At this juncture, the operatic stage presented them with a work to which they had long looked forward with pleasurable anticipation, but which caused them the most cruel and unexpected disillusionment. It was inevitable that they should be disappointed in a score which consisted of almost continuous murmurings, and which was subordinated to Maeterlinck's strange drama. To make matters worse, they were confronted with a disconcerting harmony, with novel rhythms, and a new melodic treatment which seemed to be the very negation of melody.

In spite of the general opinion, this was a really harmonious harmony; its chords vibrated with a free, individual life, unfettered by the merciless rigour of artificial laws. It was the same harmonic treatment which he had attempted in the old *envois de Rome*, and developed in the 'Prélude à l'Après-midi d'un Faune' and the 'Nocturnes'; the same that Debussy had sought for and instinctively found in his youthful days when, in the course of his alarming improvisations at the piano, he ground the colours for his future palette. His processes included: the abolition of the exclusive use of the major and minor modes; the adoption of all kinds of scales, both of the ancient and oriental types, in particular the frequent use of the whole tone-scale, and its logical exploitation; the building-up of chords by means of the continual superimposition of thirds, arranged in long, swaying, parallel lines, and chained together freely, in defiance of the absurd, century-old rules; the utilization of equally independent progressions of common chords, moving in endless festoons throughout all the keys. In a word, absolute freedom, which the musician knew how to employ with perfect tact and an

unerring instinct for appropriate expression. What a distance he had travelled from Wagner! In spite of his extreme chromaticism, the great German master remains tonal; in fact, in an article in the *Bayreuther Blätter* ('Ueber die Anwendung der Musik auf das Drama') he stated as a fundamental rule, that the composer was never to leave a key so long as it was possible to utilize it for what he had to say.

The rhythmic element was equally original. Contrary to the monotonous regularity of most music, it involved the melodic *motifs* in continual changes of accent, thus retrieving some of the infinite suppleness and elasticity of ancient lyrical poetry and of Gregorian chant whose rich resources had been contemptuously ignored for centuries past. In his analysis of 'Pelléas et Mélisande' Maurice Emmanuel quotes the first page of this score as an example of rhythmic versatility unrivalled in modern art: in twenty-two bars, he finds eight alterations in the rhythmic figures, brought about by the mingling of the three first themes, the movement and mensuration of which are entirely different.

The melodic element was of such a nature that more than one critic raised the traditional outcry: 'There is no melody!' Certainly there is no trace of square-set, symmetrical melody; but there is an almost continuous melody, moving up and down the sonorous ladder with such disconcerting freedom that it was mistaken for incoherent motion. Gone are the customary landmarks within the limits of rigid scales to which the music-lover clung from habit, not from instinct. The voices of the actors, as they soar above sustained chords or embroider their festoons upon the supple harmonic tissue, do not render either the traditional recitative with its pompous declamation, or the usual broadly-developed melodies. What they generally produce is a recitative carefully modelled on the supple undulations, the rising inflections, and the gliding cadences of the French language. (It follows, unfortunately, that translation into any foreign language is inevitably a travesty.) This was indeed an innovation at a time when the triumph of Wagnerism had caused many French composers to produce an unconscious imitation, an odious copy, of German declamation, full of jerks and bounds. Debussy's national instinct and critical taste had gradually led him to this truthful and accurate diction, his first attempts at which we saw in 'La Damoiselle Élue', the 'Proses Lyriques', and the 'Chansons de Bilitis'.

All the elements of music were renewed in their very essence. They were treated in a manner hitherto unknown, whose absolute

originality explains, if it does not excuse, the lack of understanding
which the majority of musicians manifested at the first hearing.
This fusion of the musical elements was novel and unexpected.
The instrumental treatment also assumed an unfamiliar aspect.
Discretion is the essential virtue of the orchestra in 'Pelléas at
Mélisande'. Debussy does not want us to miss a single word of
Maeterlinck's poem. He succeeded in his object in all the scenes,
except, perhaps, towards the end of the third act: the last phrases
of the breathless dialogue between Golaud and Yniold are not
quite audible. The composition of the orchestra follows the
traditional plan (the usual strings, three flutes, two oboes, and a
cor anglais, two clarinets, three bassoons, four horns, two trumpets,
three trombones, a tuba, two harps, kettle-drums, cymbals, and
triangle), but the brass is very much toned down and the trombones are heard only in exceptional cases. The percussion instruments are very discreetly used, and the kettle-drums are only
employed to reinforce the rhythm or to produce very soft rolling
effects. The wood-winds are not used together for any unnecessary
doubling; they preserve their own individual colouring and distinctive timbre. There is no Wagnerian density of tone: the
sonority is limpid, like that of Berlioz. The bassoons, in particular,
are no longer used merely for doubling, in order to emphasize the
other bass instruments; they have an expressive role of their own.[1]
The various bow instruments divide their five actual voices into
eight, ten, or twelve parts which are capable of producing the
most aerial, ethereal, effects. These processes, which had already
been utilized in the 'Prélude à l'Après-midi d'un Faune' and the
'Nocturnes', are particularly suited to this delicate symphony
which was intended to constitute a simple sonorous background—
a discreet commentary on the dramatic action—without ever
attracting attention exclusively to itself. Nothing could be further
removed from the Wagnerian procedure, which one section of
French musicians regarded as the best, if not the only utilizable,
plan; nothing could be more in keeping with the ideals of the
reformer who desired that in the lyrical drama, music should be
reduced to a state of honourable servitude whilst maintaining
her position as sovereign mistress in other domains.
    As we have seen, Debussy used the guiding themes in a very
individual manner. His themes have not the distinct aspect, or

---

[1] In 1907, when Debussy was one of the adjudicators at the Conservatoire
competitions, he wrote as follows to Jacques Durand: 'The tone of this instrument tends to become pathetic, and you will see that it will alter some orchestral
values.'

the definite, abrupt movement of Wagner's. They do not call for minute examination. The audience hardly noticed them and were considerably surprised when, later on, some musicographers analysed the themes in 'Pelléas'. In 1908 Lawrence Gilman compared Wagner and Debussy in the *Musical Standard* of the 28th of November and the 5th of December; two years later, in the *Revue Musicale de Lyon* (13th, 20th, and 27th of November; 4th, 11th, and 13th of December 1910) Étienne Destranges drew up a list—of questionable accuracy—of the *leit-motifs* that occur in the anti-Wagnerian work. We had to wait until 1926 for Maurice Emmanuel's scholarly treatment of the subject. (An article on 'Debussy and the leit-motif' was published by Mr. M. D. Calvocoressi in the *Musical Times* of the 1st of August 1925.)

The only features of this marvellous composition which can be dealt with here are those that lend themselves to analysis, that is to say, the processes of composition and the details of style. It would require a vast vocabulary of special words and metaphors, of vague literary equivalents and verbal approximations, to express the deep human significance and the exquisite feeling for nature—those eternal elemental qualities—with which this novel score overflows, and which profoundly affect not only the spectator at the theatre but even the musician who simply reads it at the piano.

In a study entitled 'Un Moment Musical', published in the *Courrier Musical* of the 1st and 15th of March 1904, Lionel de la Laurencie praised the keen, accurate naturalism which 'is expressed in the subtle, yet very simple harmonies of 'Pelléas', and he quoted some typical examples of Debussy's impressionism:

'night falling over the sea, the lighthouses being lighted here and there, and each in turn piercing with its rays the growing darkness (pp. 41–2 of the score); the murmur of the water in the fountain; the atmosphere of horror in the subterranean passages under the castle, rendered in a Shakespearean manner by the sinister chords at the beginning of the scene (p. 126) which are punctuated by grim, challenging fifths from the depths of the orchestra; the thrumming effects, suggestive of trampling, that accompany the scene of the dusty, swarming flocks of sheep (pp. 202–5); the exquisite curve of the flight of doves disporting themselves around Mélisande. . . .'

The writer of this article quoted a calmly harmonious phrase —from one of Debussy's critiques—which shows how sensitive he was to the peaceful, lofty beauty of certain landscapes: 'The fall of the golden leaves heralding the glorious death-agony of the trees, and the shrill angelus bell calling on the fields to sleep, sent up a gentle, insinuating song.'

Owing to the exceptional originality of 'Pelléas et Mélisande'—
an impression which the opera still creates to-day, although all
its harmonic formulas and instrumental processes are now in
common use—many musicians could not grasp its deep expressiveness, its pathetic grandeur, its many perfections; as so
often happens, one could not see the wood for the trees. A
characteristic of the work which very few of the spectators were
capable of appreciating was its profound and paradoxical classicism.
Indeed, it would not have been surprising if this opera had failed
in Paris, in 1902, and disappeared completely from the stage,
as happened a few years later in several provincial and foreign
towns.

One can hardly insist too much on the fact that 'Pelléas et
Mélisande' caused grievous disappointment to most music-lovers
and professional musicians, especially on the first hearing. This
was not at all the kind of music that the mass of Wagnerians
had been expecting. The whole thing sounded thin and petty
to them. Take the orchestra. Ears that were accustomed to the
Tetralogical brass, to Wotan's solemn fanfares, and the brilliant
lyricism of that exuberant orchestration, could not appreciate
the faint, distant sonorities of stopped trumpets and the gentle
caresses of muted strings. They could not understand the short
themes and the murmuring declamation, because they were
trained to follow without effort the meanderings of Wagner's
famous 'infinite' melody. Even the delicate, insinuating charm of
the harmonies did not appeal to them, for they could find no trace
in them of the logical sequence peculiar to the progressions with
which they were familiar. This sense of disappointment was very
well described by Victor Debay, in an article which we have already
quoted, but the general public were not able to discern its deep-
seated causes, nor did they realize that the condition was only
temporary. Animated by a blind faith in the music of the recent
past, they unhesitatingly condemned this new music of the future.
They clung to their old loves with a reactionary confidence, and
discovered endless reasons for preferring Wagner to a composer
whose apparition, according to some, sounded the knell of all
former aesthetics. There was a certain amount of insincerity or,
at least, of deliberate exaggeration, in the manner in which they
stressed the humble role of Debussy's music, which had made itself
' a servant of the drama, a slave to literature, a mere harmonic
framework, a sonorous background. . . .'

The series of performances of 'Pelléas et Mélisande' had not
been planned to last long, but it was in danger of being interrupted

by the departure of André Messager. Debussy repeatedly paid the most grateful homage to the talents of this conductor, and he dedicated his score to him, and to the memory of Georges Hartmann. Messager who was called away to London for an engagement at Covent Garden, was obliged to abandon the direction of 'Pelléas' on the day after the fourth performance. He handed over his baton to his chorus director, Henri Büsser, who had taken part in the preparatory work and had followed all the rehearsals. After some slight preparation, this second conductor was able to direct the fifth performance in such a manner as to satisfy even Debussy, a feat that was all the more creditable, as this was the first time he took his place at the conductor's desk. It now became possible to continue the performances regularly. Thus, little by little, the public came to appreciate this remarkable lyrical drama which had at first taken them by surprise; day by day, they took a keener pleasure in following its development.

In the letters Debussy wrote to Messager during the latter's stay in London, he briefly recorded the continuation of the first series of performances under Büsser's conductorship.

'Thursday; such rehearsal as was essential for Büsser. Between ourselves, the management of the Opéra-Comique might have allowed him a complete rehearsal! . . . My impressions are vague and nebulous, there is no knowing what may happen . . . Friday: a splendid house, including M. Jean de Reszke. An attentive audience. . . . After the fourth act, three calls compensated all these good people for their trouble. A pleasant evening in fact, the only flaw being your absence.'

The sixth performance did not go off without some hitches:

'Excuse my delay in writing. I suppose it was inevitable that I should have to pay for all these varied emotions with a fit of discouragement. I have been suffering from the consequences of it. The performance on Saturday did not go very well. A number of absurd little mishaps contributed to this failure, and I cannot be held responsible for the ironical tricks that fate sometimes plays. In order to continue the series, "Pelléas" was replaced yesterday by "Le roi d'Ys" as M. Jean Périer announced that he had lost his voice. . . . We start again tomorrow, unless some unexpected hitch occurs. . . .'[1]

On the seventh day 'people had to be turned away (explain that as best you can). But, to make up for that, the performance was weak. . . . Miss Garden and Dufrane are the only ones

---

[1] Jean Périer had created a very fine Pelléas, but his vocal powers were obviously inadequate. His role was written too high for a baritone and too low for a tenor, and it had to be 'pointed' in order to make it suitable for ordinary voices. Debussy, who never paid much attention to normal *tessitura*, seems to have written it for his own voice.

who are always in form. But it seems to have been a very good evening all the same and a great success. . . . There is sure to be a matinée on Sunday.' The opera had become a success and the receipts were increasing: 'I forgot to tell you that we made 7,400 francs last Friday! you wouldn't believe the respect they have for me! The fact that I had created "Pelléas" was of purely anecdotal significance, but to have made money, that 's what counts!'

When things went wrong, Debussy was helpless. He acknowledged this to Messager: 'You know I am no good at pretending and humbugging people in order to revive their courage.' He suffered so much from the defects of some performances, that he longed for the series to end. 'It is high time,' he wrote to Robert Godet, in June. 'They are beginning to treat it like a repertory work. The singers are improvising, the orchestra is getting heavy (a feat that seems almost fantastic and incredible), soon, people will inevitably prefer "La Dame Blanche".' . . . At such moments, his nerves were on edge and he experienced 'a degree of fatigue that suggests neurasthenia, a fashionable disease I did not believe in. But evidently, the overwork and the nervous strain of the last few months have been too much for me. . . .'

The nervous strain was not due to artistic causes alone. Debussy's extreme carelessness about money matters had got him into difficulties. The artist was a typical Bohemian, and lacked all financial instincts, as his publisher and his friends had reason to know. He was apt to look upon his cash-box as common property; he was, indeed, absolutely free from avarice. Hartmann had gradually advanced him a great deal of money, which he had no intention of demanding back from him except in kind, that is, in scores. The generous publisher died in 1901. His heir did not behave with the same consideration, but requested the thoughtless debtor to pay back the total sums advanced. This heir was General Bourgeat, 'le général' to whom Debussy alludes somewhat bitterly in some of his published letters. Just at the time of the production of 'Pelléas', the General, who was in a hurry to recover all amounts due to the testator, sent the bailiffs after the musician, and, on the 5th of July 1902, he sold to the publisher, Fromont, the entire collection of Debussy's works which had become his property on the death of Hartmann. He sold, along with the engraved plates, all his rights in: the 'Marche Écossaise', the 'Ballade Slave', the 'Tarentelle', the 'Valse Romantique', the 'Proses Lyriques', the 'Chansons de Bilitis', the 'Nocturnes', and 'L'Après-midi d'un Faune'; and, together with the unpublished manuscripts, his rights in the 'Suite

Bergamasque', the 'Rêverie', the 'Mazurka', and the arrangement of Schumann's 'Am Springbrunnen'. While these financial
negotiations were in progress, Debussy sold to the publisher
Durand, the 'Cinq Poèmes' and 'La Damoiselle Élue' with the
plates that had been engraved in 1890 or 1893. But, in spite of
his money troubles, he jealously guarded his rights in 'Pelléas et
Mélisande'; it was only three years later that, driven by a more
urgent need, he agreed to sell the opera to his friend, Durand.

In order to ensure the success of the opera from the start,
'Pelléas' was played fourteen times[1] during May and June 1902.
While the general public were growing accustomed to the new
art, Debussy was fortunate enough to be able to count on the
support of all sensitive musicians who were not fettered by prejudice
or custom, as well as on the frequenters of the symphony concerts, who were less hampered by Wagnerism and more eclectic
than the regular opera-goers; and the highbrows, too, gave their
sanction to his masterpiece almost from the first. This select
public was described by Jean Lorrain in a satirical article in the
Journal in which he made an unsuccessful attempt to launch a new,
punning nickname: the *Pelléastres*, this being the title and the last
word of the article. According to this writer, the audience seemed
to have been recruited from amongst the frequenters of the

---

[1] 'Pelléas' was revived and played ten times between the 30th of October
1902 and the 6th of January 1903; twelve times in 1903–4, still under the
conductorship of Messager; six times in 1904–5, with Alexandre Luigini as
conductor. The following year, the opera was set aside. But after the season
of 1906–7 (when it was performed eighteen times) it remained on the repertoire,
except during the war. The hundredth performance was celebrated on the 28th of
January 1913. In the spring and autumn of 1926 a few performances took place
of exceptional interest, perhaps unique in the history of opera: twenty-four years
after its first performance, 'Pelléas et Mélisande' was given practically under the
same conditions as on the day of its production. André Messager conducted the
orchestra, and restored its original style which had been distorted by his successors; the principal singers—Mary Garden, Dufranne, and Vieuille—resumed the
roles they had created. This resurrection, this miracle of rejuvenation, was hailed
with enthusiasm by the entire press.
From 1908 on, 'Pelléas' was given in the provinces, first in Lyons.
Up to the 30th of March 1928, 'Pelléas' had been given over 250 times in
foreign countries, first in Brussels and Vienna, then in Germany. The following
is a list of the number of performances held in each country: Germany, 49;
Belgium, 32; Austria, 29; England, 31; Switzerland, 14; United States, 22;
Argentine Republic, 8; Italy, 9; Spain, 6; Holland, 8; Brazil, 2; Luxemburg, 2;
Yugoslavia (Zagreb), 4; Denmark (Copenhagen), 6; Portugal (Lisbon), 3;
Hungary (Budapest), 5; Egypt (Cairo and Alexandria), 7. Accounts of some of
these performances will be found farther on. The international popularity of
this opera is hampered by the very characteristically French nature of its smooth
declamation, the meaning of which becomes lost, even in the most accurate
translations. Toscanini realized this fact, and the performances which he conducted at the Scala, Milan, in 1925 and 1926 were given in French, with Mme
Fanny Helder, and MM. Alfred Legrand and Marcel Journet.

Lugné-Poë[1] *premières*—the fervent admirers of Grieg's nostalgic melodies and of the scientific orchestration of 'Fervaal'. In other words they were, in his opinion, snobbish, pretentious, ignorant amateurs.

'Just as they were convulsed with admiration over the sunshiny *pizzicati* of that little masterpiece the "Après-midi d'un Faune", they have now decreed that we must go into raptures over the deliberate dissonances in the lengthy recitatives in "Pelléas". Those long-drawn-out chords and those perpetual beginnings of repeatedly announced phrases have an enervating effect. A kind of titillation that is at first pleasurable, then exasperating, and in the end, cruelly painful, is inflicted on the ears of the audience by the continual repetition of a theme that is constantly interrupted and which never terminates. This work, with its limbo-like atmosphere and its occasional little shocks (so very artistic! so subtilized! . . . and so bewildering!) received the united suffrages of a public consisting of snobs and *poseurs*. Thanks to these ladies and gentlemen, M. Claude Debussy became the head of a new religion, and during each performance of "Pelléas" the salle Favart[2] took on the atmosphere of a sanctuary; the audience wore an air of compunction, they exchanged meaning glances and winks full of complicity. After the preludes, which were listened to in a religious silence, the initiated greeted one another in the corridors, finger on lips; peculiar handshakes were hastily given in the semi-darkness of the boxes; faces wore a tortured expression, and eyes a far-away look. . . .'

Jean Lorrain regarded the neophytes of this new religion as quite different types from the Wagnerians, who had recently come to be regarded as sincere, and who, according to him, were recruited from all social classes. He would not admit that the Debussyists were to be found anywhere but in the orchestra stalls and the first tier of boxes: 'that fair-haired girl, too frail, too pale, too fair, who has evidently got herself up to look like Miss Garden . . . and whose fingers listlessly turn the pages of the score placed on the edge of the box', or 'that group of good-looking young men (nearly all the Debussyists are young, very young), whose long hair is skilfully brushed across their foreheads, those youths with the plump, pallid faces, deep-set eyes, velvet-collared coats, slightly puffed sleeves, frock coats a little too tight at the waist, wide satin cravats that thicken their necks, or floating lavallière ties. . . .' These are the ecstatic spectators, 'who drink in Miss Garden's gestures, Jusseaume's scenery, Carré's lighting effects; archangels with the eyes of visionaries who, at impressive moments,

[1] Aurélien-Marie Lugné-Poë, actor-manager, who specialized in foreign drama and the works of young idealistic writers.
[2] Name of the old Opéra-Comique Theatre, called after Charles Favart, manager and playwright, who was the creator of the *opéra-comique*.

whisper in one another's ears words that reach the very soul. . . .The Pelléastres!'

This article, which was eventually to form part of the first chapter of the posthumous novel, *Les Pelléastres*, was not published until the 22nd of January 1904. In spite of its tendency to exaggeration and caricature, it contained a certain degree of truth, and it may be regarded as applicable to some sections of the audiences of 1902 and 1903. Debussy's triumph was, in fact, responsible for the growth of a somewhat ridiculous, but rather useful form of snobbery. Furthermore, the rise of Debussyism—a kind of aesthetic religion, founded on the principles of the man after whom it was called—gave birth to the Debussyists—the voluntary disciples of a musician who did not wish to found a school, the fervent, intolerant devotees of an artistic sect which they had founded in spite of their god, for the exploitation of his ideas and processes.

It was indeed possible to extract from his works and statements the material for a complete doctrine. Later, when Debussy took up his pen as a musical critic, it was evident that the opinions he expressed had a definite basis, although the fact passed unnoticed at the time. We have attempted to demonstrate this in our book on *The Theories of Claude Debussy*. Yet, one essential principle was cherished by the composer above all others, namely: that musicians should be unfettered by any unjustifiable scholastic rules, that absolute independence was essential to the artist, that he should personally adapt the musical means to suit the character of his artistic creation. Debussyism, on the other hand, tended to fetter its adepts, by making them the prisoners of aesthetic opinions that did not suit everybody, the slaves of processes which Debussy had created for his own use, never meaning to preserve them intact, but to modify them constantly to suit the ever-changing needs and promptings of his intellect and feelings. Fortunately, this narrow Debussyism was practised only by a few unimportant acolytes. The best composers of that generation were inspired by a broad, intelligent form of Debussyism. They profited by its general teaching, as well as by particular examples of writing and style which were to be found in the masterpieces of their elder. Debussy also opened the eyes of some of the older composers. They not only borrowed some of his grammatical idioms, but they also appreciated the aesthetic significance of his teaching.

The sudden triumph of 'Pelléas', which Debussy himself had so little expected, was the cause of a schism amongst French musicians which lasted several years. A few months after the memorable production of this masterpiece, the musical world was

divided into two principal camps. On one side was the Schola
Cantorum, a school with spiritual ideals, which was alarmed
by Claude Debussy's sensual paganism; on the other side, the
Conservatoire, the pupils of which had rallied to the Debussyist
art in spite of the disapproval of their professors. On one side stood
Vincent d'Indy, the prophet of Franckism; on the other, Claude
Debussy, the unwilling champion of the Debussyism he abhorred.
The Schola Cantorum had been founded by Vincent d'Indy in 1896,
as a practical demonstration of the principles which were to serve
as a basis for the reorganization of the national Conservatoire, as set
forth in the official report which d'Indy had been asked to draw up
in 1890. The very existence of this severely styled Schola Cantorum, as well as the noble ideals of its founders, placed it in direct
opposition to the official school with its rather out-of-date system of
education. Although it was a nationalist institution, it tended—
with a curious, unconscious inconsistency—to place the French
school under the spiritual dominion of classical and romantic
Germany. These tendencies were beginning to arouse violent protests. Vincent d'Indy, who had not yet been recognized by the
general public, was regarded by some of the young independent
musicians as an academic composer; they thought him conventional,
heavy, dull, pedantic, and, above all, too *theological*. The revelation
of 'Pelléas et Mélisande' united these scattered malcontents. They
believed that in Debussy they had found a leader to whose standard
they could rally in order to combat the abuses of the d'Indy school.

In their enthusiasm or their folly, some partisans of both clans
indulged in absurd excesses which made them objects of ridicule.
In 1905, Camille Mauclair, a writer on art, amused himself by
analysing the acute disorders from which some frantic Debussyites
were suffering. The principal target of his irony was Louis Laloy,
whose quivering sensibility found expression in magnificent, but
extravagant lyrical outbursts. Mauclair attributed these disorders
to an actual disease rather than to aesthetic emotion. According
to him, pathologists should have recorded the discovery of
Debussyitis, a serious affection, a peculiar form of alcoholism, due
to hypertrophy and malformation of the Debussy cult, which produced in its victims a sudden loss of all critical sense.

'I should never have imagined that "Pelléas" could produce such an
effect. One would think those people had been listening to a revolutionary hymn. They smell blood and gunpowder, and they forthwith
fall under a kind of hypnotic influence. It is very curious. A mixture of
saltpetre, Cretan bhang, hashish, and curry works them up to a state
of rabid mysticism. They rush about like those Malays who become a

prey to the murderous frenzy known as *amok*. They declaim wildly and vociferously. . . .'

These unfortunate victims 'begin to turn round and round like those African sheep that have a worm in their heads'. This amusing account of the new disease was inserted in the *Courrier Musical* and gave rise to lively polemical discussion between that review and the *Mercure Musical*, a publication which had just been founded by Louis Laloy and Jean Marnold and which was unfortunately short-lived. Émile Vuillermoz took an active part in the discussion. He wrote an amusing and characteristic fantasia entitled 'Une Tasse de Thé', which the *Courrier Musical* did not dare to print, but which appeared in the *Mercure Musical* of the 15th November 1905.

The struggle between the d'Indyists or the Schola party and the Debussyists was waged fiercely until the outbreak of the war. During those ten years a great deal of talent, wit, and obvious insincerity was expended on aesthetic battles. The Debussyists held that the beauty of music was chiefly a matter of successions of chords; according to their opponents, it depended on the patterns and the interlacings of superimposed melodies. It was a case of harmonists versus contrapuntists. The latter delighted in set forms, like the sonata, that had been imposed by tradition; the former claimed complete liberty, so long as it did not lead to confusion. Debussy might occasionally make use of counterpoint, but in his more emancipated compositions one did not expect to find old forms, classical processes, or scholastic formulas; he was classified exclusively as a harmonist; his music was *vertical*. And although Vincent d'Indy is capable of a systematic use of very daring harmonic progressions—as in the beginning of his 'Wallenstein' (the *sidereal* chords) and at the end of 'Fervaal' ('Ils dorment') he was nevertheless labelled as an uncompromising contrapuntist; the classifiers described his music as *horizontal*. As Romain Rolland says in *La Foire sur la Place*, it was another case of 'Big-endians' *versus* 'Little-endians', and their futile quarrel as to the correct way of opening boiled eggs.[1]

Vincent d'Indy did not fail to support his adherents by word and deed, but Claude Debussy, intent on his inner life, his experiments, and his efforts for the renewal of art, kept aloof from the contest. Some musicians of note, like Florent Schmitt

---

[1] Echoes of these discussions are to be found in various articles, as, for instance, in Émile Vuillermoz's article on 'La Schola et le Conservatoire' (*Mercure de France*, 16th of September 1909) and in the replies of Louis Combes, Alfred Casella, and R. Lambinet (*Monde Musical*, 15th and 30th of October 1909).

and Maurice Ravel, had been either willingly or forcibly incorporated in his party, whilst Albert Roussel was committed to the
other side of the barricade. Debussy's followers were led to battle
under the command of the most ardent and energetic of his
young admirers, Émile Vuillermoz—a composer who had volun-
tarily retired from his profession, in order to devote himself
entirely to musical criticism. Thanks to his energy and ability, and
the role of 'Éminence grise' which he often assumed in order to
ensure the triumph of his ideas, he was responsible for accentuat-
ing the split amongst French musicians, and the establishment of
a kind of political division: the right wing being represented by the
Schola and d'Indy, and the left by the Conservatoire and Debussy.
Some years later, after considerable effort, he even succeeded in
setting up Vincent d'Indy and Claude Debussy against one another
officially, when he engaged the rival composers to write for the
Revue Musicale S.I.M., of which he had become the zealous editor-
in-chief. At the beginning of 1910, he founded the Société Musicale
Indépendante (S.I.M.) under the patronage of Gabriel Fauré, who
had been appointed director of the Conservatoire. This concert
society for the production of new works was established in
opposition to the old Société Nationale de Musique, which, in his
opinion, had been appropriated by the Schola. The struggle,
often rather futile, though sometimes beneficial and fruitful, was
carried on with considerable energy; but, nevertheless, in spite
of slight occasional annoyance, Vincent d'Indy and Claude Debussy
constantly professed for one another feelings of admiration, esteem,
and good comradeship.

CHAPTER IX

CHAMBER MUSIC. 'LA MER' (1902-7)

TOWARDS the middle of May 1902 Robert de Flers interviewed Claude Debussy on behalf of the *Figaro* with the object of inviting him to criticize the critiques of his opera. On that occasion he sketched the following portrait of this very reserved musician who was the object of so much discussion.

'Who was it said that the souls of musicians are hermetically sealed? Whoever it was made no mistake. It is no easy matter to discover what M. Claude Debussy thinks of the criticisms of "Pelléas et Mélisande". He smiles readily, but his answers are brief. He speaks very quietly in a soft, melodious voice. One feels that he instinctively hates advertisement, and disapproves of publicity on principle. There is something almost monastic about his reserve. One must knock very gently at the door and remove one's shoes lest any noise should disturb a soul for whom all sounds have a professional value and a definite resonance.'

Very few people knew Debussy intimately. Some months after the production of 'Pelléas', he was to be seen even more rarely than before. His second marriage cut him off from most of his former friends, and he seemed very reluctant to emerge from the seclusion into which he then withdrew. It was at this period that he began to acquire a kind of patina and ceased to resemble himself, to use the apt words of his friend René Peter. In a short literary work, André Suarès gives a portrait of the composer as he appeared just before his triumph at the Opéra-Comique. In spite of its length we think it well worth reproducing here.

'At first sight, there seemed to be nothing distinctive about him. He was not tall. Nor was he either particularly robust or delicate; and though rather flabby, he had a look of solidity. He was plump, not to say stout, with a well-rounded figure. His beard was silky and luxuriant, his hair thick and curly. His features were heavy, his cheeks full; his bantering manner concealed a subtle shrewdness. His was an ironical and sensual personality, melancholy and voluptuous. In complexion he was dark and sallow. Though highly strung, he could control his nerves but not his emotions, which must have affected him profoundly—all the more so when he struggled to conceal them. . . .

'Ironical and pleasure-loving by nature, he had a mischievous sense of humour, and openly acknowledged his love of good living. He had a barbed tongue, a certain carelessness of speech, a touch of affectation in his gestures, an ardent though cynical spirit, a strong, sensitive nature, unerring taste and great simplicity, though at times appearances suggested the contrary. Debussy was in fact as much a Montmartre

Bohemian as a man of the world. There was something of the cat in him, and something of the recluse. Although the sensuality of his expression suggested a capacity for violence, there was no sign of brutality; as a young man, his natural timidity probably developed into cynicism. I imagine that his constant, deep-seated melancholy always kept Debussy somewhat aloof from other men. The shape of his head denoted great obstinacy of mind.

'His forehead was of the kind one sees in the craftsmen of harmony, the masters of rhythm, the celebrated artisans of music. It bulged outwards in a convex curve in marked contrast to the smooth brow of the poet. Those other adepts in numbers, mathematicians, also have these prominent bumps over the eyebrows. To the close observer, Debussy's glance suggested not only the musician, but still more a man out of the ordinary. Those fine, caressing, mocking eyes, so sad and languid, so warm and pensive, were the eyes of a brilliant, imperious woman, eyes such as artists sometimes have; as if they had been women in a previous existence before becoming what they are. But his glance would at times assume a curious tenseness, a look of close concentration, characteristic of the French poet who analyses even his dreams, who must always understand.

'At first, Debussy did not disclose his real self. Many traits both in his art and his personality were misleading, for they suggested the painter or the poet quite as much as the musician. He himself helped to lead the critics astray. To judge his works by their titles, he is a painter and that is what he wants to be; he calls his compositions pictures, sketches, engravings, arabesques, masques, studies in black and white; it is evidently his delight to paint in music, and his reputation was made under false pretences. His physical appearance helped the illusion; so did the fashion of the times, for painters were never so much in vogue as during the last quarter of a century. There was nothing tragic or violent about him. He was as different as possible from Beethoven and Berlioz; he did not suggest the inspired prophet nor the caged eagle protesting against its fate. He was no frock-coated lightning-flash; he had not the enormous forehead so conveniently devastated by baldness, which devout worshippers regard as the seat of genius, nor the nose of the bird of prey that ravishes the sheep.

'Although there was nothing of the South about him, least of all about his music, Debussy was not unlike some Provençal or even some Italian types. . . . He had the same look of experience, that patina which the centuries produce on men's faces, and which signifies that they have been civilized longer than others without forfeiting the freshness and fervour of their sensations. In fact, no one could have been less of a barbarian, and he had every right to turn his back disdainfully on the very virtues of the barbarian.'[1]

This studied portrait may be contrasted with the following picturesque sketch by Léon Daudet, who used to meet Debussy at

[1] Andre Suarès. *Debussy* (1921).

the Restaurant Weber, rue Royale, Paris, about 1900–5. 'Occasionally, less often than we should have liked, we were joined by Claude Debussy, a musician of genius, who has the forehead of a Pekinese dog, a horror of his neighbour, a fiery glance, and a slightly husky voice. . . .' At the restaurant the musician would choose some dainty dish, 'nibble a few of those potato chips which are served in bars to induce thirst, smoke a little Oriental cigarette, sniff audibly, make a few cutting remarks, and then set off, lifting his forehead and his fantasies to the stars.'[1]

Amongst other literary men whom Debussy used to meet 'Chez Weber' or at the Brasserie Pousset was the fantastic poet, J. P. Toulet. The keen intellectual sympathy that united the two men led them to plan a dramatic collaboration of which the beginnings date from the time of the production of 'Pelléas'. Toulet was to adapt Shakespeare's 'As You Like It' under the title of 'Comme il vous plaira', and Debussy was to write the music. Their recently published· correspondence enables us to follow the progress of their plan at least in its early stages.

Writing in 1902 from Bichain in the department of the Yonne, where he was spending the summer holidays with his family after the performances of 'Pelléas' had been discontinued, Debussy asked for news of 'that little human fairy-tale' from which he thinks something admirable can be made. Of the two plans submitted to him by Toulet, he prefers the second. He wishes the musical and choral possibilities to be developed. For example, in the first scene, in order to stress the incidents of Orlando's wrestling-bout, he suggests having a chorus behind the scenes uttering various exclamations which, from a musical point of view, 'would be rather novel'. He would like to have the various songs sung by a group of people. He remarks humorously: 'the Duke is rich enough to bring the Chanteurs de Saint-Gervais and their conductor to the Forest of Arden'. He makes the following general observation: 'do not hesitate to replace the exact word by its lyrical equivalent whenever possible. This does not mean to say that I do not like the manner in which the two scenes are written. I do; I only wish to reassure you as you express a fear of being too rhythmical. Do not be afraid, it will all reappear in the music.' He is also concerned about the dramatic composition and suggests some modifications in the original plan. He is particularly anxious to have a joyous ending and wishes the betrothal rites to be carried out with attractive ceremonies so as to conclude the work on a cheerful note. 'It suggests to me the possibility of a scenic treatment in

which marvellously attired personages would make their appearance
to a rhythmic accompaniment preparing the entrance of Orlando's
Rosalind. The whole thing would be interspersed with songs
in the antique manner, that is to say, forming part of the action.'
We can discern here Debussy's anxiety not to repeat 'Pelléas', to
write an entirely different work, especially as the atmosphere of
the Forest of Arden might possibly evoke the memory of the forest
in which Mélisande had strayed.

Toulet left for Tonkin in October. No doubt the correspondence
was continued, but it has not been traced. Eight months later,
notices appeared in all the musical reviews in Paris announcing
that Debussy was composing or completing the score of 'Comme
il vous plaira'. The *Ménestrel* took advantage of the opportunity
to describe Debussy as a '*pointilliste* musician (we do not say
punctilious)'. The *Courrier Musical* of the 15th of June 1903 gave the
following details: 'Here is an interesting point. It was during a
voyage to Indo-China, to visit the Hanoi exhibition from which he
has just returned to Paris, that M. Toulet wrote the libretto of
"Comme il vous plaira", forwarding the text scene by scene to
M. Debussy.' These indiscreet revelations were certainly not
supplied by the musician, who was just then becoming interested
in a new dramatic subject, 'Le Diable dans le Beffroi'. It is probable
that Debussy had merely thought out the scenario of the Shakespearian play without doing any actual writing. The composition
of 'As you like it' was destined to remain in abeyance for some
fifteen years, and to be resumed in a different form in 1917.

A few months before the production of 'Pelléas et Mélisande'
a suite of Debussy's, entitled 'Pour le Piano', had been performed
at the Société Nationale. On this occasion, the work had not been
played as usual by Debussy himself, but by Ricardo Viñes, who
was becoming his accredited interpreter. The performance took
place on the 11th of January. The suite met with great success,
the final 'Toccata' being encored. Though some musicians of the
Franckist school found it rather perplexing, no one could remain
insensible to the charm of the new work. In his feuilleton in the
Temps of the 28th January, Pierre Lalo praised its nimble grace,
its supple, luminous fluency, its brilliant, unobtrusive charm, its
studied nonchalance, its whimsical, careless skill, its light, vague
form—nevertheless so sure and definite—and the unexpected
sequences of its modulations.

In this suite, the first piano composition published after an interval of ten years, there are several passages of a rather classical
character, reminiscent of the clavecinists, Bach and Scarlatti. But

the work also displays Debussy's individual harmonic colouring and a new style of writing. For, even though the device be copied from Chopin or more especially from Balakiref, the repetition and the insistent reiteration of certain processes results in a surprisingly novel effect. A short, compact, undulating *motif*, a tightly coiled ornamental figure, or an arabesque may be stated twenty times in succession without intermission, and yet these repetitions do not produce an impression of monotony. Although continuously constructed upon the same theme, these tiny patterns with their persistent rhythms seem ever new. For, as they occur with identical intervals on the different notes of the theme, at each step they awaken different harmonies in which they reflect themselves; they build up unexpected chords; they sweep the hearer along through jostling, conflicting tonalities whose caressing contact produces novel and delightful sensations.

The 'Prélude' consists of a rapid *martellato* theme which is now blurred by the reiterated figures that encircle it, now emphasized by brilliant, overlaid chords. The 'Toccata', with its richly chased patterns, its broad, decorative *arpeggios* and its brilliant colouring, seems intent on pursuing its upward path throughout all the tonalities. Between them, the 'Sarabande' is perhaps all the more effective by contrast, with its graceful, noble melody steeped in rich, sumptuous chords. Some people ascribed to Debussy's friend, Erik Satie, a certain influence on the development of his harmonic genius. One wonders whether in writing this piece Debussy did not intend to point out politely that that other 'Sarabande', written by his so-called precursor in 1887, was but the crude sketch of an untalented bungler. This is quite possible. Perhaps he composed this beautiful dance measure with a vague desire to claim his own property, for with supreme artistic skill he utilizes systematically and deliberately those daring successions of sevenths and ninths which he delighted to produce on his piano even in his student days at the Conservatoire.[1]

His pianistic writing showed evidence of considerable progress and from that time on, it bore the essential marks of the Debussyist manner which became the object of careful study.[2] The correct

[1] See Appendix C.
[2] See Mr. M. D. Calvocoressi's article 'A Few Remarks on Modern French Pianoforte Music' in the *Monthy Musical Record*, 1st of June 1906; 'The pianoforte works of Claude Debussy' by E. Burlingame Hill, in the Boston *Musician*, August 1906 (of which a French translation appeared in the *Mercure Musical*, 15th of October 1906); and Léon Vallas's article 'Le Nouveau Style Pianistique: I. Claude Debussy' in the *Revue Musicale de Lyon* of the 14th and 21st of October 1906.

rendering of this music demanded a special style of interpretation in keeping with the ideas and intentions of the composer. According to the notes published by Louis Laloy in 1909, which reflect Debussy's own ideas, pianists should avoid all romantic affectations, they should not attempt to emphasize the melody, but leave it to achieve of itself such slight prominence as is necessary; nor should they, in the gymnastic, acrobatic manner of the virtuoso, stress the chords which form the harmonic framework of the principal themes: they should rather aim at blending the patterns into one sonorous halo. As regards the notes which are surmounted by a small stroke, these should be neither detached nor emphasized; they should be rendered with a transparent tone, which can be achieved by attacking them boldly, but not harshly, then letting go the keys and allowing the pedal to prolong the sound. That was how Debussy played. But some of the mysterious, delightfully subtle effects of his playing were lost in large halls and, as we shall see later, its good points were not always obvious to the ears of the critics.

'Pour le Piano' was the last work published by Fromont. The letter which Debussy wrote him on the subject of the red clover-leaves with which the cover of this piece is decorated shows what an interest the composer took in the general appearance of his works, an interest which he retained to the end of his days. The sale contract of this work was signed on the 25th of April 1905. Debussy wished to make a condition that Fromont should not publish his old Mazurka. 'I dislike that type of piece, especially at the present moment', Debussy wrote on the 21st of April. But the publisher, who owned the rights of this little work, composed fifteen years earlier, printed it all the same.

Two years later, the 'Estampes' which were composed in 1903 and published immediately, gave further opportunity for admiring this new style of writing, in a transformed, improved, embellished form, parts of which perhaps imitate Ravel's 'Jeux d'Eau'. (The letter reproduced here shows once more how concerned Debussy was about the typographical appearance of his works.) The 'Estampes' were performed by Ricardo Viñes at the Société Nationale on the 9th of January 1904. These very diversely coloured pieces gained immediate appreciation; the third had to be repeated by the virtuoso. 'Pagodes' contains reminiscences of the Oriental dances of Cambodia and Java which the composer had seen at the exhibitions of 1889 and 1900. This piece attracted considerable attention by reason of the systematic, almost exclusive use of a Chinese five-note scale, and the persistence of the principal theme which is repeated at different octaves in changing

158   CLAUDE DEBUSSY: LIFE AND WORKS

rhythms, amid continuous bell-like effects produced by irregular *motifs*. The effective dissonant ending also aroused much interest and discussion. 'Jardins sous la Pluie' delighted both readers and hearers by its skilful utilization of two French songs which are heard through a deluge of *arpeggio* figures that splash like rain upon leaves. The songs utilized are the *ronde* 'Nous n'irons plus au bois', which Debussy had already introduced into one of his vocal compositions in 1880, and the lullaby, 'Do do, l'enfant do'. This 'Estampe' was soon to become a favourite with virtuosi who, unfortunately, could not refrain from altering the character of the work and upsetting its balance. The second part of the suite, 'La Soirée dans Grenade'[1] is distinguished by its careless, supple *Habanera*-like movement, its alternating rhythms, and a persistent pedal on C sharp around which languid, drooping chords slowly move and turn. This composition was destined to cause a certain amount of discreet commotion in the musical world.

On the 5th of March 1898 the Société Nationale had produced a suite of two pieces for two pianos which had been composed two or three years previously by Maurice Ravel, then twenty-three years old. The audience had considered the music as strange as its title, 'Sites Auriculaires'. The first piece, 'Entre Cloches', had been rendered unintelligible by the confused rendering of the interpreters. The second piece was a *Habanera*. This dance-measure had interested Debussy so much that he had asked his young confrere to let him see the manuscript of the work. The question is: did Debussy study the score as would have been expected; or did he, as has been stated, mislay it and only find it again many years later without having ever examined it? The latter hypothesis has seemed the more probable one since the autumn of 1926, the date of the publication of 'Lindaraja', a work for two pianos which Debussy wrote in 1901, and which had lain forgotten for a quarter of a century between the pages of one of his orchestral manuscripts. For this mediocre work, 'Lindaraja', is likewise a *Habanera* in the course of which a C sharp pedal-note appears surrounded by the novel harmonic effects which young Ravel had discovered as early as 1895 and which, by a remarkable

[1] In the *Revue Musicale* of December 1920 Manuel de Falla was to comment on the intensely Spanish atmosphere of this piece. 'The descriptive skill which is condensed into the few pages of the 'Soirée dans Grenade' seems nothing short of miraculous when one considers that this music was written by a foreigner, guided almost entirely by his own insight and genius. . . . This is indeed Andalusia that he depicts for us: unauthentic truth, we might call it; seeing that not one single bar has been directly borrowed from Spanish folk-music and that, notwithstanding, the entire piece, down to its smallest details, is characteristically Spanish.'

coincidence, are also voluptuously displayed throughout the entire
length of the 'Soirée dans Grenade'. Obviously, if Debussy was
haunted by a vague memory of these shifting chords, he would not
have taken long to reproduce them, whether he frankly borrowed
Maurice Ravel's invention or unconsciously imitated it. But Ravel,
having so confidingly shown Debussy his *Habanera*, had every
reason to complain that his illustrious colleague had overstepped
the limits of legitimate reproduction, especially as Debussy showed
a natural tendency to borrow. The matter aroused some controversy
in artistic circles, and although the incidents were not made public,
they caused considerable excitement in the little world of music.
The affair had an unexpected and highly interesting sequel in 1907,
when Maurice Ravel composed a 'Rapsodie Espagnole' for
orchestra into which he inserted his old *Habanera* of 1895, giving
it the exact date, in order retrospectively to assert his paternal
rights to a charming, effective harmonic discovery.

Particular interest was aroused by this little controversy because
the majority of the critics were at that time unable to distinguish
between the harmonic treatment and pianistic style of the two
composers—surprising as this must seem to-day. Several old
critiques testify to this confusion which was openly acknowledged by many writers, in particular by E. Burlingame Hill in
an article in the *Mercure Musical* (15th of November 1906). In a
detailed study, published in the *Grande Revue* (10th of May 1907),
M. D. Calvocoressi fully explained the points of resemblance and
the differences in the musical style of these two composers, a subject with which he had already dealt briefly in the *Courrier Musical*
of the 1st of March 1905. He pointed out that Debussy's construction was obscure and difficult to analyse, and that his developments consisted of repetitions, slightly varied after the manner of
some of the Russian composers; whereas Ravel's plan and development were classical. He also showed that the tonal and harmonic
feeling, the rhythmic movement, and the melodic line of the two
composers were quite different.

Debussy was never to lose the position he had acquired in the
foreground of the musical world after the first performance of
'Pelléas et Mélisande'. Thanks to the efforts of Jules Combarieu,
the musicographer, who was then *chef de cabinet* to the Minister
for Education, Debussy was awarded the Cross of Chevalier de la
Légion d'Honneur on the 1st of January 1903. This unsolicited
distinction had an interesting musical sequel. At the suggestion
of Louis Laloy, editor-in-chief of the *Revue Musicale*, then under
the management of Combarieu, Debussy offered the latter the

publication rights of his *envoi de Rome* 'Printemps' which had not yet been printed. 'In addition to the fact that it has not yet been published', wrote Debussy to Laloy, 'it has a certain historical interest, for it reveals a *manner* which I have never recaptured.' Thus, after a delay of twenty years, this composition was published at last, in the form of an arrangement for chorus and piano duet. Thanks to the success of 'Pelléas', another *envoi de Rome* which had been practically forgotten since its production in 1893 reappeared on the concert programme. On the 21st of December 1902 Colonne performed 'La Damoiselle Élue', the principal role being taken by Mary Garden; but although invited to do so, Debussy refused to conduct his old work, a new edition of which was being prepared by Durand.

About this time Debussy accepted the position of musical critic to a Paris paper, *Gil Blas*. He made his début on the 12th of January 1903, with a feuilleton devoted to the first performance of Vincent d'Indy's 'L'Étranger' which had just been produced at the Théâtre de la Monnaie in Brussels. He held this post until the end of the 1902–3 season. At the end of April he was sent to England as musical reporter. He did not overdo his temporary journalistic duties. He sent only two articles from London, which dealt with the performances of Wagner's 'Ring'. The first, comprising his reports of the 29th and 30th of April, appeared on the 5th of May, the other on the 1st of June. He took the opportunity to write a few lines full of enthusiastic praise of Hans Richter, and indulged in a lively and humorous satire on the art of Wagner. One of his reports contained some ideas on the ballet suggested to him by an enjoyable performance at the Empire Music Hall, 'which', he wrote, 'corresponds to our *Folies-Bergère*, but with the addition of a luxurious comfort that is characteristically English'. The essential points of all these articles are reproduced in the author's book *The Theories of Claude Debussy*.

On his return Debussy found to his annoyance that he had to spend a good deal of time on the orchestral score of 'Pelléas et Mélisande' as his publisher Fromont was anxious to get the plates engraved.

At the end of June 1903 he went, out of curiosity, to hear the cantatas composed by the competitors for the Prix de Rome. He was appalled by the very theatrical style of the scores that had been sent in to the Institut. 'You have no idea of the sort of thing they are concocting', he wrote to Messager on the 29th of June, '. . . it makes one absolutely disgusted with music. These gentlemen are now awarding prizes for cantatas that do not even follow the sacrosanct traditions, but belong to the type of music known as *dramatic*.

I wish you could hear it. . . . It is painful!' He described a certain laureate as 'Leoncavallo's best pupil. Heavens, what music! It might have been written by a pork-butcher.'

After listening to these distressing performances he had the pleasure that same evening of attending a special festival organized by the Schola Cantorum; a summer concert given in an open-air theatre. The programme consisted of the prologue of Campra's 'Fêtes Vénitiennes', Duni's 'Sabots' and a pastoral ballet by Rameau entitled 'La Guirlande'. The last-mentioned work, a revival by Charles Bordes, aroused Claude Debussy's keenest enthusiasm. Only a few months previously, in one of his articles in *Gil Blas*, he had extolled the genius of the great French master, comparing him to Gluck, very much to the latter's disadvantage. So great was his enthusiasm that he could not refrain from shouting: 'Long live Rameau! Down with Gluck!' On the 29th of June he wrote as follows to Messager on the subject of 'La Guirlande': 'I was sorry you were not there. No one would have appreciated the delicate charm of this music more than you.'

A short time previously he had undertaken the disagreeable task of composing a work to order, namely the 'Rapsodie' for saxophone, intended for Mrs. Elisa Hall, President of the Boston Orchestral Club. For the sake of her health, this lady had devoted herself to an instrument which had not yet achieved the popularity it has since acquired, thanks to the triumph of Jazz. Wishing, regardless of cost, to build up a special repertoire for herself, she had given various French composers orders for important compositions. Debussy was very dilatory in the matter; he was almost incapable of composing to order, and, besides, he knew very little about the technique of this solo instrument. On the 8th of June, he wrote to Messager: 'The Americans are proverbially tenacious. The Saxophone lady landed in Paris at 58 rue Cardinet, eight or ten days ago, and is inquiring about her piece. Of course I assured her that with the exception of Rameses II, it is the only subject that occupies my thoughts. All the same, I have had to set to work on it. So here I am, searching desperately for novel combinations calculated to show off this aquatic instrument . . . I have been working as hard as in the good old days of "Pelléas". . . .' About the same time, the composer wrote as follows to Pierre Louÿs: 'Considering that this "Fantaisie" was ordered, and paid for, and eaten more than a year ago, I realize that I am behindhand with it. . . . The saxophone is a reed instrument with whose habits I am not very well acquainted. I wonder whether it indulges in romantic tenderness like the clarinet?'

In spite of all his efforts, the 'Rapsodie' remained unfinished. The following year, at the Société Nationale, Mrs. Hall played one of the pieces of her new repertoire, the 'Choral Varié' by Vincent d'Indy. But this performance did not expedite the work of the dilatory composer. In fact, he was anything but encouraged. He thought it ridiculous to see a lady in a pink frock playing on such an ungainly instrument; and he was not at all anxious that his work should provide a similar spectacle. The composition still remained in an unfinished state. On the 11th of September 1905 he wrote as follows to his publisher, Durand: 'Mrs. Elisa Hall, the Saxophone lady, is politely demanding her "Fantaisie"; I should like to satisfy her, for her patience deserves to be rewarded.' But Debussy did not satisfy her yet. In 1911, he again set to work on the instrumentation. But he wrote nothing more than a rough draft on three or four staves, and in this form the work was delivered to Mrs. Hall. He had not the courage to finish the score: he even left some bars blank, and some of the 'bridges' incomplete.

The title was to have been 'Rapsodie Orientale', as Debussy mentioned to André Messager in 1903. It then became 'Rapsodie Mauresque', the name that is inscribed on the Conservatoire manuscript, though not in the composer's handwriting. The adjective was omitted in the final edition which, like the first performance of the work, was posthumous. The score was completed by Roger-Ducasse in 1919, and it is his manuscript of the work which is included in the collection of Debussy's autograph manuscripts in the library of the Paris Conservatoire. That same year (1919), on the 11th of May, the Société Nationale was at last able to give the first performance of the 'Rapsodie' under the conductorship of André Caplet, and with the collaboration of the saxophonist, Mayeur. The work is enlivened by Spanish rhythms, and has the definite lines and rather concise expression that distinguish the works Debussy composed about the year 1903. In spite of its pleasing qualities and the present-day vogue of the saxophone, the 'Rapsodie' has not been placed on the repertoire of the symphony concerts, in Paris at any rate; for up to 1929, there has been no second performance with orchestra.

Several piano works were composed or published by Debussy in 1904. He took one piece from one of his note-books and gave it the simple title 'D'un Cahier d'Esquisses', which indicates its origin. The little work was not performed until the 20th of April 1910, when Maurice Ravel played it at the first concert of the new Société Musicale Indépendante. This piece, which is very little known, was first published in an *Album de musique* brought out by the

journal, *Paris Illustré*, early in 1904. It was subsequently bought by
a Belgian publisher, who retained the rights of the work and had it
arranged for cinema orchestra. Some of these new, or newly published, compositions seem reminiscent of earlier works. 'Masques',
which is dated July 1904, recalls the rhythmical scheme of the old
'Tarentelle Styrienne' or 'Danse' of 1890. 'Hommage à Rameau',
one of the first of the 'Images', is a new 'Sarabande', rather laboured
and formal in style, which lacks the simplicity, freedom, and charm
of the 'Sarabande' in the suite 'Pour le Piano'. It was written
at the time when Debussy was revising the score of the 'Fêtes de
Polymnie' and loudly proclaiming himself an enemy of Gluck.
But most of these works are original and show the fruits of the
composer's continuous technical experiments. 'L'Isle Joyeuse',
which was inspired by Watteau's 'Embarquement pour Cythère',
is brimful of gaiety and animation. It opens with a kind of cadence,
and the whole piece is written in a brilliant, sparkling style that has
made it a favourite with virtuosi. Debussy realized that it was
difficult of execution. In a letter to his publisher, dated September
1904, he writes gaily: 'Heavens! how difficult it is to play. . . . This
piece seems to embrace every possible manner of treating the
piano, combining as it does strength and grace . . . if I may
presume to say so.' In spite of its very pianistic style, 'L'Isle
Joyeuse' called for symphonic treatment; and, in accordance with
the instructions given by the composer in 1917, a very successful
orchestral transcription was made by the Italian conductor,
Molinari.

'Masques' and 'L'Isle Joyeuse' were performed by Ricardo Viñes
at the Société Nationale on the 18th of February 1905. They met
with great success. Julien Torchet's very honest critique of this
concert in the *Guide Musical* is worth quoting, for it describes the
frame of mind of many musicians at that period.

'The 325th concert . . . was a triumph for M. Claude Debussy. This
composer, who usually soars amidst the misty clouds of artistic vagueness, was represented on this occasion by two very rhythmical and
characteristic pieces: "Masques" and "L'Isle Joyeuse. . . ." But the programme contained other works derived from his school. I dare not
express any opinion as to whether they are better or worse than his.
Those who admire M. Debussy, worship him; those who do not admire
him, detest him. Some ten years ago I could not endure any of his works.
To-day, long habit has rendered them bearable; in fact, I go to listen to
them again and again, they attract me like some forbidden pleasure,
some vicious habit. I am afraid of growing to like the music of M.
Debussy and his imitators. . . .'

Two series of 'Images' appeared, one in 1905, the other in 1908. The honour of giving the first performance of these works was reserved for Ricardo Viñes. He played the first at the Société Nationale on the 3rd of March 1906, the second at the Cercle Musical on the 21st of February 1908. A third series bearing the same title had been planned for two pianos and had even been announced by the publisher Durand, in 1905, as being 'in the press'. Debussy intended to finish it by September. It was to include three pieces: 'Gigue Triste', 'Iberia', and 'Valse'. But the project was altered. The first two pieces were written for orchestra, and nothing is known of the last. Possibly it took the form of the little piece published in 1910 under the title of 'La plus que Lente.'

The first series of 'Images' includes 'Reflets dans l'Eau' and 'Mouvement' which form a framework for 'L'Hommage à Rameau' with its solemn sonorities suggesting an organ or wind instruments. The composer was pleased with the series. He wrote to his publisher on the 11th of September 1905: 'I think I may say without undue pride, that I believe these three pieces will live and will take their place in piano literature . . . either to the left of Schumann (as Chevillard would say) or to the right of Chopin . . . *as you like it.*' The groundwork of the first 'Image' is formed by a slow trailing theme and its transformations. Three times in succession, the three notes: A flat, F, and E flat, are mirrored in their harmonic reflections, as the title indicates. They are *Variations* of a kind, and once written, they were remodelled, as their composer explained, 'on a new basis, in accordance with the latest discoveries in harmonic chemistry'. The last of the three 'Images' is a *moto perpetuo*. Its motion, represented by a succession of triplets, is uninterrupted, except in the middle of the piece where a slower theme is introduced. Here and there we find delightfully humorous touches, such as the *motif* in octaves and fifths which the two hands ironically pass on to one another. There is a fine example of accumulation towards the end, where an original triplet figure climbs up the keys uninterruptedly in a series of whole tones, only stopping to end the piece at the extremity of the keyboard.

When these three 'Images' were subsequently performed at one of the Concerts Durand, the programme contained notes by Maurice Emmanuel drawing attention to some of the characteristics of the new Debussyist style and its ultra-modern chemical ingredients, such as: the enveloping of the real notes of a chord in notes alien to it; harmonic ellipses and omissions; passing chords traversed by the persistent outline of an unchanging pattern. In

his critique in *La Liberté*, Gaston Carraud drew attention to the felicitous and very individual manner in which Debussy had adapted devices from the technique of other composers like Balakiref. 'We find the processes of subdivision and inlaying common to the Russian composers, and all their voluptuous, capricious picturesqueness, treated with a superior skill, subordinated to a keen, subtle sense of logic, and transformed by unity of thought.' But this style of writing and this type of sensibility did not appeal to all. Many of the audience, though moved by this subtle art, seemed dumbfounded. According to the *Guide Musical*, Ricardo Viñes succeeded 'in making the composer's ideas intelligible, expressed though they were in the most abstract formulas and the most complex equations. But it was highly entertaining to watch the expressions of the audience who were obviously overwhelmed by mingled feelings of bewilderment, delight, and ecstasy.'

It was inevitable that these works should produce the complex impressions described in these vague epithets. The public would have preferred Debussy to repeat himself, to reproduce his former works, by supplying, as far as possible, exact replicas of them. But the composer, bent on discovering new means of expression, had no intention of becoming the slave of his own inventions. He was beginning to renew himself, to adopt a different manner, and in developing it, he sometimes showed a very natural uncertainty and a carefulness and attention that astonished, alarmed or delighted those who admired his former spontaneity. The distinguishing marks of his new style were already noticeable in the 'Trois Chansons de France', dated 1904, and dedicated to Mme Sigismond Bardac, who was soon after to become Mme Claude Debussy.

Amongst these songs, the first 'Rondel' of Charles d'Orléans, 'Le Temps a laissé son Manteau', is remarkable for the breadth and symmetry of its melodic line, especially in the refrain of the first verse which is repeated three times. A lively rhythm carries it along through harmonies that are as brilliant as 'le soleil riant, clair et beau', and their modernity is in striking contrast to the antiquity of the mode in which the luminous little work is written. The other 'Rondel' too is set in an ancient mode, and its harmonic and rhythmic contrasts are equally fascinating. The principal melody recalls Ernest Chausson's 'Chanson Perpétuelle'; but its movement, as well as the harmony and metre of the accompaniment, so transforms it that one scarcely recognizes the theme—an unconscious reminiscence, suggested by the similarity of the sentiments expressed

in the poems of Charles d'Orléans and Charles Cros. 'La Grotte', the third of the 'Chansons de France', written to a poem by Tristan Lhermitte, was to reappear later in the 'Promenoir des deux Amants'.

A new series of songs published about the same time under the old title of 'Fêtes Galantes', testifies to his change of style. Judging by his manuscript, Debussy had first intended the series to include only two songs: 'Le Faune' and 'Crépuscule du Soir'. Eventually, he chose three of Verlaine's poems: 'Les Ingénus', 'Le Faune', and 'Colloque Sentimental'. These songs show his love of persistent patterns, particularly the first and second, in which the rhythmic bass never changes. In 'Les Ingénus' the piano plays a very modern kind of pastiche of an old dance rhythm, to a detached declamation in which the accents do not always conform to those of the accompaniment. Likewise in the following song, 'Le Faune', the piano accompaniment no longer envelops the voice in chords. Gone is the vague harmonic halo of former days. Two independent elements are added to the voice: a flute theme and the muffled but persistent beating of a tambourine, which occasionally forms harmonies. In the 'Colloque Sentimental' the background is rendered by a very simple melodic line ending in a long pedal point which continuously sustains the dialogue in which the shades recall the past. The declamation is very faithfully modelled on the words. The colloquy itself recalls one of the first of the 'Fêtes Galantes' of 1892 by its use of *tenuti* and of a phrase suggesting the sighing of a flute, effects which had been already utilized in 'En Sourdine'. Thus, in spite of the difference in style in the first two songs, the new series is a continuation of the old.

The new style which the composer was adopting was to be displayed in all its brilliance and splendour in a big symphonic work. But there were also some unobtrusive manifestations of it in the second series of 'Images' for piano. In this series, dated October 1907, the writing can be more clearly followed as it is set out on three staves, which serve to bring out the skilful blendings and the subtle combinations of the new pianistic and harmonic elements. These three pieces: 'Cloches à travers les Feuilles', 'Et la lune descend sur le temple qui fut', and 'Poissons d'Or', are a very free type of variations. The first, as its title suggests, reproduces the complex resonances of harmonics, heard through the rustling of leaves. The third is a glorified description of the scintillating movements of its living models fixed on a lacquer tray by the hand of an Oriental artist. The composer greatly admired this *objet d'art* which inspired him to portray this endless succession of gold fishes.

The second piece has a very curious and novel character. The calm moonlight scene and the impressions awakened by its contemplation are reconstructed or translated by the musician by means of a simple melody without the support of any accompaniment whatever. Needless to say, the long phrase chanted by the piano is not completely unadorned; it is clothed in harmonies—chiefly combinations of fifths and seconds—which seem to spring and to radiate quite naturally from the melody itself. Thus Debussy, the reputed scorner of melody, declared his faith in this essential element of music—no traces of which had been discovered by some critics in the entire score of 'Pelléas et Mélisande.' 'My music', he was to say some years later, 'aims only at being melody. . . .'

The melodic value and the beauty of this moonlight picture, this new type of Nocturne, were not evident to all; indeed, they completely escaped some of the critics. Take, for instance, the extraordinary opinion expressed by Luc Marvy. In 1912, five years after the publication of this work, he wrote in the *Monde Musical* the following incredible lines, in which he alludes to a joke then current in the studios:

'I find it hard to believe that this piece is anything but a practical joke. M. Debussy and his confederate (Ricardo Viñes), must be laughing in their sleeves at the poor simpletons who take it seriously. It reminds one inevitably of the illustrious painter, Boronali, of happy memory; "Et la lune descend sùr le temple qui fut" is in the same category as "Et le soleil se couchait sur l'Adriatique".'

The most extraordinary opinions are to be found in musical journals between the years 1900 and 1914, especially during the two or three years following the production of 'Pelléas et Mélisande'. The simplest compositions called forth statements that sound incredible to-day. Here is an example from an article by Hugues Imbert, editor-in-chief of the *Guide Musical*, which appeared in that journal on the 15th of November 1904. The Concerts Colonne had just performed the 'Danses' ('Danse Sacrée', 'Danse Profane') which had been written the previous spring for chromatic harp with string orchestra. They had been commissioned by the firm of Pleyel for the competitions at the Brussels Conservatoire, where a class had been inaugurated for the study of the ancient harp in its modernized form. The music is simple and pleasantly harmonious. The use of the ancient modes, as well as certain details of the instrumentation, may possibly recall Erik Satie's 'Gymnopédies', more especially Debussy's own

orchestral transcription of his so-called precursor's little work. The critique was as follows:

'In M. Debussy's music dissonance has become the rule and consonance the exception. Consequently, those who admire the former style applauded his "Deux Danses" ("Danse Sacrée", "Danse Profane") for chromatic harp and orchestra; whilst the devotees of the latter type of music made grimaces. M. Debussy's music is either a choice or a bitter fruit, according to one's tastes and point of view. Perhaps the young composer would have succeeded in pleasing everybody if he had maintained a happy medium; he could have been as subtle as M. Gabriel Fauré without indulging in such far-fetched formulas. But M. Debussy did not wish this. His musical plan has, so to speak, no architectural quality; it is vague, hazy, disturbing, almost morbid. Its counterpart in impressionist painting is to be found in some of M. Carrière's canvases, where the subjects are so submerged in a misty atmosphere as to be barely visible, and where suffering seems to be the dominant note. . . .'

As is evident from this article, Debussy was exposed to the recriminations of most music-lovers; his admirers and adversaries alike considered his art too subtle, too free, and above all, too unstable. Ever since the triumph of 'Pelléas', people had been looking forward, in a friendly or hostile spirit, to the appearance of the big symphonic work on which he had been engaged ever since 1903 during his sojourns at Bichain, in the department of the Yonne, as well as when he was in Paris or at the seaside. His work had been hindered by certain serious events which occurred during the summer months. Most people, even the composer's friends, were ignorant of the particulars until they returned to Paris in October. André Messager heard nothing on the subject from Debussy. In a letter dated the 19th of September 1904, the composer only gave his friend the following vague hints:

'My life during the last few months has been strange and bizarre, much more so than I could have wished. It is not easy to give you particulars, it would be rather embarrassing. I would rather wait and tell you over some of that excellent whisky of the old days. I have been working . . . but not as I should have liked. . . . Perhaps I was overanxious, or perhaps I was aiming too high. Whatever the cause, I have had many a fall, and have hurt myself so much that I have felt utterly exhausted for hours afterwards. There are numerous reasons for this of which I shall tell you some day . . . if I have the courage, for it is all very sad. There are times when one spends one's days mourning for the past, and I have been mourning the Claude Debussy who worked so joyfully at "Pelléas"; for, between ourselves, I have not been able to recapture him, and that is one of my many sorrows.'

The events which occurred during the summer of 1904 involved

DEBUSSY AT POURVILLE
(September 1904)

DEBUSSY OUTSIDE HIS HOME
(about 1910)

Debussy in all kinds of complications, financial included. In spite of the intimate, personal nature of these incidents, one cannot avoid a passing allusion to them. Besides, various published statements, as well as numerous lawsuits and decrees, have made them public property. The subject was even treated by a dramatist twenty-five years ago.

At the time of Debussy's marriage with Mlle Rosalie Texier, the couple had become very friendly with Mme Sigismond Bardac, née Moyse. This lady, the wife of a financier, was very well known in musical circles. She had a son, a composer, who had studied at the Paris Conservatoire in 1901–2 and who was a devoted disciple of Debussy. She herself was an excellent amateur musician and vocalist. In recognition of her talents, Gabriel Fauré had dedicated to her in 1892, one of his finest compositions, his 'Bonne Chanson', which she had been the first to sing in public and which she interpreted delightfully. Deserting his wife—for whom this incident had at first dramatic and well-nigh fatal results—Debussy fled with this lady. The date was probably June 1904, for Debussy expresses his gratitude to this month in the very obvious dedication of the second series of 'Fêtes Galantes'. Double divorce suits ensued, which continued for several months, indeed years, and which ended by severing the legal bonds that united the Debussy-Texier and the Bardac-Moyse couples. Debussy was later to contract a second marriage. By his second wife he had had a daughter, Claude-Emma, known as Chou-chou.[1]

Debussy's financial circumstances were now very different. Up to this he had been a poor man, a Bohemian—in 1905, more than three years after 'Pelléas', the sale of his copyrights had not brought him in more than 2,400 francs. Although his second marriage meant separation from all his old friends, a complete rupture with his past life and all the ties of his youth, yet the prospect attracted him; for it effected a considerable improvement in his social position. He hoped and believed that he would now be relieved of the material cares that had always weighed him down, especially since the death of his publisher, Hartmann. During the lengthy divorce proceedings, he still had to endure hard times. It was then that he was obliged, much against his will, to sell the copyright of 'Pelléas' which he had hitherto jealously preserved. The publisher, Fromont, could not afford the 25,000 francs which

[1] In his Memoirs (*La Musique Retrouvée*, 1928) Louis Laloy gave the public a romantic version of Debussy's marriages. In this connexion, he wrote something in the nature of a defence of the composer, whose conduct had been mercilessly condemned by all his friends with the exception of Erik Satie and of Laloy himself.

the composer asked for the transfer of his rights. This important transaction was carried through by the firm of Durand. Whilst preparing a new edition of the opera, to include the orchestral interludes which had been written during the Opéra-Comique rehearsals, Durand published these interludes in a separate volume in 1905. Three months later, just before the divorce decree was pronounced against him, on the 2nd of August 1905, Debussy signed a contract pledging himself to submit all his future works to this publisher who, as a matter of fact, brought out all his new scores. Now that he was a father and married to the mother of his child, Debussy thought that all his difficulties were over. Things had reached such a pass during the last few months that, as he wrote to Louis Laloy, 'he had become incapable of even thinking except through the medium of a process-server'. But the period of complications and lawsuits was to be prolonged till the end of his life, and indeed, his heirs were involved in them long after his death.

In the midst of his matrimonial troubles, he had managed to finish his composition, 'La Mer'. The rough draft of the orchestral score was terminated on 'Sunday, 5th March at six o'clock in the evening', as he wrote on the manuscript at present preserved in an American library.[1] This work, which had been looked forward to with lively interest, consisted of three 'Symphonic Sketches', three sea pieces, inspired by recollections some of which, no doubt, dated back to his childhood and the days of his sojourns in Cannes. The titles he had originally planned for these pieces were: 'Mer Belle aux Îles Sanguinaires' (this name was chosen for the sake of the verbal contrast between the words *belle* and *sanguinaire*; Debussy was never in Corsica), 'Jeux de Vagues', and 'Le Vent fait danser la mer'. The first and last were altered to the more general and more picturesque titles: 'De l'Aube à Midi sur la Mer' and 'Dialogue du Vent et de La Mer.' He had been working for a short time at this score—not at a quintet as had been rumoured—when he wrote to his friend Messager on the 12th of September 1903. (He was then spending the summer holidays at a country place in Burgundy, the home of his parents-in-law the Texiers.)

'You may not know', he wrote, 'that I was destined for a sailor's life and that it was only quite by chance that fate led me in another direction. But I have always retained a passionate love for her (the sea). You will say that the Ocean does not exactly wash the Burgundian hill-

---

[1] In this rough copy, the date 'Sunday, 5th March, 1905', is written in a different ink from that used for the hour and the signature; and one can see that another date has been scratched out.

sides . . . and my sea-scapes might be studio landscapes; but I have an
endless store of memories and, to my mind, they are worth more than
the reality, whose beauty often deadens thought.'

Most of Debussy's admirers had anticipated that this work would
afford them pleasant recollections of the sea-music in the second
act of 'Pelléas'—the grotto scene; they expected that it would be
derived directly from his masterpiece, which was now accepted,
sanctioned, classified. But their conjectures proved false. Debussy,
who was always obsessed by a constant desire to renew his art, had
been at pains to write an entirely new type of composition. The
result was that most of the musical public were disappointed.
Possibly too, the carefully studied, but very vigorous interpretation of the work which Camille Chevillard had given at the Concerts Lamoureux on the 15th of October 1905 was not suited to
this type of music, which the spirited conductor did not appreciate
in the least. Louis Laloy evidently had Chevillard in mind in
1909 when he condemned the manner in which symphony conductors performed Debussy's works—in particular their tendency
to alter the composer's perspective, their love of contrasts, and the
sentimental outbursts which a romantic training prompts them to
indulge in whenever expression is required. The genuine Debussyites did not attach any importance to that performance once they had
heard the real first production at the Concerts Colonne on the 19th
of January 1908. On that day and on the following Sunday, the 26th
of January, Debussy took his place at the conductor's desk. Showing very obvious signs of the nervousness of the *débutant*, and a
paradoxical stiffness of manner, he confined himself to beating strict
time with his baton and the first finger of his left hand; but the
experienced orchestra knew better than to follow such rigid directions. He had at least one of the qualifications essential to the
conductor, namely, an extremely acute sense of hearing, which
enabled him to seize the smallest details of the execution. But only
his most zealous partisans could discover any outstanding merit
in the few performances he directed, for his conducting was
always stiff and awkward.[1] The presence of the very original and
much-discussed composer himself greatly heightened the interest
in this interpretation of 'La Mer' at the Concerts Colonne; it was
received with loud applause and some hissing. On the 19th of

[1] This personal opinion is contrary to that of Louis Laloy; for, on hearing
Debussy conduct 'La Mer', in January 1908, he described him as a conductor
who showed authority, precision, and power. And on the same occasion,
Pierre Lalo praised his precision, authority, and restrained energy. But we shall
see later that Debussy himself, in 1914, acknowledged to an Italian journalist
that he had not the gifts necessary for a conductor.

January, the battle between the composer's partisans and enemies was particularly lively—cries of bravo were mingled with hisses and abuse. At the conclusion of 'La Mer', the commotion lasted ten minutes; and during the ensuing performance of Bach's Chaconne by Jacques Thibaud, the disturbance began again and there was such a din that the violinist was obliged to stop playing. A few days later, on the 1st of February, Debussy's work achieved a triumphant success in London; there was no discordant note. On that occasion he again conducted the work himself, as well as 'L'Après-midi d'un Faune' and 'La Damoiselle Élue' which was then performed for the first time in England.

Interminable arguments arose in 1905 on the subject of these symphonic sketches of 'La Mer'; for in texture they were more complex, denser, and more polyphonic than had been expected and, at the same time, more powerful and grandiose. And yet, they lacked the violence, the tense romantic feeling, which according to some people must inevitably animate a seascape, producing an atmosphere of agitation and upheaval. To-day, after a lapse of a quarter of a century, the controversy may be reduced to two schools of opinion: one reproaching Debussy, more or less unconsciously, for not have repeated 'Pelléas' or the 'Nocturnes'; the other congratulating him on the marvellous manner in which he had renewed his art. No one seems to have noticed that the new score was a development of the third 'Nocturne', the 'Sirènes', which is also a sea piece. Some of the more characteristic criticisms are worth recording.

The opinion expressed by Pierre Lalo, the critic of the *Temps*, has been much discussed and frequently quoted. It reflected the feelings of those music-lovers who were disappointed.

'If the three pieces included in "La Mer" were the work of any one but M. Debussy, they would have delighted me. It is only when I compare him to himself that I am disillusioned. . . . You will ask the reason for my disappointment. . . . Think of the grotto scene in "Pelléas": a few chords and a single orchestral rhythm give you the entire atmosphere of night and of the sea. . . . It seems to me that in "La Mer", the sensibility is neither so intense nor so spontaneous; I think that Debussy desired to feel, rather than actually felt, a deep and natural emotion. For the first time in listening to a descriptive work of Debussy's I have the impression of beholding not nature, but a reproduction of nature, marvellously subtle, ingenious and skilful, no doubt, but a reproduction for all that. . . . I neither hear, nor see, nor feel the sea.'

A cruel verdict to pass on a composer who had always shown such a delicate and subtle feeling for nature, who had always loved

the sea, and who had endeavoured to render faithfully all the varied aspects of that ever-changing scene. A similar opinion was expressed by Gaston Carraud in *La Liberté* in an article which revealed his keen musical judgement. This impartial and very discriminating critic considered that the composer had misnamed this work, and went on to describe in detail its novel style and its good and bad qualities.

'The three symphonic pieces . . . do not give any complete idea of the sea, they depict only a few of its aspects as seen at close quarters. Nor do they express the essential characteristics of the sea, but rather those ever-delightful frolics in which she exhausts her divine energy, and the lively interplay of water and light that so bewitches us: the magic spell of foam and wave and spray, swirling mists and splashes of sunlight. Nor is the term "sketches" well adapted to these pieces, for their structure, though slight, is logical and strong, as in all Debussy's compositions; in fact it is clearer and more definite than in his previous works. There is also less originality and inventiveness in the ideas, which suggest now the Russians, now César Franck; the atmosphere is less subtle, less exact; the vision is rendered with a sensibility that is as delicate as ever but which seems to lack freshness. And the rich wealth of sounds that interprets this vision with such accuracy and intensity, flows on without any unexpected jolts, its brilliance is less restrained, its scintillations are less mysterious. It is certainly genuine Debussy—that is to say, the most individual, the most precious and the most subtle expression of our art —but it almost suggests the possibility that some day we may have an americanized Debussy.'

The points that Gaston Carraud criticized as defects were regarded as good qualities by M. D. Calvocoressi, a very close observer of French and foreign music. This writer, who is of Greek origin, was for fifteen years a musical critic in Paris before he settled in London. He wrote as follows in the *Guide Musical* of the 22nd of October 1905:

'I consider that "La Mer" marks a new phase in M. Debussy's evolution; the inspiration is more robust, the colours are stronger, the lines more definite. . . . One has the impression that M. Debussy, after diligently exploring the domain of sonorous possibilities, has here considerably condensed and clarified the sum total of his discoveries, and his music tends to acquire the absolute eurythmic quality that characterizes all masterpieces. . . .'

This judicious statement was developed by Louis Laloy in 1908 in an article quoted further on. Jean Chantavoine was of opinion that in 'La Mer' Debussy had been prodigal of all his most fascinating qualities as well as of all his defects. He wrote in the

Revue Hebdomadaire: 'Never was music so full of fresh, spontaneous, unexpected, novel rhythms; never were harmonies richer or more original; never has an orchestra possessed more voices and sonorities with which to interpret compositions overflowing with such a wealth of fantasy....' 'This music,' he went on to say, 'absorbs and enthralls our sensibility, caressing and wounding it by turns.... I think no one, who was not deliberately hostile, could listen to this music without its awakening a thousand memories, dim impressions which he thought he had entirely forgotten: the reflection of a sunbeam, the swift rush of a billow, the booming of a rock, or the caressing murmur of a wave as it breaks into foam on the sands and recedes.... It is a succession of subtle impressions, exquisite details, dazzling surprises, interspersed with short intervals of rest that are soon broken. M. Debussy's "La Mer" deserves a place beside his "Nuages", a little below it, perhaps, as is but in the nature of things....' He adds, however, that these sketches 'with all their brilliant effects, too often suggest a glittering kaleidoscope, for though original and attractive, they are superficial and incoherent.'

The rhythm of the work, which Jean Chantavoine praised so highly, struck Jean d'Udine as its weakest and most commonplace element. This very original and highly cultured musician was to become one of the most zealous partisans of rhythmical gymnastics, first under the guidance of Jacques Dalcroze, and later as a schismatical member of the Dalcrozian sect. In an article in the *Courrier Musical* he expressed his dislike of Debussy's new score. Seeking for the cause of his disapproval he attributes it to the obvious symmetry of Debussy's rhythm, which contrasts so strangely with the elaborateness of the harmony and the richness of the orchestration; he stigmatizes this rhythm as elementary, insipid, almost Mozartian in its symmetry. In his opinion, the whole of Debussy's music was turned out mechanically like a schoolboy's Latin verses:

'Choosing his themes and harmonies, and excluding rhythm, so that they are as lifeless as dried plants in a herbarium, M. Debussy next distributes his material, lays it out, and fits it as best he can into four, eight, or sixteen bars, which four, eight, or sixteen other bars will presently reproduce more or less exactly. Such a proceeding cannot give life to sounds which did not originally possess any individual or congenital rhythmic coefficients.... In any case, it is enough to see M. Debussy conducting an orchestra—I am not blaming him for his lack of experience, which is no crime—to realize that this composer regards the bar division as an unavoidable limitation, a hateful yoke,

from which he cannot free himself; and I pity him very sincerely. For, if he is not a genius, it is perhaps solely on account of this dynamic weakness; and if he is a genius, he is certainly an incomplete one.'

The criticism published by Luc Marvy, the editor of the *Monde Musical*, on the 30th of January 1908, was still more unfavourable, but of little significance. 'A complete systematic absence of all unity of ideas,' he wrote, ' . . . a continuous succession of vague, glittering effects. . . .' In his endeavour to depict all the undulating movements of the sea, the composer 'was faced with this dilemma: either he must give an incomplete reproduction and render the work meaningless, . . . or else all the sounds must be imitated and the result will be noise, not music. M. Debussy managed to concoct a regular salad of sonorities. One hearer was so overcome that he cried out: "I feel sea-sick!" The phrase was apt enough.' This article, which sounds so incredible to-day, does not seem to have offended many of the readers of the *Monde Musical* who were present at the second performance of 'La Mer' at the Concerts Colonne.

Jean Marnold, on the other hand, gave Debussy unrestricted praise in the *Mercure de France*.

' "La Mer" ', he wrote, 'has both power and charm; grandeur and delicacy are blended together, and interweave their shimmering colours into one fascinating polyphonic tissue full of extraordinary verve and brilliant fantasy. There are pages where one seems to tread the edge of an abyss and gaze into limitless depths. The orchestra contains undreamt-of sonorities; the inspiration is equally true in its tenderness and in its vehemence; it is at once supple, rich, and poignant. All these elements combine to form an admirable symphony. No doubt, its harmonious and novel eurythmics would have been more easily appreciated if the work had been conducted by the composer himself or one of his friends.'

Nor were any grave defects evident to the composer's most fervent admirer, his friend and confidant, Louis Laloy, who published an important article full of the most enthusiastic praise in the *Grande Revue* on the 10th of February 1908. He stated that the composer had inaugurated a new style with 'La Mer', the second set of 'Fêtes Galantes', and the first, and more particularly the second volume of 'Images' for the piano. Until then his music had been 'an art made up of suggestions, nuances, allusions; an evocative art which awoke in the hearer's soul echoes of thoughts that were not merely vague, but intentionally incomplete; an art capable of creating delightful impressionistic pictures out of atmospheric vibrations and effects of light, almost without any visible lines or substance'. The writer considered that the

'Nocturnes' and 'Estampes' belonged more particularly to this type of art. 'Without in any way abandoning his delicate sensitiveness, which is perhaps unequalled in the world of art, his style has to-day become concise, decided, positive, complete; in a word, classical.' He pointed out that in this big, powerful work, Debussy had not limited himself to delicate, ethereal, unreal effects, but had utilized strong, conspicuous colours.

Laloy went on to analyse in detail the component elements of the new score. He justly remarked that the melody, instead of remaining in suspense as formerly, or dissolving in the air, had now become definite, enduring, self-contained. He drew attention to developments that were fully worked out without any recourse to scholastic processes such as Debussy unexpectedly utilized in a subsequent work. He considered that the plan was almost classical, especially that of the first piece which, when analysed, reveals a first subject in D flat, a second in B, and a third reintroducing the original key of D flat (a theme that was destined to reappear in the last piece, according to the cyclical plan). As regards the harmony, he wrote:

'Instead of being presented in the primitive form of chords and confining itself once and for all to a chorus of instruments, it is distributed throughout the entire orchestra, it passes from one group to another, expands and shrinks by turns; above all, it takes the form of strong accents, definite *motifs*, even complete melodies, which give animation to these hitherto motionless backgrounds, dividing them into separate planes and conferring movement on them.'

The result is a vital polyphony. Instead of the loose, undulating rhythm of his previous compositions, we now find 'real dance measures: pursuits, replies, interlaced rhythms which suddenly appear, call to one another, and take their places in gay dances or in processions that are continually disbanding and re-forming in a harmonious tumult.' We find, in fact, evidence of a vigour that is not merely latent or implied, but as strikingly displayed as in the most dramatic pages of 'Pelléas et Mélisande'.

Such an appreciation, such a detailed musical analysis, is most valuable and interesting; all the more so, as it is probably the outcome not only of a minute study of the score but also of the confidences made by Debussy to his devoted friend and admirer. This article clearly indicates the change in the composer's style, a change so definite that Ladislas Fabian, the author of a German book on Debussy, regards it as the end of his impressionist period and the beginning of a new style described as *expressionism*.[1]

---

[1] Ladislas Fabian also distinguishes in the evolution of Debussy's art, a period of 'simplified melodic style', the dates of which include the afore-

In judging 'La Mer', too many of the critics had followed the convenient traditional custom of basing their opinions on superficial statements or on fruitless comparisons with the past; they indulged in uncertain forecasts and hazardous deductions, instead of considering the new work from a calm objective standpoint and placing their trust in a musician of genius who was ever seeking new means of expression.

From that time on, until an artistic truce was imposed by the European war, Debussy was the centre of ceaseless controversies between the partisans and the adversaries of his art. Both sides wrote well-meaning articles in which they pointed out the path his genius should follow, and the musician must have been greatly annoyed by the aggressive diversity of their opinions—some over-enthusiastic, others over-censorious—which served to increase his own natural doubts and perplexities. Early traces of his exasperation against both his friends and his enemies are apparent in the series of feuilletons he published in *Gil Blas* during the year following the production of 'Pelléas'. He expressed his feelings even more strongly later on in the various interviews he granted to journalists, as well as in the hastily written articles which he published in the *Revue musicale S.I.M.* from 1912 to 1914. He often told his friends that he longed to go away to some distant country where he could behold new horizons, where he would not be drawn into disputes, where, in an atmosphere of perfect liberty and peace, he could achieve a renewal of his art—the desire that obsessed him constantly during his entire career—where he would be free from the exacting, tyrannical, exasperating devotion of the Debussyites.

Debussy never ceased to rebel against this tyranny as well in his music as in his conversations and correspondence. This can be easily seen even from a superficial comparison between the first and the second set of 'Images' for piano, and becomes still more obvious if one compares the first and the second series of 'Fêtes Galantes' for voice and piano, which are separated by an interval of twelve years.

His correspondence, when it comes to be published later, will furnish numerous proofs of his constant desire and his continual efforts to renew himself. His aim was not so much to find new processes to replace those which his imitators borrowed from him so unceremoniously, but rather to achieve a style that would

mentioned period; and a 'neo-classical' period, in which he places: 'Le Martyre de Saint Sébastien', all the works written during the war (1914–17), as well as a few of his earlier compositions.

remain entirely his own. The following lines which he was to write to his friend, Godet, in 1914 betray his ceaseless strivings: 'The longer I live, the more I dislike this deliberate disorder that deceives the ear, those bizarre, beguiling harmonies that are nothing more than parlour games. . . . What a number of things one must first discover and then reject, before one can express emotion naked and unadorned.' We find unexpected evidence of his unsettled state of mind in a letter of Puccini's who, in spite of his realism, always showed his appreciation of the art of the new school of composers. In this letter, dated the 5th of April 1918, the Italian composer, writing to a journalist, says:

'When I hear people speak of *Debussyism* as a system which one may or may not adopt, I feel that I should like to tell young musicians about the doubts which, to my personal knowledge, assailed the great artist during his last years. Those harmonic processes, when they were first revealed, dazzled everybody and seemed to hold an immense reserve of ever-fresh treasures of beauty. After the first delightful shock of surprise, they grew less and less surprising, and in the end, they surprised no one. Even their author realized that they offered a very restricted field and, I repeat, I know how hard Debussy tried to escape from it. As a fervent admirer of Claude Debussy, I was anxiously waiting to see what form Debussy's revolt against Debussyism would take.'

The directors of orchestral societies often demanded new works to suit the tastes of the members. For lack of something better, Debussy's publisher would offer them old compositions that had been more or less revised. In the beginning of 1906, in answer to a request from Édouard Colonne, Jacques Durand offered to let him have the 'Cortège et Danse' from 'L'Enfant Prodigue', the Prix de Rome cantata, which the composer intended to re-orchestrate completely the following year. When the publisher informed him of the project, Debussy answered as follows on the 26th of March, 1906:

'You are very good and Colonne is most kind. . . . I am sure you will think me very annoying, but to my mind "Cortège et Danse" are hardly interesting or important enough to be played during a season in which "La Mer", the "Nocturnes", and "Images" have been successively given. I think they would be quite suitable in an historical programme of my works; but otherwise, I should be afraid that people would accuse me of dragging out all my old compositions in order to keep my name constantly on the concert posters. . . .'

This reproach was, as a matter of fact, often levelled at Debussy.

At the beginning of 1907, his admirers began to complain of his over-long silence. But Debussy was incapable of composing

unceasingly. At times he felt that he was stagnating 'dans les usines du Néant', and he suffered tortures because he could not think, because his brain was 'blind'. People also complained that he allowed old works of his to be published under new titles. But he was not responsible for the publication of works that no longer belonged to him, the rights of which he had sold to various publishers ten or fifteen years previously. These complaints found an echo in *La Nouvelle Presse*, a Paris daily, on the 26th of February. 'Jet d'eau', a vocal composition written in 1887, had just been performed at the Concerts Colonne, in the form of an orchestral transcription which failed to reproduce the transparent, fluid, atmosphere of the piano version. On this occasion, the following curious article appeared in the above-mentioned paper.

'Sincere admirers of the creator of "Pelléas"—who daily increase in numbers—have long been deploring the silence of their favourite composer. From the depths of his no doubt laborious retreat, M. Debussy does not condescend to send them anything but old compositions that have been lying by, and revivals or republications of early works. These old productions, under new titles and in new shapes, are being systematically passed in review to the great sorrow of musical epicures who are partial to first editions and unpublished works. This "Jet d'eau" (a mere extract from the "Cinq poèmes de Baudelaire" which all the Debussyites know by heart) will not satisfy their thirst for novelty. Besides, there is something contemptuous about the facile manner in which the composer of the "Nocturnes" has orchestrated this old song, in order to ensure that his name should not be banished from the Colonne concert posters during the entire winter season. The instrumentation of this piece lacks fluidity, freshness, and brilliance. The dear familiar processes that characterize "Pelléas" occur in haphazard fashion, without any descriptive justification. The piano version is preferable to an orchestral score that has neither coherence nor colour. And neither the harps nor the inevitable stopped trumpet reproduce the exquisite vision of "la gerbe d'eau qui berce ses milles fleurs que la lune traverse de ses pâleurs". One wonders whether, during his long period of idleness, M. Debussy is not losing that marvellous skill, that instinct which have made him one of the most remarkable poets of the modern orchestra. If that is the case, I see only one remedy for this disastrous situation. Let the composer of "Pelléas" read the works of the young composers who are regarded as his pupils; let him listen to this "junior class" which contemporary critics are ridiculing—a little too readily, perhaps. There, very skilfully treated, he will find all the new sonorous effects which he seems to have forgotten. The master can draw a useful lesson from the works of his impudent disciples, and he will realize with amazement the dangers that lie in wait for him. If he does not resolutely take his place once more at the head of the contemporary musical

movement, the composer of "Pelléas" will find that the young generation of parasites which has grown up around his work is writing *Debussyist* music—better than he!'

This querulous critique was written and signed by a young Debussyite, Émile Vuillermoz, who was one of the cleverest spokesmen of this 'junior class'. It makes strange reading to-day, after the lapse of a quarter of a century; but no one was astonished at it in 1907, especially as it contained a note of irony which the writer further emphasized in the course of a controversy with Louis Laloy (see the *Revue S.I.M.*, 15th of April and 15th of June, 1907, and the *Mercure de France*, 1st of June 1907). Moreover, his more or less deliberately exaggerated statements referred only to the orchestration of the 'Jet d'eau'; he did not confuse the genius of the composer with his processes, nor did he fail to distinguish between the two expressions: 'faire du Debussy' and 'être Debussy' [to imitate Debussy and to be Debussy]. This criticism seems to have had the indirect result of inducing André Caplet to re-orchestrate the piece, or at least to lighten the instrumentation; and his alterations were inserted in the orchestral score after the composer's death.

Between the years 1907 and 1910, everybody assumed the right of dictating to Debussy. French musicians were animated by a violently combative spirit; they were sharply divided into two great hostile parties, or to say the least, they belonged to creeds of conflicting tendencies. Camille Mauclair, a highly cultured critic, who had on a previous occasion invented the term *Debussyitis* and humorously described the symptoms of this new disease, wrote an important article in the *Revue* of the 15th of November, 1907—this time in a serious vein—which treated of the various musical creeds in France ('Les Chapelles musicales en France'). This article makes even more interesting reading to-day than at the time it appeared; in it we find definite mention of the faithful who belonged to the various creeds, the belligerents of the two rival clans. Descriptions of the battles that were fought in this little art war are also to be found, boldly and vividly drawn, in one of the volumes of Romain Rolland's *Jean-Christophe*, *La Foire sur la place*, which was published at that time. It describes the various activities and reactions of the classical party whose members had once been looked upon as revolutionaries; of the new rebels who, in their turn, were to end in a kind of neo-classicism; of the ageing conservatives, and the youthful explorers. . . . A never-ending struggle, but one which is more obvious during periods that are illumined by the genius of a great creative artist.

CHAPTER X

VARIOUS COMPOSITIONS. 'LE CAS DEBUSSY'
(1907–10)

IN 1905 and 1906 the issue between French musicians had been a clear one of Debussyists versus Franckists, but the situation was complicated in 1907 by an event which was deemed of sufficient importance to be described as 'L'Affaire Ravel'. Various circumstances led up to it. Some were of ancient date, such as the incident of the 'Habanera', whose harmonic innovations were still a matter of dispute; others were recent, like the disturbances at the Société Nationale on the occasion of the first performance of Ravel's 'Histoires Naturelles' (which was described as *café-concert* music to chords of the ninth'). The result was that the composer of these humorous illustrations to Jules Renard's whimsical verses was by some people ranked with Debussy, and set up as a rival of the creator of 'Pelléas'. Some regarded him as a disciple or imitator, others as an original creative artist. And Maurice Ravel at the age of thirty-two found himself, to his surprise, involved in a conflict which neither he nor his older confrère and so-called rival desired. *Ravelism* was now contrasted with *Debussyism*, although it was obvious that many amateurs, professional musicians, and even critics, were still incapable of distinguishing between the very dissimilar characteristics of the art and mentality of these two composers.

The confusion became complete on the appearance of Paul Dukas's 'Ariane et Barbe-Bleue'. The *première* of this opera had been eagerly looked forward to, and even during the rehearsals at the Opéra-Comique the work was compared and contrasted with 'Pelléas et Mélisande'. Again, in this case, the two composers, who had been friends for more than twenty years, neither desired nor encouraged this systematic comparison of their operas. It was, however, an easy matter to establish a regular parallel between the two works, and it was considered an opportune and clever thing to do. No two scores could have shown a greater disparity; their sole resemblance was the fact that both had been constructed on dramas by Maeterlinck; their only point of contact was the theme of Mélisande which Dukas had borrowed and utilized in 'Ariane'. The spirit of the music itself was utterly dissimilar in the two operas: one was highly intellectual; the other somewhat sensual. Even before the first performance of

'Ariane et Barbe-Bleue', the members of Schola, as became connoisseurs of architectural design, were lost in admiration on seeing the substantial framework of its solid symphonic form; but in hailing the work as a masterpiece they were no doubt influenced by their anti-Debussyist spirit. The Debussyites held various and contradictory opinions; they hesitated between enthusiasm and disparagement. In the solution of artistic problems there was no middle course for them: they were either Guelphs or Ghibellines—so their ranks became divided. As happens in Parliament during periods of crisis, parties coalesced and formed new groups. Rather complicated tactics were indulged in by the principal critics in 1907. Pierre Lalo and Gaston Carraud took up a hostile attitude; they were adherents of the Schola and admirers of both Dukas and Debussy, but opponents of Debussyism.[1] Louis Laloy, a former pupil and partisan of the Schola, had undergone a sudden conversion at the Opéra-Comique in the spring of 1902, and his violent Debussyist sentiments took the form of brilliant prophecies which delighted some of his readers and exasperated others. Jean Marnold was pro-Debussy, pro-Ravel, and anti-Schola, though personally favourable to Vincent d'Indy; but in spite of the scientific and mathematical trend of his articles, they were not free from juvenile exaggerations. Young Émile Vuillermoz, a champion of both Debussyism and Ravelism, though, as we have seen, occasionally critical of Debussy, was above all an implacable enemy of the Schola and Vincent d'Indy, of the partisans of contrapuntal exaggerations and 'the Jansenists of the augmented fifth'; both in public and private he acted as the leader of a powerful and widespread conspiracy against the neo-Beethovenian spirit of the Franckists. The history of the Debussyist feuds and of 'L'Affaire Ravel' has been recorded in the author's own musical review (see the *Revue française de Musique* of the 5th of October 1905, and of the 14th of April, 1st of May, 15th of June, and 15th of December 1907). The author took part in a friendly controversy with 'L'Ouvreuse du Cirque d'Été', and with Jean Marnold and Émile

[1] A feuilleton which appeared in the *Temps* of the 24th of March 1908, on the occasion of a revival of 'Ariane et Barbe-Bleue' at the Opéra-Comique, shows the narrow-mindedness of some professional musicians. In this article Pierre Lalo deplores the fact that in 'the battle of Pelléas', people of taste had curious allies in the shape of some 'degenerate aesthetes'. He adds 'There were days when, in our annoyance at finding ourselves in the same ranks with them, we concluded that, in order to attract such partisans, "Pelléas" must contain some unsuspected blemishes. This will not happen in the case of "Ariane". . . .' Debussy was more hurt by these controversies than he cared to show. In a letter to Jacques Durand, bearing the same date as the feuilleton, he alludes somewhat bitterly to this article of Pierre Lalo who, Debussy complains, seems to regard 'Pelléas' as music 'for debauchees'.

Vuillermoz. As usual, his tolerant attitude resulted in his being regarded as a Guelph by the Ghibellines and as a Ghibelline by the Guelphs.

Occasionally Debussy made the classification of his works a difficult task by writing compositions of an utterly unexpected type. In the *Children's Corner*, published in 1908, he displayed a sense of humour which some of his earlier compositions had already revealed, though the seriousness of 'Pelléas' had made people forget this characteristic. This little suite for piano was played at the Cercle Musical on the 18th of December 1908, by Harold Bauer, who interpreted it with all his usual skill but in a rather romantic style, indulging in uncalled-for contrasts and effects. The work had been specially written for Debussy's little daughter, and the English titles seem to suggest the games played by a child in charge of an English nurse or governess. The composer made an original design of his own for the cover illustrating the title, and the work is dedicated to 'my dear little Chouchou, with her father's affectionate apologies for what follows'. This very gifted child, who was not to survive her father, was studying the piano, as may be inferred from the title of the first piece, a parody of the 'Gradus ad Parnassum': both the technical exercise, which begins in a very easy form, and the Latin title with its doubly classical significance, are reminiscent of Clementi. Writing to Jacques Durand, who had inquired as to its tempo, the composer ironically described it as: 'a kind of progressive, hygienic, gymnastic exercise to be played every morning fasting, beginning *moderato*, and working up gradually to an *animato*.' In the *Revue Hebdomadaire* Jean Chantavoine gave a delightful literary transcription of this 'tiny masterpiece full of mischievous wit'. The third piece, the 'Serenade of the Doll', had been printed separately in 1906, the year of its composition, under the title of 'Sérénade à la Poupée' (the English title is of course incorrect, the word *of* being used in mistake for *to*). The sixth, and best known piece, is the 'Golliwog's Cake-Walk', in the middle of which occurs an unexpected passage marked 'with great emotion'—an ironical reference to the Prelude of 'Tristan and Isolde'; this little composition is a witty imitation of the newly imported negro music which preceded the now triumphant jazz. It was written for sheer amusement. The great musician, who was at times something of a snob, managed very cleverly to bring his art to the level of his little daughter, whose games he loved to share. According to Harold Bauer, whose reminiscences appeared in the *New York Times* of the 21st of December 1930, Debussy felt somewhat uneasy as to the result of his public excursion into the domain of

humour. He remained outside the concert hall during the performance and was delighted when his interpreter informed him
that the audience had laughed at his musical witticisms.
André Caplet made an orchestral transcription of the work
which he produced in New York in 1910. Debussy himself
conducted it at the Cercle Musical in Paris, on the 25th of
March 1911; and the Concerts Lamoureux performed it on the
25th of February 1912. The adaptation though skilful, is uninteresting and at times awkward, and the purely pianistic 'Gradus
ad Parnassum' is of course deprived of all its significance.
During that same year, 1908, Debussy published 'Trois
Chansons de Charles d'Orléans', a new set of songs written in
an unusual form to verses by the courtier-poet, the first performance of which was conducted by Debussy himself at the Concerts
Colonne on the 9th of April 1909. They consist of unaccompanied
choruses, modern in harmony, but written in an old-world contrapuntal style which was obviously inspired by the Renaissance
masters, so dear to the Schola. In an article in *Gil Blas*, in 1903,
Debussy had proclaimed the intense admiration for these Renaissance composers, which he had already expressed in his Roman
correspondence, as well as in his letters to Chausson.
The variety of tendencies displayed in Debussy's new works,
the unusual style in which they were written, and his continual
attempts to transform his art, were disconcerting to people of
a conservative mentality. Such minds are always disturbed by
the slightest evolution on the part of musicians the characteristics
of whose art and genius they imagine they have indefinitely determined once and for all. In an interview, given in February 1908,
Debussy declared that the days of the *chef d'école* were over: 'the
chef d'école implies a special technique, not merely a few processes, but a complete individual doctrine. Now in these days
the musician (or artist) who has achieved great celebrity has only
one desire, namely: to produce individual works, works that will be,
as far as possible, ever new. He can no longer find time to train
disciples, or even to draw up such rules as would enable him to
train them.'
Early in the spring of 1909 Debussy gave admirers and calumnia-
tors alike two opportunities to display their feelings openly. At
the Concerts Sechiari, on the 25th of March, he conducted his
'Prélude à l'Après-midi d'un Faune', an accepted masterpiece,
a safe composition which gained unanimous success. As soon as
he took his place at the conductor's desk, Debussy was greeted
with frenzied applause; but, immediately, a hostile counter-

demonstration broke out which was obviously aimed rather at the ultra-fervent Debussyists than at the composer himself. When he conducted his new polyphonic choruses at the Concerts Colonne, a fortnight later, on Good Friday, these unknown compositions were received with such warm applause that the last two items had to be repeated and no dissentient voice was heard.

This display of enthusiasm evidently exasperated some of the critics. The archaic, yet novel beauty of the 'Chansons de Charles d'Orléans' did not procure them unalloyed pleasure, but rather dis-illusion; they expected more from the composer—they were inclined to demand from him something better than these charming imitations. This almost general feeling of disappointment led the journalists to pronounce a formal censure both on the novel characteristics that did not conform to their vague aesthetic ideals and on those that were old, and consequently out of date. From amongst the numerous examples of this attitude of hostility towards Debussy, we quote the following lines from the *Guide Musical* in which the writer attacks 'La Damoiselle Élue'. The work which had been performed once more at the Concerts Colonne on the same day as the 'Chansons de Charles d'Orléans' appeared somewhat old-fashioned on account of its literary, if not musical, pre-Raphaelitism. ' A great disillusionment has saddened all our hearts', wrote this malcontent. 'The beautiful maiden who won our love of yore, is to-day a wrinkled, insipid, irritating old maid, whom the author of her being conducts with a weary arm. It is heart-rending. Let us weep for her, for him, and for ourselves.' Reading between the lines we find that this unfair criticism records a feeling that was very widespread at that time, though usually less brutally expressed. As we have already seen from the article quoted at the end of the preceding chapter, Debussy's intolerant worshippers considered it the absolute duty of their deity to rise above all human contingencies, and to go on, unceasingly and unflaggingly, creating sublime works inspired by a stupendous genius.

Meanwhile, gradually and not without difficulty, Debussy's works were becoming known. 'Pelléas et Mélisande' was produced in Brussels in January 1907. The composer went to Belgium to super-intend the last rehearsals, which necessitated a great deal of work. The interpreters were Mary Garden, the baritone Bourbon (Pelléas), the bass Arthus (Arkel), Mme Bourgeois (Geneviève), and Mlle Das, 'a singer with a light voice,' wrote Debussy on the 3rd of January, 'who is somewhat disconcerted by the lack of vocaliza-tion in the part of Yniold'. The unfortunate composer, who had

little experience of the almost miraculous extemporizations common to operatic performances, was greatly worried. He could not believe those who assured him that everything would go well. He confided his anxieties to his publisher, to whom he wrote as follows on the 7th of January:

' They have a bell here which ought to ring on G but which, out of a spirit of contradiction, rings on C. It sounds like the dinner-bell of the castle, and it mars the sad scene of Mélisande's death. So far, I have only seen half a tower . . . a fountain in white wood . . . and the subterranean regions are so realistic that it is impossible to get into them. Little Yniold is so young that he hasn't learnt music yet, and the *dress rehearsal* is to-morrow. . . . Better to be a dead celebrity with whom they can do as they like. Indeed, I fancy both the singers and the orchestra are seriously thinking of casting me for that rôle, for it seems that they have never come across a composer who is so hard to please. . . . So, my friend, you will witness a performance that will be anything but perfect; I apologize beforehand, I have made every effort to have things otherwise, even to the extent of making myself disagreeable. . . .'[1]

In spite of all his anxieties, the Brussels production on the 9th of January 1907 was a triumph. Eight performances were given in a month. The critics were enthusiastic. In his report in *L'Éventail*, the novelist, Georges Ekkhoud, declared that in future the beautiful drama of his compatriot, Maeterlinck, should never be deprived of the 'suave, subtle, musical atmosphere with which the French composer has imbued and impregnated it'; from a literary man this was the highest possible praise.

Not until 1908 was 'Pelléas et Mélisande' produced in a French provincial town, and then in the most Wagnerian of all. One of the directors of the Grand Théâtre in Lyons was Philippe Flon, the Belgian conductor who had conducted the first performances of the 'Ring' in France four years previously. This musician whose talents were of a vigorous order and who was no Debussyite, had taken the precaution of getting the composer to go over the score with him at the piano. He conducted the first performance at Lyons on the 1st of April 1908, the principal singers being: the tenor Geyre, Mlle Berthe César, the baritone Gaidan, and the bass Lafont. The audience, utterly Wagnerian in sentiment, was inevitably disappointed; only three performances were given, to half-empty theatres. It was a *succès d'estime*, in other words, a failure. The general public were completely apathetic

[1] These two letters were written on the 3rd and 7th of January 1907, but Debussy inadvertently dated them 1906, so that they have been erroneously classified amongst the letters of that year in his correspondence with his publisher.

in spite of the Belgian conductor's romantic interpretation of the opera, and the eloquent appeals which the critics of Lyons had made to their fellow citizens, before and after the first performance. In the very same month, the masterpiece was transplanted to a country to whose aesthetic ideals it did not conform, namely to Italy, where the prevailing taste is all for *bel canto* and lively dramatic effects. It was given for the first time at the Scala in Milan in April 1908. This production, under the musical direction of Toscanini, was a tardy realization of a project conceived as early as 1905 by Gatti-Casazza, the manager of this famous opera house, at the suggestion of Toscanini's predecessor, Campanini. The opera was sung in Italian, the interpreters being: la Ferrani (Mélisande), la Lollini (Geneviève), la Schinetti (Yniold), Fiorelli Giraud (Pelléas), Pasquale Amato (Golaud), and Giulio Cirini (Arkel). This great artistic event was the occasion of very lively incidents. Both at the dress rehearsal and the first performance, hostile demonstrations took place which developed into a real battle. The noise was so great that from the stage the manager could hear neither the orchestra nor the singers, and he feared that the performance would have to be stopped. It was only after a determined struggle on the part of some young pupils of the Milan Conservatoire that the performances were allowed to proceed. This artistic battle eventually attracted crowded audiences to the eight performances which were given in the space of three weeks. A year later, the opera was staged in Rome. There, too, violent scenes occurred at the *première*; the public began hissing from the very start of the performance. The critics, however, were favourable, and the frequenters of the gallery demanded a special performance, at popular prices, to enable the real music-lovers to form a true opinion of the value of the work. The disturbances were so violent and prolonged that the daughter of the French Ambassador to Rome, Mademoiselle Hélène Barrère, thought fit to write an explanatory article on the subject, which was published in the *Revue Musicale*, on the 1st of May 1909. This able and diplomatic young lady stressed the fact that the Italians usually showed keen interest in modern French music. She stated that the disturbances, unseemly though they were, were not directed against Debussy or his opera, but solely against the manager of the theatre in person, with whom the public were so dissatisfied that they objected to all his undertakings, no matter how felicitous. The musicians of Rome were to make amends to Debussy in person, in 1914, when they acclaimed him both as conductor and composer at a concert in the Augusteo.

Before reaching Italy, 'Pelléas' had penetrated into Germany, the first experiment being made at Frankfurt-on-Main on the 17th of April 1907. The work was conducted by Rottenberg, the singers being: Frl. Sallin (Mélisande), and Herren Wirl (Pelléas), Breitenfeld (Golaud), Schneider (Arkel). At first the public was perplexed, especially as, owing to the emphatic accentuation natural to the German language, Otto Neitzel's exact translation could only give an approximate idea of the work, being constantly at variance with Debussy's smooth-flowing style. Nevertheless, the reception given to the opera on that occasion ensured its success in Germany. The Press was favourable, although the usual reservations were made on the score of monotony, lack of colour, and the harmony, which some critics regarded as mere cacophony. Hugo Schlemuller declared in the *Signale* that he had heard nothing in the entire opera but successions of chords, false relations, and series of consecutive fifths; in fact, in his opinion, the whole score, with its vague tonality, was like a collection of outlandish curios, a cabinet full of harmonic monstrosities.

'Pelléas' caused great disappointment at Munich, where it was given on the 9th of October 1908, and at Berlin, where it was performed a fortnight later. The public were incapable of appreciating a work that was so characteristically French in style. In countries that were entirely impregnated with romantic art, especially that of Wagner and Mahler, the music, declamation, orchestration, must all have appeared excessively restrained and depressingly colourless. In some towns, after the first night, the performances were given to half-empty theatres. Although the ground for the Berlin production had been prepared by a lecture given by the translator, Otto Neitzel, a well-known critic, some of the audience, who had expected to hear an opera in the traditional style, gave angry vent to their disappointed feelings. In Munich, the musical direction had been left to the conductor, Roehr, as Felix Mottl had declined the honour. The conductor of the Berlin performances was Alexander Birnbaum, who came from Lausanne for the occasion. In both towns the Press was very favourable to Debussy. One critic, P. Schwerz, in an article in the *Allgemeine Musik Zeitung*, observed that German composers could glean valuable hints from Debussy's free treatment of the words and the voice. In 1909 the same paper published an article by Theodor Tagger, which concluded with a paraphrase of Schumann's famous allusion to Chopin: 'Hats off, gentlemen, Debussy is a genius!'

The United States welcomed the dramatic work of Maeterlinck and Debussy about the same time as did Germany and Italy.

'Pelléas et Mélisande' was produced in New York in February 1908, when a series of performances in French was organized at the Manhattan Opera House under the direction of Hammerstein. Four of the artists who had created the roles in Paris took part: Mmes Mary Garden and Gerville-Réache, MM. Jean Périer and Dufrane. The musical direction had been entrusted to an Italian conductor, Campanini, who greatly admired the work and had seen it performed at the Opéra-Comique in Paris in the spring of 1905, when he himself was conducting a season of Italian opera at the Châtelet theatre. As usual the public were taken by surprise, but they gave the work a very warm reception. A year later, the same conductor directed similar performances at Covent Garden, London, where, more than in any other foreign country, the public was prepared to appreciate 'Pelléas.'

Some twenty years previously, Debussy had tried in vain to win recognition in England; he now achieved a great and personal success. He made his first appearance at the Queen's Hall on the 1st February 1908, when he conducted his 'Prélude à l'Après-midi d'un Faune', and also 'La Mer', which was then performed for the first time in England. Debussy, who was very nervous, especially because of his lack of experience in conducting, had the satisfaction of achieving an exceptionally brilliant success. The public and the critics were equally enthusiastic. The English were particularly struck by his remarkable resemblance to the late Dante Gabriel Rossetti, the librettist of 'La Damoiselle Élue'. A year later, he had to return to London to conduct further performances of his work given by the Queen's Hall Orchestra. The programme again included the 'Prélude' and, in addition, the 'Nocturnes'. Once more the reception was enthusiastic; 'Fêtes' had to be repeated, as the first rendering had been somewhat marred owing to the composer's inexperience. Debussy was to have gone on to Edinburgh and Manchester, but he fell ill. He had to abandon the idea of continuing his journey and return to Paris. He went to England a third time in May 1909, to superintend the rehearsals of his opera in which the principal singers were Rose Féart, Warnery, Bourbon, and Marcoux.

Campanini had only been allowed three rehearsals with orchestra, including the dress rehearsal. The maestro conducted very well, though rather too showily in the opinion of the composer who, in a letter to Toulet, gave the following amusing sketch: 'The conductor answers to the charming name of Cleofonte Campanini; he beats time in a most peculiar manner, exactly as if he were working a hand pump. . . .' Debussy was exasperated by the behaviour of

a stage-manager from Marseilles, and disgusted with the whole atmosphere of the opera house, which he had always found unbearable both in France and elsewhere. 'No matter what efforts one makes', he wrote to Durand, 'there is always an element of mediocrity that is horribly upsetting.' He had not the courage to attend the *première* on the 21st of May; but it went very well, according to the invariable rule, for the dress rehearsal had been execrable. The opera was in fact a brilliant success. A few days later, on the 25th of May, Edwin Evans gave an important lecture on the recently produced work at the Royal Academy of Music, London. He made a very able and comprehensive analysis of 'Pelléas' which was published in the *Musical Standard* of the 5th of June 1909 and which appeared in a French translation in the present writer's musical review (*Revue Française de Musique*) of the 1st of January 1910. Several other lectures on the art of Debussy were given about this time, and his compositions were discussed in numerous articles, usually in a very sympathetic spirit. In March 1909 the *Revue S.I.M.* published a study by Jean Aubry, pointing out the importance of the favourable reception given to Debussy's music in England.

On the eve of his second journey to London, that is to say, about the middle of February 1909, Debussy, the former revolutionary, became a public official. He was appointed a member of the Supreme Council of the Musical Section of the Paris Conservatoire, thanks to the efforts of Gabriel Fauré, to whom he was not united by any bonds of friendship. Some journalists took advantage of this opportunity to interview him. He did not hesitate to give his candid opinion of the National School of Music of which he had now become adviser. He criticized the method of teaching harmony, the system of public competitions, and the institution known as the Prix de Rome; the essential points of these criticisms will be found in the author's book on his theories. It was part of his new functions to adjudicate at some of the competitions. In 1907 he was one of the judges for the wind-instrument tests, and was delighted with the sonorities of the flutes, oboes, clarinets, and bassoons. This experience interested him so much that he consented to write the two test pieces for the clarinet candidates in the 1910 competitions: a competition piece and a sight-reading test.

The test piece bears the promising title of 'Première Rapsodie'; it was composed in December 1909 and January 1910, being first written with piano accompaniment, and subsequently arranged for orchestra in 1910–11. The other piece, published under the title of 'Petite Pièce', was also transcribed for orchestra. In 1910, Debussy again adjudicated at the wind-instrument competitions.

The majority of the candidates showed little talent. The composer considered that only one competitor, Vandercruyssen, who obtained the first prize, had interpreted the piece 'like a real musician'. The 'Rapsodie', which was dedicated to P. Mimart, was played by this virtuoso, to piano accompaniment, at the Société Musicale Indépendante, on the 16th of January 1911. This piece, which was orchestrated during the summer of 1911, was a valuable addition to the repertoire of an instrument for which neither Mozart nor Weber disdained to write, and the 'romantic charm' of which Debussy had always appreciated. Although written in the showy style suitable for a solo instrument, the work maintains a high artistic level; its melodic breadth, the graceful ease of the instrumental coloratura passages, and the charm of the orchestral accompaniment are equally noteworthy. One of the first performances of the work, if not the very first, was given in Russia towards the end of the autumn of 1911. The audience showed a perplexity which surprised Debussy; he wrote on the 8th of December: 'Surely this piece is one of the most pleasing I have ever written. . . .'

Notwithstanding the halo of glory which Debussy had worn for some years past he was quite aware of the endless controversies which the versatility of his art still called forth, and which caused him intense annoyance. Battles continued to rage around this artist who ardently desired to keep aloof from all party conflicts. The production even of some of his early works gave rise to discussions at home and abroad. For example, during the winter of 1906–7, 'L'Après-midi d'un Faune' and two Nocturnes were performed at Christiania (Oslo), under the conductorship of Johan Halvorsen. The Norwegian public received the works with enthusiasm, and 'Fêtes' had to be repeated—the applause being led by Grieg. But the critics indulged in lively disputes; for even then, seven and thirteen years after the publication of these delightful works, some refused to admit that music could develop along the lines chosen by the French composer, instead of following the paths already marked out of it.

In October 1909 the *Revue du Temps Présent* published a long article which betrayed an utter lack of musical understanding. The author, Raphaël Cor, basing his argument on a principle wrongly attributed to Wagner, to the effect that melody was the only essential of music, proceeded to state that the works of the French composer did not contain any trace of melody ('according to Debussy's own admission. . . .' though Debussy's stated opinion was to the contrary!) On this basis, he built up an elaborate aesthetic theory, and having analysed Debussy's art, he ventured

to express, quite solemnly, opinions such as the following: 'His originality is supremely negative. If you deprive music of all rhythm, melody, and emotion, you will not be far from a definition of his art.' So foolish a statement does not call for any answer. Two journalists took advantage of the opportunity to investigate what they termed 'le Cas Debussy'. They approached several writers, artists, philosophers, composers, and critics, and put to them three questions which were expressed in the following jargon: 'What is the actual significance of M. Claude Debussy, and what should be his role in the evolution of contemporary music? Is he a really original personality or merely an accidental phenomenon? Is he the representative of a fecund innovation, of a formula or a tendency capable of creating a new school—should he, in fact, create such a school?'

Some of his appointed judges, amongst them Gaston Carraud, Camille Chevillard, and Jules Écorcheville, declined the honour in appropriate and witty terms. A great many were quite willing to answer, and of these Albert Bazaillas, Professor of Philosophy, the critic Willy, and Ernest Ansermet, did so judiciously (the last-named, a future conductor, stated in a letter of the 25th of October 1909 that 'M. Debussy's important contributions to technique find their repercussions in most contemporary composers, particularly in Richard Strauss, in nearly every page of "Electra" . . .'). Most of the others who replied unconsciously displayed their own stupidity. All the answers were published in a little volume entitled *Le Cas Debussy*, bearing the names C. Francis Caillard and José de Bérys. The book is worth its weight in gold. Sâr Péladan declares that Debussy's music makes him suffer physically, he describes the composer as 'a deformer of music and impressions, who is possibly the victim of some nervous affection difficult to classify'; a 'Salon d'Automne musician, akin to M. Matisse'. Camille Bellaigue is of opinion that his former fellow pupil at the Conservatoire is of very little importance in the evolution of art; and to the last question, he replies with desperate intensity: 'No, no, and again, no!' The composer, Edouard Trémisot, professes a certain degree of appreciation for Debussy so long as he is only treated to 'short auditions' of his works, but he dreads the thought of 'a school founded on the accumulation of his solecisms'. As a general rule, the adversaries of the new art were convinced of its decrepitude. One music-lover, A. Chéramy, expressed a very widespread opinion when he wrote: 'I feel sure that in ten years' time there will be very little mention of "Pelléas et Mélisande" . . .'

Some German composers who were approached by the investigators expressed disconcerting views. Siegmund von Hausegger

stated that 'Debussy makes a principle of the absence of melody and rhythm, thus renouncing the two essential elements of music. . . . Debussy's originality is rather the outcome of his morbid nature than of any real depth of personality. . . .' Even his harmonies 'cannot always be regarded as original; instead of the challenging audacities one had anticipated, one is quite surprised to meet with harmonies that are rather commonplace in spite of their insinuating charm and seeming complexity. His originality is due rather to eccentricity than to genius. His art will certainly be of the greatest interest to historians, but it will not be an active and living influence in the future.' Hausegger concludes his curious statement with the hope that 'the rhythmic feeling which is such an important element in French music, and the charm of his melodic inventiveness, will prevent him from going astray in these regions of vague, flattering dreams'. The conductor, Felix Mottl, who had such a keen and lively appreciation for the music of Emmanuel Chabrier, expressed his admiration for 'l'Après-midi d'un Faune', 'a delightful, refined little work, exquisite in tone-colouring', to which he considered 'Pelléas' 'was not in any way related'. Regarding music drama Wagner's principles remained the only ones he could accept, and he declared that he was quite incapable of judging a work like Debussy's, which differed entirely from his ideal. This verdict was not lightly given. Already in May 1907, in the interval between the two performances of 'Tristan and Isolde' which he had conducted at the Théâtre de la Monnaie in Brussels, Mottl had read Debussy's orchestral score. He immediately resolved to produce the French work at the Royal Opera House in Munich, and in the following autumn he had conducted a few performances of 'Pelléas' there with all his usual skill.

Comment is superfluous in the case of Siegfried Wagner's scornful reply written from Bayreuth on the 21st of October 1909, when his French colleague had been publishing for ten or fifteen years such compositions as the Quartet, 'L'Après-midi d'un Faune', and the Nocturnes. 'I must confess,' he wrote, 'that I do not know the works on which you have asked my opinion. "Pelléas" has been given in Germany, but I was advised not to go and hear it, as the German translation is a bad one. I followed this advice in part, by hearing one act only, and one cannot judge from one act. . . .' [1]

[1] In 1911 Siegfried Wagner took occasion to state that he persisted in this deliberate ignorance which also extended to the works of his compatriot, Richard Strauss. 'My object', he said, 'is to endeavour to remain faithful to myself. I am anxious to avoid all contact with ultra-modern productions. Thus, for instance I know none of Debussy's works. . . .'

The verdicts of Joachim and Rimsky-Korsakof are also of interest. In January 1905, in a letter quoted by Maurice Emmanuel, the famous German violinist wrote that he could not account for the success of 'Pelléas'; he had discovered nothing in the score but utter disorder, haphazard effects, mere improvisations. As for the Russian composer, on hearing 'Pelléas' at the Opéra-Comique in 1907, he declared that there was nothing about it that he liked; he complained of the monotony of the music, the uniform softness of the orchestra, and the harmonic combinations, which he found incomprehensible. . . . The impression he had received on reading the score at the piano was confirmed when he heard the work performed, and he was of opinion that this 'curious experiment' of Debussy's had no future before it.

In the midst of so much nonsense, it is a pleasure to come upon the threefold answer of Jean d'Udine which is remarkable for its conciseness, moderation, and wisdom. This author was an admirer of the Nocturnes, but did not care for 'La Mer'.

'M. Debussy', he writes, 'is obviously a composer of the utmost importance, for nearly all the musical scribblers are now engaged in writing either hypo-Debussy or hyper-Debussy. M. Debussy is certainly *without an equal*; and if he is only an accident, he is at all events an accident that has had serious consequences, since he has disturbed the entire musical organism of his day. I do not know whether he *ought* to create a school . . . but I notice that he *has* created one. As for saying whether his influence promises to be fruitful, or whether he is really an original composer . . . we shall know that in a century or two, and if you wish, we can discuss the matter further, in the Elysian Fields. . . .'

Besides the thirty published letters, this inquiry comprised a large number of evasive answers. The matter aroused comment in various reviews and newspapers. Some writers made a lively and justifiable attack on the promoter of the controversy, Raphael Cor, who, with a grievous lack of sensibility, almost amounting to deafness, ventured to state that Debussy's scores 'contain notes and sounds, but they are not music!' All these discussions must have had a disturbing effect on the musician; they certainly irritated him. And there was more to follow.

CHAPTER XI

'IMAGES' FOR ORCHESTRA; PRELUDES AND SONGS
(1910–13)

AN important composition was published between 1910 and
1913 which aroused considerable opposition and gave rise to
lively controversies. This was the great triptych, 'Images', a set of
symphonic pieces, of varied aspects and contrasting styles, which
constituted a further attempt on the part of Debussy to strike out
a new path. In writing this series Debussy borrowed from the
popular music of three countries: from English folk-music, in
'Gigues'; from Spanish dances, in 'Ibéria'; and from French songs,
in 'Rondes de Printemps'. In the last-mentioned 'Image', the
second in order of performance, he has recourse to academic processes, any strict application of which he had avoided in his previous
works.

In this symphonic triptych, 'Images', the three pictures which
depict England, Spain, and France, are too uniformly subtle
and too full of brilliant, sparkling effects, to be performed with
advantage at the same concert. They took a long time to complete.
'Rondes de Printemps' and 'Ibéria', which had originally been
planned and announced as compositions for two pianos in 1905,
were eventually written for orchestra. Both these works as well as
'Gigues' were to have been ready by July 1906; but at the end of
the rough draft of the orchestral score of 'Ibéria' we find the date
25th of December 1908; the 'Rondes' were finished only in 1909,
and the 'Gigues' in 1911. The days were over when Debussy,
untrammelled by publishers' contracts and heedless of public
opinion, could write spontaneously what his emotions dictated.
His youth had fled. By formal contract with his publisher, he had
relinquished his cherished freedom as a composer; the Bohemian
of former days, who followed only his own inspiration, had reluctantly become a bourgeois, a purveyor to the firm of Durand,
a kind of galley-slave of music. Meanwhile, attention was focused
on the productions of a composer whom much to his annoyance the
entire musical world persisted in regarding as the leader of a school.
Musicians watched out for the appearance of his new works with
more eagerness than sympathy, expecting to find faultless examples, flawless models, perfect works of art.

The composer's correspondence with his publisher, Durand,
betrays his misgivings; as his fame increased, he became more and

more a prey to doubts. By the 8th of August 1906, Debussy, who was then staying at Puys, near Dieppe, had thought of three different ways of ending 'Ibéria'. 'Shall I toss up between them', he wrote, 'or try and find a fourth solution?' A year later, on the 5th of August, he was hoping to finish the 'Images' at Pourville. 'There were a number of passages that I was dissatisfied with. . . . It was well written, but in the well-worn professional manner that is so difficult to avoid and so tedious. I really believe that I have now discovered what I want, something different from that mandarin-like style which certainly does not suit me.' What the composer describes as a mandarin-like style is possibly the academic treatment of the 'Rondes de Printemps'. On the 3rd of September he anticipates that the three 'Images' will soon be ready, if he can succeed in finishing the 'Rondes' 'as I should like, and as it should be done. The music of this piece has a distinctive ethereal quality, and consequently one cannot treat it as one would a robust symphony that has four feet to walk on (sometimes they have only three, but get along all the same).' After another six months, 'Images' were still awaiting completion. The reason was that Debussy, as he stated in March 1908, had been trying 'to achieve something *different*—an effect of *reality*—what some imbeciles call *impressionism*, a term that is utterly misapplied, especially by the critics; for they do not hesitate to use it in connexion with Turner, the finest creator of mysterious effects in the whole world of art.'

The 'Rondes de Printemps' (which bear as an inscription these words from 'La Maggiolata': 'Vive le mai! Bienvenu soit le mai avec son gonfalon sauvage!') were finished about the same time as 'Ibéria', the original orchestral score of which is dated 25th of December 1908. On the 19th of May 1909, just before leaving for London, Debussy was able to send in the manuscript of the 'Rondes', of which about a dozen bars were still incomplete. They were played in Paris at the Concerts Durand, on the 2nd of March 1910. The composer himself conducted that day. One wonders whether the programme notes, which bore the signature of Charles Malherbe, were inspired by Debussy.

'. . . These are real pictures' one reads 'in which the composer has endeavoured to convey, aurally, impressions received by the eye. He attempts to blend the two forms of sensation, in order to intensify them. The melody, with its infinitely varied rhythms, corresponds to the multiplicity of lines in a drawing; the orchestra represents a huge palette where each instrument supplies its own colour. Just as the painter delights in contrasts of tone, in the play of light and shade, so the

musician takes pleasure in the shock of unexpected dissonances and the fusion of unusual timbres; he wants us to visualize what he makes us hear, and the pen he holds in his fingers becomes a brush. This is musical impressionism of a very special kind and of a very rare quality . . .'

Both from the aesthetic and the historical point of view, this notice is of the highest interest if, as seems probable, it was inspired by Debussy himself; but the definiteness and the trite, elegant style of these notes cannot have entirely satisfied this subtle artist who disapproved of all such indiscreet analytical annotations.

This 'Image' did not please the majority of the audience although the assembly was a select one and had greeted Debussy's appearance with warm applause. This may have been an unforeseen and paradoxical consequence of his use of the popular song, 'Nous n'irons plus au bois', which runs right through the 'Rondes', though in a very unobtrusive manner. 'Springtime Rondes'? queried some of the audience; 'they are more like wintry dances!' The very high pitch of the violins, the sudden gusts of thirds that shake the wind instruments, the rough sonorities of certain passages, suggested to some people icy blasts rather than the gentle breezes of spring. In spite of the freshness of the rustling orchestra— which was perhaps too much subdivided—an impression of melancholy was produced by the continuous distortions of the old French song which Debussy had already utilized more obviously in some of his previous works. It did not infuse the gaiety that permeates 'La Belle au bois dormant' of 1880, nor did it sparkle with the shimmering brilliance that illumines that bright 'Estampe' for piano, 'Les Jardins sous la Pluie'. Debussy's enemies concluded, with visible signs of satisfaction, that he had reached the decline of his powers. They clearly saw the traces of the effort he had made in torturing—according to academic procedure—this pretty, childish *ronde* which, when forced to undergo augmentations, diminutions, and other contrapuntal contortions, gains nothing and loses its innocent charm.[1]

Scornful and even contemptuous reports appeared in some journals, as, for instance, the following note by Luc Marvy in the *Monde Musical*: 'the "Rondes de Printemps", a pleasant but unimportant little work, crumbles away to nothing in an orchestral

---

[1] 'Nous n'irons plus au bois' reappears continually throughout the piece under various rhythmic forms. In the eleventh bar, one can also distinguish the first notes of 'Do, do, l'enfant do'; the analytical critics do not seem to have noticed his utilization of this other popular song.

treatment which grows more tenuous every year. . . .' The opinion of a large number of musicians was voiced by Gaston Carraud. This excellent critic, whose weekly notes in *La Liberté* were read with great interest, devoted an important article in the *Revue S.I.M.* to a series of concerts which the publisher, Durand, had organized with the object of demonstrating the magnificent vitality of French music.

Carraud began by drawing attention to the two divergent currents noticeable in contemporary music, but he made no secret of the fact that he greatly preferred the movement led by Vincent d'Indy. He remarked that ever since the production of his master-piece at the Opéra-Comique in 1902, Debussy had disappointed some of his original supporters, whilst others expressed a growing enthusiasm, and even went so far as to maintain that 'Pelléas' was the last of his youthful works and that it marked the beginning of a period of conscious maturity. In order to explain this difference of opinion amongst the musical public, the critic drew a distinction between those who think and feel like musicians, and those who judge works from the point of view of the writer or the painter. The former, whilst rejoicing that these new works remained musical in form, deplored the fact (which was a matter of indifference to the others) that this was no longer true of the emotional feeling: 'that emotion, of a type unique in the world of art, which embraced in its mysterious unity a whole multitude of sensations of the most marvellous intensity, accuracy, delicacy, and novelty; it was the soul condensing the evidence of the senses. But now, the sensations alone subsist, and they seem to have become at once shrunken and ponderous, to have lost something of their freshness and originality; instead of blending, they clash. . . .'

This prejudiced article which seems exaggerated both in its wording and intent, drew a very sharp retort from Maurice Ravel. This composer, who seldom indulged in musical criticism, wrote as follows in the *Cahiers d'aujourd'hui* of February 1913:

'You were quite well able to understand, you who yielded yourself up without effort to the vivid charm and exquisite freshness of the "Rondes de printemps"; you who were moved to tears by that dazzling "Ibéria" and its intensely disturbing "Parfums de la nuit", by all this novel, delicate, harmonic beauty, this profound musical sensitiveness; you, who are only a writer or a painter. So too was I, and so were Messrs. Igor Stravinsky, Florent Schmitt, Roger Ducasse, Albert Foussel, and a host of young composers whose productions are not unworthy of notice. But the only musicians, the only people with real sensibility, are M. Gaston Carraud, to whom we owe three songs and a symphonic poem,

M. Camille Mauclair, who has become known for his literary and
pictorial works, and M. Pierre Lalo, who has not produced anything
at all.'

Having made the general statement, to which Maurice Ravel
replied so trenchantly, Gaston Carraud proceeded to a minute
examination of the new score. He considered that its unity was
based on artificial technical processes, instead of on emotional
feeling:'The"Rondes de Printemps" 'he says 'which are constructed
on a single theme, and follow almost exactly the principles laid down
for the nurslings of the Schola, do not give such an impression of
cohesion as was achieved with a number of themes in the works of
M. Debussy's first style. . . . It is a curious phenomenon that to-
day M. Debussy's music is a reflection of that of his imitators. . . .'
According to the critic this original artist has now come to resemble
Maurice Ravel: the method of construction is more visible, more
studied; the writing loses its conciseness, it becomes emphatic and
cumbersome; the colouring takes on cruder tints without gaining
in sincerity; sobriety of treatment, naturalness and simplicity
are no more. He concludes his harsh verdict with these blunt
words: 'The diversity and complexity of technical means in use
to-day, cannot conceal pettiness, superficiality, and triviality of
conception. This music was certainly written by an incomparable
artist, but it deserves only too well the title of "Images"; one is
conscious of the labour, the method, the exertion involved.'

For all its judicious tone, this article must have offended Debussy.
It called forth a reply from one of his friends. Writing in the
Revue S.I.M. of August–September 1910, Louis Laloy admitted
Debussy's obvious change of style, but insisted that this 'Image',
like the others, as well as the twelve Preludes for piano, and the
clarinet Rhapsody, were all admirable examples of a new type of
art, more substantial than the older form of Debussyism.

' Now that Claude Debussy has made it possible for music to
interpret impressions that were hitherto inexpressible', he wrote, 'the
time has come for him to utilize these elements according to the dictates
of his genius. Consequently, taking into consideration all the marvellous
innovations he has endowed us with, we are to-day in a position to
determine to what race of artists he belongs: he ranks with the very
noblest, those who in their art ignore hatred, strife, opposition, violence,
and all ugliness, and who are capable only of love. . . .'

Louis Laloy then proceeded to make a vigorous attack on those
who criticized Debussy even in a friendly spirit:

'Those who call Mozart *divine* might very well apply the same term
of praise to the modern musician; but, needless to say, the majority

refuse indignantly. And this lack of appreciation for Debussy's work is shown not only by the short-sighted champions of a tradition which they regard as dead, but which is reviving, not merely by the Wagnerians who proclaim, as articles of faith, the theories of their master or by the disciples of M. d'Indy who gird themselves with an armour of austerity; but even some Debussyites follow suit, though surely such appreciation should be given freely to a type of music that is much more orthodox and definite than that of his earlier works. They seem to consider the artist guilty of treason because he has overstepped the limits of their conception of him. They had to make such a violent effort to understand him in the beginning, that nothing more can be expected of them. . . .'

The state of mind which Louis Laloy describes really existed; we shall come across numerous examples of it. In fact, if they were sincere, a great many musicians who belonged to the musical life of Paris or the Provinces at that time would acknowledge that they more or less shared these views. One might instance the case of a conductor belonging to the Schola party who rejoiced, as over a victory of his clan, at the unfavourable reception given to a certain score of Debussy's, though this was chiefly due to the defects of his own interpretation. Debussy was annoyed and intensely irritated by the quarrels of the anti-Debussyites and of the former Debussyites, who were unable to follow his continuous evolutions; whilst the whole-hearted Debussyites were, in their own way, as troublesome as the others. In speaking of them Debussy declared one day: 'They are killing me!'

In this article Louis Laloy extolled the beauties of the 'Rondes de Printemps' which were not obvious to the majority of music lovers: 'great audacity is shown', he wrote, 'in the development of the single idea which now glides, now runs, through light fronds of melody, till it joins in a breathless dance, whirls wildly for an instant, then grows calm and vanishes in the clear air. And the orchestra, having rejected the flamboyant brass, achieves with more luminous tints, all the clear, yet hazy, charm of a Corot landscape.' But it was precisely this deliberate attempt to attain unity by cyclical methods, and this novel treatment of the orchestra, that were made the basis of a fresh attack on Claude Debussy's art.

On the 20th of February 1910—a few days before the 'Rondes de Printemps' were performed at the Concerts Durand—the Concerts Colonne produced the second of the 'Images', entitled 'Ibéria', with reference to which Debussy remarked to the writer of the annotated programme: 'It is useless to ask me for anecdotes about this work; there is no story attached to it, and I depend on

the music alone to arouse the interest of the public.' The work was greeted with prolonged applause, and the audience of the Châtelet— those, at least, who occupied the upper galleries—demanded an encore. Gabriel Pierné, who was conducting the orchestra, seemed inclined to grant the request, when immediately, a hostile counter-demonstration broke out with the result that the work was not repeated. The critiques expressed divergent opinions; some were enthusiastic, others disparaging. A certain number of music-lovers and journalists showed their dissatisfaction openly and declared that they were disappointed in the hopes they had entertained of Claude Debussy ever since the production of 'Pelléas'. The opinions of this disillusioned group found expression in Jean Chantavoine's terse phrase in the *Revue Hebdomadaire*: 'It was high time for M. Debussy to give those who admire his talents or genius an opportunity of agreeing with those who do not.'

Many musicians regarded 'Ibéria' as a dainty tit-bit, too unsubstantial to satisfy their artistic hunger. According to Luc Marvy, whose anti-Debussyist views—no doubt quite sincere—found expression regularly in the *Monde Musical*, this work was just 'one more rhapsody *tra los montes*, neither better nor worse, and certainly not better constructed, than the ones we have been listening to for the last twelve years'. A very indiscriminating criticism, surely, for 'Ibéria' is obviously much superior to the other Spanish rhapsodies.

Nevertheless, even some impartial judges reproached Debussy with imitating his own imitators and held that he was no longer the original creative artist of former days. An explanation, which occurred to no one, could have been found in the fact that the composer was nearing his fiftieth year: maturity had withered the fresh emotions that had animated his youthful compositions and had inspired him to write such novel music. Even the most individual artists find that advancing age dries up the springs of their sensibility. If they are incapable of Rameau's courageous, though brutal, candour, they should admit at least to themselves— it would be painful to acknowledge it to the public—what the French eighteenth-century master did not hesitate to declare in his old age: 'Day by day my taste improves, but I no longer have genius. . . .' It is then that professional craftsmanship and architectural methods must supplement the faltering powers of the artist.

This opinion can be found on reading between the lines of Gaston Carraud's report in the *Liberté* of the 22nd of February 1910: 'Curiously enough, M. Debussy would now seem to be taking back out of the hands of his successors his own processes

after they have degraded them; like them too, he is putting more brains than emotion into his music.' In this new score, the critic found a realistic note which did not suit the composer's genius. This realism had also been noticed by a temporary critic on the *Figaro* who drew a parallel between 'La Mer', which he described as a sonorous transcription of impressions of colour or light, and 'Ibéria', which he regarded as impressions of sound rendered in terms of music. A number of articles, in newspapers and reviews, betray a definite feeling of dissatisfaction which is seldom justified by any technical or aesthetic criticisms; the great artist had undergone another evolution, and the music-lovers were disappointed. He was offering them distinct, broadly drawn outlines, when they had looked for the iridescent haze and the soft effects that distinguished his earlier scores. One of the few entirely favourable critiques was that of Alfred Bruneau in the *Matin*.

' These delicate Spanish sketches', wrote this critic-composer, 'bear no resemblance to the bold canvases of Albeniz and Chabrier. One recognizes M. Debussy's personality in the smallest details. They contain no trace of violence or roughness, in spite of the lively gaiety that animates the first and last sections. They are delightfully poetical, exquisite in colouring, full of fascinating charm and marvellous artistry.'

The general opinion of the work seems to have changed and it now almost coincides with the favourable verdict expressed by Alfred Bruneau alone in 1910. Many musicians, it is true, still accord only a qualified admiration to the big central panel of this triptych, whose side-panels present such complete contrasts; many deplore a certain scrappiness of effect which is partly due to the excessive subdivision of the orchestral parts, especially in the quartet. But even these are ready to appreciate the vividness of the promenade 'Par les rues et par les chemins', the charm and the suggestiveness of 'Parfums de la nuit', the purely musical brilliance of the final scene 'Au matin d'un jour de fête'; and, above all, the supreme art displayed in the very effective transition from night to day when, amid the slow pealing of bells, the hearer is gradually led into the radiant sunlight. To-day, prejudices are forgotten; no one feels any ill-will towards the composer for having refused to repeat what he had successfully accomplished before; no exacting demands are made on the artist who having attained maturity, both in years and talent, was perhaps nearing the natural decline of his genius; people listen to the work sympathetically, without scrutinizing too closely the thematic and instrumental processes, which are of little importance. We are now able to appreciate the general effect of this harmoniously composed pic-

ture, executed according to new methods with a rather novel orchestral colouring. It was not Debussy's aim to write Spanish music, but rather to express truthfully his own impressions of Spain, a Spain of which he knew little or nothing, but which his imagination depicted with marvellous accuracy.

A foreign musician of standing, whose opinion is invaluable, has written of 'Ibéria' as follows:

'The echoes from the villages, a kind of *sevillana*—the generic theme of the work—which seems to float in a clear atmosphere of scintillating light; the intoxicating spell of Andalusian nights, the festive gaiety of a people dancing to the joyous strains of a *banda* of guitars and *bandurrias* . . . all this whirls in the air, approaches and recedes, and our imagination is continually kept awake and dazzled by the power of an intensely expressive and richly varied music. . . .'

This is the verdict of Manuel de Falla. In an article in the *Chesterian* from which this passage is quoted, the celebrated Spanish composer extols the originality of this 'Ibéria', which is so Debussy-like and yet so French in spite of its title and subject. He goes even further, and ventures to state that Debussy had a considerable and decisive influence on young Spanish composers, especially on Albeniz, to whom he demónstrated the art of utilizing merely the fundamental elements of popular music, instead of following the usual method of employing authentic folk-tunes.

This theory is very flattering to Debussy but, in the face of chronological data, we cannot accept it. When the French composer began to write his 'Ibéria', he already knew his Spanish colleague's work of the same title, or he had seen at least the first part, which was published as early as 1906. He took a great delight in playing these pieces, in rendering at the piano the scintillating effects of these varied and brilliant reflections of Spanish life. Indeed, he himself praised the vivid beauty of this work in one of his musical critiques, an extract of which will be found in the author's book on his theories. We are forced to conclude that it was Debussy who came under the influence of Albeniz; an influence in the contrary direction would not have been possible. For the French 'Ibéria' had not been published or performed in February 1909, when the fourth and last part of the Spanish 'Ibéria' appeared. But, as Manuel de Falla has stated, other young Spanish composers were inspired by the example of the French master.

The three parts of 'Ibéria', of which the last two are played without a break, are connected by the repetition of certain themes.

'Not only have we complete melodies', wrote Louis Laloy in the previously quoted article, 'but these develop prolifically, and give birth

to other melodies around them, which intersect one another without concealing the principal melody; this stands out like the stalwart trunk of a luxuriant tree. Thus they reappear under aspects that are ever new; and except for minor incidents, two such melodies are sufficient to fill one of the movements completely. There is here no question of vague suggestions; on the contrary, everywhere the melody stands out in relief, the phrases are definite, the rhythm compelling. And yet, this distinct style is capable of expressing infinite subtlety, as we can see by the middle section, the 'Parfums de la nuit'. In this suave, dreamy piece, the ideas seem to emanate from a dim distance; they draw near, take shape, vanish, and reappear, transfigured by some inward alteration which changes all the details whilst maintaining the feeling intact. In obedience to some deep, instinctive sense of order, these ideas arrange themselves almost in the form of a verse set between two refrains; yet a continuous development links them together. And when the first theme reappears, a new atmosphere of voluptuous sadness envelops all. Thus, everywhere vitality accompanies the equilibrium of the work or rather, engenders it, as in some supernatural world where harmony is an attribute of existence.'

In such polished terms, Louis Laloy describes the plan of this work, with its tapering lines and its definite, though not too obvious, cyclical form. It was thus the composer deliberately planned it, giving it a delicacy and subtlety that are in marked contrast to the conventional stiffness and the clumsy emphasis of solemn architectural music.

The third of the 'Images' did not appear until long after the first two. After several delays, Debussy informed his publisher, on the 5th of August 1911, that he thought he could promise it to him for the month of October. On the appointed date, only the piano duet arrangement was ready; the orchestral score was not yet completed. The rough draft, scored on four staves, bears the dates 4th of January 1909, and 10th of October 1912. The 'Gigues', originally entitled, 'Gigues Tristes', were not published by Durand until 1912–13; they first appeared in the form of a transcription for piano duet arranged by André Caplet, later as a miniature orchestral score. They were played at the Concerts Colonne on the 26th of January 1913, and repeated at the short-lived Concerts Monteux (at the Casino de Paris) on the 8th of February 1914. This remains the least known of all Debussy's works; it is very rarely performed, perhaps because its execution is rendered difficult by the fact that the orchestra includes an oboe d'amore, and that the wood-winds are in groups of four; but possibly the cause lies deeper. André Caplet, who knew the score better than any one, and who witnessed its slow completion, wrote a little-

known article in 1923, pointing out the reasons why this work was so neglected, and at the same time giving interesting details regarding its emotional contents.

' "Gigues" . . . Sad Gigues . . . tragic Gigues. . . . The portrait of a soul . . . a soul in pain, uttering its slow, lingering lamentation on the reed of an oboe d'amore. A wounded soul, so reticent that it dreads and shuns all lyrical effusions, and quickly hides its sobs behind the mask and the angular gestures of a grotesque marionette. Again, it suddenly wraps itself in a mantle of the most phlegmatic indifference. The ever-changing moods, the rapidity with which they merge, clash, and separate to unite once more, make the interpretation of this work very difficult. That is perhaps the reason why it is so seldom to be found on the programmes of our big symphony societies. And yet, "Gigues" is not eclipsed by the proximity of "Ibéria", the central panel of that admirable triptych, which is completed by "Rondes de Printemps", a youthful, shimmering vision of Spring. Underneath the convulsive shudderings, the sudden efforts at restraint, the pitiful grimaces, which serve as a kind of disguise, we recognize the very soul of our dear, great, Claude Debussy. We find there the spirit of sadness, infinite sadness, lying stretched as in the bed of a river whose flow, constantly augmented from new sources, increases inevitably, mercilessly. And that is why, though I have no definite preference for that "Image", I feel for it a very special affection.'

These 'Gigues', which Caplet possibly preferred to the other 'Images' because he had collaborated in the finishing of the score, seem to have been inspired by memories of England of old or recent date. Debussy had visited that country at an early age, and more than one of his compositions recall some aspects of the life there or some English books he had read; we shall find further proof of this in the piano Preludes. When passing through London in 1905, he had listened with pleasure (as he wrote to Louis Laloy on the 13th of September) 'to the grenadiers' band that passed by every morning, with cheerful bagpipes and savage-sounding little fifes, playing marches in which Scottish airs seemed to mingle rapturously with the rhythm of the cake-walk'. One of the essential elements of this score is a popular air, a jig, which Debussy borrowed, perhaps unconsciously, from a song by Charles Bordes, entitled 'Dansons la gigue'.[1] Possibly the plaintive melody played by the oboe d'amore is also derived from English folk-music.

The composition is limpid in style, the melodic lines are easy to

[1] This is not the only musical link with Charles Bordes, one of the founders of the *Schola Cantorum*, who has composed some very beautiful songs for voice and piano.

follow, the emotion is simple, the expression direct, in spite of the superimposed or alternating moods of nostalgic melancholy and dashing humour. But the delicacy of its subtle harmonies, the minute detail of the orchestration, which is also more subdued than usual, the very swing of its jerky rhythm (though the gigue is after all a traditional dance) aroused the disapproval of those music-lovers who are hostile to all innovation. Possibly they also objected to the harshness of the melodic outlines and rhythms, the obscurity of occasional voluptuous appeals, the sudden outbursts of violence quickly repressed—to which Paul Landormy drew attention in the annotated programme.

It is evident from many of the critiques that these 'Gigues' produced rather confused impressions. On the day it was produced, the other two 'Images' were also played; consequently this was one of the very rare complete performances of the symphonic triptych. In his critique in *La Liberté*, Gaston Carraud stated that, of the three 'Images', he preferred the one that had not been heard before: ' "Gigues", first known as "Gigues Tristes"—a very appropriate title. The really delightful interplay of the rhythms and sonorities is enveloped in an atmosphere of sadness whose penetrating fragrance reaches the heart. This work is no mere impressionist sketch; one cannot regret that all the tiny sparkling, scintillating touches with which this artist usually covers the firm, though light, arabesques of his compositions, should here blend in an atmosphere of grey, so rich and delicate that it must delight all musicians. . . .' The same verdict was expressed in the *Ménestrel* by Joseph Jemain. This pianist-composer and occasional critic also regretted that the word *triste* should have been omitted from the title: 'It would have made his meaning clearer, and brought out the paradoxical idea that inspired this piece—which, in my opinion, is the best in the work. For the jig-rhythm, which is after all only intermittent, is used merely as a contrast to the mood of intense melancholy which the entire movement expresses by means of its veiled, blurred, remote instrumentation, which is so strikingly effective.' In the *Guide Musical* André Lamette, on the other hand, expressed his preference for the firmer texture of 'Rondes de Printemps' and 'Ibéria': ' "Gigues",' he wrote, 'does not lack either charm or attractiveness; on the contrary, if one wished to find fault, one might say that these qualities are over-emphasized, to the detriment of the musical tissue, which to my mind lacks consistency—a defect (or a virtue, according to one's point of view) which one does not find in the other pieces. And if one's attention were not constantly held by the fascinating details of the vivid, brilliant orchestration, one

would gladly give one's self up to the sheer enjoyment of a charm so rich in exquisite beauty of sound.'

Very divergent opinions were expressed in the Paris press. In his critique in the *Matin*, Alfred Bruneau praised this work as 'the logical sequence of the composer's refined, sensitive, disturbing art'; but the writer asks rather anxiously whether Debussy 'is right or wrong in not varying his style more. I fancy it would be very difficult for him to change his manner now; and in attempting to do so, he would run a grave risk'. In his clever article in the *Figaro*, Henri Quittard remarked shrewdly that 'Debussy has attempted to create to his own image a form of development in keeping with his very individual conception of tonality and harmony. This effort, possibly unconscious because inevitable, which can be clearly seen in many of the details, does not seem to have met with entire success.' Jean Chantavoine, in the *Revue Hebdomadaire*, described the work as 'a dazzling kaleidoscope of sounds which simultaneously arouses and disappoints our curiosity. . . . We should now like M. Debussy to give us something better than the small change of his incomparable talent.' Writing in the *République*, Gustave Samazeuilh questioned whether 'the deliberately subdued atmosphere and the subtle harmonic effects of 'Rondes de Printemps' and 'Gigues' were quite in keeping with the spontaneous character of the popular airs on which they are based. . . .' It is evident that Debussy once more alarmed or disappointed even the most intelligent and sensitive of his hearers.

Very few criticisms expressed wholehearted praise of the new 'Gigues'; the only enthusiastic opinions on record are those of Louis Vuillemin in *Comoedia*, of Adolphe Boschot in the *Echo de Paris*, of Paul Locard in the *Petit Journal*, and of Paul Landormy in *La Vie Parisienne*. All these articles taken together enable us to ascertain the varied views of music-lovers, most of whom took up a rather aggressive or grudging attitude towards Claude Debussy.

In 1910, whilst his recent orchestral works were the subject of the most impassioned controversies, the much discussed composer again submitted a large number of chamber music works for the consideration of an undecided public. These included: the first volume of the piano Preludes, consisting of twelve pieces; two sets of songs: 'Le Promenoir des deux amants' and the Villon 'Ballades', each containing three items; works for clarinet with piano or orchestral accompaniment, which we have already mentioned; a little waltz, 'La plus que lente' (which later he was to orchestrate himself 'for the countless *five o'clock* tea parties frequented by beautiful listeners whom I remembered'; he treated it in the

'brasserie style', utilizing the tympanon, a gipsy instrument which he had learned to appreciate during his early trip to Russia, and which he had further opportunity of enjoying during his concert tours in Austria-Hungary); and lastly, a short piece, also a kind of slow waltz, written to order for a special occasion to a set theme. It was one of the works written by a few French composers, at the request of the *Revue S.I.M.*, in honour of Joseph Haydn, on the occasion of the centenary of his death.

Claude Debussy himself played some of his Preludes at the Société Musicale Indépendante, on the 25th of May 1910, namely: 'Danseuses de Delphes', 'Voiles', 'La Cathédrale engloutie', and 'La danse de Puck' (which last he had to repeat). At the Société Nationale, on the 14th of January 1911, Ricardo Viñes played three other pieces from the same volume: 'Les collines d'Anacapri', 'La Fille aux cheveux de lin' and 'La Sérénade interrompue'. At another concert given by the same society on the 5th of April 1913 this virtuoso also played three Preludes from the second book (which was only published that same year, 1913): 'Les Fées sont d'exquises danseuses', 'La Terrasse des audiences au clair de lune', and 'Feux d'artifices'.

Owing to their picturesque titles, which Debussy, for purely musical reasons, inserted only at the end of each piece or in the index, the twenty-four Preludes aroused the interest of commentators, many of whom displayed great ignorance. Debussy does not adopt any very strict form in these pieces, but gives them the character of an improvisation or *fantaisie* which is best suited to this very free type of composition. He utilizes all the varied means of expression the value and effectiveness of which he had tested during so many years; and thus he succeeds in rendering the impressions produced on his mind by the contemplation of actual or visionary scenes, by his memories of people, landscapes, works of art, incidents, legends, poems, and stories.

In styles ever-varied but always concise, the series file past. 'Danseuses de Delphes', three bacchantes performing a dignified dance, as they are depicted in sculpture on the top of a pillar found in the ruins of an ancient villa, and as we can still see them in the Louvre Museum; 'La Fille aux cheveux de lin', probably a reminiscence of a 'Chanson écossaise' by Lecomte de Lisle, which bears this title, or of an English portrait by some pre-Raphaelite painter, like Rossetti (in his youth, Debussy wrote an unpublished song to the same title); the fantastic beings in the 'Danse de Puck' inspired by 'A Midsummer's Night Dream', or some character from Dickens, like the famous Pickwick (the tribute to Mr. Pick-

wick is based on 'God save the King'); music-hall types, like
'Minstrels' and 'General Lavine, eccentric'—'the fellow was made
of wood', Debussy used to say to indicate the mechanical stiffness
required in the interpretation; legendary or mythological characters
like 'Les Fées sont d'exquises danseuses', or 'Ondine'—reminiscent
of her sisters, the 'Sirènes' of the 'Nocturnes'; the antique cinerary
urns which are evoked by the funeral march of 'Canope'; 'Voiles',
full of floating effects of major thirds that suggest sailing boats
anchored to a fixed pedal-point; the lively strains of 'Collines
d'Anacapri' in which the joyous rhythm of the tarantella, and an
expressive melody in the Neapolitan style, are heard now alternately, now simultaneously; 'Brouillards', 'Feuilles mortes', and
'Bruyères'; 'Feux d'artifices' in which the allusion to the 'Marseillaise' suggests a reminiscence of 14th of July celebrations; 'Les Pas
sur la neige', where, according to the composer's picturesque
directions, the rhythm, represented by a simple appoggiatura,
'should have the sonorous value of a melancholy, ice-bound, landscape'; 'Puerto del vino', a vision of Spain and of the Alhambra—
a new 'Habanera' which, we are told, was written on receipt of an
picture postcard; 'La Sérénade interrompue', another Spanish
scene, based on guitar effects, which suggests either a preparatory
sketch for the 'Ibéria' of the symphonic 'Images' or a reminiscence
of it; a Baudelaire landscape in which 'Les sons et les parfums
tournent dans l'air du soir' and dance a 'melancholy waltz' full of
'vertiginous langour'; yet another picture, that of the 'Terrasse des
audiences au clair de lune' (slightly suggestive of the melodic and
rhythmic elements of the popular air 'Au clair de la lune', supported
on chords of the seventh)—a picture that was not inspired, as many
imagined, by the chapter in Pierre Loti's 'L'Inde sans les Anglais'
which describes the 'Terrasses pour tenir conseil au clair de lune'
and actually bears that title, but by a few words in a letter written by
the French author, René Puaux, to the *Temps*;[1] the legend of Ys and
its 'Cathédrale engloutie'; the vivid impressionism of 'Le Vent dans

[1] Debussy had been keenly interested in the letters which René Puaux sent
to the *Temps*, in December 1912, describing the Durbar (the ceremonies for
the coronation of King George V as Emperor of India). In reading one of
these letters, which is reproduced in a book by René Puaux entitled *Le beau
voyage* (Paris, Payot, 1917, p. 85) Debussy was struck by a phrase in the following passage: 'the hall of victory, the hall of pleasure, the garden of the sultanesses,
the terrace for moonlight audiences. . . .' He chose these last words for the title
of his Prelude; and it is probable that he attempted to reproduce the atmosphere
of the Indian scenes described by the writer, whose talent he greatly admired—
as is testified by a letter to Alfred Bruneau, dated 29th of May 1915, in which
he praises his 'individual sensibility which is far above the average'. This
circumstance enables us to determine that 'La Terrasse des audiences' was
composed in December 1912.

la plaine' and the tragic nightmare scenes of 'Ce qu'a vu le vent d'ouest'. . . . Of the twenty-four Preludes, only one, 'Les Tierces alternées', has a purely musical title and a technical significance. The Preludes were planned to consist of two sets of twelve—the fateful number! This fact probably accounts for the delay in the publication of the second book, as well as for the inequality of the pieces. There are a few which the composer probably only published in order to complete his two dozens. He did not like the complete series to be played as a whole, according to the present custom: 'They are not all good', he himself admitted; and pianists do not always choose the best. Georges Pioch, a prolific critic and fervent admirer of Debussy, stated that in listening to a performance of the first twelve Preludes he had been 'thrice enraptured and nine times disillusioned'. The proportion of really admirable pages can be reckoned at a higher figure than that. Still, the fact remains that the twenty-four pieces include a good deal of repetition and padding. It is probable that in some cases Debussy utilized old sketches, as an examination of the harmonies would suggest. Again, many of the Preludes have the intimate quality of genuine chamber music, and lose a great deal of their effect in big concert halls. His English biographer, Mrs. Liebich, recorded in the *Musical Times* of June 1918 a statement of Debussy's to the effect that some pieces, such as 'Danseuses de Delphes' and 'Les Pas sur la neige', should only be played '*entre quatre-z-yeux*'. People are also apt to forget the meaning of the word *Prelude*, which the composer did not choose heedlessly. Debussy regarded these little pieces less as works intended to be played by themselves than as real preludes, short introductions to more important pieces in the same keys. This so-called revolutionary showed many traits characteristic of the conservative upholder of tradition.

One of the Preludes in the first book, 'La Cathédrale engloutie', is particularly celebrated both on account of its musical characteristics and the legend which its title recalls. Some regard it as a masterpiece, others as a mediocre work. Perhaps musicographers will one day discover in it traces of an Oriental influence—which is however non-existent—for both its principal theme and its harmony, which is modelled on the medieval organum, bear a curious but quite accidental resemblance to a certain old Chinese air.[1] The suggestive quality of the piece impresses all who hear it; but as a rule people notice only the harmonic features and overlook the melodic element, which is obviously Gregorian in origin or inspiration. André Obey, a musical critic and poet, has utilized

[1] See Lavignac's *Encyclopédie de la Musique*, vol. i, p. 28 (Ode Kwan Tshyn).

this subject for a very effective cinema scenario, which has not yet been filmed. The magnitude of the idea seems to exceed the limits of the piano, the instrument for which the composer wrote the work. An orchestral arrangement was undertaken by Henri Büsser with Debussy's approval. But the orchestral version, which is a literal transcription of the piano score, did not produce the anticipated effect. A free adaptation would have been preferable, but such a liberty could not be taken after Debussy's death. With a different object in view, Gabriel Grovlez arranged four other Preludes for orchestra: 'Ondine', 'General Lavine', 'La Danse de Puck' and 'Minstrels'; they were included in the orchestral score of 'L'Antre des Gnomes', a fantastic legend which was staged at the Olympia, Paris, in the beginning of July 1920.

Ever since 1904 Debussy had sought inspiration for his songs in the works of the poets of medieval France; a felicitous manifestation of his patriotic feelings which the European War was soon to intensify. He first wrote music to five poems by Charles d'Orléans, some for solo voice and piano, others for several voices unaccompanied. He next collaborated with Tristan Lhermitte, a rather neglected seventeenth-century poet, choosing his 'Promenoir des deux Amants', which Jane Bathori sang at the Société Nationale on the 14th of January 1911. (The first of the three songs in this series, which is perhaps the most beautiful, had already been published in 1904 as one of the 'Trois Chansons de France' under the title of 'La Grotte'.) The music is very subtly adapted to the preciosity of this old-world ode, and emphasizes all its delicate traits. In an article published in the *Guide Musical* on the 13th of April 1913, Georges Servières draws attention to the sympathy, the perfect harmony between the poet and the musician:

'Tristan Lhermitte's madrigal-like style is so full of subtle expressions and soft-sounding words that the composer was naturally prompted to envelop them in caressing rhythms and suave, mellow harmonies. The images suggested by this poetry, with its grottoes and fountains, where gentle zephyrs blow, where the waters throw back shimmering reflections, have enabled him to give free scope to his taste for imitative effects which evoke the mysterious aspect of the grottoes, the splashing of the water, and the quivering of light breezes. . . .'

The critic also praised the increased breadth of Debussy's melodies, a noticeable feature for some years past: 'The vocal line is no longer reduced to a mere declamation. Whilst respecting the rules of punctuation and natural pronunciation, it has regained a melodic form, particularly in the first and last numbers.'

This change of style was not obvious to all. Charles Cornet, a

critic on the *Guide Musical*, showed that he was unable to distinguish between the new melodies and the preceding ones, and he expressed his displeasure at having to listen to songs so lacking in vocal qualities. He reported the first performance of the 'Promenoir' in a long article obviously inspired by ill-feeling. The critic discerned nothing in the series of songs but 'charming boudoir sounds, the rustling of silken linings, subtle, voluptuous murmurings; the most graceful, effeminate, elegant, improvised effects one could wish for; everything, in fact, except a song for a singer with a voice, and for lovers of song who pay their money to hear people sing....' In the opinion of this merciless critic the composition was of little account. He expressed an equal contempt for the four piano Preludes that were performed at the same concert, the titles being the only things about them that interested him.

In May 1910 Debussy delved still more deeply into the poetical past of France and composed a new set of songs to the verses of a famous fifteenth-century poet: the 'Trois ballades de François Villon'. They exist in two forms. The original version, with piano accompaniment, was sung for the first time by Paule de Lestang on the 5th of February 1911; and the orchestral arrangement was performed at the Concerts Sechiari on the 5th of March of the same year, when Debussy himself conducted, the soloist being the baritone, Clarke, who replaced Jean Léner. These three songs are utterly different in character. In the first, the sorrowful 'Ballade à s'amye', broad melodic phrases 'expressing anguish as much as regret' are contrasted with equally expressive rhythmic appoggiaturas; the vocal declamation is also full of intense feeling. The third is the very lively song of the 'Dames de Paris' whose chattering talk, interspersed with musical allusions, is rendered by detached notes and a bounding rhythm. The second, an exquisitely beautiful song, is the 'Ballade que Villon fit à la requête de sa mère pour prier Notre-Dame'. Here Debussy achieves a medieval colouring that is neither artificial nor archaeological by means of a modal melody in the vocal part which alternates with a hesitating, psalm-like recitative, by the use of certain successions of chords and by a contrapuntal style of writing. Debussy's restrained art here attains its highest perfection. One need only indicate the stammering refrain 'En cette foi je veux vivre et mourir', or the marvellously suggestive quality of the simple common chords which by the sheer effectiveness of their gentle mobile harmonies, seem to open the doors of the 'Paradis peint, où sont harpes et luths'.

Debussy had taken great pains with his musical adaptation of the

old French poet's verses, and his melodies are closely wedded to the words. He had found it very difficult 'to follow exactly, to mould the rhythms satisfactorily whilst keeping one's own inspiration'. He made some public statements on the subject which are recorded in the author's book, *The Theories of Claude Debussy*. As usual, he took a keen interest in the typographical appearance of his 'Ballades'. He wished them to be brought out in a style suggestive of Villon's period. He was pleased with the edition, but wrote to his publisher on the 17th of September 1910: 'I should have liked the parchment to be a little yellower (plus jaulni). . . .' He added: 'A day will come when it will all be withered (desseiché), the music as well'. But the truthful accents of his 'Ballades', the perfection of this work, will postpone indefinitely the withering he apprehended.

Owing to his celebrity, as well as to certain financial exigencies which he had not foreseen when he contracted his second marriage, Debussy was obliged to undertake concert tours, though he did so very reluctantly. He refused to take part in the sorry French Festival which was held in Munich in the summer of 1910; he considered the financial arrangements unsatisfactory. In this connexion, he made some statements that were rather offensive to German musicians, exaggerated criticisms, uttered out of sheer caprice and vexation, which we have recorded in a previous work.[1] In December 1910 he accepted an invitation to Austria-Hungary to conduct concerts in the two capitals.

In Vienna the 'Prélude à l'Après-midi d'un Faune' had already been performed under the conductorship of Ferdinand Loewe; Richard Strauss had also conducted it in 1907 on the day his 'Domestic Symphony' was given for the first time in that town. 'La Mer' had also been performed, and had been received with mingled applause and hisses. Some untoward incidents occurred during the preparations for Debussy's concert. Several big works were to have been included in the programme: 'La Mer', the Nocturnes, the 'Petite Suite', 'L'Après-midi d'un Faune', and 'Ibéria'. But as the composer was not an experienced conductor, he was obliged to confine himself to the three last-mentioned works, the time being too short for the necessary rehearsals.

'I can assure you that it was hard work to get "Ibéria" into shape in two rehearsals', he wrote to his publisher. 'I do not claim that

---

[1] In 1908, 1909, 1910, and 1911 Debussy had to reply to a number of questions put to him by journalists in the course of interviews he reluctantly granted. The essential points in his replies are to found in *The Theories of Claude Debussy*.

this remarkable feat should be engraved on the tablets of eternity, but it was no joke all the same, and my nerves are shattered. Remember that these people could understand me only with the help of an interpreter—actually a doctor-of-law—who, for all I know, may have transmitted a distorted version of my ideas. I made use of every possible means of expression: I sang, I gesticulated like a character in an Italian pantomine . . . it was enough to move the hardest heart. Well, they managed to understand in the end, and I got what I wanted out of them. I was recalled as often as a dancer; the only reason why the idolizing crowd did not unyoke the horses from my carriage was that I was in a taxi-cab.'

Soon after his return to Paris, Debussy, in speaking to a journalist connected with *Comoedia*, praised the excellence of the Austrian orchestras and, especially, their perseverance and industry.

The Budapest concert, which was held in the huge Redoute Hall, consisted of chamber music works. 'Fifteen hundred people to hear "Children's Corner",' wrote Debussy to Robert Godet, 'it seems startlingly out of proportion.' The most appreciated item was the early Quartet, which was played by the Waldbauer Quartet. The French composer was warmly applauded by an audience which included not only music-lovers, but also a number of young painters who had come to listen to a type of music which, like their paintings, was regarded as impressionist. He heard gipsies play in a café, as had happened once before when he was seventeen. He expressed great admiration for one of the gipsies, named Radicz, 'who loves music much more than a great many celebrated musicians do. In an ordinary, commonplace café, he gave one the impression of sitting in the depths of a forest; he arouses in the soul that characteristic feeling of melancholy we so seldom have an opportunity of indulging in. . . .' It was no doubt on this journey that he got the idea of orchestrating his waltz, 'La plus que lente', using the tympanon as solo instrument.

He remained only a few hours in the Hungarian capital where the audience struck him as very similar to the French.[1] His coming was regarded as a sensational event; the musical review, *Zenekoslony*, devoted a special number to him, and the newspapers published long articles in praise of his genius, of which the most important

---

[1] In November 1913, Gabriel Pierné conducted a concert in Budapest at which the Nocturnes were warmly applauded. On the 9th of November Debussy wrote him a few words of thanks: 'The Hungarians are charming people', he said, 'there is something *French* about their enthusiasm which brings us more quickly into sympathy with them than with our so-called Latin brothers. . . .' He went on: 'Have you ever seen anything more beautiful than the Danube (which Johann Strauss insisted on calling blue)? Have you heard a gipsy of the name of Radicz. . . .? He is the *violin* itself.'

was Emile Haraszti's feuilleton in the *Budapesti Hirlap*. He made a longer stay in Vienna where, to his great annoyance, official receptions were given in his honour. In proposing a toast at the end of a banquet, one ill-advised orator attempted to congratulate him on having abolished melody—a hazardous statement, which immediately drew from Debussy this lively protestation: 'But, Monsieur! my music aims at being nothing else but melody!' He was irritated by the lack of understanding displayed by some musicians who adhered to rigorous classifications and a terminology which he refused to accept. He told his publisher that he had not the qualifications necessary for the musical composer travelling in foreign lands: 'one would need the heroism of a commercial traveller, and one must be willing to compromise, and that is most repugnant to me.'

His annoyance found vent in his statements to a Viennese journalist, which amount to a declaration of independence. They are partly reproduced in *The Theories of Claude Debussy*. The French composer asserted with some heat: 'There is no school of Debussy. I have no disciples. I am I. . . .' He added, in mockery of those who insisted on labelling his works: 'See how easily people are deceived: some praise me for being a man of the North, a melancholy type; others regard me as a representative of the South; Provence, Daudet, tireli, tirela! And I am simply a native of Saint-Germain, half an hour from Paris. . . .'

Whilst Debussy was issuing these declarations of independence, his illustrious colleague Saint-Saëns was engaged in drawing up an aggressively conservative profession of faith, obviously directed against Debussy, which appeared in the *Courrier Musical* of the 1st of January 1911. In an article entitled 'L'Anarchie Musicale', the venerable composer protested against the possibility of their being an 'atonal system', and expressed his sorrowful indignation against the atrocities of his day, in the following ironical lines: 'Every one is to make his own rules; music is free, boundlessly free; there are no common chords, there are no dissonant chords, there are no wrong chords; any combination of notes is legitimate. And, would you believe it, that is what they call developing one's sensibility! . . .'

In spite of Saint-Saëns's condemnation, some serious theorists thought it worth while to make a minute study of the harmonic system of Debussy and of those who were more or less his disciples. In 1912 the composer René Lenormand wrote a brief study, entitled *Étude sur l'harmonie moderne*, chiefly based on an examination of the scores of this master whom the young school, 'la petite

classe', had chosen as their leader in spite of himself. 'Pelléas' and his other works were carefully dissected with a view to finding a classical basis, an academic explanation, for his most novel harmonies. A naïve, painstaking, classification of this kind was not likely to appeal to a composer who had always shown his hatred of strict scholastic rules. The author of this meticulous *Étude* asked Debussy's opinion of his article. The composer replied in a letter, dated the 25th of July 1912, which betrays a certain humorous anxiety.

'It is all quite correct', he wrote, 'and almost mercilessly logical. You evidently received the somewhat ironical impression that all these experiments, all these colours, plunge one eventually into a state of alarm from which one emerges with a note of interrogation firmly implanted like a nail in one's brain. Whether you so intended it or not, your essay is a severe censure of modern harmony. There is something almost savage about your quotations of passages which, being necessarily separated from their context, can no longer justify their "curiousness". Think of all the inexpert hands that will utilize your study without discrimination, for the sole purpose of annihilating those charming butterflies which are already somewhat crumpled by your analysis. Well, so much the worse for the dead, and for the wounded that will be despatched in this wise. . . .'

Thus Debussy once more expressed his contempt and hatred of all the classifications and systems into which people insisted on forcing his art and what they called his aesthetics.

CHAPTER XII

DRAMATIC MUSIC, VARIOUS PLANS. 'LE MARTYRE DE SAINT-SÉBASTIEN' (1911)

ON his return to Paris, Debussy had to submit to the ordeal of being interviewed. In speaking to a representative of the *Gaulois*, he expressed his astonishment at the commercial attitude taken up by some of his colleagues when protesting against the neglect of their works by the directors of the Opéra and the Opéra-Comique; he was indignant at their attitude which, he declared, savoured of the 'shopkeeper'. 'Have I filled the air with noisy protests because the Opéra-Comique has not given "Pelléas" for over a year? No, I am biding my time. . . . I was hissed in Italy; perhaps the day will come when I shall be applauded. We should not expect our works of art to be recognized in our own epoch. We do not write music to become millionaires; we should be able to see a little further than the end of our scores. . . .'

In spite of these haughty statements, the composer was toiling 'like a labourer', working with all his might at tasks that were not all to his liking. He began with a piece of hack work, an Egyptian ballet, entitled 'Khamma', which the English dancer, Maud Allan, had asked him to write for her. It was to be a short music-hall number. But this music was never danced to, nor was it performed until quite recently, and then as a casual item at symphonic concerts: it was played for the first time at the Concerts Colonne as late as November 1924. Claude Debussy merely sketched out the work. He scored the first few pages in full, and left the rest of the instrumentation to Charles Koechlin. The composition was only completed in 1913, and published in 1916, although the publication was registered in 1912. The composer was not in the least interested in this 'légende dansée' in which the characters were the dancing girl, Khamma, and a high priest, surrounded by a crowd of worshippers of the god Aman-Ra. There was nothing in this conventional plot to appeal to his artistic tastes. In a letter to his publisher he alluded to it sarcastically as 'that queer ballet with its trumpet calls, which suggest a riot, or an outbreak of fire, and give one the shivers'. In speaking to his friends he made no secret of the fact that his sole interest in this ballet was of a financial nature.

The composer's contempt for this composition is easily explained by the fact that Gabriele d'Annunzio had just then

suggested to him a particularly interesting collaboration. He asked Debussy to compose incidental music for the curious tragedy he had just written, a long work in French verse, entitled 'Le Martyre de Saint-Sébastien.' The undertaking was of such importance that Debussy gave up all his other plans and devoted himself exclusively to this project.

Since the triumph of 'Pelléas et Mélisande', several dramatists, poets, and actors, had offered him librettos to set to music. He had considered a few of these schemes, but only two had really interested him, and none of them materialized. His first operatic score, 'Pelléas', the work into which he had put his entire youth and all his genius, was to remain unique.

Through the agency of his young friend, the dramatist, René Peter, Debussy, always an admirer of Shakespeare, was commissioned to write incidental music to 'King Lear', for André Antoine, the actor-manager, who was then about to produce this drama. This was in 1904, the year Debussy composed 'La Mer', the second series of 'Fêtes Galantes', 'L'Isle Joyeuse', and the 'Danses' for chromatic harp and string quartet. This score was never written; but Debussy was not entirely to blame if it is true that unforeseen circumstances deprived the musician both of the plan which Antoine had sent him, and of his own musical notes for the composition. The famous theatre-manager himself relates in his memoirs[1] that he received a letter from Debussy on the 20th of September 1904, stating that he could not have the music ready by the appointed date and that an orchestra of thirty players would be required for his score. 'That is the minimum I can manage with,' he wrote, 'otherwise we shall have a miserable little noise, a sound like flies rubbing their legs together. . . .' Antoine, who was not in the least interested in the music, which he considered unnecessary, replied in rude and contemptuous terms; he was quite satisfied with some incidental music that was hurriedly put together for his Shakespearian performances by Edmond Missa, a former fellow-pupil of Debussy at the Conservatoire and a rival competitor of his at the Prix de Rome competitions of 1884. In 1905–6 Debussy again set to work at 'King Lear', as the conductor Colonne wished to perform it at one of his concerts. Probably the two movements that were discovered and published in October 1926 were written at that time. They consist of a rough draft in pencil of the *Fanfare* written for three trumpets, four horns, two harps, three kettle-drums, one drum; and a berceuse, 'Le

[1] André Antoine, *Mes souvenirs sur le Théâtre Antoine et sur l'Odéon* (Paris, 1928).

Sommeil de Lear', a completed work scored for flute, horn, harp, and strings. The only performance ever given of these two rather insignificant little pieces proved disappointing, and it is unlikely that they will be included in the repertory of our symphony orchestras.[1]

Debussy planned some more incidental music. One score, sketched in June 1917, was written to another play of Shakespeare's, 'As You Like It'; J. P. Toulet undertook the dramatic side of the work, which was intended for the actor Gémier. It was a transformed, condensed version of a very early project conceived in the Villa Medici days, which Debussy had resumed after the completion of 'Pelléas', and subsequently abandoned. The history of the work is to be found further on where it belongs chronologically. Prior to this, he had planned to write music for Gabriel Mourey's 'Psyché'; but when the work came to be performed at Louis Mors' on the 1st of December 1913, Debussy had only written one short page for the flute. It was played behind the scenes by Louis Fleury, who kept the manuscript jealously to himself, and performed it frequently at concerts in France and elsewhere, always with great success. This very expressive little work represents Pan's song as he breathes his last. It was published in October 1927 under the title of 'Syrinx', instead of the original one, 'Flûte de Pan', which would have duplicated the title of the first of the 'Chansons de Bilitis'. Debussy wrote another detached piece for René Peter's 'La Tragédie de la Mort'—a little Berceuse, which, as he informed his friend Peter, on the 15th of February 1898, he decided to write himself, 'after a fruitless search amongst collections of folk songs'.

Debussy had also thought of writing an 'Orphée-Roi', on choral lines, in collaboration with Victor Ségalen, his close friend and confidant in artistic matters. They worked at it for over two years, but no trace of the musical plan remains. It was intended as anti-Gluck propaganda. In Debussy's opinion, Gluck's 'Orpheus' represented solely the anecdotal, lachrymose aspect of the subject. He conceived 'something absolutely novel'. We can form some idea of what he intended by reading the libretto of 'Orphée-Roi' and the preface in which Ségalen describes the very close collaboration planned by the author and the musician.[2] Another original

---

[1] Some time before the first orchestral performance took place in Paris, the present writer produced Debussy's music for 'King Lear' in an unusual form at one of the meetings of 'La Musique Vivante' held at the Salle Gaveau, on the 22nd of October 1926. On this occasion the work was performed at the piano, and simultaneously Debussy's orchestral score was shown on a screen by the aid of a magic lantern.   [2] Victor Ségalen, *Orphée-Roi* (Paris, Crès, 1921).

scheme had been proposed to him about 1900 by Paul Valéry, a writer whose 'Monsieur Teste' suggested to Debussy the idea of his 'Monsieur Croche'. This was a plan for a lyrical drama to consist of instrumental music, choruses, and miming. The project was soon abandoned, but it was subsequently resumed by the dramatist, who has just completed this work, 'Amphion', in collaboration with Arthur Honegger.

Debussy wished to write music to another poem by Rossetti, the librettist of his early work 'La Damoiselle élue'. He chose his 'Willow-wood', which Pierre Louÿs translated. In 1909, at the request of Serge de Diaghilef, he composed an Italian sketch in one act for the Russian Ballet. He wrote the libretto himself and was undecided whether to call it 'Masques et Bergamasques', 'L'Éternelle Aventure', or 'L'Amour Masqué'; the scenario was published under the first-mentioned title, but the music was never written. The rather conventional setting was to consist of a scene in eighteenth-century Venice, the characters being: Barbarina, 'l'Eau qui danse', 'la Pomme qui chante', Arlequin, the Bolognese Doctor, Captain Piribiribombo, Scaramouche, &c.

In 1914 he had an idea for another ballet which he did not write, 'Le Palais de silence' or 'No-ya-ti'. He also planned a work after Verlaine, entitled 'Fêtes Galantes', a subject he had already treated, and for which Louis Laloy had written a synopsis. Owing to a question of priority, however, Debussy was obliged to collaborate with Charles Morice, with the result that the project was soon abandoned. Debussy mentioned the work to a representative of *Comoedia* who reported his statements on the 1st February, 1914: 'As regards the "Fêtes Galantes" which Charles Morice and I have put together from Verlaine's poems, it is to be ballet, an *opera-ballet*. It is not finished—far from it! I am working at it at present, but I cannot say exactly on what date I shall deliver the work to our Academy of Music.' It was announced, perhaps as a joke, that a work of his, entitled 'Crimen Amoris', was to be included in the repertoire of the Opéra for the season 1912–13. Debussy told a reporter (see *Excelsior*, 15th September 1913) that he thought it essential to discover some new formula, suited to the special conditions prevailing at the National Opera. He thought it necessary either 'to adapt and rejuvenate the venerable opera-ballet of our ancestors, by removing all its wrinkles; or else . . . to create an entirely new form of lyrical art'. It was rumoured during the summer of 1904 that Debussy had arranged to write orchestral and choral music to Joachim Gasquet's 'Dionysos' which was to be produced at the Roman theatre in Orange. Of all these numerous plans, some

of which were never definitely decided on, none held the composer's attention to such an extent as 'Tristan', 'La Chute de la Maison Usher', and 'Le Diable dans le Beffroi'.

Early in August 1907, the Paris newspapers announced that 'L'Histoire de Tristan' was finished and was to be performed at the Opéra-Comique the following year. This rumour was quite unfounded. Debussy had merely discussed the subject with Gabriel Mourey, who thought of writing a new drama on Joseph Bédier's modern adaptation of 'Tristan et Yseult'. A semi-official notice appeared in the *Revue Musicale S.I.M.* of the 15th of November 1907, announcing definitely that Mourey and Debussy were collaborating at this lyrical drama; it concluded with these words: 'All previous and subsequent statements may be disregarded.' In a letter to Jacques Durand the composer declared that he almost dreaded the moment when the libretto would come into his hands, so wonderfully 'attractive and tempting' did the idea appear to him. By the end of September 1907, after working for a whole day with Mourey, he thought he had got hold of 'a rather good idea'. But nothing came of this French 'Tristan', conceived by one who was an equally passionate enemy and admirer of Wagner. One gathers, from various rumours, that it was to have been a descriptive, anecdotal, epic drama, tragic and comic by turns. Its episodic character would have made it akin to the romances of chivalry and utterly unlike the Germanic conception of the other 'Tristan'. Nothing is known of the work except the twelve bars which the composer inserted in a letter dated August 1907; he described the passage ironically as 'one of the 363 themes in the "Roman de Tristan"'. See illustration facing p. 261.

Debussy had already worked at 'Le Diable dans le Beffroi' during the summer of 1902, as he mentioned at the time in a letter to André Messager:

'I wish you would read or re-read this story and give me your opinion of it. There should be material there for a play which would be a happy blending of the real and the fantastic. The devil is represented as cynical and cruel—much more devilish than the red, brimstone-breathing clown that has, so illogically, become a tradition with us. I should also like to put an end to the idea that the devil is the spirit of evil. He is simply the spirit of contradiction; perhaps it is he who inspires those who do not think like everybody else.'

The following year Debussy sent the same musician further particulars about the work he was engaged on:

'It is too soon to say that I am done with the "Devil". The scenario is nearly finished; I have almost decided on the colouring of the music;

but I have still many a sleepless night before me, though I see a ray of hope at the end of it all. . . . As for those people who are so kind as to hope that I shall never be able to escape from "Pelléas", they are very much mistaken. Surely they must realize that if such a thing were to happen I should immediately devote myself to the cultivation of pine-apples, for I think it is quite disastrous to repeat *oneself*. I dare say the same people will think it scandalous of me to have deserted the shade of Mélisande for a cynical, pirouetting devil, and they will once more make it a pretext for accusing me of eccentricity.'

To get away from 'Pélleas' was Debussy's constant preoccupation. It was this desire that led him to abandon the idea of adapting Shakespeare's 'As You Like It' to music; its legendary setting suggested an atmosphere too similar to that of his masterpiece.

Debussy's attempt to escape from 'Pélleas' by devoting himself to 'Le Diable dans le Beffroi' involved a formidable imaginative effort, which was facilitated by his droll sense of humour. The work was to contain only one singing part, that of the crowd; the devil himself was to remain dumb, and only whistle. He wished the crowd to be really alive; in his opinion, this genuine animation had never been properly rendered. As a proof to the contrary, Pierre Lalo one day quoted as examples the finale of the second act of 'Meistersinger' and the Coronation scene in 'Boris Godunof'. But Debussy replied:

'The populace in "Boris" does not form a real crowd; first one group sings, and then another, there is no third group; they sing alternately, and usually in unison. As for the populace in the "Meistersinger", that isn't a crowd, but an army, highly organized in the German manner and marching in ranks. I should like to achieve a more scattered effect, something more divided, more detached, more indefinite, something that would appear unorganized, and which would yet be regulated, a real human crowd in which each voice would be independent, but where all the voices, when united, would produce an impression of concerted movement.'

On the 7th of July 1906 Debussy thought he had found the means of achieving his ideal. 'A propos of the "Devil",' he wrote to Jacques Durand, 'I think I have discovered a rather novel method of handling the voices; it has the additional merit of being simple. But I hardly dare to have faith in it, and it must remain a secret between us. . . . I am still afraid that one of these mornings I shall realize that the idea is idiotic.' In 1911 he was still dissatis-fied with the result: there were a good many *accents* that he did not like, and the setting was not sufficiently accurate. In a letter to Robert Godet, dated 6th of February 1911, he rejoiced that his new

project, 'Le Martyre de Saint-Sébastien', obliged him to postpone his other compositions indefinitely.

'I should like', he wrote, 'to achieve a choral style that would be at once perfectly simple and perfectly mobile. . . . I do not consider the *placage* in "Boris" any more satisfactory than the persistent counterpoint in the "Meistersinger" finale, which is nothing else but cold-blooded disorder. . . . There must be some other solution, some clever device to cheat the ear. It is the very devil! Not to mention the stupid way they have of arranging the chorus as if they were in a bathing establishment: one side for the men, the other for the women—another difficulty that I shall have to overcome. And then you will see what long outlandish words people will use to describe a very simple thing. . . .'

The composer spent a long time over 'La Chute de la Maison Usher' the libretto of which, like that of 'Le Diable dans le Beffroi', was adapted from a tale by Edgar Allan Poe. He often mentioned the work in letters to his publisher. We see from his correspondence in June and July 1908, that the 'heir of the Usher family' had become an obsession with him; he says: 'I am guilty of about ten acts of impoliteness per hour, the exterior world hardly exists for me. It is a delightful frame of mind, but has the disadvantage of being incompatible with the twentieth century.' In 1909 and 1910 the obsession still continued: 'These last days, I have been working at "The Fall of the House of Usher", and I have nearly finished a long monologue of poor Roderick's. It is sad enough to draw tears from a stone . . . as a matter of fact, it is all about the influence of stones on the minds of neurasthenic people. It has a delightfully mildewed atmosphere which I have achieved by blending the deep notes of the oboe and the harmonics of the violins (a patent device of my own). Don't mention this to any one; I am very much taken with it' (26th of June 1909). It made him forget the 'Images' he was composing, 'for I have got into the way of thinking of nothing else but "Roderick Usher" and the "Devil in the Belfry" . . . I fall asleep with them, and I awake either to the gloomy sadness of the former or to the sneers of the latter' (21st of September 1909). On the 2nd of June and the 8th of July 1910, he mentions that he hardly ever leaves 'the House of Usher'. Louis Laloy describes this work as a 'symphony of presentiments—growing constantly stronger until the catastrophe is reached and an atmosphere of mourning restores the feeling of calm'. Debussy believes that if he can achieve 'this progressive sense of anguish', he will have done good service to music—and to his publisher. When he leaves this 'House' his nerves are often 'as tense as the strings of a violin' (15th July 1910). After a long interval he took up this dramatic work once

again in September 1912, but completed only the libretto, which he handed over to his publisher in the autumn of 1917. The music has completely disappeared.

According to an interview published in the *New York Times* of the 15th of March 1925, these three compositions—'La Légende de Tristan', 'La Chute de la Maison Usher', and 'Le Diable dans le Beffroi'—had all been promised, rather vaguely, but by formal contract, to the impresario, Gatti-Casazza, a former director of the Scala, Milan, who had become manager of the Metropolitan Opera, New York, in 1908. Gatti-Casazza had been responsible for the first Italian performances of 'Pelléas' at Milan in the spring of 1908. He was, however, unable to produce the work in the United States, as the Manhattan Opera House had acquired the exclusive rights. He went to see Debussy in Paris in May 1908, and asked him to sell him the copyright of the three forthcoming operas. The composer replied that nothing was yet written except rough sketches of the librettos and a few vague suggestions concerning the music. As Gatti persisted in his request, Debussy consented to sign a contract and accepted a small advance fee, saying, as he did so: 'Don't forget that I am lazy and that it sometimes takes me weeks to choose between two chords. And don't forget either that it was you who insisted on the contract, and that you will probably get nothing for it.' Debussy made a number of interesting statements in the course of further conversations which took place at intervals ranging over several years, whenever the Italian manager came over to Paris from New York. 'My dominant characteristic', he once said, 'is not genius, but uncertainty and laziness. . . . Edgar Allan Poe had the most original imagination in the world; he struck an entirely new note. I shall have to find its equivalent in music. But I am growing old and becoming lazier than ever. . . .' Hesitations, delays, and postponements were the result.

But delays and postponements were out of the question in the execution of the new scheme which made him the associate of the celebrated Gabriele d'Annunzio. Debussy was immediately bound by a formal undertaking to be ready by a definite date, and the important orchestral score had to be improvised at very short notice. A journalist who interviewed him on behalf of the *Excelsior* about that time gave a pen-portrait of the musician signed with his pseudonym, Henry Malherbe. It appeared on the 11th of February 1911.

'M. Claude Debussy', he wrote, 'in his quest for light and silence, has withdrawn to a bright, secluded little corner, not far from the Bois de Boulogne. In his narrow study which is most artistically decorated

in fabrics of bronze and tawny hues a deliberate simplicity reigns. The only objects that reveal the musician are a long Japanese kito and the bulky form of a small black piano. The composer of "Pelléas" has the dusky, golden countenance of an idol. His aspect is at once powerful, noble, and unusual. His short beard and black hair help the illusion; he looks like one of the Magi, who has strayed by mistake into our times. His gleaming forehead on which the light plays, is thrust forward in convex curves of unusual prominence, indicating violent impulses. He is slow to give his confidence. He has withdrawn within his mortal shell, into the domain of pure feeling, where he entertains all the emotions and gives himself up to the intoxicating delights of ecstatic raptures. In these elegant surroundings, M. Debussy rolls a cigarette like any artisan, and speaks in a voice at first high-pitched and drawling which, as it increases in tone, becomes deep and pleasant.'

He explained to this journalist the difficulties that beset him. He had been attracted by the mixture of intense vitality and Christian feeling that characterize this subject, 'in which the worship of Adonis is united with that of Christ,' but he was hampered by lack of time. 'It would take me months of concentration to write adequate music to this subtle, mysterious drama of d'Annunzio. I feel obliged to limit myself to such music as will be worthy of the subject—probably a few choruses and some incidental music. I labour under the distressing obligation of having to be ready by May as "Le Martyre de Saint-Sébastien" is to be given at the Châtelet that month. . . .' The composer went on to mention his theories with regard to religious music: 'In my opinion the writing of sacred music ceased with the sixteenth century. The beautiful, childlike souls of those days were alone capable of expressing their passionate, disinterested fervour in music free from all admixture of worldliness. . . .' He made a pantheistic profession of faith:

'I do not practise religion in accordance with the sacred rites. I have made mysterious Nature my religion. I do not believe that a man is any nearer to God for being clad in priestly garments, nor that one place in a town is better adapted to meditation than another. When I gaze at a sunset sky and spend hours contemplating its marvellous, ever-changing beauty, an extraordinary emotion overwhelms me. Nature in all its vastness is truthfully reflected in my sincere though feeble soul. Around me are the trees stretching up their branches to the skies, the perfumed flowers gladdening the meadows, the gentle grass-carpeted earth, . . . and my hands unconsciously assume an attitude of adoration. . . . To feel the supreme and moving beauty of the spectacle to which Nature invites her ephemeral guests!—that is what I call prayer. . . .'

Given the conditions in which he was composing—the extreme

haste, the novelty of the conception, the remarkable nature of the drama—Debussy could not help thinking of the critics who were soon to pronounce on his sacred music. In this connexion, he made some noteworthy statements during the same interview:

'Who will discover the secret of musical composition? The sound of the sea, the curve of the horizon, the wind in the leaves, the cry of a bird, register complex impressions within us. Then suddenly, without any deliberate consent on our part, one of these memories issues forth to express itself in the language of music. It bears its own harmony within it. By no effort of ours can we achieve anything more truthful or accurate. In this way only does a soul destined for music discover its most beautiful ideas. If I speak thus, it is not in order to prove that I have none. I detest doctrines and their impertinent implications. And for that reason I wish to write down my musical dreams in a spirit of utter self-detachment. I wish to sing of my interior visions with the naïve candour of a child. No doubt, this simple musical grammar will jar on some people. It is bound to offend the partisans of deceit and artifice. I foresee that and I rejoice at it. I shall do nothing to create adversaries, but neither shall I do anything to turn enmities into friendships. I must endeavour to be a great artist, so that I may dare to be myself and suffer for my faith. Those who feel as I do, will only appreciate me the more. The others will shun and hate me. I shall make no effort to conciliate them. On that distant day—I trust it is still very far off—when I shall no longer be a cause of strife, I shall feel bitter self-reproach. For that odious hypocrisy which enables one to please all mankind will inevitably have prevailed in those last works.'

Shortly before the work was produced, Debussy made some equally interesting remarks on the religious character of his music to a representative of *Comoedia* (18th of May 1911). Two days previously, the 'Martyre' had incurred the censure of the Archbishop of Paris who declared the performance to be 'offensive to Christian consciences,' and forbade Catholics to attend.

' Do you imagine', said Debussy, 'that my works do not contain what I may call religious precedents? Do you propose to fetter the soul of the artist? Is it not obvious that a man who sees mystery in everything will be inevitably attracted to a religious subject? I do not wish to make a profession of faith. But, even if I am not a practising Catholic nor a believer, it did not cost me much effort to rise to the mystical heights which the poet's drama attains. Let us be clear about the word *mysticism*. You see that this very day the Archbishop has forbidden the faithful to assist at d'Annunzio's play, although he does not know the work. But let us not dwell on these annoying details. . . . From the artistic point of view such decrees cannot be considered. I assure you that I wrote my music as though I had been asked to do it for a

church. The result is decorative music, if you like, a noble text, interpreted in sounds and rhythms; and in the last act when the saint ascends into Heaven I believe I have expressed all the feelings aroused in me by the thought of the Ascension. Have I succeeded? That no longer concerns me. We have not the simple faith of other days. Is the faith expressed by my music orthodox or not? I cannot say. It is my faith, my own, singing in all sincerity. In case it interests you, I may as well tell you that I wrote in two months a score which in the ordinary way would have taken me a year, and that I put into practice what I might call my theories on incidental music. It should be something more than the vague buzzing that too often accompanies verse or prose, and should be closely incorporated with the text.'

As the time was so short, Debussy was not able to write the entire score himself. He invited André Caplet, who was to be the conductor, to collaborate with him. Caplet developed the orchestral canvas which the composer sketched out on several staves according to his usual custom. As soon as the pages were written, they were copied and sent to be engraved. Émile Vuillermoz—who, with D. E. Inglebrecht and Marcel Chadeigne, directed the singing and rehearsed the dances of the principal character— has recorded his reminiscences of those days in his *Musiques d'aujourd'hui*. 'The music,' he says, 'was sent to the theatre page by page, corrected in pencil. Debussy remained invisible in his house, engaged, up to the last minute, in writing and revising this work, the importance of which was realized only by a few of his intimate friends.' Debussy did not put in an appearance until the day of the ensemble rehearsal, which was given in the foyer of the theatre in the Italian manner. The performance was an unprecedented success. The composer was moved to tears. But, although on that occasion the work had seemed flawless and marvellously effective, the performance in the theatre was unfortunately spoiled by an unavoidable misunderstanding between the conductor and the stage manager. It was also marred by the absurdly inadequate interpretation of the principal role by the foreign dancer, Ida Rubinstein, who had absolute control of the production. To further her theatrical ambitions, she had commissioned two of the most celebrated artists of the day to write this work for her.

Misfortune continued to pursue 'Le Martyre de Saint-Sébastien'. The ecclesiastical censure was not revoked in spite of the following respectful statement signed by both Debussy and d'Annunzio: 'We declare . . . that this deeply religious work is a lyrical glorification not only of this splendid Christian athlete, but also of all Christian heroism.' This protestation did not remove what the

Archbishop of Paris regarded as the extremely objectionable nature of the performance: the representation of the saint by a Jewish woman dancer; and the ecclesiastical interdiction kept a great many people away from the theatre. Nor was that all. The dress rehearsal of the new work was to have been a gala performance, the date of which was fixed for Sunday the 21st of May. On the morning of that day, when an aeroplane race was starting from Issy-les-Moulineaux, a member of the French government, the Minister for War, was caught by the propeller of an aeroplane and killed; on account of the official mourning the gala performance could not take place. It was decided to give the rehearsal in private and to admit only journalists. But throngs of guests whose invitations had been cancelled too late forced their way into the Châtelet, with the result that there were uproarious scenes at the doors of the theatre which completely upset the performance.

The first performance of the 'Martyre de Saint-Sébastien' took place on Monday, the 22nd of May. It achieved only a mediocre success, in fact, it barely escaped being a failure. The musicians were hampered by the Italian poet's phraseology, which was rather laboured, though at times magnificent, and by the incidental nature and subordinate role of the music which, to their mind, should have been supreme. The criticisms were very varied; some expressed boundless enthusiasm, others the most violent disparagement. The *Rappel* remarked that during the course of the performance 'the audience poured out gradually, like water from a broken vase'; the writer came to the conclusion that the work was a *beffa*, a practical joke, that had been played on the Paris public; he even went so far as to record the vulgar saying of a well-known personage: 'Ça, le Saint-Sébastien? C'est la Sainte-Barbe!' According to the *République Française*, the music consisted entirely of 'disconnected pieces, without any sequence which, most of the time, had no relation whatever to the scenes they accompanied'. The *Gaulois*, 'out of consideration for its readers', refused to give any account of the drama itself: 'There is something inherently sacrilegious about it which necessarily offends Christian feeling.' However, this paper gave Debussy every praise: 'I thought the musical side of the performance superb; the instrumentation was full of rich effects and showed masterly virtuosity.'

The reports of the performance were for the most part entrusted to the musical rather than the dramatic critics. More than one writer pointed out the essential differences between the art of d'Annunzio and that of Debussy. They considered that Debussy's themes and melodic formulas were not intimately welded to the

essence of the drama; they remarked that the music had difficulty
in making itself heard and seemed to be submerged beneath 'the
extraordinary flood of words'. Many reporters also pointed out the
novel nature of the score, and contrasted it with the composer's
previous works. Here are some of the opinions expressed.

The *Courrier Musical* published an article which condemned the
poem in the strongest terms, but expressed lively admiration
for the music. The writer, Paul de Stoecklin, distinguished in
this score a fourth manner of Debussy's.

'In his first period', says the critic, 'he followed in the footsteps of
Massenet. He next created a manner of his own under the influence of
the Russians and the Orientals, and then proceeded to exploit that
manner, to his own detriment and our annoyance. And now, he is
writing tonal music, music with characteristic themes, full of common
chords, music that recalls "Parsifal"! We find once more the well-known
caressing harmonies, the remarkable, unusual, orchestral sonorities of
which M. Debussy knows the secret, and which seem to be an efflo-
rescence of pianistic sonorities, even as the flower is the development of
the bud. But there is a new element also and the exquisite manner in
which M. Debussy has treated the choral masses is an additional
attraction.'

Paul de Stoecklin regretted that so much skill should have been
devoted to the production of a still-born work, and expressed the
hope that the composer would take up the score again and transform it into a concert suite or some kind of oratorio.

According to Louis Vuillemin, in *Comoedia*, Debussy had undergone a transformation. He considered that the essential parts of the
work were very fine, but not solidly welded owing to over-hasty
composition. 'There are great things in this new score', he wrote.
'Above all—as d'Annunzio's superlatively lyrical text demanded—
we have an utterly new and remarkably powerful Debussy, a
Debussy who has definitely resolved no longer to imitate his
imitators. Will they forgive him?' Paul Souday, in *L'Éclair*,
recognized Debussy's 'usual qualities with all their fascinating
originality; but this incidental music is not broadly developed, nor
of any great importance. The final choruses are very beautiful
and full of real religious feeling.' In a long and extremely verbose
article in *Gil Blas*, Georges Pioch described the score as being
full of the characteristic charm of the Île-de-France, 'so called
simply because it is the heart and soul of our nation'. He
recorded the varying impressions produced on him by the different acts: the fascination of the first act, the comparative weakness
of the second; whilst, in the third act, the music 'is richly

profuse; in turn solemn and voluptuous, now vibrating to ardent
embraces, now appeased by prayer. Above all, it is most moving;
it is the work of a great pagan musician who sees a god in all
things. . . .' The *Figaro* gave the work high praise:

'For the first time in the history of the *mélodrame*', writes Robert
Brussel, 'the music is intimately united and identified with the poem;
it heightens and prolongs the effect without ever altering the atmosphere, except to render it more intense. The four preludes, the
choruses and soli, will certainly be numbered amongst M. Debussy's
most perfect works. Without indulging in the slightest imitation of
antique forms, he has managed to interpret Saint-Sébastien most
fittingly, in a simple lyrical style full of natural feeling. The orchestral
writing, the tier-like disposition of the voices in the choruses, the manner in which he regulates their entries, the softness or brilliance of their
effects, their rhythm, their vigour or subordination, all go to form a
work that is self-sufficing, and possesses a significance and beauty of
its own.'

According to Paul Abram, critic to *La Petite République*, the
score is conceived on the same lines as 'L'Après-midi d'un Faune'
and 'Pelléas', 'but there are occasional pauses which produce an
impression of calm serenity, and gusts of solemn melody that
are marvellously seductive'. In the *Journal* Reynaldo Hahn remarked that 'this music is singularly lacking in continuity, breadth,
and power'. In *L'Action* an article signed merely 'L. S.' praised
the simplicity and clarity of the music: 'wonderful to relate, one
can listen to it without wearing out one's brain.' A critic in
Excelsior, who signed simply 'C.', remarked that Debussy had
hitherto 'never indulged us with such a continuous outpouring
of melodic expression. "Le Martyre de Saint-Sébastien" is exceptional in this respect. It is true that it abounds in the most
subtle Debussy harmonies, and I rejoice thereat. But throughout the entire work the composer is constantly preoccupied with
genuine themes, with phrases in fact.' A similar opinion was
expressed by Adolphe Aderer, to whom the score revealed
'a Debussy who has grown more vigorous and powerful, who has
extricated himself from the subtilized Debussyism of his imitators
and attained to the noble simplicity that characterizes all great
works'.

Pierre Lalo (in the *Temps*) considered that the novel aspect of the
music had been deliberately and artificially achieved:

'Debussy has been led to modify the character and form of his
musical ideas, of his music itself, even of his orchestra; he has given
them greater breadth and expansiveness, more assurance, almost more

form; the idiom is more definite, less restrained and subtle. . . . This is excellent music, but it is foreign to M. Debussy's real nature; it forms an incident, a parenthesis, in his work and in his artistic development.' He adds that the breadth, assurance, and symmetry one notices here 'are far from being deeply imprinted marks revealing in the musician a new form of sensibility; this is a casual, transient manner, which he has assumed for a special piece of work, which is perfectly suited and adapted to that work, but which has no affinity with his real nature and remains foreign to his art.'

There were no such reservations in the reports of two other important critics, both composers, who had so far been rather sparing in their praise of the works Debussy had published since 'Pelléas'. Alfred Bruneau and Gaston Carraud both expressed the greatest enthusiasm for the success their colleague had achieved in that difficult, in fact rather objectionable, form, incidental music. In the *Matin*, Bruneau gave particular praise to the perfection and power of the vocal ensembles, 'which are constructed with remarkable skill and are full of striking and curious effects'. He also praised 'the hieratic, fantastic preludes, at once religious and voluptuous; the brilliant fanfares, and the lively dances. . . .' For some years past, owing to repeated disappointments, Carraud's faith in Debussy had grown lukewarm. But in the new work he found once more 'M. Debussy's finest qualities, whose existence had seemed imperilled in the works subsequent to "Pelléas" '. He found these characteristics expressed with 'a melodic precision, a breadth of inspiration, a boldness of colouring and accent, such as he has never before exhibited'. He concluded his report in *La Liberté* with the following enthusiastic lines:

' It impressed me as being one of the finest things M. Debussy has ever written. In spite of the sumptuous colouring and the fanciful originality and marvellous diversity of the instrumental combinations, the emotion in the essential parts of the work remains intensely spiritual and of a rare purity. There are moments of ecstasy and of pain when the emotional atmosphere of the "Martyre de Saint-Sébastien" recalls that of "Parsifal", although the works are so dissimilar in feeling and style.'

In the *Revue S.I.M.*, Émile Vuillermoz wrote as follows: 'This curious work, written in a novel style, which belongs to no category and shows no respect for form, has an absolutely miraculous quality.' But the writer of this enthusiastic panegyric realized that the full importance of the 'Martyre' could not be gauged till after the orchestral performances of the following winter; for only then would the divine spell exert its miraculous power on the great mass of music-lovers and 'a marvelling public will

insist on the revival of this masterpiece which has been so misunderstood.'

A very different forecast was given by the Abbé F. Brun in *La Croix Illustrée*. In his analysis of the new score this critic, himself a composer of sacred music, drew attention to the frequent use of Gregorian modes and paid homage to Debussy's lofty conception of religious music. He concluded that there was reason to hope that the illustrious composer would write 'some charming cantatas, some beautiful motets which would render in music what the religious pictures of the English pre-Raphaelite school, particularly those of Burne-Jones, expressed in painting'. He added: 'Perhaps we shall see this within the next ten years.'

On the 14th and 17th of June 1912 the orchestral score was conducted by D. E. Inglebrecht at two concerts of the Société Musicale Indépendante. In order to make the unlucky composition more widely known, André Caplet subsequently arranged it as a symphonic suite without choruses, a form which is necessarily disjointed and does not enable one to reconstruct the original atmosphere. When divorced from the drama of which it is the appropriate accompaniment and commentary incidental music loses its significance; its original colouring disappears entirely when the score is transcribed for instruments, no matter how accurately the work is done. This purely symphonic performance did not arouse any enthusiasm in the audience. On the contrary, as Émile Vuillermoz recorded, the work sounded dull and remote; in the following fine passage he described the vanished beauties of the score:

'. . . In vain the trumpet endeavours to replace the absent voices. We no longer witness the building up, from the basses to the sopranos, of the magnificent stairway of mystic invocations whose steps reach up to heaven; the twin brothers, Marc and Marcellien, no longer utter their double cry of light at the moment of the miracle, and no longer do the seven witnesses of God rise up like lilies above the orchestra, as their pure notes soar aloft with indescribable majesty. Gone are the black sorceries of the Magic Chamber and its polytonal brilliance, so prophetic in effect, the voice of the Virgin Erigone whose song floats on the air like a loosened scarf, the sensual lamentations of the women of Byblos who warble of grief and love like wounded cooing doves, the dazzling magnificence of Paradise, with its fierce act of faith and the savage joy of its psalms. . . .'

Since 1912 the work has been played at various concerts, sometimes in the complete version and sometimes in the form of extracts with or without chorus. In June 1922 and February 1924

it was revived at the Opéra in its original form but with some alterations in the poem; these performances were not satisfactory. The
prophecy of the admirer of 'Saint-Sébastien', who confidently
believed in the future success of this remarkable work, has not
been realized. 'Le Martyre de Saint-Sébastien', wrote Émile
Vuillermoz once more in 1920, 'is a masterpiece which has not yet
been understood. It remains to be discovered. Debussy wrote
his "Parsifal" that day. But his "Parsifal" is still waiting for its
Bayreuth.'

There are no immediate signs that the hoped-for Bayreuth will
materialize. The score alone, freed from its cumbersome poetic
text, is to be heard fairly often, and some excellent performances
have been given by the talented conductor D. E. Inglebrecht. But
the rights of the complete dramatic work remain in the possession
of the dancer for whom the two great artists were commissioned
to write it, and whose interpretation was marked by a bland
incomprehension on the three or four occasions on which the
complete work was performed. Meanwhile, until we witness some
decisive test that may never take place or may come too late, it is
difficult to pronounce judgement on a score consisting of a varied
series of unequal, disconnected, hastily-written pieces. Certainly
no musician can remain insensible to the pure beauty of the first
prelude in which the wood-winds reproduce the cold, even-toned
sonorities of the organ, to the glittering brilliance of the *Magic
Chamber*, or to the sombre or radiant beauty of the various interludes, with their poignant lamentations. One cannot but admire
the very novel melodic vigour; the admirable writing of all the vocal
ensembles, some of which are full of intense expression; the lofty
beauty of the new contrapuntal style towards which the composer
seemed to be tending, with the deliberate intention of resuming the
traditions of the fifteenth- and sixteenth-century masters whose
melodic interlacings he had always admired; and the richness of
the orchestration which is so much stronger in colouring than that
of 'Pelléas'. But, in spite of Debussy's magnificent efforts to
achieve now an extreme complexity, now an utter simplicity, a kind
of sonorous bareness that was not natural to him, it is on the whole
doubtful whether the music of 'Le Martyre de Saint-Sébastien' can
be placed on the same level with such consummate masterpieces as
the 'Prélude à l'Après-midi d'un Faune' and 'Pelléas et Mélisande'.

Debussy was aware of the abnormal character of the work and
realized that if it was not more widely known, this was partly
because of the 'incidental' nature of the music. In 1914, at the
request of Jacques Rouché, the new director of the Opéra, he began

to make an operatic version of the work, having received full authorization from Gabriele d'Annunzio to adapt the poetical text. But he was soon obliged to abandon his plan on account of the misgivings of Rouché, who feared that the Archbishop's previous condemnation would still influence an important section of his subscribers. During the war of 1914–18, anticipating that d'Annunzio's political activities would modify the opinion of the ecclesiastical authorities, or, at any rate, alter the views of the frequenters of the Opéra, Rouché decided to carry out his original plan. The Italian poet had already authorized the necessary cuts and alterations, and the literary adaptation was begun; but it was already 1917, and Debussy's new opera was never written. Nor did he ever begin the Indian drama which Gabriele d'Annunzio had planned for him during the war.[1]

[1] The Italian poet alluded to this project on the 31st of March 1928, in a telegram which he sent to the committee engaged in organizing the Debussy monument. 'I spent hours and hours working with Claude', he said, 'and no one realizes better than I do what might have been expected from this transformation of his art. I had planned an Indian drama for him, and was looking forward to meeting him again as to the highest reward for my four years of ceaseless warfare. . . .'

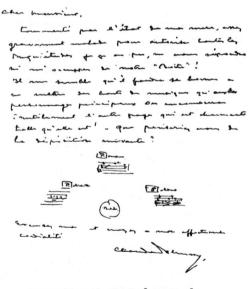

LETTER TO ANDRÉ HELLÉ
(27 August 1913)

CHAPTER XIII

'JEUX'. 'LA BOÎTE A JOUJOUX' (1913)

AT the request of several theatre managers and dancers Debussy and his publishers decided to sanction, or at least to permit the adaptation of his symphonic works as ballets. In May 1913 Loïe Fuller floated on shining, flame-coloured veils to the strains of the Nocturnes. This ballet consisted of a curious adaptation of 'Nuages' and 'Sirènes'. Unfortunately, owing to practical considerations connected with the specially designed stage setting, the choreographic rendering of 'Fêtes' had to be omitted. Consequently, this section, the most rhythmic and animated portion of the work, was performed only as an instrumental item while the curtain was lowered; it became a mere interlude to which no one listened, but which destroyed the unity of the dimly luminous spectacle.

The Russian Ballet next expressed a wish to adapt some of Debussy's works. Serge de Diaghilef's famous artistic enterprise has had such a deep influence on music and musicians and, indeed, on all the arts, that it deserves to be seriously studied from the historical, aesthetical and technical points of view. The Russian Ballet had just produced Stravinsky's 'Le Sacre du Printemps', which had given rise to violent scenes among the audience. The dancer, Nijinsky, undertook to adapt the 'Prélude à l'Après-midi d'un Faune'. He illustrated this delightfully delicate, undulating music with a horribly angular choreography—a stereotyped, unintelligent, ridiculous reproduction of the classical style. His interpretation was condemned by all musicians, and gave rise to a lively controversy. Diaghilef appealed to Odilon Redon and Auguste Rodin to state their opinions; they both approved highly of the performance. But Gaston Calmette, the manager of the *Figaro*, questioned the authority of a painter and a sculptor to give judgement in a matter that was quite as important from the musical as from the artistic and plastic points of view. On the whole, this experiment of the Russian Ballet was considered a blunder.

In the spring of 1912 the Russian Ballet had announced that they were about to produce 'Fêtes' (from the Nocturnes). They next asked Debussy to write music to a very modern theme for which the dancer Nijinsky had planned a ballet entitled 'Jeux'. The subject was 'a plastic vindication of the man of 1913', and the

synopsis was as follows: 'The scene is a garden at dusk; a tennis ball has been lost; a young man and two girls are searching for it. The artificial light of the large electric lamps shedding fantastic rays about them suggests the idea of childish games: they play hide and seek, they try to catch one another, they quarrel, they sulk without cause. The night is warm, the sky is bathed in a pale light; they embrace. But the spell is broken by another tennis ball thrown in mischievously by an unknown hand. Surprised and alarmed, the young man and the girls disappear into the nocturnal depths of the garden.'

Debussy managed to express the general idea of this subject in musical sketches full of delicate effects. He evidently also attempted to reproduce in his music the agile, restless, bounding technique of this favourite English game.

'This supple music is extraordinarily nimble, always ready for sudden movements. It is constantly on the alert like the tennis players it describes. Every few bars its movement and colour changes. It quickly abandons a design, a timbre, an impulse, and rushes off in another direction. Presently, the melody is returned with a skilful back-hand stroke; the theme, dexterously taken, is sent to and fro in volleys or half-volleys, now stopped short in its course, now taken on the rebound like a cut ball.'

The clever effects described by Émile Vuillermoz in the above passage were not noticed by the public and the critics. So fascinated were the members of the audience by the modern atmosphere of the subject, by the realistic setting and the conventional stiffness of the mathematical choreography, that they paid little attention to the music itself.

And yet the work was worth listening to, if only from curiosity, for it contained new experiments in composition and showed evidence of a further harmonic evolution. Debussy had taken a great deal of pains with it, and, in some details, he had followed the advice of Diaghilef; he rewrote the ending and kept revising the score until the last minute. A whole series of dates are inscribed at the end of the rough draft of the orchestral score (Legouix collection); first, we read: 23rd, 28th, 29th of August 1912; then, 1st, 2nd (of September, no doubt). As he wrote to Jacques Durand on the 12th of September 1912, the end of 'Jeux' was 'very difficult to get right, for the music has to convey a rather *risqué* situation. But of course, in a ballet, any hint of immorality escapes through the feet of the danseuse and ends in a pirouette.'

In this composition, which is really too delicate and subtle for mere incidental ballet music, Debussy managed to achieve a degree

of unity and thematic variety which permits us to bracket the 'Jeux'
of 1912–13 with the old Quartet of 1893, and to include them with
the 'cyclical' music of an earlier period. But the connecting links
between the various musical ideas, and the spontaneous processes
by which they are constantly transformed to suit the incidents of
the graceful game they illustrate, are not readily perceptible to
most music-lovers, or even musicographers. For, with subtle art,
Debussy discreetly shrouds the delicate mechanism in a light veil
which it would be both difficult and futile to remove.

The harmonic evolution is more obvious. Certain processes
which Stravinsky had recently inflicted on the ears of the audience
in his 'Sacre du Printemps' in a harsh, abrupt, form are here
treated by Debussy with great lightness and skill. Already in the
mysterious prelude, he introduces, over a pedal-point in the strings,
a succession of descending chords composed of all the notes in the
whole-tone scale; and later, he ventures to superimpose major and
minor seconds, thereby utilizing a system that was not yet generally
known by its future name of harmonic counterpoint or polytonality.
A scale rambles off in two parallel lines a semitone apart; or a
melody is twice superimposed upon itself, one part being a minor
second, the other a minor third above the original, thus producing
a continuous double series of changing intervals of a second.
He was in future to make frequent use of this device. It is, for
instance, employed in a very obvious manner in the first bars of
the Sonata for flute, viola, and harp.

'Jeux' was danced for the first time at the Théâtre des Champs-
Élysées, on the 15th of May 1913. This was three and a half
months after the date of the first performance of 'Gigues' at
the Concerts Colonne, and of the hundredth performance of 'Pelléas
et Mélisande' at the Opéra-Comique, and a month after the Société
Nationale had produced the re-orchestrated version of the 'Printemps' of 1887 (18th of April 1913). 'Jeux' was not a brilliant
success. The applause was moderate, and there was some hissing:
the public seemed undecided. Debussy cannot have been very
much surprised, for he did not approve of the peculiar choreography
of his collaborator Nijinsky. 'Nijinsky's perverse genius', wrote
Debussy to Robert Godet, 'is entirely devoted to peculiar mathematical processes. The man adds up demi-semiquavers with his
feet, and proves the result with his arms. Then, as if suddenly
stricken with partial paralysis, he stands listening to the music
with a most baleful eye. . . . It is ugly; Dalcrozian in fact.'
The composer also realized that by constantly transforming
his art he was disappointing the expectations of most music-

lovers who thought that he owed it to himself to remain the *Maître* of 'Pelléas et Mélisande'. On the 1st of March of the following year (1914) the score was played at the Concerts Colonne without the accompaniment of any miming or dancing. It was received with mingled cheers and hisses. The hostile manifestations were chiefly caused by the novel harmonic treatment, although the programme contained notes by Paul Landormy which clearly explained the derivation of these dissonances. Since then 'Jeux' has never been revived except by the Swedish Ballet, who performed it at the Théâtre des Champs-Élysées in 1920 and 1923. Diaghilef has entirely given them up. In collaboration with other composers he has made further interesting experiments, some of which have been highly successful.

The press opinions were very divergent. Writing in *La Liberté*, Gaston Carraud ranked the music 'far above "La Mer" and a considerable portion of the "Images" with their minute, rather dry, effects. . . . I also prefer it on account of its rich, expressive tone-colouring, its breadth, the clarity and graceful spaciousness of the lines which sustain its extremely subtle and astonishingly profuse details.' This critic thought he could discern 'something reminicent of M. Dukas'. When 'Jeux' was given without its choreographic setting, the same musician wrote that it had 'a warmth of colouring, an intimacy of feeling, above all, a mellowness and grace of line which are too often lacking in M. Debussy's recent compositions'. The *Ménestrel* published two successive reports of the concert performance of 'Jeux'. The first, by Amédée Boutarel, was very enthusiastic and praised, in particular, the poetical feeling for nature which was noticeable in the work; the other, by Joseph Jemain, was less favourable and pointed out that 'the original and novel effects seemed less natural, more strained, more artificial'.

The *Revue du Temps Présent* published a very eulogistic article containing a brief defence of Debussy by Paul le Flem, a composer who was then making his debut as a critic. After praising the subtlety of this music 'with its broken rhythms, which are so perfectly adapted to the ever-changing choreography', the musician went on to reply to those of his colleagues who found fault with Debussy because he had not treated every detail in the score of 'Jeux' in a completely novel manner.

'The musicians who level this reproach at Debussy are the very people who constantly wave the banner of tradition. Why should not Debussy be faithful to *his own* tradition, to his intensely individual manner? Why should he utilize processes that are not his? Is he to be forced to use

an idiom that is repugnant to his very nature? In short, what is all this critical hair-splitting but an attempt to trump up a meaningless charge against the composer of "Pelléas"?'

Side by side with such enthusiastic eulogies of 'Jeux', there appeared a few articles full of merciless censure, such as that of Auguste Mangeot, a sincere, but impulsive critic who lacked the finer shades of musical sensibility. Although the performance had left him in no doubt as to the excellence of the score, he ventured to state in his review, *Le Monde Musical*, that the work was 'devoid of rhythmic and plastic elements', and that evidently 'M. Debussy's sole concern had been to experiment with the chords and timbres of the orchestra, without paying any attention to the musical structure of the work'. As regards the harmony, he thought it harsh and discordant and none the less unpleasing because of the 'confused medley' Debussy had achieved. 'You feel as if you had penetrated courageously into a thorny bush hoping to discover some rare flower, and have come away with empty, bleeding hands, exasperated and disheartened. . . .'

During part of 1913 Debussy was engaged on another ballet which he found entertaining and interesting. André Hellé, a painter who specialized in writing and illustrating children's books, wanted some musician to collaborate with him in the dramatic version of his 'Boîte à Joujoux'. Besides writing the original text of this pretty little story and designing the illustrations he had also extracted from it the scenario for a ballet. He discussed the subject with Debussy in February. The composer immediately agreed to collaborate with him and set to work in the beginning of the summer.

The subject of Hellé's little play narrates a tragic love story which takes place within the narrow limits of a toy-box; but, as the librettist's synopsis indicates, this box had a secret compartment full of thoughts and sentiments.

'Toy-boxes', he said, 'are really towns in which the toys live like real people. Or perhaps towns are nothing else but boxes in which people live like toys. Some dolls were dancing; a soldier saw one of them and fell in love with her; but the doll had already given her heart to a lazy, frivolous, quarrelsome polichinelle. The soldiers and the polichinelles fought a great battle in which the poor little soldier was seriously wounded. The doll, who had been deserted by the wicked polichinelle, took in the soldier, nursed him, and grew to love him; they got married and were very happy and had lots of children. The polichinelle became a *garde-champêtre*, and life went on as before inside the toy-box.'

This little moral tale probably appealed to the sense of humour, the philosophic mind, and the paternal instincts of Debussy, now in his fiftieth year. In writing the score he constantly had in mind the little daughter he loved so tenderly. In order to put himself on the childish level of his subject, which moved him more than might have been imagined, he used to amuse himself, he declared, by 'extracting confidences from some of Chouchou's old dolls'. The two first parts were written rather quickly, but he wrote to his publisher on the 27th of September: 'The third part is dragging. The soul of a doll is more mysterious than even Maeterlinck imagines; it does not readily tolerate the kind of clap-trap so many human souls put up with. There is to be a money-box, but that I have no hope of interpreting, knowing too little about them. But I hope to get through with it all the same. . . .' By October the work was done, or at least the piano score was finished. The orchestral score was not sketched until the spring of 1914; it was partly written by the end of 1917, and was completed by André Caplet after Debussy's death. The work was to be brought out in the usual style of André Hellé's productions. As will be seen from the letter here reproduced facing this page, Debussy took a keen interest in the artistic presentation of the work and the make-up of the piano score.

He was equally interested in the stage production, but left it to André Hellé to superintend the setting and the costumes, which the artist had designed himself. Debussy anticipated that the acting and the dancing would be done by children; he did not think it necessary to have a ballet-master, as his music was intended to accompany simple movements, not set dances. He even stated, in a letter dated the 31st of October 1913, that 'only marionettes could interpret the meaning of the text and the expression of the music'. The production, which had to be postponed owing to the war, did not take place at the Opéra-Comique. It was at the short-lived Théâtre Lyrique du Vaudeville that 'La Boîte à Joujoux' was performed for the first time, on the 10th of December 1919, under the direction of P. B. Gheusi. The parts were played by adult dancers, as was also the case later at the Opéra-Comique and the Swedish Ballet performances. Debussy was no longer there to decide whether the artists were carrying out the intentions he had explained so clearly in an interview to a representative of *Comoedia* on the 1st of February 1914. 'You see', he said, when he had related the subject of his ballet, 'you see how utterly simple it is. But the difficulty is to get that effect on the stage . . . to achieve that natural simplicity . . . to see that these cardboard personages

retain their air of burlesque, in a word, their character, without
which the play becomes meaningless. . . .'

In the course of the same interview, the composer explained
how modest his aim was: 'La Boîte à Joujoux' was to be a mere
'pantomime to the kind of music I have written for children in
Christmas and New-Year albums . . . a little work to amuse the
children, nothing more!' In writing this music, which he considered was 'conceived in a characteristically French spirit',
Debussy told his publisher that he had endeavoured 'to be clear
and even *amusing*, without posing or indulging in any unnecessary
acrobatic feats'. The score is full of allusions to such songs as 'Il
pleut bergère'; there are bugle calls, musical-box effects, even
parodies of well-known operas and bizarre tunes. The style of the
whole work, though very Debussyist and full of subtle, daring
harmonies, is extremely simple and natural. And yet, as is pointed
out in the manuscript letter reproduced above, one can easily distinguish leit-motifs, each of which applies to a particular character.
When 'La Boîte à Joujoux' was produced in Paris in 1919, the
critics were unanimous in praising its charm. The *Monde Musical*,
a paper which, as we have seen, was not always very favourable to
Debussy, hailed the little play as a masterpiece of French music:
'What charming music', wrote Auguste Mangeot. 'It is of to-day
with its novel rhythms and its melodic patterns new to our ears;
yet belongs to all time, through its lively feeling, its harmonious
sense of measure and proportion, the discreetness with which it
suggests without ever insisting, and the harmonious quality
which is blended both with its laughter and its tears. . . .'

During the summer of 1913, when he was composing 'La
Boîte à Joujoux', Debussy also wrote a group of songs entitled
'Trois Poèmes de Stéphane Mallarmé'. Thus, after an interval of
twenty years, he returned once more to the poet who had inspired
his famous symphonic Prelude, 'Le Faune'. Intensely subtle, the
compositions 'Soupir', 'Placet futile', and 'L'Éventail' bring out
all the essential feeling of the abstruse poems, and underline
the verbal refinements in which the poet indulges. The music,
which some declare to be superfluous, is not of a type calculated
to arouse enthusiasm at the first hearing, even amongst cultured
amateurs; the songs are consequently rarely sung in the concert
hall. But Debussy himself was pleased with these 'Poèmes'.
Comparing them to the compositions of the masters and
disciples of the Schola Cantorum, he wrote: 'I venture to say that
they do not stock this article in the rue Saint-Jacques.' One
notices his twofold preoccupation: to give an accurate rendering

of the poetical text and to achieve a broad melodic line. This is particularly and very distinctly noticeable in the second poem, 'Placet futile', which is declaimed with meticulous exactness to the undulating line of a slow minuet, closely resembling the old sarabandes whose stately elegance Debussy had always loved, and which he imitated so well.

During the last few years before the war Debussy played a part in public life. His activities were limited by his natural love of solitude and by the fact that being at last, after many vicissitudes, able to enjoy a degree of comfort very much to his taste, he found great satisfaction in a peaceful home life with his wife and little daughter in their house near the Bois de Boulogne. But his craving for luxury and his extravagance led him, nevertheless, to appear at concerts either as conductor or as pianist. On these occasions he usually interpreted his own works, very rarely those of other composers. Immediately after the performances of 'Saint-Sébastien', he went to Turin to conduct a symphony concert, on the 25th of June 1911. He gave a fine programme of French music including: Emmanuel Chabrier's 'Gwendoline' Ouverture, Roger Ducasse's 'Sarabande', the Prelude to the third act of 'Ariane et Barbe-Bleue' by Paul Dukas, as well as three of his own works, namely: André Caplet's orchestral transcription of 'Children's Corner', 'L'Après-midi d'un Faune' and 'Ibéria'. (On the 10th of October of the same year Vincent d'Indy conducted the two first Nocturnes for the same Concert Society in Turin.)

Debussy was warmly applauded at the Cercle Musical, on the 25th of March 1911, when he conducted Erik Satie's 'Gymnopédies', followed by the orchestral version of 'Children's Corner', which was not yet known in France, although André Caplet had conducted it in New York, also the 'Chansons de Charles d'Orléans'. He also accompanied a few songs sung by two interpreters of 'Pelléas', Jean Périer and Maggie Teyte (an artist who had succeeded Mary Garden, chiefly because the high-brows considered it essential that Mélisande should have an English accent). Four days later, on the 29th of March, at the Concerts Durand, he played a group of piano Preludes: 'Les Sons et les parfums', 'Le Vent dans la plaine', 'Des Pas sur la neige' and 'Minstrels'. On the 5th and 12th of March 1912, he achieved a triumphant success at a performance of the same concert society, when he accompanied his second Mélisande in the 'Promenoir des deux Amants' and 'Fêtes Galantes'; he also played some Preludes in his usual very delicate manner. His playing, so full of intimate feeling and subtle

effects, was not heard to advantage in the big Salle Gaveau. The surprise of the audience at his performance was described in the *Monde Musical* in a harshly-worded critique. Several of the writers on this review disliked or misunderstood Debussy's versatile and subtle art. This article, by the editor, Auguste Mangeot, accused the pianist-composer of having maintained an almost continuous *pianissimo* during his entire performance.

The present writer expressed a similar criticism of the distinguished composer one day in the spring of 1914 when Debussy had taken part in a concert devoted exclusively to his own compositions. On this occasion the author wrote in his *Revue Française de Musique* of the 15th of April 1914:

'The performance was not lacking either in interest or monotony. M. Debussy gave a charming rendering of his "Preludes" which sound like clever pastiches written *in the manner of* . . . *Debussy*; he also played in a dim, veiled tone, that was at times almost inaudible, some accompaniments of songs which Mme Vallin-Pardo, skilfully muting her powerful voice, rendered in a soft unchanging murmur. This subdued colouring, evidently desired and insisted upon by the musician, is in keeping with the general tradition that composers are apt to be the least successful and least convincing interpreters of their own works. The extremely elegant audience enjoyed a pleasant doze during the music, and woke up to join in the unanimous applause. . . .'

The composer's over-subtle interpretation is no doubt partly responsible for the impressions recorded by Auguste Mangeot. In the above-mentioned article he also upbraids Debussy for writing works which are not 'important enough for the concert hall. They are lacking in expressive accents, and the few one notices here and there have nothing new to offer; for instance, those in "La Cathédrale engloutie" had already been utilized by Rachmaninoff in his "Prelude".' The critic of *Le Monde Musical* regarded 'Children's Corner' as Lilliputian art; its characters did not suggest children's toys to him but rather 'trinkets, the substance of which may be very precious, but which have neither life nor brilliance. . . .' His opinion of the 'Poèmes de Mallarmé' was equally unfavourable. 'Fortunately', remarked the critic, 'the String Quartet was there to remind us that Debussy had been a great musician; that work by itself is sufficient to justify his fame.' This article is an example of the comparisons that were constantly made at that time between Debussy's first manner and his new style: of course, as usual, the past seemed more attractive than the present.

Whenever a new work was published, and especially whenever Debussy himself appeared in public, a section of the critics gave

vent to their dissatisfaction in very unfair articles. For instance, at one of the Concerts Durand, in March 1913, the composer played three of his 'Preludes', pieces to which he probably did not attach any very great importance. There were a number of critiques similar to the following by E. Stoullig which appeared in *Le Monde Artiste*:

'M. Debussy, *in person*, played three of his new Preludes. The first, "Bruyères", has no significance at all; the second, "Feuilles Mortes", has very little more; the third, "Puerta del vino" . . . is an improvement on the two first pieces, without being at all remarkable. But what was remarkable, was the behaviour of a section of the audience. There were enthusiastic cheers and numerous calls, and some girls even threw flowers to the celebrated composer, who picked them up with evident pleasure . . . M. Debussy is undoubtedly a man of great talent and a very clever pianist. But he must realize himself that his trifling little pieces do not deserve the same ovations as the masterpieces of Gluck, Beethoven, or Mozart.'

On the 26th of April of that same year (1913), Debussy, in his capacity as critic to the *Revue S.I.M.*, had an opportunity of witnessing the varied impressions produced by a complete performance of his three 'Images' at the Concerts Colonne. He recorded the event in the following brief and haughty terms: 'It was owing to reasons, into which reason did not enter, that the integral performance of 'Images' aroused such divergent opinions. The execution was as vigorous and animated as one could have wished.' On the 2nd of April, he took part in an inaugural concert given at the new Théâtre des Champs-Élysées, when he conducted 'L'Après-midi d'un Faune'. In this important festival of French music, Saint-Saëns, Vincent d'Indy, Gabriel Fauré, and Paul Dukas also took part as conductors. At the end of the month Debussy was present at a performance given in his honour at the Comédie des Champs-Élysées. The interpreters were: Ricardo Viñes, Ninon Vallin, Gaston Poulet, and the actor Signoret, who read a paper written by Émile Vuillermoz. On the 15th of October 1913 he conducted 'Ibéria' at the Nouveaux Concerts des Champs-Élysées. 'La Damoiselle Élue' and the 'Marche Écossaise' were also played that day under the conductorship of D. E. Inglebrecht; this was the first performance of the old 'Marche Écossaise' which had been composed twenty-two years previously.

On the 21st of March 1914, Debussy took part in another concert of his works which was held at the Salle Gaveau; on that occasion his "Trois Poèmes de Stéphane Mallarmé' were heard for the first time. They were sung by Ninon Vallin who had become his

favourite singer ever since the production of the 'Martyre de Saint-Sébastien'. That day the composer played 'Children's Corner' and, departing from the printed programme, also gave 'Feuilles mortes', 'La Cathédrale engloutie', and 'La Fille aux cheveux de lin'.

A writer connected with *La Critique Musicale*, who had already praised the pianist's 'ease and fluidity, and his insinuating, though rather monotonous tone', expressed his appreciation once more on this occasion. 'I confess', he wrote, 'that I prefer his playing to that of any other pianist. His restraint and discretion make one forget all considerations of technical dexterity. Thus the naked soul of the work is placed before the audience; its action is direct; the interpreter is lost sight of.' Louis Laloy expressed equal enthusiasm in *Comoedia* (his verdict was quoted in Vuillermoz' feuilleton of the 9th of February). 'The power of magic will be realized by all who have ever heard his marvellous playing; the sounds seem to be produced without any impact of hammers or vibration of strings; they rise up into a transparent atmosphere where they unite without merging, and then dissolve in iridescent mists. M. Debussy puts the keyboard under a spell, the secret of which is unknown to any of our virtuosi.'

At a concert held in the Salle des Agriculteurs on the 5th of February 1914, Debussy, in collaboration with his friend, the violinist Arthur Hartmann, played Grieg's violin and piano sonata and three vocal or piano works of his own, transcribed by Hartmann for violin and piano, namely: 'Il pleure dans mon cœur', from the 'Ariettes Oubliées', 'La Fille aux cheveux de lin', and 'Minstrels'. The unusual circumstance of Debussy's appearance at a violin recital was regarded, and rightly so, as a public protest against the action of certain adherents of the Schola who had openly expressed their contempt for Grieg. In order that there should be no misunderstanding as to the significance of this tribute which was intended as a vindication of Grieg, Louis Laloy, acting as Debussy's spokesman, devoted an entire feuilleton in *Comoedia* to the Norwegian composer. In this article, which appeared on the morning of the concert, he attacked the 'pedants' who seemed unable to recognize the fact that the end and object of music was to please, and who insinuated 'that fashion is capricious, that the music which has been the delight of one generation is sure to be quickly forgotten, and that fame is in inverse proportion to celebrity'. He compared these unhappy people to 'benevolent sextons, already engaged in digging the grave into which, so they assure us, posterity will cast "Pelléas et Mélisande"; even as they

themselves would already like to bury the entire works of
Chopin, Liszt, Grieg, and even Mozart'. This calumnious statement aroused no surprise in musical circles where an aggressive,
indeed absurdly controversial spirit was rather the rule.

In an article which was published in the American review, *The
Musical Courier*, immediately after Debussy's death in 1918 and
which has often been reproduced, especially in Canadian papers,
the violinist Arthur Hartmann gave an account of his relations
with the French composer. With reference to the alterations that
occur in his transcriptions, he pointed out that he himself was
responsible for those in the violin part, and Debussy for those in
the piano part. He also mentioned a vague plan for a concert tour
with Debussy in North America—a plan of which Debussy had
approved, but on one condition: 'my friend Hartmann must appear
with me at each concert and play my "Poème" for violin and
orchestra'. This unknown 'Poème' was begun; only a few pages
of it are in existence, preserved by Hartmann in an autograph
book.

In June 1914 Debussy made a short trip to London solely for
the purpose of taking part in a private concert. He wrote to
Jacques Durand: 'Caruso would demand for his accompanist the
fee that I am getting. But, at any rate, it is a drop of water in the
desert of these dreadful summer months.' This letter and a few
others that have been published show that his financial situation
was not so flourishing as people imagined; indeed, his circumstances were at times difficult, if not distressing. Only the most
pressing financial reasons could have induced Debussy to undertake journeys that were intolerable to his love of tranquillity and
ceremonious public appearances that were highly distasteful to one
of his reserved disposition.

In December 1913 Koussevitsky engaged him to conduct a
concert in Moscow and another in Petersburg. The journey
proved a triumphal success. He met several of his Russian colleagues, but had no opportunity of hearing their works; he regretted that he did not know the compositions of any of the younger
men except Igor Stravinsky. According to an article by Lazare
Saminsky, the Russians regarded Debussy as the spiritual son of
Rimsky-Korsakof and Mussorgsky, and as the one master of French
art who had established a link between East and West. The estimate is a very accurate one and well founded, as the study of
Debussy's musical development proves. His face, which resembled
that of a Byzantine ikon, his aloof manner, and his indifference to
the public were all characteristics which helped to surround him

with a halo. Although realizing that he did not possess the requisite talents for a conductor, the musicians accorded an enthusiastic reception to his interpretations of his own works, which had been minutely studied before his arrival during the course of long and careful rehearsals. Debussy addressed a letter to the readers of his critiques in the *Revue Musicale S.I.M.* which was published in the issue of the 1st of January 1914. He praised the high artistic standard of Koussevitsky's orchestra, and mentioned the interesting activities of this organization and the nomadic wanderings in which they indulged during the summer months, when they went up the Volga giving concerts in different places to the most varied audiences.

Early in 1914 Debussy was again obliged to accept engagements to conduct concerts in Rome, The Hague, and Amsterdam, 'in order to earn quite inconsiderable sums', as he wrote to his publisher. Towards the end of February, he had the pleasure of revisiting the Italian capital where he had lived as a young Prix de Rome. 'But, alas, I am no longer twenty', he wrote. His visit aroused considerable interest in artistic circles. The 'advanced' music-lovers were anxious to take advantage of this opportunity to make public amends, and atone for the disgraceful manner in which he had been insulted during the performances of 'Pelléas et Mélisande'. As one of the newspapers, *La Tribuna*, expressed it, they wished to set a seal on this public reconciliation between musical Rome and Claude Debussy. Their anticipations were brilliantly realized.

The concert took place at the Augusteo. The moment the French composer appeared on the platform, he was greeted with enthusiastic applause by the entire audience with the exception of 'a few groups made up of anti-modernists, and old-school nationalists'. After the magnificent performance of 'La Mer' there was prolonged applause. It was less enthusiastic at the end of 'Rondes de Printemps', for the harshness of this composition grated on some of the audience.

'The nationalists regained their courage and attempted a sudden attack. There was a moment of tense anxiety. But, fortunately, Debussy did not allow himself to be intimidated. Secure in the knowledge of his coming victory, he turned round and looked straight at his adversaries in the upper galleries; then, in a spirited manner, he attacked the "Prélude à l'Après-midi d'un Faune". It was indeed a victory—a brilliant one. As the work ended the Augusteo shook with applause. It was a scene of delirium. Those amongst us belonging to the "Art for Art's sake" group who had feared for the good name of our city breathed a sigh of relief.'

This dramatic article from *La Tribuna*, in which one must, of course, allow for the Italian tendency to exaggeration, shows the attitude of the public in other lands towards the musical innovator. In France too, as we have seen, each first performance was the occasion of a regular battle of applause, hisses, and invectives, between Debussy's partisans and adversaries.

During the interval in the Augusteo concert the composer had some conversation with the writer of the above critique who described him as 'a true son of France, courteous, unaffected, and a good conversationalist'. During the informal interview, he expressed his confidence in his art, but confessed that he was not a good conductor, having neither the necessary talents nor experience. He also stated that he had been greatly disappointed in Nijinsky's adaptation of 'L'Après-midi d'un Faune' for the Russian Ballet; that he liked working in Paris, and that he had composed the entire score of 'La Mer' there, because the sight of the sea itself fascinated him to such a degree that it paralysed his creative faculties. One cannot, of course, take in too literal a sense these snatches of desultory conversation carried on during such nerve-racking circumstances as the interval of an important concert.

There was no likelihood of any such exciting incidents occurring during the concerts at which he appeared in Holland. They consisted of two performances given in collaboration with the Concertgebouw orchestra; the first took place at The Hague on the 28th of February 1914; the second at Amsterdam, on the 1st of March. The same programme was given in both towns. The first part, conducted by Gustave Doret, consisted of two works by Saint-Saëns (the 'Marche du Couronnement' and the 'Second Symphony'), and one by Duparc ('Aux Étoiles'); the second part of the programme was reserved for Debussy, who appeared as composer, conductor, and pianist. The French musician, then making his début in the Netherlands, conducted the 'Prélude à l'Après-midi d'un Faune', two Nocturnes ('Nuages' and 'Fêtes'), and the 'Marche Écossaise'; and at the piano he played: 'Danseuses de Delphes', 'La Fille aux cheveux de lin', and 'Puerta del Vino'. The official programme contained a notice in which the organizers of the concert welcomed Debussy to Holland, and praised his originality, adding: 'It is not surprising that this composer should have encountered implacable enemies as well as enthusiastic admirers. But he has never ceased to hold his own against all attacks; he has bravely accomplished his task and won the victory. To-day he is recognized as an authority not only in France but in the entire musical world.'

In November 1912 he once more took up his pen as musical critic and at irregular intervals sent contributions to the *Revue S.I.M.*, the substance of which is to found in *The Theories of Claude Debussy, musicien français*. It was only by dint of much persistence that Émile Vuillermoz, the editor of the review, obtained these articles,[1] and they were not always up to the standard of the old critiques of 1901 and 1903. The composer did not profess to write more than mere *notes*, and he himself declared one day that they were 'much too hastily written'. This haste, and a touch of contempt, indifference, or annoyance, are occasionally evident in the confused expression of his jostling ideas and the looseness of his style. One feels that he is handicapped by his celebrity and by the ceremonious role he is expected to play; only at the last minute does he make up his mind to fill with his fine handwriting the pages he must supply to the printer, now that he has become, in spite of himself, a critic, an authority on aesthetics, the leader of a school. His difficulties were increased by the fact that whilst he strongly disapproved of hasty or premature criticism, he no longer felt any desire to hear new music. He would have liked to live apart from the musical world, to withdraw within himself, and concentrate. He admitted, in the beginning of the winter of 1913–14, that he had made it a rule to hear as little music as possible. He knew none of Schoenberg's works and intended to do no more than read a Quartet by that composer.

Notwithstanding the controversies which the continuous evolution of his new works aroused, Claude Debussy had become a very important and representative personage. Now that the whole world honoured him as a great master—as the programme of his concerts in Holland proclaimed—he was considered worthy of the highest civic dignities. About the middle of July 1914, when Ch. M. Widor was elected permanent secretary to the Institut de France, a chair became vacant in the Académie des Beaux-Arts. Several of the 'Immortals' belonging to the different sections decided to support the candidature of Debussy, including Widor himself—who immediately wrote to Debussy offering him his place—and some former students of the Villa Medici, like Marcel Baschet and Gaston Redon. They were anxious to forget the disrespectful behaviour of the former Prix de Rome, especially as it belonged

---

[1] Louis Laloy had never succeeded in obtaining from Debussy anything more than his promise to collaborate in the *Mercure Musical* which he and Jean Marnold had founded and which he edited in 1905–6. In the issue of the 15th of June 1906 he had thought he was in a position to announce that the following numbers would contain 'the beginning of Monsieur Croche's colloquies, by Claude Debussy'.

to a bygone century. Debussy had a very good chance of being elected. Owing, however, to the underhand, stubborn, though passive, opposition of Saint-Saëns—an intolerant reactionary and the implacable enemy of his distinguished colleague, or, at least, of the artistic independence he represented—the preparations for the election were delayed, although the result was a foregone conclusion.[1] Debussy was not able to send in his letter of candidature until the 17th of March 1918, when he barely had the strength to write a trembling signature with his dying hand. Nothing was lacking to Debussy's glory; but death deprived the Institut de France of the glory of his name.

[1] Saint-Saëns, as we have seen, often gave public expression to his detestation of Debussy's art. In his 'Rimes Familières' which have been published in book form, we find his anti-Debussy sentiments expressed in very indifferent verses. Under the title of 'Mea culpa', the composer begins his diatribe in these words:

> Mea culpa! Je m'accuse
> De n'être pas décadent. . . .

He then alludes to the 'imprudent young people' who compose

> . . . des salades
> De couleurs avec des sons.

His attitude of critical disapproval becomes quite clear in the following verse which obviously refers to Debussy:

> Je deviendrais vite aphone
> Si j'allais en étourdi
> M'égosiller comme un faune
> Fêtant son après-midi.

CHAPTER XIV

THE WAR. LAST YEARS (1914–18)

THE war came. Debussy, now fifty-two years old, was profoundly affected. This artist, aloof, reserved, who seemed so preoccupied with his musical plans, had often given proof of his French outlook, his typically national tastes, his dislike of German exuberance and over-emphasis. Eighteen months before the outbreak of hostilities, he had once more proclaimed his abhorrence of the Munich formulas in the *Revue S.I.M.* 'Let us retrieve our own good taste', he wrote. 'Not that it is quite lost, but we have smothered it under the eiderdowns of the North. It will be our mainstay in our warfare against the Barbarians, who have become much more dangerous since they have taken to parting their hair in the middle.'

He was keenly sensitive to the terrible disasters that were overwhelming his country. The formidable conflict provided him with a special opportunity—a very melancholy one—of protesting, more earnestly and solemnly than ever, against the German tyranny to which his musical fellow countrymen had so long submitted. He rebelled against their 'powerful hold on our thought and on our forms to which, with amiable carelessness, we have submitted. This is a serious, an unpardonable fault on our part and difficult to correct because it is in our system, like vitiated blood.' He asked himself: 'Where is French music to be found? What has become of our old clavecinists, in whom there is so much genuine music? They knew the secret of that penetrating charm, that emotion, free from epilepsy, which, like ungrateful children, we have disowned . . . ' In a short preface to a series of lectures on French music which he wrote in December 1916, he pointed out the remedy for this deep-seated disease from which a number of French musicians were still suffering. 'Let us get back our freedom and our own forms', he wrote. 'Since we ourselves invented most of them, it is only right that we should preserve them; there are none more beautiful. . . . Let us be on our guard against those who accuse us of frivolity. This charge has always come from the mealy massiveness which has ineffectually concealed its desire to stifle us. . . .'

He had already expressed similar ideas in the spring of 1915, in a signed article which appeared, under the title of 'Enfin seuls!', in the Paris daily, *L'Intransigeant*, on the 11th of March, and later in the *Bulletin musical de la S.I.M.* In this article Debussy deplored

the break in French tradition that had occurred after Rameau; he lamented the fact that we had left off cultivating our native garden; he expressed the hope that we should understand the eloquent voice of the guns: "To-day, when all the virtues of our race are valiantly asserting themselves, the coming victory should make our artists realize the pure, noble quality of French blood. We have a whole intellectual province to reconquer. And so, whilst Fate is turning over the pages, Music must meditate in patience, before she breaks the affecting silence which will ensue after the bursting of the last shell.'

At the commencement of hostilities, Debussy remained for weeks without touching a piano. Composition seemed such a senseless occupation to him during that time of anguish that he completely abandoned it—all the more readily because, ever since the unhoped-for triumph of 'Pelléas et Mélisande', he had suffered from a kind of inhibition, natural enough in a highly sensitive artist who was constantly exposed to extremes of praise and censure. He did not wish his works to be performed even in other countries. He wrote as follows to his publisher with reference to 'No-yati,' a ballet of his that was in course of preparation and which there was a question of staging at the London Alhambra: 'I should not like that work to be played before the fate of France has been decided, for she can neither laugh nor weep while so many of our men are heroically facing death.'

In this letter, dated the 9th of October 1914, Debussy confesses: 'If I had the courage, or rather, if I did not dread the inevitable blatancy natural to that type of composition, I should like to write a "Marche Héroïque" . . . But, I must say, I consider it ridiculous to indulge in heroism, in all tranquillity, well out of reach of the bullets. . . .' He had an opportunity of gratifying his wish. In November 1914 he wrote a work of this type for the King of Belgium's Book, but it was discreet in colouring and delicately shaded. This 'Berceuse Héroïque' was written 'as a tribute of homage to His Majesty King Albert I of Belgium and his soldiers'. In the course of this simple piano piece, which he scored for orchestra in the month of December, the 'Brabançonne' is introduced. Mournfully, in muffled timbres, the Belgian National Anthem is given out first by the bassoons, horns, and clarinets, then by the violas and 'cellos. The music of the surrounding bars seems to depict the dismal trenches of Flanders full of harassed, home-sick soldiers, who are soothed by the strains of the patriotic melody. During the 1915–16 season the symphonic version of the work was played by the Concerts Colonne et Lamoureux which

had then united. Generally speaking, the heroic element in the work was not considered sufficiently conspicuous; its significance was not understood. With this exception, Debussy abstained from all creative work for a whole year.

In order to compensate his publisher for the advance fees which were mounting up alarmingly every month, Debussy consented to revise Chopin's works in preparation for a new edition which the firm of Durand were just bringing out. This meant a considerable amount of work both of a purely musical and historical nature, work for which, in spite of his admiration for the Polish Master, Debussy was not altogether fitted. Then more than ever, he regretted the death of his former piano teacher, Mme Mauté de Fleurville, 'to whom I owe the little I know about piano playing. . . . She knew a great deal about Chopin.' He wrote thus to Jacques Durand on the 27th of January 1915. In another letter to him dated the 1st of September, Debussy says: 'I have a very clear recollection of what Mme Mauté de Fleurville told me. Chopin advised his pupils to study without the pedal, and not to hold it except in very rare cases.' Left to himself, with only his own musical instincts and very remote memories to guide him, Debussy often found himself faced with unsoluble problems. His correspondence with his publisher betrays his recurring anxiety. 'The Chopin manuscripts simply terrify me,' he wrote on the 24th of February 1915. ' . . . How can *three* manuscripts, which are obviously not all in Chopin's hand, be all three correct? You may be quite sure that only one is . . . and that is where the trouble begins. . . .' He was alarmed to think that in the preface of the coming publication he would have to discuss the different editions and the various fanciful interpretations. Fortunately for himself, he managed to condense the introduction into a few lines. He limited himself to paying homage, in enthusiastic and appropriate terms, to a composer whom he had always admired and who, as he pointed out, still exercised a considerable influence on contemporary music.

After devoting himself to Chopin, he had next to undertake the revision of J. S. Bach's sonatas for violin and clavecin. Sheer necessity forced him to accept this task which gave him no pleasure, his distaste for which he humorously expressed in a letter to Jacques Durand on the 15th of April 1917. He had spent 'a rainy Sunday' correcting the proofs of these sonatas and the result was a 'rainy' mood within himself.

' . . . When the old Saxon Cantor is short of ideas, he starts off with anything at all, and he is really merciless. In fact he is bearable only

when he is absolutely admirable. Well, you will say, that in itself is something. All the same, if some friend—or publisher—had gently advised him to stop writing on, say, one day of the week, we should have been spared some hundreds of pages through which we have to wander between long rows of dreary bars which succeed one another relentlessly, repeating the same rascally little *subject* and *counter-subject*. Sometimes—in fact, often—his marvellous style of writing (which, after all, is nothing more than a gymnastic feat peculiar to this old Master) does not succeed in filling the awful void, which increases in proportion as he insists, at all costs, in turning some insignificant idea to account.'

Debussy appeared in public in March 1915, when he accompanied the singer, Mme Ninon Vallin, at a concert in the Salle Gaveau. About this time he finished revising his 'Six Épigraphes Antiques', and sent them to the printers. We have already mentioned (pp. 110–11) the hitherto unknown origin of this work. It was in order to satisfy the legitimate demands of his publisher that Debussy decided to make this piano-duet arrangement of one of his early compositions. It is said that he had previously considered the possibility of transforming it into an orchestral suite. In some of the pieces, it is true, we find the principal theme slightly developed, or adorned with changing harmonies and accessory rhythms; and one can distinguish the tinkling of Chinese bells, the instrumental colouring of flutes, and the plucking of harp-strings, effects that he had utilized fifteen years previously in incidental music. There is also a suggestion of symphonic and even cyclical treatment in the manner in which the first Epigraph is repeated so as to form an ending for the last. Again, if we compare this work with the unpublished incidental music written to the 'Chansons de Bilitis', we can discover the germs of terse, concise developments which Debussy could have worked out for either full or small orchestra. He could thus have achieved a highly modern interpretation of these significant inscriptions whose bold melodies, originally inspired by Pierre Louÿs' word paintings, are based on the supple modes of the Orient and ancient Greece.

On being asked to undertake the revision of some classical music towards the end of June 1915, Debussy expressed a wish to postpone this task. 'I have a few ideas at the moment,' he wrote, 'and, although they are not worth making a fuss about, I should like to cultivate them for the benefit of the duet for two pianos, and of the "Fêtes Galantes".' He had already used this title for two series of songs written in 1892 and 1904, yet, as we have already mentioned, he was planning to write an operatic work under the same title after Verlaine's poems—a work which he eventually

either could not, or would not compose. The pieces for two pianos just referred to are those which were published in 1915 under the rather vague title, 'En blanc et noir'.

When his letters come to be published we shall no doubt find in them numerous allusions to the joy Debussy experienced on resuming his creative work. This is evident in the extracts from his letters to Robert Godet which have already appeared. Debussy's point of view had changed. He had decided to break his long silence, caused in the first instance by the disturbing effects of the war, but which had subsequently become deliberate and intentional. 'I have come to the conclusion,' he wrote, 'that, all things considered, it would be cowardice on my part to join the ranks of the disabled, and spend my time dwelling on the atrocities that have been committed, without reacting against them by creating, to the best of my ability, a little of that beauty which the enemy is attacking with such fury.' He was soon able to write to his friend: 'At long last, I have got back the power and, as it were, the right, to think in terms of music—a thing that has not happened to me for the last year. It is, of course, not indispensable that I should write music, but it is the only thing I can do more or less well; I humbly regret my state of latent death. Now, I have been writing like a madman, or one who has to die next morning.'

He was not to die so soon, but it is possible that he occasionally suffered from the effects of the almost incurable disease which was to carry him off two and a half years later. Meanwhile, he was conscious of the revival of his powers, and the first work he composed at that time was very quickly written. It was the above-mentioned set of pieces for two pianos, the original title of which, 'Caprices en blanc et noir', was simplified at the time of publication.

These three pieces are very different in style, though written in the same manner; they are quite independent of one another, each has its own inscription, its own individual significance. The first piece illustrates four short lines of poetry by Gounod's librettists. It is taken from 'Roméo et Juliette': 'Qui reste à sa place—Et ne danse pas—De quelque disgrâce—Fait l'aveu tout bas.' This verse is obviously an ironical allusion to the men who during the war stood aside from the macabre dance of the battlefields, thus silently confessing to some physical defect. The third piece does not seem to suggest any reminiscence of the war. It is a simple commentary on a line from an old poem by Charles d'Orléans which Debussy had already set to music: 'Yver, vous n'estes qu'un vilain!' The middle piece of the series is war music.

.

Everything points to this: its inscription, its dedication, its musical contents. At the beginning we find inscribed the *envoi* from François Villon's 'Ballade contre les ennemis de la France'; it is dedicated to the memory of Lieutenant Jacques Charlot, killed on the 3rd of March 1915, and the entire little work constitutes a rather obscure war picture. Here and there we hear suggestions of military bugle calls, and the distant rumbling of guns; a calm, contemplative mood, rendered by broad harmonies, gives way to a tumultuous uproar, now dull, now shrill in tone; and, at intervals, in ponderous discords, Luther's Choral resounds—a symbol of warlike Germany and of the old German god.

Debussy was rather pleased with this second piece which he thought the most successful and original of the three. He had spent a great deal of time at it, and had revised it with minute care. He alluded to it on several occasions when writing to his publisher: 'I must tell you that I have slightly altered the colouring of No. 2 of the "Caprices" (the "Ballade de Villon contre les ennemis de la France"); it was inclined to be too sombre and almost as tragic as a "Caprice" of Goya's' (14th of July 1915). He sent it to the printers on the 22nd of July: 'You will see', he wrote, 'how Luther's hymn catches it for having imprudently strayed into a French "Caprice". Towards the end a modest little carillon rings out a pre-*Marseillaise*. I apologize for this anachronism, but I think it permissible at a time when the very pavements and the trees of the forests are vibrating to this ubiquitous song.' There were, however, a few bars that worried him, and with reference to them he wrote to his publisher two days later: 'I warn you at once that there are a few bars to be inserted between the episode in E flat and the six bars in E natural. . . . That is to say, they existed in my sketch, but when copying it out I omitted them, fearing that they would make it too long. After several nights, one of which brought counsel, I have decided to put them in again . . .' Finally, on the 5th of August, he sent in an altered version of a few bars, with the remark: 'This alteration was absolutely necessary for the sake of the balance of the work; besides, it makes things clearer, and cleanses the atmosphere of the poisonous fumes which were spread for a moment by Luther's Choral, or rather by what it represents—for, after all, it is a fine thing.'

In June and July 1915 the composer acknowledged how much he had previously suffered from what he described as his cerebral drought brought on by the war. He once more felt the desire to compose. On the 1st of September 1915, writing from

Pourville, near Dieppe, where he spent three months, he mentions that he has got back 'the capacity of thinking and working. It gives me the cold shudders to think of the empty void of last year, and I dread the thought of returning to Paris and to that "usine du néant" that my study had become.' He left off revising the Chopin edition, for, as he wrote, 'the Muse, whom you kindly believe to be inspiring me at the moment, has taught me to put little faith in her constancy, and I would rather hold her fast than run after her'.

It was then that he wrote his piano 'Études'. When sending them to his friend, André Caplet, on the 22nd of July, 1916, he described them sarcastically as containing 'a thousand different ways of treating pianists according to their deserts. . . . They are not always particularly entertaining, but they are at times very ingenious.' This judgement is too severe. The 'Études', which consist of two series of six pieces each, are all very 'entertaining', that is to say, they are most musical and attractive. This extremely artistic work exemplifies in its fascinating pages all the composer's characteristic processes—harmonic, rhythmic, and pianistic—besides being invaluable from the point of view of piano technique, an art which, thanks to Debussy's own influence, had been considerably altered, if not transformed, during recent years. Each study is devoted to some particular difficulty which it is intended to overcome. Debussy, in his casual role of teacher, expressed in his brief, ironical preface his contempt for the strict fingering on which so many pedagogues insist.

'The fingering', he says, 'is intentionally omitted in these "Études". . . . It is obvious that the same fingering cannot suit differently shaped hands. The modern method of writing several fingerings over one another is supposed to solve the difficulty, but it results only in confusion. . . . It makes the music look like a queer sum in arithmetic in which the fingers, by some inexplicable phenomenon, have to be multiplied by one another. . . . Our old masters—I mean *our own* admirable clavecinists—never marked the fingering; no doubt because they had confidence in the ingenuity of their contemporaries. It would be unseemly to mistrust the skill of our modern virtuosi. To sum up: the absence of fingering provides excellent practice, it abolishes the spirit of contradiction which prompts us to avoid the composer's fingering, and proves the truth of the old saying "If you want a thing well done, do it yourself". Let us then choose our own fingering.'

His letters to Jacques Durand enable us to follow the progress of the composition of the 'Études' and to form an idea of Debussy's industry. By the 12th of August, 1915, he had finished the

twelfth 'Étude', a study in ornaments, '*pour les agréments*, but not *for the entertainment*[1] of pianists, the facetious virtuosi will say. It takes the form of a "Barcarolle" on a rather Italian sea.' In the same letter, he mentions the 'Étude' for chromatic passages 'which is, I fancy, a new way of treating this rather worn-out device'; whilst another 'trains the left hand to perform a gymnastic exercise which might almost be called Swedish; and another. . . . But if I tell you about them all, there will be no surprise in store for you. At any rate, these "Études" conceal their severe technical aspect beneath flowers of harmony—you don't catch flies with vinegar On the 19th of August he had finished revising six of the 'Études', the music of which, he said, had not 'come to him whilst listening to the sound of the sea on the shingle'. He was already thinking about the practical side of the publication: 'I should like the cover of the said "Études" to retain something of its present aspect notwithstanding the simplicity of my modest decorations—which I should like printed in red. They will be dedicated to either F. Chopin or F. Couperin. I have an equal respect for these two composers, both so admirably intuitive.'

On the 28th of August he sent further particulars, still from Pourville. He first mentions the Study in sixths: 'for a long time,' he says, 'continuous passages in sixths made me think of affected young ladies sitting sulkily in a drawing-room listening enviously to the wanton laughter of the giddy ninths. . . . I am now writing a study in which the sixth plays such an important part that the harmonies consist entirely of combinations of these intervals— and it isn't ugly. (Mea culpa. . . .)' With reference to the six 'Études' he had first written he says: 'These six Studies are nearly all in quick tempo; don't be uneasy, there will be some quieter ones too. The reason I began with these is that they are more difficult to write and to vary . . . owing to pre-determined requirements the most skilful combinations are quickly exhausted.' With regard to the other studies, he says that they are devoted 'to special experiments in sonorities; amongst others, there is one in *fourths* where you will find effects you have never heard before, despite the fact that your ears are inured to all sorts of strange sounds'. The original manuscript of nine of the 'Études' (Legouix collection), contains a number of interesting corrections.

Both the composer and his publisher realized the extreme difficulty of some of these studies, which, Debussy wrote, 'terrify your fingers. . . . You may be sure that mine sometimes halt at certain

[1] A play on the word *agrément*, which means entertainment, as well as ornaments or grace-notes in music.

passages. I have to stop and recover my breath as after a stiff climb. . . . Truly, this music soars to the summit of execution. Some fine records will be established.' This letter was written on the 1st of September. By the 27th of September the 'Études' were finished. 'I must confess that I am glad to have successfully completed a work which, I may say without vanity, will occupy a special place of its own. Apart from the question of technique, these "Études" will be a useful warning to pianists not to take up the musical profession unless they have remarkable hands.' By the 30th, the last note had been copied out, and the composer was greatly relieved and pleased with himself: 'For', he wrote, 'the most minute Japanese engravings are child's play beside the transcription of some of the pages; but I am satisfied, it is good work.' Already on the 28th of August he declared that he had great hopes of the future prospects of these 'Études'. Anticipating, however, that musicians, or rather professors of music, would take up a critical attitude, he added: 'I am sure you will agree with me that there is no need to render technique more depressing for the sake of making a serious impression; a touch of charm has never spoiled anything. Chopin proved that, and he makes my attempt seem very presumptuous, as I am well aware. I am not sufficiently dead to be safe from the comparisons that will inevitably be made to my disadvantage by my contemporaries—colleagues and others. . . .' After hesitating for some time between the great Polish composer and François Couperin, he decided to dedicate the work to the memory of Chopin.

The summer of 1915 was to witness the beginning of an important undertaking. Debussy's first Quartet was written in 1893; about the same time he had begun a second, which remained unfinished and which has disappeared, and had also planned to write a piano and violin sonata. He now decided to return to pure music and traditional forms. This kind of neo-classicism was partly induced by his national tendencies, and partly, perhaps, by the instinctive need which had prompted him shortly before the war to return to the processes he had formerly condemned. He now proposed to write six sonatas for various instruments. He succeeded in writing three; the first for 'cello and piano, the second for flute, viola, and harp, and the third for violin and piano. On the manuscript of the last-mentioned work, he wrote the following note which seems to have passed unnoticed: 'The fourth will be for oboe, horn, and clavecin.' (See Illustration facing p. 261.) This interesting blending of sonorities would have greatly restricted the performance of the work, but it would have been the first instance

in modern music of the use of that old double-key board instrument which composers and interpreters are endeavouring to revive to-day.[1]

Prompted by national feeling and the desire to link himself up with the old French composers whose descendant and heir he claimed to be and was, Debussy decided to seek inspiration in the old French forms which had fallen into disuse rather than in the models which everybody had adopted after the example of the great German composers. He resolved to imitate the sobriety of his compatriots of yore, their discretion which had always appeared to him so commendable. He determined not to overload compositions so classically designated with the romantic redundance that encumbers sonatas written in the Beethoven manner. In addition, he decided to emphasize his deliberately chosen filiation by signing these sonatas with his Christian name and surname, followed by two words which he used as if they were a title of nobility: 'Claude Debussy, musicien français.'

This title, which he wished to have engraved with a quaint ornamentation in imitation of the old French style, was his by right. It is true that from his earliest youth he had shown a keen interest in the original art of all countries—an interest which he always retained. Nevertheless, he never ceased to struggle against those deeply-rooted foreign influences which seemed to him to hinder and crush the art and genius of his race. In his songs, and in the vocal part of his opera, he sought to obtain an intimate fusion of the words and the music, to adapt the melody of his recitative to the supple undulations of French diction, so distinctive, so utterly different from the bounding declamation that characterizes German opera. Even in his instrumental music he seems to have tried to imitate the gently-flowing curves, the sinuous movements of his national tongue. He endeavoured to link himself up with all the musical traditions of his country. The works he composed were at all times distinguished by clarity and simplicity, by conciseness, reserve, restraint, discretion— qualities that are generally recognized as characteristic of French art; and on many occasions his example, his writings, his critiques bore testimony to his steadfast, at times rabid, fidelity to France. To one foreign musicographer, however, Debussy's wish and claim to be essentially French in his art seemed an impertinence.

[1] Manuel de Falla has utilized the clavecin in his orchestra in the 'Retablo de Maese Pedro' and has recently published a concerto for clavecin. With a different object in view, Francis Poulenc has written a 'Concert Champêtre' for the same instrument. Paule de Lestang, a French singer and clavecinist, has successfully adapted some modern pieces to the old instrument and, thanks to the different sonorities of the two manuals, these works take on a new colouring.

According to this writer, Debussy was the least French of all musicians. We quote this highly debatable opinion, for what it is worth.[1]
All the compositions Debussy wrote during those tragic years
were intended as a secret, fervent, tribute to the youth of France
mown down by the scythe of war. When, after a year's silence,
he determined to set to work again, toiling with the ardour of a
young man, it was not, as he wrote on the 5th of August 1915, 'so
much for my own sake as to prove, in a small way, that not
thirty million Boches could destroy French thought even though
they had attempted to degrade it before annihilating it'. This
instinctive patriotism, or rather this genuine, conscious, and
reasoned nationalism, is expressed with ardent eloquence in every
page of his literary writings and private letters.

The first sonata for 'cello and piano was composed without
effort; the joy that fills the work is evident to all who read or hear it.
It was written during the end of July and the first days of August.
Debussy himself confessed that he liked 'its proportions and its
form, which is almost classical in the true sense of the word'. His
continuous desire to improve and transform his art had in this case
brought him a most felicitous inspiration, although the general tone
of his musical idiom was calculated to annoy conventional musicians—the conservatives, who hold that the sonata should preserve
a general atmosphere of solemnity. But even more disconcerting
than the style and writing of this sonata was its ironical, sarcastic,
almost facetious character. We are told that the musician had
thought of calling it 'Pierrot fâché avec la lune', and that he wished
to evoke characters from the old Italian comedy.

Debussy gave the first performance of the sonata himself
with the assistance of the 'cellist Joseph Salmon. In this composition he does indeed seem to have rediscovered French forms of
long ago and to have joined up instinctively as well as deliberately
the broken thread of national tradition. The work is not at all
on the Beethoven plan. It bears a resemblance to the French

[1] The English critic, Cecil Gray, expresses this opinion in an essay on
Debussy in his book, *A Survey of Contemporary Music* (1924). He writes:
'Debussy is the least French of musicians. . . . His best work is that which is
most exotic and least French; his greatest quality, his only quality, lies in the
wholly personal and entirely original nature of his art, owing very little, and
giving nothing, to any one . . . genealogies have been elaborately constructed
in order to show that he is descended from Rameau and Couperin. They are
obvious forgeries. In so far as he is French at all his descent is very different,
and not nearly so distinguished. 'L'Enfant prodigue' and 'La Damoiselle Élue'
are the guilty fruit of liaisons with the Manon Lescaut and Marie-Magda-
lène of Jules Massenet. The influence of Massenet is the only French
element in the music of Debussy. . . . It is apparent even in "Le Martyre de Saint-
Sébastien".'

sonatas of the seventeenth and eighteenth centuries. It is the continuation, after a long interval, of the manner or rather the simple form employed by J.-M. Leclair and his predecessors. The twentieth-century 'musicien français' managed, in addition, to impart to his work a graceful charm, an irresistible verve. This is noticeable in the 'Prologue', whose lively theme, resembling some beautiful melody by Couperin, recurs in the other movements in the cyclical style of the early String Quartet but here very subtly and delicately treated as in Debussy's big recent works; it is noticeable also in the metrical development *sur la touche* amid successions of rich parallel chords; in the at times pathetic banter of the 'Sérénade', with its almost continuous *pizzicati* during which the violoncello seems to strike the tambourine, to pluck the guitar, to play the flute; and in the 'Finale', whose rhythmic gaiety gives way, for a few moments, to a flowing movement of the most affecting *morbidezza.* . . .

This 'cello and piano sonata is also remarkable for its widely spaced instrumental writing and its experiments in novel sonorities in the extreme registers. Nevertheless, this highly fanciful composition recalls more than one of Debussy's early works, especially the 'Prologue', some bars of which remind us of 'Pelléas', of 'La Cathédrale Engloutie', and of the Caprices 'En Blanc et Noir'; whilst in the 'Finale' one can distinguish the style, if not the formulas, of 'Fantoches', written thirty-five years previously. Above all, this sonata shows the versatility of this creative artist whose evolution was continuous. The progress of the ageing composer is noticeable at once in the rhythm, with its sudden bounding movements, in the harmony, whose tonalities are more mobile, more oscillating and undulating than ever, and also in the melody. Debussy, always concerned about the melodic element, here finds inspiration in French folk-songs which he utilizes with the most delicate discretion; he imitates the free movement of Gregorian *vocalises* and of the supple melodies of certain Trouvère songs. The entire melodic material escapes naturally from the stiff major and minor keys, and finds its true setting in modes inspired more or less by ancient and medieval music.

Nor did the second sonata cost Debussy much trouble. It was written at the end of September and the beginning of October 1915, and was performed at the Société Musicale Indépendante on the 21st of April 1917. The flute was played by Manouvrier, the viola by Jarecki, and the harp by Jamet. The composer had originally planned and sketched out the sonata for flute, oboe, and harp. A happy inspiration prompted him to exchange the oboe

for the viola and the veiled timbre of this deep-toned violin blends harmoniously with that of the flute. The colouring resulting from the combination of these three instruments was so novel and attractive that it was subsequently imitated by several other composers. It helps to give the trio a character of mournful tenderness; it emphasizes the vague atmosphere of despair that characterizes the work, in contrast to the humorous nature of the preceding sonata. 'It is terribly sad,' wrote Debussy himself, 'and I do not know whether one ought to laugh or cry at it. Perhaps both.'

This Trio, with its rich flood of melody and its vigorous rhythms marked by novel metrical effects, displays a very daring but exceedingly pleasing harmony which is occasionally, even in the exposition (ninth bar, the harp part), definitely though agreeably polytonal. The results of his successful quest for melodic novelty are equally interesting. As in the first sonata, and in a more marked degree, we find supple instrumental *vocalises* inspired by Gregorian chant, by pastoral songs, or by the broader melodies outlined long ago by the Trouvères and Troubadours: numerous arabesques, rapid in movement and complex in rhythm, which embellish the capricious line of the melody. The 'Interlude' (tempo di minuetto), which connects the 'Pastorale' with the 'Finale', is based on a flexible, sinuous theme whose rhythm and mode are alike supple and smooth. The various movements show a remarkable unity of feeling and colouring, emphasized by discreet reminiscences of themes, especially the last movement, whose ending recalls the first. This genuine and essential unity derives from the themes themselves which, in spite of their diversity, are closely related.

The novelty, the striking originality, of the first and second sonatas, the broad spaciousness of their themes—so modern in spite of their slight imitation of the antique—their free symphonic treatment, and the obvious relationship of their plastic forms to the old traditional French patterns, make them a kind of artistic last will and testament, the full scope and import of which have perhaps not yet been gauged or understood. They may be regarded as the supreme musical expression of the doctrines Debussy preached as a critic and illustrated as a composer for over thirty years.

This happy period of facile composition did not last long. Debussy fell ill and had to undergo an operation soon after his return to Paris. In December 1915, on the eve of this ordeal, which might easily have been fatal and which checked only for a few weeks the development of an almost incurable disease, Debussy

wrote the words and music of a little piece which, in spite of its brevity and the fact that it was written for a special occasion, may be counted among his masterpieces. This was 'Le Noël des enfants qui n'ont plus de maison'. Nothing could have been simpler or more moving. The short poem is a naïve prayer addressed to 'Le Petit Noël' (Santa Claus) by the children belonging to the regions that had been devastated by the Germans during the war. Against the panting rhythm of the piano accompaniment a tender, pathetic melody unfolds—an exact transcription of the words which, like their enveloping harmonies, are reminiscent of 'Pelléas et Mélisande'. The composer wrote two versions of this work: a well-known arrangement for solo voice with piano accompaniment, and another, which is almost unknown, for children's two-part chorus. In the invaded Belgian territory, during the last three years of the war, all who heard this little work recognized, in addition to its artistic merit, the deep patriotic emotion which had inspired both the poem and the music.

From a letter he wrote to the violinist Arthur Hartmann, one realizes the misery of Debussy's life during the months that preceded his first operation:

'. . . Of course', he writes, 'this illness had to come at the end of a spell of good work. I tell you, old man, it made me weep. And in addition to all this misery, there were four months of those morphine injections that turn you into a walking corpse and completely annihilate your will. When you want to go to the right, you go to the left, and do all sorts of stupid things of that kind. If I were to give a detailed account of my misfortunes, you would be reduced to tears, and Madame Hartmann would think you had lost your wits. I was ready to work like a whole plantation of negroes and was preparing to write that violin and piano sonata you are kindly looking forward to. . . . But now, I do not know when the impulse to write will return. There are times when I feel as if I had never known anything about music. . . .'

From December 1915 on, Debussy was a sick man in the hands of doctors and surgeons. In spite of operations and radium treatments he was in constant pain and growing ever weaker. Nearly the whole of 1916 passed without his writing a single note of music. Life had become almost unbearably hard. 'Since Claude Debussy is no longer writing music, he has no excuse for being alive,' he wrote on the 8th of June. 'I have no hobbies, I was never taught anything but music. . . . Things are endurable only on condition that I can compose a great deal; but to keep tapping a brain that sounds hollow is an unpleasant business.' On the 3rd of July he informed his publisher that he intended to work in spite of every-

thing: 'I cannot say that I feel any better, but I have made up my mind to ignore my health, to get back to work, and to be no longer the slave of this over-tyrannical disease. We shall soon see. If I am doomed to disappear soon, I wish to have at least tried to do my duty.'

What did he accomplish during the course of his slow agony? He made laborious efforts, but only one of which resulted in a complete work. He went to Moulleau-Arcachon in October. He was very ill at the hotel there and realized immediately that he would not bring back any masterpieces from his country holiday; '. . . but perhaps a few valuable ideas for future use'. He was seized by his usual artistic misgivings. They were increased by an untimely visit paid him on October the 15th by an importunate but well-meaning person, who insisted on voicing his vapid criticisms. The worried artist wrote to his publisher:

'For a moment, he made me regret having ever written a sonata, and I began to lose confidence in my writing. . . . This incident has greatly upset me; it is fraught with all sorts of consequences, and I am no longer surprised at the lack of understanding my poor music so often meets with. Without being unnecessarily melodramatic, I assure you it terrifies me. Why was I not taught to polish spectacle-glasses like Spinoza? I should never have had to depend on music for my daily bread. . . .'

The sick man was overwhelmed by grief and material worries. His ordinary income and the sums his music yielded did not suffice to defray the expenses of his costly manner of living. Meanwhile, he was thinking out the violin and piano sonata. It was to have nothing in common with the work which he had planned for the same instruments twenty years previously and mentioned to the publisher Durand in 1894. The new work was to be the third of the French series he had so brilliantly begun. 'During a recent visit to Cap Féret,' he wrote on the 17th of October 1916, a week before his return to Paris, 'I found the germ idea of the last movement of the violin and piano sonata. . . . Unfortunately, the first and second movements are holding back. . . . Knowing myself as I do, you may be sure that I shall not force them to endure my unpleasant company.' By February 1917 the first and second movements were finished. The third was emerging with difficulty. As Debussy wrote to Robert Godet, he was attempting to render 'the play of a theme turning back on itself, like a serpent biting its own tail'. He copied out the first version of 'that terrible final movement', the 'Neapolitan' one. He abandoned it, however, because it 'savoured too much of the surrounding

atmosphere of anxiety'. He began another version, then returned to the first and altered it. 'It is one of those countless little intimate tragedies that overwhelm you without making any more noise than a rose shedding its petals, leaving the rest of the world at peace. In a few days, therefore, you will see Naples again and . . . you will not die.' A month later he was still engaged on the revision of this work, but thought he could promise to let his publisher hear the first informal performance of it on the 26th of March. He was, however, delayed by a concert which he organized in aid of an army charity, as well as by his usual artistic scruples. Two redundant bars in the last movement spoiled the whole structure, and he was not able to repair the damage until a few days later. The manuscript, which is preserved in the Conservatoire library, contains the first line of the rejected finale. We reproduce (facing p. 261) this little passage, a mere phrase, which has hitherto never been noticed.

The third sonata, for violin and piano—originally described as for 'piano and violin'—is an unequal work. Like the preceding sonatas, it shows obvious attempts at melodic originality, a tentency to utilize folk-songs, free cantilenas, and even oriental melodies, especially in the first movement. In spite of its animation, the whole work betrays fatigue and effort. There is an impotent vehemence about it. It suggests a fight for life, a struggle against death, particularly noticeable in the repetition of yearning melodies with their laboured and unnecessary anacruses. The composition ends like a ballet, in a bounding, whirling vortex, somewhat reminiscent of the 'Cortège' in the very early 'Petite Suite' for piano. In spite of all the energy expended by the failing composer, the work lacks inspiration. The unity is more deliberate and artificial than in the two preceding works; the academic processes of augmentation and diminution are fairly obvious; one notices repetitions, replicas, pastiches of earlier compositions; the principal melodies are padded out with arabesques and ornaments of various kinds; these main ideas themselves are mediocre and lacking in originality. Alone the intermediary section, marked 'fantasque et léger', in which several tonalities are at times superimposed, is developed with the utmost freedom. If the work falls short of real excellence, the period and the circumstances in which it was written offer sufficient explanation for its defects.

Debussy had the courage to play the piano part of his last sonata himself, with the violinist Gaston Poulet, at the Salle Gaveau on the 5th of May 1917. This first performance of the work was his farewell to the Paris public. He had promised to

interpret some of his own piano works at the first concert announced by the Société Nationale de Musique after its reorganization in the spring of 1917. The performance was subsequently postponed till the 1917–18 season, when Debussy was too ill to keep his promise. At the end of June 1917 he was seen for the last time in the audience at a Franco-Italian concert during which Molinari conducted an admirable performance of 'La Mer'. Then Debussy disappeared. In his own mournful words, which recall a phrase in 'Pelléas et Mélisande', death's old retainer, sickness, had singled him out for his prey and condemned him to complete retirement.

In the beginning of the winter of 1916–17 he planned to write a big patriotic work for solo voices, chorus, and orchestra, for which he had asked Louis Laloy to write words. This 'Ode à la France' was to have a deep national significance. The two collaborators wished 'to take Jeanne d'Arc as the personification of suffering France, a victim sacrificed to appease an unjust fate, and save future generations'. It was the sublime theory of redemption through suffering—Jeanne d'Arc who offers herself to the flames to deliver her people. Early in January 1917, Debussy received the poem which was to form the beginning of the ode, 'La Ballade de la Pitié du Royaume de France'; and a few days later he was sent the verses which describe Jeanne raising up the wounded body of France and summoning the warriors to the rescue. Debussy immediately began to compose the music, though he asked for several alterations in the literary text. His collaborator furnished him with two alternative versions of the remainder of the poem. In one part he suggested a soldiers' chorus to a march tune the rhythm of which he indicated by a sample verse.

Nothing was known about this 'Ode à la France'. It was only after the composer's death that the rough copy of the score was found; it was incomplete and, in parts, the words were missing. Several musicians amongst Debussy's friends considered that it would be inadvisable to undertake any arrangement or completion of this last effort. Nevertheless, in spite of their verdict, the composer's heirs decided to subject the manuscript once more to a minute examination. Louis Laloy reconstructed the missing text from his own notes, and a young virtuoso, who was an excellent interpreter of Debussy's piano works, had the audacity to develop the musical sketch and to add an orchestration of his own. On the 2nd of April 1928, a performance of this unpublished work arranged for full orchestra and chorus was given at the new Salle Pleyel, Paris. This presentation of the work was both unworthy and

inexpedient. It does not seem fitting to express any opinion on this work, which Debussy left in the form of a mere sketch—especially as, in the printed version, we do not know for which portions the composer and the transcriber are respectively responsible. Whilst awaiting the possible publication of a facsimile of the original manuscript, we must deplore the fact that a French publisher, duly authorized by the composer's heirs, should have published an arrangement of an incomplete sketch without indicating, even in a short note, the state in which the manuscript was found and the exact nature of the score, part of which was incomplete. We notice in the very beginning of the printed version, a suggestion of the second piece in 'En Blanc et Noir', and a reminiscence of the 'Ballades de Villon'; indeed the work vibrates with all the emotional feeling that animated the great French musician.[1]

At the end of March 1917, André Suarès saw Debussy taking part in a charity concert which he had organized and which had cost him considerable trouble and worry. Suarès has left us the following sad portrait of the composer, a contrast to that of 1902, which we have quoted earlier (p. 152).

'I was very much struck', he wrote, 'not so much by his wasted, emaciated appearance, as by his absent-minded, weary expression. His face was like wax and the colour of ashes. The flame of fever did not glitter in his eyes, their light suggested the dull reflections from a pool. There was no bitterness in his gloomy smile, but rather the utter weariness of suffering, with now and again spasms of anguish, like quivering reeds on the quiet shores of a marsh, breaking the deceptive calm of an autumn evening. His hand, which was rounded, soft, plump, episcopal, weighed down his arm, his arm dragged down his shoulder, his head pressed on his whole body; and on that head weighed life itself, unique, exquisite, and cruel. A few people affected to speak of him with confidence, and found him in better health than they had expected. Meanwhile, having seated himself, he looked at the audience with dull eyes from under flickering lids; like one who seeks to see without being seen, who steals a furtive glance at something his eyes hardly seem to light on. He was overwhelmed with confusion, as alone an artist can be who loathes and is almost ashamed of suffering. It was even said that he allowed his disease to develop through concealing it. The voluptuous are often more anxious than others to hide their bodies, especially if they are blemished. The mind partakes of this shy reserve, this voluptuousness, this desire for perfection, that are inseparable from art. . . .'

[1] On the eve of the public performance of 'L'Ode à la France' Louis Laloy published a preliminary notice in several papers. He related the complete history of this posthumous work in an article in the review *Musique* (Paris, March 1928). It was skilful special pleading in a bad cause.

His lamentable condition did not prevent Debussy from considering a new project early in June. Meeting the actor Gémier at a performance of 'Shylock', Debusssy told him of the interest he had for thirty years taken in Shakespeare's 'As You Like It'. In case the famous theatre manager decided to stage this drama, Debussy wished to reserve for himself the honour of composing incidental music for it. This conversation gave rise to an exchange of letters with J. P. Toulet. The composer immediately suggested to his friend that they should resume their former scheme of collaboration. As had been originally planned in 1902 and 1903, Debussy intended to give importance to the vocal element in the new version. He wished to make use of all the songs that embellish the text, and asked his friend to devote his lyrical gifts to them. He had no illusions as to Gémier's interest in the score he was about to write.

'As regards the music', he wrote on the 9th of July 1917, 'Gémier is a follower of Antoine who "didn't care a damn" about "that sort of thing". As that charming actor used to say, it costs a lot of money and no one pays any attention to it. Even though we don't quite share his views, we must try and manage to do it at the least possible cost. It is contrary to my usual habits, but there is no use in being too clever . . . I am too anxious to write this music not to be willing to make some sacrifices. . . .'

Unfortunately, sickness and pain soon obliged the composer to give up all work.

In the beginning of July 1917, Debussy went to stay at the 'Chalet Habas' at Saint-Jean-de-Luz. He wrote to his publisher that he was planning 'a series of little Concertos, similar to the series of Sonatas, for piano and certain groups of instruments'. He was not able to write them. A terrible fatigue, a disinclination for all exertion, overwhelmed him. The lightest work exhausted him. He wrote to Jacques Durand on the 22nd of July 1917:

'There are mornings when the effort of dressing seems like one of the twelve labours of Hercules. I long for anything to happen that would save me the trouble, even a revolution or an earthquake. Without being unduly pessimistic, I may say that my life is a hard one, for I have to fight against both disease and myself. . . . I feel that I am a nuisance to every one. Lord, do people think it's any fun for me! If they are looking for some one to conduct the Music of the Spheres, I think I am perfectly fitted for that *high* office. . . .'

This same despair is also apparent in the few published letters written to his friends Robert Godet and André Caplet. Debussy feels that he is near the end of his 'life of waiting—my waiting-room existence, I might call it—for I am a poor traveller waiting

for a train that will never come now'. He bewails his inability to compose: 'I cannot work, or rather, I work in a void and exhaust my strength on schemes which only increase my despair. Never before have I felt so weary of this pursuit of the unattainable.' At times his lamentations were more resigned: 'Is this to be the end of me . . . of my constant desire to go forward, that meant more than bread or life to me? . . . There are some ruins that should be hidden; and although I am old, I cannot expect people to feel any historic thrill on seeing the ruin that I have become.'

Nevertheless, the unhappy musician was able to make a last public appearance in the month of September. He played his last sonata at Saint-Jean-de-Luz with the assistance of the violinist Poulet. The 'Intermezzo' was received with continuous applause, and an encore was called for. Debussy objected to repeating it, 'mainly for the sake of the unity of the composition', he wrote to Jacques Durand, 'the entire sonata should have been encored. . . .' At two concerts given by the Société Charles Bordes he had the pleasure of seeing and hearing Francis Planté perform the 'Toccata' from the suite 'Pour le piano', as well as 'Reflets dans l'Eau' and 'Mouvement'; 'that man is a marvel', said the composer. He returned to Paris about the middle of October. When his friend Alfred Bruneau visited him about that time, Debussy showed him some sheets of paper on the piano on which he had scribbled a few rebellious ideas in his minute, aristocratic writing: 'Here you are; look at it', he said, 'I can't compose any more.' Soon he became a prey to terrible tortures and took to his bed.

There was no hope now of his completing the series of his 'Six Sonatas', of his writing the incidental music to 'As You Like It', or his 'Concertos' (nothing remains of these plans but a few indecipherable pencil notes); nor could he finish the great patriotic work he had sketched out under the title of 'Ode à la France'.

Claude Debussy lived his last sorrowful days to the sound of the bombardment of Paris by airships and long-distance guns. He had not even the strength to allow himself to be carried down to the cellar of his house when warning was given of the approach of the enemy 'Gothas'. He died on the 25th of March 1918, during the last German offensive, when the military situation of France was considered desperate by many.

Circumstances did not permit of his being paid the honour of a public funeral, or of ceremonious graveside orations, or 'Festivals' of his works. He was buried at the Père-Lachaise cemetery on the 28th of March, the eve of the Good Friday on which a shell from 'Big Bertha' fell on the church of Saint-Gervais, claiming

numerous victims. The small funeral procession was obliged to make its way right across Paris, from west to east, in the midst of the bombardment. An ironical fate decreed that this reserved and reticent artist should be laid to rest amidst the crash of artillery. A little later his remains were transferred to the Passy cemetery. In spite of the appalling international situation, the news of his death created a considerable stir. The newspapers of the allied and neutral countries devoted lengthy articles to his memory, amongst which we may mention a remarkable study by Ernest Newman in the *Musical Times*. A few German, Austrian, and Hungarian papers proclaimed the deceased musician as a great artist belonging to all humanity. In Italy and Spain the musical world mourned him. Bossi, the director of the Santa Cecilia Academy in Rome, assuming that the director of the Paris Conservatoire was the most exalted representative of music in France, telegraphed to Gabriel Fauré that Italy owed its renaissance to Debussy 'for in the art of Debussy we have found its spiritual roots and flowers'. In Spain, during the course of an important concert, Manuel de Falla declared that the composer of 'Pelléas et Mélisande' 'was a Latin, one of our own people, belonging to that great and noble race—immortal and unconquerable'.

One would seek almost in vain for obituary articles in the French papers of the end of March 1918. At most, there were a few news paragraphs, but no critical articles, with the exception of two impartial notices, one by Adolphe Jullien in *Les Débats*, the other by Paul Landormy in *La Victoire*. The newspapers were at that time published only in a very curtailed form; their few columns were naturally taken up with war news, concise reports of the movements of the armies, and dramatic accounts of the bombardment of Paris (which incidentally made it impossible to hold any memorial concert). As for the journals, most of the music reviews had ceased to appear on the outbreak of hostilities, and the small number of other reviews that continued to be published devoted their articles to the frightful conditions of the day. Amongst the very rare articles published immediately after Debussy's death one might mention two expressing contrasting views, one by Camille Bellaigue, the other by Gaston Carraud, the former condemning, the latter extolling, the art of the illustrious artist who had just passed away.

Camille Bellaigue's article appeared in the *Revue des Deux Mondes* on the 15th of May 1918. Debussy's former fellow-student at the Conservatoire, his fortunate rival in Marmontel's

piano class, his persistent adversary in the artistic field, was not moved by the tragic circumstances to alter his point of view or to modify his previous opinion—based on lack of understanding and sympathy. He admitted that 'Debussy drank out of a glass of his own; it was not a big one, but it was made of a thin crystal in which the play of vague, changing colours produced iridescent reflections'. He admitted that the reaction against Wagner had been brought about by this delicate artist who aimed at economy of sonorous material, and who wished to transform music into something 'light and almost silent', the art of singing and speaking softly. But as he had done on the appearance of 'Pelléas' in 1902, still animated by the same obsession, the writer persisted in denying the existence of any trace of melody, of almost any sign of rhythm or architectural structure, in Debussy's works. They still remained closed books to him.

Gaston Carraud, on the other hand, delivered on two occasions fitting and worthy funeral orations. Fifteen years previously this composer-critic had been one of the first to draw attention to the lasting qualities of the art of the composer whom he had always regarded as a genuine classical artist. In *La Liberté* of the 1st of April and in the *Courrier Musical* of the 15th of April, he extolled the dead composer, laying stress on his characteristic French qualities. He considered him as genuine an example of French genius as Watteau, Fragonard, or Houdon—so essentially national that he was misunderstood in other countries. He pointed out that he was national in the extraordinary subtlety of his most intimate emotions, in his very vision, so to speak, and in his delicate conception of form. This form, though definite, was marked and sustained by lines and links so malleable, so light, and clothed in such an airy fantasy that in order to grasp their illusive significance it was necessary to have a profound knowledge of our language, indeed of the very spirit of our language and our race; just as one understands by a kind of intuition those who express themselves only by allusions. . . .' He described how, between the years 1892 and 1905, roughly speaking, this Frenchman, who was still not acknowledged by some of his compatriots, 'overthrew the very foundations of musical art, destroyed its highways, opened up a horizon of almost illimitable discoveries, at the same time renewing the entire material of musical expression'. Carraud, whilst admitting that Debussy's art was rather limited and over-refined—the natural endowment of a highly original artist—remarked that even if Debussyism is of limited appeal, it is a fact of capital importance and must be taken

into careful account. It separated the music of the twentieth
century from that of the nineteenth, in the same manner as the
art of Beethoven (with all due sense of proportion be it said)
separated the nineteenth and eighteenth centuries. . . . 'Even if
the art that follows should turn aside from him, art can never be
what it was before he came.'

Public opinion seems to have ratified this verdict. How much
do we not owe to the composer of 'Pelléas'! He renewed all the
elements of melody, harmony, rhythm, recitative, symphonic form,
architectural structure, and pianistic treatment. Neither the in-
transigence of his theories, the violence of his reactions, the obvious
exhaustion of his very individual art—noticeable from about the
year 1905—nor the shortcomings of some works composed
during his last years under the stress of material necessities, can
prevent us from recognizing in Claude Debussy one of those
musicians who exert a profound and effective influence on the
artists of their day—in a word, one of the most original creative
artists of all time.

ONE OF THE 363 THEMES IN *ROMAN DE TRISTAN*

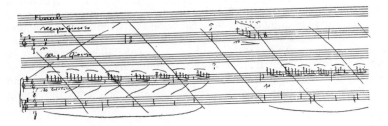

DEBUSSY'S NOTE FOR THE FOURTH OF A
PROJECTED SERIES OF SIX SONATAS

OPENING OF THE FINALE OF THE VIOLIN SONATA

APPENDIX A (*See page* 112)

THIS connexion with the art of Whistler becomes still more apparent when one reads a hitherto unpublished letter written by Debussy on the 22nd of September 1894 to his friend the violinist Ysaÿe. This letter supplies, in addition, some very interesting information concerning the history of the work. The composer informs the virtuoso that he is writing three Nocturnes for him, for violin solo and orchestra, with an unusual instrumental grouping. The first piece was to be for strings; the second for three flutes, four horns, three trumpets, and two harps; the last was to combine the two groups of instruments. 'It is in fact,' wrote Debussy, 'an experiment in the different combinations that can be achieved with one colour—what a study in grey would be in painting.' This experiment in tone-colouring seems to correspond to the first version of the three Nocturnes for orchestra. In the two first, especially, one can distinguish traces of the original instrumentation as first planned by the composer. Two years after this letter—on the 7th of November, 1896—Debussy wrote to Ysaÿe that he would prefer to forgo the performance of his three Nocturnes for violin and orchestra unless the famous violinist himself would undertake the interpretation of the work in Brussels. The result was the abandonment of the original project, of which the public had heard nothing and to which the composer never seems to have alluded.

The Nocturnes for orchestra, which are probably a transcription of those intended for Ysaÿe, bear the date 1897–9 ; it is entered on the big MS. score in the possession of the publisher, Jobert.

APPENDIX B (*See page* 121)

THE composition of 'Pelléas et Mélisande' was so far advanced in 1896 that the violinist Eugène Ysaÿe attempted to get the work accepted by the Théâtre de la Monnaie, Brussels; but without success. He then conceived the idea of performing portions of the opera at one of the symphonic concerts he conducted in Brussels. Early in October 1896, it was announced that the programme of his second subscription concert would include excerpts from the music composed by Claude A. Debussy to Maeterlinck's drama 'Pelléas et Mélisande', to be performed with the assistance of Mlle Duthil, vocalist, and the baritone Demest, Professor at the Conservatoire. Debussy immediately wrote his friend an affectionate letter of protest. His very legitimate remonstrances were based on aesthetic considerations. He objected to a partial performance in the concert hall on account of the close connexion between the scenic action and the music. He also pointed out that it was only in the theatre that one could appreciate the 'remarkable eloquence of the silent intervals with which the work is strewn'. Nor would the simplicity of the means he had utilized have any significance in the concert hall. 'Wagner's American opulence' would inevitably be held up as an example to the young

anti-Wagnerian composer, and people would taunt him with being financially unable to afford contrabass tubas. He suggested that instead of 'Pelléas' they should give 'La Saulaie' which he had written to a poem of Rossetti's ('Willowwood'), and in the composition of which he had turned his 'latest experiments in musical chemistry' to account. He also proposed the three Nocturnes for violin and orchestra he had written specially for Ysaÿe, his 'Marche Écossaise', the instrumentation of which he had just revised, and an orchestral arrangement of two of his 'Proses lyriques'. The vocal part in the last-named work could have been interpreted by Mlle Duthil, and that in 'La Saulaie' by the baritone Demest. The only work by Debussy that eventually figured on the programme of Ysaÿe's concert was the 'Prélude à l'Après-midi d'un Faune'. From which we may conclude that, as usual, Debussy did not finish either 'La Saulaie' or his new version of the two 'Proses lyriques' in time.

If Ysaÿe's sponsorship had had sufficient weight with the directors of the Théâtre de la Monnaie, 'Pelléas' would probably have been finished in haste, and it could have been produced in 1897. In that event, Debussy's masterpiece would have appeared at the same period as Vincent d'Indy's 'Fervaal'. The great Belgian theatre would have witnessed an interesting juxtaposition of Wagnerism *à la française* and French anti-Wagnerism.

Two years later, in 1898, the score of 'Pelléas et Mélisande' was practically finished.

APPENDIX C (*See page 156*)

IF this was his intention, it was of early date. For the 'Sarabande' of 1901 had been composed at least five years previously, and had indeed been published in a Paris paper, the *Grand Journal*, on the 17th of February, 1896. It was mentioned as forming part of a series of pieces about to be published by Fromont under the title of 'Images' and the following picturesque note indicated its movement and expression: 'In "Sarabande" *tempo*—that is to say, with a slow, stately elegance, suggestive of an old portrait, a reminiscence of the Louvre, &c.' The 1896 version differs but slightly from the final form and only in a few details. For instance, the C and D natural in the first and third bars of the 1896 edition alter the harmonic colouring considerably. The following shows the beginning of the first version. It may be compared with that of 1901, which will be found in the thematic list.

DEBUSSY, *photographed by* PIERRE LOUŸS
(about 1900)

LISTE DES

ŒUVRES DE CLAUDE DEBUSSY